Contained within this book are stories I've heard since my youth. Some — like my mother's recollections of comical childhood battles with her older brother — I practically know by heart. Other memories I only learned by reading this memoir, which provides invaluable perspective about a young girl's life in Germany, before and after Hitler, Nazism and World War II. It's the story of how my mother's family life was turned upside down by world events and how rural communities like her hometown were uprooted from a simpler way of life by global winds of change.

Thanks to my mother's great capacity for oral history and my father's journalistic commitment to factual accuracy, I know that anytime I open this book I'll be getting a truthful account of a world I'll never truly experience, that is nonetheless a part of me.

While it's a tremendous gift to our family and friends, I believe this book will offer something beneficial to readers in general, namely an understanding of how world events can impact personal destiny as well as an appreciation for how perseverance and courage can transform tragedy and misfortune into a new lease on life — a fresh start 'on a green twig.'

— Kristopher Erich Peter Spencer

Kristopher Spencer is the author of
Film And Television Scores, 1950–1979:
A Critical Survey by Genre
McFarland and Company, 2008

On a Green Twig

⇜A Memoir⇝

By Anna Klein Spencer
With
Tim Spencer

ISBN 978-0-578-00227-9

ILLUSTRATIONS BY TINA VANOSS
COVER DESIGN BY LAURA LANGA-SPENCER

Notes and Acknowledgments

"Am grünen Zweig gibt es immer eine andere
Möglichkeit zu einem neuen Anfang."
('On a green twig there is always another
chance for a new beginning.')

All his life, my father believed in the 'green twig' approach to whatever the fates handed him. There was an overwhelming need for that kind of relentless optimism just to survive during the years I was growing up in Germany. That period of 1930 to 1955 saw the world turn up-side-down by extreme economic depression, the rise of Nazism, world war, German defeat and military occupation. Yet, my memory lingers on the fate of a single place and two families.

Both my parents' people came from villages situated on the eastern slopes of the Donnersberg, the highest elevation in the highlands of Rheinland/Pfalz. The Pfalz, as most Germans call it, was once a part of Bavaria, but came into its own as a state early in the 20th century. This heavily forested, hilly area, bordered on the east by Germany's famous wine region, is special to the native Pfälzer. It became so as well to British and American bombers heading for targets along the Rhein river in war. These included Mainz, Ludwigshafen, Mannheim, Worms, Speyer and Neustadt along the river, and on south toward very industrial Kaiserslautern.

I'm blessed with a clear memory of my youth, for which I credit the absence of television and other such diversions while growing up. Even listening to the radio and recordings didn't enter my life until the age of seven, and then sparingly. Daily entertainments revolved around simple play with friends in a sheltered environment, school studies, and a constant flow of stories told within the family. All of it is indelibly etched in my memory.

Aiding my recollections are hundreds of family documents, letters, diaries, school workbooks and notes. There's even my handwritten cookbook filled with recipes from Mama. I have also included photos from my personal collection and the generosity of family and friends.

No fictional characters live in this book, but I have changed a very few names for what I hope are obvious reasons. All places mentioned are real, and all events and dates are true to the best of my knowledge. Dialogue quoted throughout the text comes solely from actual conversations involving myself or spoken between others in my presence. While the words quoted can't be

i

exact in all cases, the content is always true.

I'm indebted to my brother Erich for confirming all incidents to which he was a witness, and also for his interest and support.

Extensive research through the archives of Kirchheimbolanden provided vital facts about the city's role in the war and what followed. My full gratitude to Fräulein Baab and Herr Buhrman of the city administration, allowing us generous personal access to documents during the archival search.

Fräulein Baab also led us to Konrad Lucae, Director Emeritus of the Kirchheimbolanden Museum, and a leading expert on local history. For me, Herr Lucae proved to be much more. In two long interviews, his patient answers came with large doses of humor and charm. During the second interview, I was jolted to learn he had actually known my grandfather Peter Klein, whose reputation radiated through the next two generations of my family.

Peter was a major influence on my life, though I never met him. Herr Lucae's description of the unforgettable 'Seppel' matched everything I had ever heard about him. Herr Lucae told me that in his youth he often worked in his father's restaurant and pub. Old Peter had been a frequent patron.

So many of the houses and street scenes identified in this book have changed or have disappeared over the years, and many of the photos available were unsuitable for use. My daughter Kristina VanOss came to the rescue with a series of pen and ink drawings, either from the dim old photos or her own visit to Kirchheim. A fine artist and mother to my grandchildren, she faithfully captured scenes from that long ago time. Likewise, my writer son Kristopher read the text and offered valuable advice.

My husband's constant encouragement drove my pen over reams of paper. A stickler for accuracy — Tim insisted on double and even triple checking on people, events and timelines. He was a part of all research, often posing questions I hadn't considered. We traveled a number of times to the Donnersberg region to double check the content of my writings. We were both surprised, and pleased, to find any mistakes or lapses were few. From this research and wealth of materials, it was Tim who wrote my story. After a long career in broadcast news and writing, he had retired — it seemed like the right time to ask him.

I dedicate this work to the memory of my father, who never stopped believing, — to older brother Erich, who shared with me the best and worst of times — and to young brother Peter, who gave me more joy than I deserved.

Anna Spencer
Hamilton, Michigan

Language Notes

In this book the correct spelling for proper names of people and places is used, including the double-S (ß) as in Langstraße, and the umlaut (two dots above certain vowels). Examples of the latter include München and Köln (Munich and Cologne). And for me, the Rhine will always be the Rhein. In German it is customary to combine words such as street names: Breitstraße instead of Breit Straße (Broad Street). In all cases of formal address, I use Herr, Frau, and Fräulein for Mr., Mrs., and Miss. The German titles for Mayor and Teacher are also used: Bürgermeister and Lehrer. In dealing with family members, I use Papa (Father), Mama (Mother), Bruder (Brother), Opa (Grandfather), Oma (Grandmother), Tante (Aunt), and Onkel (Uncle). All others are identified in English.

Many German words and phrases are commonly known or correctly guessed: Guten morgen/tag/abend (Good morning/day/evening), Gott (God), Himmel (Heaven), Ja (Yes), and Nein or Nay (No). In dialogue, the guttural expression "Ach" is commonly used to add emphasis. Examples: "Ach, Gott im Himmel!" (Oh, God in heaven!) or "Ach, ja or nay." (Complete agreement or disapproval/denial). A very meaningful phrase to me and said to me only by my father — "Sei brav," pronounced 'sigh brah-vuh.' Its common meaning is simply "Be good." To Papa and to me it gave a stronger message: Behave, be responsible, and do nothing that will bring shame on you or the family.

In reading my story, it may help to remember these tips on pronouncing certain letters. One good example is the A, most often pronounced as a soft 'Ah,' whether in upper or lower case. My name Anna would be said Ah-nah. The endearing Annchen becomes Ahn-shun. The A is rarely said as in the English late, mate, great.

It is generally known to English speakers that Germans say the W like a V — the letter V sounds more like an F — and Th is almost always said like a T only, thanks becomes tanks. There are other differences, but these are the more common.

All other German used is clarified in the text.

— AS

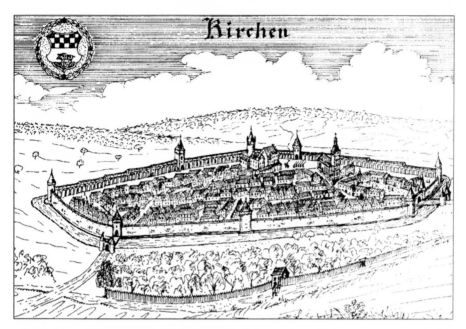

An unknown artist's view of the old walled community of Kirchen in the 1400's. It was the forerunner of what is today Kirchheimbolanden. Only five kilometers away was my place of birth, the farm village of Marnheim. It too claims existence in the 13th century, and perhaps back to Celtic times.

Prologue

In the mid-1980's, my husband and I fulfilled a long delayed wish to re-visit my birth home in Germany. Excitement made it impossible to sleep on the long overnight flight, but all our weariness vanished in the bright, crisp morning air of Luxembourg. The small hassle-free airport there is only a half-hour drive from the German border. Crossing that boundary put us just where I wanted to be — the Rheinland/Pfalz.

Despite knowing that family waited with a welcoming party, just an hour away on the high-speed Autobahn, an irresistible urge came over me. I simply couldn't bear the idea of seeing my Pfälzer forests, hills and valleys zip by at 140 kilometers an hour. In those first hours back my heart ached to stop when and where I wanted, to smell the sweet wild violets, the heavy scent of pine — the rich soil itself. Most of all, I wanted to hear the "Pälzisch," a dialect that had always been music to my ears.

My driver resisted the idea of making my family wait two or three extra hours, wondering where we could be.

"They'll understand," I insisted. "You'll see. Besides, it won't take that much longer." Reaching into the glove compartment, "I have a map right here!"

Behind the wheel, my partner rolled his eyes, shook his head, smiled, and turned off the Autobahn at the first exit. As we passed through villages, forests and farmland, all my reasons and excuses for constantly putting off our return came up empty.

That my family would understand our tardy arrival in Kirchheim was only a hope. The emotional moments of reunion between sister and brothers at six rather than three o'clock, held more forgiveness than understanding. Erich, my brother and oldest friend, was my first and longest embrace. I was surprised that he hugged me so tightly, and apparently, so were many others gathered around the scene. To them, I was a total stranger. Standing patiently on the sidelines was brother Peter, fourteen years younger than me, and my first baby to care for. With him were his wife, Christa, teenage son Michael, and little sister Sybille. I had never met my young nephew and niece.

All of my many uncles and aunts, and some peer cousins, had died during the intervening years. Feeling both guilty and sad about it, I was determined to get to know those who came into the world during my absence, and to again enter the lives of at least a few close cousins still alive.

❧

It was only days later that I had a chance to restore relations with my second cousin Adam Herbst, the youngest son of one of my mother's uncles. While Adam was first cousin to Mama, he was just ten years older than me and, over the years, I was often treated as more of a younger sister. An incident on the occasion of his confirmation celebration at the end of eighth grade set the later course of our encounters on a humorous note. I stuck my tongue out at the camera taking the mandatory formal family photo. I have a rather long tongue, so there was no doubt in the photo about my five-year-old behavior. The image made Mama mad, but Adam thought it hilarious, teasing me about it for years to come.

Ida wanted me to call ahead. After all, she said, Adam hadn't seen me in over thirty years. I refused — wanting to see Adam's shocked expression. I was certain he wouldn't know me at first glance. It would be sweet revenge for all the years of his teasing.

We drove the few kilometers to Ilbisheim at mid-morning, as I was sure the party would be an evening affair. By going early, it would head off any teasing about "ruining" another big event in his life. Besides, I'd never met his wife and children. After he married, Adam moved to his wife's village, which meant we had to find the right farmhouse, a small matter in a tiny village. A red-faced, pig-tailed girl kindly pointed it out, but upon entering an open back door into the kitchen, we were promptly told by a flour-dusted woman that her "husband wasn't resting at home on his birthday!" She directed us to a sugar beet field outside the village.

Driving slowly into the countryside, we soon caught sight of a single figure working far off the road in a huge field of young sugar beet plants. After parking, Tim and I began the long trek down a row toward the man with a hoe. I couldn't help remarking that the field was clean of weeds. Maybe Adam was out there just to escape a hot kitchen. I couldn't blame him. It was a lovely day of cool June sunshine, so clear that the air seemed to sparkle, and just breezy enough to make me glad I wore a scarf. It would also add to the mystery of my identity.

With about twenty feet to go, the man with the hoe suddenly turned around, dropped the implement, clapped his hands and shouted, "Ach, Annchen." A bear hug followed. It was Adam alright, with his large moon face and the stocky build of a Herbst. However, most of the Herbst clan were not of the hearty, easy-to-grin kind. Adam was a happy exception, and I favored him for it. Shocked by his instant recognition of me, I nearly forgot to introduce Tim.

As Adam and I talked of the memories of youth, it dawned on me that I stood in the middle of a vast panoramic view of the Pfalz. Behind Adam, to the east, there were the high rolling hills and farmland that gradually gave way to the lower flat plain around Worms on the Rhein. From our high crest, the towns, villages, vineyards and fields of all sorts dotted the landscape to the far horizon. Long-tailed swallows flitted and circled overhead, sometimes swooping close to the earth, then darting upward as if challenging gravity. In my youth, I had worked in many fields like this and would pause from laboring now and then to watch the swallows playfully swooping about in the sky overhead.

Behind me, to the west, lay the tree-covered Donnersberg (Thunder Mountain) and the start of the Pfälzer forest. Though kilometers away, Kirchheimbolanden was visible at the edge of the forest. All these vistas, out of sight to me for so very long, suddenly interfered with the flow of our reminiscing. After a brief awkward pause, we were invited to Adam's party that evening, but I declined. There were too many places to visit, so many people to see.

"Adam, you must tell me something," I said, hugging him one last time. "How did you know me? It's been at least thirty-five years!"

"Ja, ja, Annchen," he replied, patting his stomach with a chuckle. "Some of us change a lot over the years, but you will always be Seppel's daughter."

Tim and I walked back to the car in silence. My husband could understand German, especially dialect, and sensed that I needed time to reflect. Adam's words, and all that surrounded me, had unleashed a flow of vivid memories from another life.

I was a small child the first time I heard someone refer to me as 'Seppel's daughter.' It was in the courtyard of the house where I was born in Marnheim. Four years old and quite shy, I stood close to Mama as she talked to a man who had come to see Papa. He seemed to know my father well, and was telling Mama he was sorry not to find him at home. His eyes fell on me, standing half way behind my mother. With a smile, he reached down to tousle my thick curly hair.

"So, this is Seppel's daughter," he chuckled.

"No, I'm Fritz's daughter," I said firmly, clinging to Mama and looking up to her face for support. The man laughed louder.

"Ach, child," Mama said, somewhat impatiently. "You'll soon learn that your father is known far and wide as 'Kleine Seppel'."

While it was a comfort to be reassured I was not another man's child, all the rest had to wait a while before I'd understand it.

3

Remembering...

The story began with my father's grandfather. Joseph Klein was born in March 1841, in Bolanden, a small village on the eastern slope of the Donnersberg. From the start everyone used the endearing form of Joseph so that, in time, everyone would know him only as 'Seppel.'

He was a young farmer in 1865 when he met Philippina Schlicker from the village of Schiersfeld, on the other side of the mountain. There is some mystery about the circumstances of their marriage, but a little digging revealed a few interesting facts.

Philippina had joined her parents in relocating temporarily to the village of Marnheim to await the outcome of her out-of-wedlock pregnancy. She gave birth to a son on August 30, and named him Peter. He would become my grandfather. The name of his father was at first not revealed on the birth papers. One family legend has it that Seppel was the lover, but was unprepared to marry. Another says he met Philippina only after she and her parents arrived in Marnheim. The last is plausible — folks of Bolanden and Marnheim mingled daily. In either case, an event two years later satisfied the official record of Peter's parentage.

Philippina was pregnant again, and three months along when she became Seppel's wife. Son Theodore was born February 21, 1869 in Bolanden. When Seppel went to the Kirchheimbolanden district office, he put his name on the birth certificates of both boys, but in pencil not ink on Peter's. Did this mean that he was simply giving the boy an honorable name?

The next birth on December 18, 1871 brought double tragedy. Philippina died three days after delivering another boy, Jakob. He followed her in death nine months later.

Somehow Peter and brother Theo managed to survive until Seppel married in March of 1873 to a Katharina Weschan. She hailed from Odenbach-am-Glan, another of the many villages nestled around the Donnersberg. It was said Katharina had been Seppel's housekeeper for some months before he married her, not an unusual act for a widower with young children. Though they had no children of their own, the union lasted forty-three years. Seppel was seventy-five when he died, a ripe old age in those days. Katharina lived another four years.

Papa was fifteen years old in 1916 when his grandfather died, but never ran out of tales to tell about him to my brother and I. "Old Seppel," as he called him, knew no strangers. As a farmer, Joseph never made much money, but was always generous with his time and labor to help others where it was needed. Over a lifetime, he became widely known and respected around the Donnersberg. Never a war hero or holder of public office, Papa found it hard to credit anything except a wonderful nature as the reason why his grandfather was so widely revered.

Long before his father's death Peter had begun taking on the Seppel name and mantel. More specifically Peter became widely known as "Kleine Seppel," a play on the family name Klein, hence 'little Seppel.' Papa said his father didn't mind being called by his father's name. He was determined to make the goodwill, the name engendered, a foundation for his many ambitions. Young brother Theo saw early on that he couldn't compete and left the area. Both in inheritance and personality, Peter had the advantage. In 1888 he married his beloved Charlotte and took up residence in Bolanden. When a house fire killed their first two children, they began again in Kirchheimbolanden, the region's commerce and government center three kilometers away. Most people had long before stopped saying the whole name in everyday conversation. The simpler Kirchheim or Kibo (key-bow) is used. Best of all, for me, is the dialect name Kerchem.

The next seven Klein children were born there, including my father. Papa said that Kleine Seppel believed Kirchheim offered a better place to get on a green twig — a place to make money. He was a well-read man, and saw a new age coming in agriculture. Though no longer a farmer himself, he knew local farmers and believed they must modernize the planting and harvesting of crops. Manual labor in farming was still the way because mechanization was too costly. Having upwards of a dozen children to help do the work was still common. Even as a non-farmer, Peter sired twelve children, all the while predicting an end to the custom.

In the meantime, he supported his dreams and family with an appointment as a government forestry agent. The position proved very useful before and after World War One. The Pfälzer forest is Germany's largest, and the harvest of timber quite lucrative. As a forestry official, he was a key person in deciding location and number of trees to be removed.

The records show that he profited much when demand for timber grew during the "Great War," as it was called, and later under French occupation. Papa had many stories of working long days for his father, driving teams of horses to haul logs down to main roads. He was not yet thirteen when his father took him out of school. An older brother Robert escaped the toil by going to München in Bavaria to eventually become a chef and restaurant owner. Papa stayed on to work with his father in all his schemes for success.

After the first Seppel died, Peter returned to make Bolanden his home base on a large scale. The family moved into a leased estate at the edge of the village called Kloster Hane. The kloster (cloister) had been a Catholic monastery hundreds of years before, and later became a cloister for nuns. After 1800 and the French revolution, the church gave the property over to private hands. Along with a section of fields, the property boasted many structures including a chapel and one large building converted into several apartments. In time, the growing Klein family would occupy all the apartments. The ancient chapel went into use as storage for hay and straw, and a few animal stalls.

There's a rare photograph of Peter and Charlotte posing for the camera in the cobblestone courtyard. Between them is "Fuchs" (Fox), the family carriage horse. Papa said "Füchschen," as they called him, was a beautiful roan without fault in form or blemish in coloring. It was quite a sight, he said, watching his father, dressed in dark suit and vest, and wearing a wide-brim black hat, hold the reins as horse and carriage appeared to fly down the road. Peter always leaned far forward on the seat as though pushing to go ever faster. Ceaseless ambition had him gone on business so much, a common joke in the neighborhood asked how he found time to have so many children! It's doubtful anyone put the question to Charlotte.

I was two years old when my grandfather died, so everything I learned about him came from other people. I have wondered if he would be surprised that 'Kleine Seppel' is a name only now beginning to fade in the villages around the Donnersberg. I was certainly shocked in later years to find that I'm still remembered as 'Seppel's daughter.'

Aside from brother Robert, my father's other older siblings included Käthe, Elizabeth and Lina. Younger than him were Gusta, Rudi, Adolf, Otto and Ludwig. Käthe and Lina were sent away to a girl's finishing school while Elizabeth and Gusta stayed at home to learn domestic work. Rudi left home as soon as he came of age, going to Stuttgart. Adolf, Otto and Ludwig were all too young while their father lived to either leave home or take on much of a workload. Peter and Charlotte never spoke of the two children who died, so Papa knew little of them, except that fire was the cause.

My father's responsibilities around the estate grew as Seppel's trips away kept Füchschen in constant harness. Always there were deals to be made, including the import of grain from the Russian Ukraine. I grew up hearing antidotes from family and strangers alike of how Seppel worked with local banks to help area farmers finance new labor saving equipment. The so-called Great War (1912–18), and French occupation after, only halted Seppel's drive forward for a brief time. Even the massive war-debt and uncertain politics just slowed his progress in the early 1920's. It took the monetary system crash at the end of the decade to break his grasp on the 'green twig.'

Long before that final collapse, however, came an event very important to me. Marie Herbst of Marnheim village married Fritz Klein in 1922. He brought her to Bolanden and the Kloster Hane estate. Already there in one large apartment were his parents and three younger brothers. In their own apartments elsewhere in the huge building, were two married sisters and their families. These were Tante Elizabeth and her husband Jacob and their three children. Jacob owned and operated a small sand quarry. Tante Gusta and her husband Ernst did not yet have children. Ernst had joined the family all the way from Switzerland and was, in fact, a cheesemaker. My parents soon welcomed their first son Raul to the Kloster Hane clan, but sadly at the age of two; the boy died of burns sustained in a boiling water mishap in Oma Charlotte's kitchen. Brother Erich came next in 1925.

People unprepared to barter when money turned worthless in the late 1920's suffered the most. The Kleins were ready to trade and did so to keep going, but Papa believed the family's longer survival was more the result of an enormous reservoir of trust created by his father. Banks foreclosed quickly on others, but stayed with 'Kleine Seppel' until the inevitable final collapse of the world economy in 1929. Soon after, in a court ordered auction, Kloster Hane simply vanished. Only property brought into my grandparent's marriage by Charlotte was saved. That was a good thing, Papa later said, otherwise, his parents would not have had a chair to sit on. Their new home was found in an old part of Bolanden. It was all of three small rooms, not much considering that three unmarried boys were still at home.

My two aunts with their husbands and children were also forced to find survival elsewhere, and like Peter, both families were able to find apartments in Bolanden. A new home for my parents and Erich was found in an unexpected place, at Mama's family homestead in Marnheim.

Papa often spoke of his father's last years. "Seppel never gave up. To the very end you'd see him on the move in and around Kirchheim, and any of the other villages he could reach on foot. And always, he cheerfully believed there was a new beginning just around the corner." In the verbal tradition of daily life at the time, tales of my grandfather were never lacking. The repetition of these stories over the years, in and out of the family circle, put the image of 'Kleine Seppel' indelibly in my mind.

Peter Klein died on April 14, 1932. He was sixty-six years old. I was only two, but heard about his funeral in later years, especially from Mama. "The burial procession was so long," she said, "the end of it was still in the village when the casket reached the cemetery high on the hill." Sometimes, when she was in a bitter mood, she would add that the scene was also one of shame. "So many of those black-clad people owed Seppel their respect, but also a lot of money."

My Opa, Peter Klein (1865–1932)

The Marnheim Years

No doubt, this has to be the first picture taken of me. I was perhaps one and a half years old.

As for the quality of the photo, I can imagine that it was taken by one of the neighbors using a primitive box camera. So it goes!

Chapter One

The personalities of my father and mother were so strikingly different; anyone might wonder what had brought them together. I've come to believe that in the beginning, Papa's attraction to Mama was ninety-percent physical. He was a hard-working optimist; bowled over by a petite Marnheim girl with an ivory complexion and the most beautiful hair he'd ever seen. Was he so bewitched that he hadn't noticed her dark, pessimistic nature? Apparently so, for while her face was only mildly pretty, few other women around could claim such a heavy mass of shining, almost black hair. It fell far past her waist, a sight that always captivated Papa when she released the two braids she kept pinned into large mounds behind her ears. At bedtime Mama released the braids to hang free. Even now, in my mind's eye, I can see Papa playfully grabbing at her heavy braids during breakfast while she prepared his lunch box. His attentions to her weren't returned in kind if Erich and I were present.

What Marie Herbst saw in Fritz Klein was more complicated. Only slightly taller than herself, he was a fairly handsome man, but looks had little to do with her decision to marry him. Mama had wanted escape from a stifling life in Marnheim. What could be better than marrying an ambitious young man whose father was one of the area's most successful businessmen. Not a bad reason to marry maybe, but not strong enough to change her true nature. Papa never accepted superstition and defeat. Mama did. Being forced to return to Marnheim, the last place she wanted to be, only deepened her pessimism. My father took the setback in stride, knowing somehow he would find a way back to a better life.

Tante Anna, Mama's youngest sister, had her reasons for offering shelter to the Klein family in the old homestead. Taking care of an invalid mother had become too much. Grandfather Herbst had died a few months earlier leaving young Anna with no help at all. The move to Marnheim for Mama, Papa and Erich came shortly before my birth in July 1930.

Mama came from a family of many children — five sisters and five brothers. Of the brothers, Jean was killed in the World War of 1914. He had been named after the father, who preferred to go by the French version of his real name, Johannes. Like my father, Mama was a middle child. Before deciding to stop just short of a dozen, Jean and Christine gave the world Wilhelm, Carolina, Jean, Dina, Adam, Heinrich, Maria (always called Marie or Mariechen), Katharina, Elisabeth, Philip, and Anna. A family portrait was taken after 1916.

Though young Jean had been killed in the war, it does seem eerie that he is in the picture, in the exact proportion and pose as the rest of them. At the family's request, Jean's image was lifted from an earlier photo and expertly inserted.

Later in life I was startled to learn that Mama's parents were both Herbst, and cousins. Oma came out of the Herbst farm estate called Heyerhof near Marnheim, and Opa was from another branch of the family living near the city of Worms. A perfunctory story of them, told by my reluctant Mama to an insistent child was all I got. She said Jean showed up one day at Heyerhof and quickly asked for Christine's hand in marriage. She was only sixteen years old.

My Opa Herbst was a saddler and upholsterer. After he married Christine, it was decided they remain in Marnheim where they bought an old farm property fronting the main street in the village. He set up shop in a small building across a courtyard from the main house, and started producing harnesses and mattresses. The production of children also took up a good part of his time. All the boys were trained in his saddlers trade, but only two, Adam and Heinrich, stayed with it. Heinrich, being older, took over the business after Opa's death. He continued operating there even after marrying and moving to his wife's village nearby. Adam married a local girl and established his trade in a different Marnheim location. All through the late 1800's and on into the Second World War, the making of leather saddles, reins, collars, and other horse equipment remained a lucrative business. Germany still fielded large army cavalry units, and farmers continued using horses to till the land and pull the wagons.

Philip, the youngest boy, eventually moved out of the area. As for the oldest, Wilhelm, he played a minor role in my life, though he was sole inheritor of the homestead. All the girls received grammar school education, but after eighth grade, their training was limited to cooking, housekeeping, and sewing. Elisabeth was born hunchbacked, and did not live past her twenty-first birthday. Mama said the whole family adored "Lisbeth" for her sweet nature and her talent for doing fine needlework. Why she died so young was never spoken.

When my parents moved back to the Herbst homestead, Mama's mother was bedridden. I was to spend the first year of life in bed with my Oma, who was well enough to care for me while shouting out orders to my mother and aunt on the household chores.

Tante Anna lived in the big house with Oma and there were plenty of rooms available to house us, but Mama refused. Wanting even a small bit of independence, she and Papa took the two small rooms above the saddlery across the enclosed courtyard that had no electricity or running water. The room at the top of stairs became the kitchen. The bedroom where I was born was just large enough for a single bed, a youth bed and my crib next to a chest of drawers. In all the eight years we lived there, Mama and Papa slept in the single-sized bed. Being small individuals they seemed to like it that way — not that they had much choice.

Downstairs Onkel Heinrich allowed Mama the use of a side room for storing foodstuffs and washing laundry. We also had use of one room in the big house for storage. Water came from a pipe and faucet just outside in the courtyard. Evening light in the apartment came from a single large oil lamp. In winter, the only heat was from a wood burning cook stove in the kitchen.

As I grew older, I often wondered what Mama thought as she gazed from our kitchen window across to where she was born and grew into adulthood. Long after Oma Herbst died when I was two years old, Mama often stared at the decaying old structure. Papa liked to joke that when Christine shouted orders from her bedroom 'throne,' you could hear her from one end of the property to the other. Thinking about it now, maybe my mother thought she heard Oma's ghost demanding attention. Papa always looked upon his mother-in-law's eight years in bed with some humor.

"The way I see it," Papa said, laughing, "Old Christine probably decided that after the hard years she needed some pampering!"

It was easy for him to joke. He had landed a job driving a delivery truck for a local flour mill from dawn to dark, leaving little time to help at home.

Oma's death altered our living arrangements somewhat. We stayed where we were, but started paying rent to Wilhelm, who inherited the property. A bachelor, he wasn't respected much by his siblings. Since Tante Anna had no means of paying her brother, she accepted an offer of marriage to a man who lived in a village nearer the Rhein River. The ground floor of the big house was then rented to an outside family with four young children. Onkel Heinrich and my mother and father, of course, joined the list of rent payers for space occupied in the saddler's building. Wilhelm reserved the entire second floor in the main house for himself, though he rarely visited. In time I learned just how bitter my mother was toward Wilhelm. I never sensed the same feelings in Papa or my uncle outwardly. They may have felt resentment, but preferred to give the matter a humorous spin. I think they were probably happy Wilhelm wasn't around much. "I'd travel too if I had his money," Papa said, after one of the landlord's snap visits.

I remember Wilhelm as a very tall, good-looking man. Having no interest in small children, he paid little attention to Erich or me. Perhaps trying to make us feel better, Mama said not to worry. "He was aloof with all the family." I do know that years later when he died not one relative attended the funeral. Fortunately, he was one of a kind among the men in the Herbst family.

To a growing child all of these adult concerns mattered little. I was busy discovering the boundaries of Marnheim life. I never gave it a worry that my home was just two small rooms over a workshop. I felt no differently even after discovering that most families around had dining rooms and many more bedrooms. In any case, the kitchen was center of family life in all households. Papa had fixed ours up with shelves and a sideboard with a wash basin on top. Above it, on the wall, hung a small mirror. Fresh water for washing and cooking came upstairs in a pail from the faucet in the courtyard.

Along one kitchen wall sat the table and chairs, with a glass oil lamp hanging overhead, our only light in the evening hours. On the opposite wall stood a large pantry cabinet for storage. It also had a pull-out surface area that was used to prepare food. Saturday evenings the kitchen doubled as a bathroom. Water was heated on the stove and poured into a washtub on the floor.

My outside world was the entire family property. I pestered my uncle in his workshop, and investigated every level of the big barn. Behind the barn I could roam in the spacious garden, and help water the flowers and vegetables, one of my early chores. Across the courtyard in the big house, I made friends with the Brandenmeier's children — Marianne, Willie, Reinhard, and Dieter. Along with Hänschen, another boy from across the street, we left few things untouched.

The courtyard was completely surrounded by buildings and walls. Like most farm village properties, Oma's house was right on the edge of the street. On the other side of the driveway leading into the courtyard, was the workshop building with our tiny apartment. It also faced the street, and a high wall with big double doors connected the two houses, allowing animals and vehicles to pass through. Built into one of the doors was a small door for people to use. Most of the time, the big doors were kept shut.

When I was considered old enough to play outside the walled courtyard, the broad cobble-stoned street remained a matter for caution. It was the main thoroughfare in the village, but few cars were seen during those poor times. Mama still worried about occasional horse drawn carts and carriages running me over — not to forget the animal herds being driven through morning and evening. Thinking back on it, the street was probably much safer than the barn. We played in the barn almost daily, fearlessly climbing ladders, jumping into the straw and hay piles, and bothering the hogs in the stalls. This could be a dangerous business for small children playing around 300 hundred pound animals. Play in the barn could get a bit rough. It was on such an occasion that my friend Hänschen was marked for life. We were chasing around, carrying little Swastika flags on sticks, when Hänschen fell down. The sharp stick rammed through his open mouth and out his cheek. The flag part hung out over the bottom lip like a limp, badly discolored tongue. Onkel Heinrich heard the screaming and came running to rush the boy to a barber down the street who took care of such problems. We didn't have a doctor in the village, so it was up to the barber to close the wound. Hänschen recovered, but with a scarred cheek to forever recall the childhood mishap.

Once, when I was around five, playmate Marianne tried to turn the barn into a sex education center. She had led her brother Willie and me into the barn and, upon closing the door announced, "We will now learn about our bodies." Being older, she always took the teacher role. Told to take my panties down, I obeyed. Turning to Willie, who was my same age, she ordered him to drop his trousers. "There," Marianne gleefully declared. "That's what a boy looks like naked!" I was disgusted — not with poor Willie — but with Marianne. She had wasted my time.

Mama never knew about the barn incident, and it was a good thing. She frowned heavily on child play that hinted at male-female relationships. Any game involving make-believe family, however innocent, was forbidden.

My name Anna was given to me after Mama's youngest sister. A second name, Katharina, came from another sister. So that I would have something of my own Mama added Elfriede. That was a mouthful for anyone. I was glad most family members and friends decided to call me "Annchen" the endearing form of Anna.

The Marnheim of my youth was not the typical postcard German village. It was and still is a small place almost unmarked by quaint steeples, interesting architecture, or other features to attract a tourist trade. In recent years, most older buildings and houses have been renovated to make a more colorful appearance. In my childhood, everything seemed shaded gray. On dreary days, it was downright dark and gloomy along the narrow streets and passageways.

Not far from my house, and down one of those tight streets only wide enough for a large wagon to pass, stood the school I first attended. Of more interest to me was an old and massive round bell tower just a few yards away. It had to be the tallest structure in Marnheim. I had heard the bells long before I saw the tower up close. Through an open doorway off the school yard my brother and I once had a chance to sneak a look inside. There wasn't much to see except a big round empty space with a stone floor. Once our eyes got used to the darkness, we easily recognized three long ropes hanging in the center. Erich said a caretaker from a nearby church was in charge of making the bells "talk" to the villagers. A frantic ringing signaled fire. The call to church seemed beckoning and weddings ended with a joyous ringing. The most unmistakable sound was the funeral bell. Its long mournful ring always seemed to bring village life to a standstill. During my childhood, an evening bell heard far into the surrounding countryside still called farmers home from the fields.

In the 1930's Marnheim still had a town crier. He, along with the tolling bells, were the official sources for news. The town crier was also our only police officer. At least twice a day, he walked the streets ringing his hand bell. As he passed, windows flew open, in summer or winter, to hear him shout out village news. And he often had some news items thought to be of interest from around Germany and the world. The town crier was one of a handful of people in town who had a radio or telephone. It's why folks came running when they heard his bell.

Marnheim and surrounding villages had nothing like today's grocery stores. Vegetables and fruit were available only in season from our garden or from local farmers. The farmers brought in small wagons loaded with fresh garden produce almost every day to sell directly to the town folk. Since we didn't have an open village square, they'd set up on one of the wide streets.

The Hauptstraße, where we lived, was one of those streets.

As I said, we enjoyed fresh greens in season, but not in winter. Mama became so used to not having green salads after frost that even later, when we could go to a green grocer in winter, she rarely thought of it.

Marnheim had two small stores where we could purchase sugar, flour, spices and the like, in bulk. Very few foods came pre-packaged, and you had to have your own shopping bag when several things were needed. There wasn't a housewife who didn't own more than one shopping bag, plain or fancy.

Our creamery shops also had many grocery items to supplement their milk, cream and cheese business. One shop owner, Herr Schäfer, also made several kinds of cheese. Mama favored him and started sending me there when I was barely five, giving me a liter-size milk can to be filled. All that kept me from splattering milk all the way home was a tight fitting lid.

At home, Mama poured the milk into a pan and brought it to a boil on the stove. This made it safe she said. I didn't care so much about that. I was waiting for the milk to cool. A rich skin of cream formed on top, and I could then have my favorite treat. Mama sliced a piece of hard crusted rye bread. I'd cover it with homemade jam and top it off with the creamy skin carefully lifted off the milk. I had to be sure Erich wasn't around during all this or he would grab it away.

Small as it was, Marnheim also had two bakeries to satisfy our needs with various breads. These were usually all dark grain with a heavy texture and thick crust. The only white bread came in the form of Brötchen, crusty rolls in several styles. We rarely bought Brötchen. Mama thought they were less nourishing. Housewives baked their own loaves of bread at times, but preferred to rely on the local baker, since he made a better crust. And, in those days, women seldom bought dessert cakes at a bakery. They could bake cakes just as well at home.

An exception was for funerals. Households usually relied on the baker for sweet braided breads, or Streußel cakes, served at wakes following burials. A wake commonly took place in the home of the deceased person's family, and food and drink was provided to all mourners. Because Mama and Papa both came from large families, I attended many funerals and wakes. It was often the only time I would see many of my relatives, including over thirty-five first cousins. Even in hard times, there was usually food and drink for everyone. Wakes were mostly for visiting anyway.

One of two butchers in town lived just two houses down from us. Looking out our second floor window I could see a huge wood beam structure in his courtyard. In winter it became a primitive icemaker as the butcher continuously sprayed water on the crossbeams to form long, thick icicles. I marveled at the sight.

The icicles were cut into big chunks and stored in a special room with straw. He would repeat the process until there was enough ice for several months cold storage of butchered meat. Our butchers also turned fresh meats into delicious cold cuts and sausages.

Mama raised a few pigs each year to sell, as well as for our own pork needs. She bought fresh beef from the butcher only on occasion, usually to make Papa's favorite meal of boiled beef, salt potatoes, green beans, and horseradish sauce. Simple food, Papa would say, but still to his liking.

The pigs Mama fattened into hogs were kept in stalls in the barn. As they grew, the stalls had to be cleaned often, and the floor covered with fresh straw. It was the only time the pigs saw daylight, bolting out the barn door into the enclosed courtyard. When I was small, stall-cleaning day with all its loud squeals, snorting and grunts frightened me into the house. Later I came to feel sorry for hogs, living all of their short lives in tight barn stalls with just an occasional glimpse of sky.

The worst part came in late fall, when the Hausmetzger (house-butcher) showed up. Mama had sold all the hogs except one for money. The remaining hog became our meat and lard supply for the year. The Hausmetzger called in wasn't the local village retail butcher. In our case, he was an area farmer qualified in the slaughter of animals. He was busiest in early spring and late fall. Animals raised for their meat were hardly ever slaughtered in winter or summer, except when mishap and injury necessitated it.

The courtyard became a lively scene on butchering day. With the butcher in charge, everyone in the family, and sometimes a couple of neighbors, were put to helping in the day long work. The butcher brought with him all the needed equipment — several knives, meat grinders, big kettles and tubs, and the rope to tie the animal for killing. After tying and binding the legs of the hog, and hanging the animal from a beam, a hard blow to the head with the blunt side of an ax stunned the animal long enough for the butcher to swiftly slit the throat. A terrible squealing filled the ears, as two or more men struggled to hang on while the animal bled to death. My first time to watch this spectacle was from behind our kitchen window.

Nothing would be wasted in the process. Even the blood streaming from the dying hog's throat was caught in a large pan to be used later in making blood sausage. Once the animal was dead and most of the blood drained, the hog was then lifted into a large tub filled with very hot water, making it easier to remove the bristle from the skin. Mama did the same with a chicken to make it easier to remove feathers.

The slaughter ordeal left me with little desire to eat meat, though I realized at the same time that it was a natural part of my family's survival. From one hog there would be hams, sausages, canned pork roast, cracklings and lard. Some of the meats not canned, like the hams and sausage, were put in salt brine and then smoked. This process, done by my parents, required several weeks.

The day's services of the butcher always ended with him joining us in the evening meal. It featured Metzelsuppe, a soup made from the broth of the cooked meat, and accompanied by roasted pork, potatoes, sauerkraut and an onion cake called Zwiebelkuchen. In fall, drinking Neuewein (new wine) was traditional. In the midst of visiting over good food, I could forget the sight and sound of an animal's death. At least, for a while.

Mama could raise pigs and chickens because the Herbst homestead was a part of the old Marnheim built when the village was a true farm community. Until modern times, Farmers didn't build homes and barns on the land. Reasons were rooted in the added security during times of turmoil, the scarcity of tillable ground, and the social nature of man. The clustering of farmers into villages began to change only in the twentieth century. I grew up seeing farmers leave the village each day to work in their fields, or driving their livestock from barnyards down main streets leading to pastures on the outskirts of town. It was still unusual to see a tractor pulling a wagon or plow. The normal sight was two large cows, or a cow and a horse together, doing the pulling. Except for raising pigs and chickens, my parents didn't farm, but both helped farmers for money or for food in bad times.

There were no shops in Marnheim for men and women to buy ready-made clothes, or furniture for the home. One place did have some fabrics and notions for sewing, but it required a trip to Kirchheim or elsewhere to do any real shopping. We had a sewing machine that Mama used only for simple garment repairs. She had many talents, but fancy machine sewing wasn't one of them. Sewing notions she invariably bought from a peddler who came through the village regularly, riding a bicycle with small suitcases strapped on the back. Going from door to door, he hung one suitcase on a strap around his neck, enabling him to open the lid to show all his wares neatly arranged inside, mostly things like ribbons and threads. In another case were linen tablecloths, bed sheets, and the like. If there was something needed that he didn't have with him, your wishes were written down and brought the next time.

A peddler with a horse drawn wagon also showed up frequently. He didn't go house to house, but instead found four or five good locations and began to holler out his wares. These may be crockery, pots, pans, and other useful items for anyone in need. He would continue to holler until he had enough housewives gathered to begin his spiel. A few men, not otherwise occupied, might come up to spy over the wagon sides to inspect the wares out of curiosity. The peddlers usually ignored them. After all, it was the ladies who made the household decisions.

The peddler I liked best also had cookware, but more importantly, he had toys. Though I didn't realize it at the time, he was my first contact with the German tendency to recycle. His goods were not sold for money. He only traded for scrap metal and old cloth. It must have been a good business because, at the time, he was the one peddler I remember having a motor truck.

One of the more interesting craftsmen to visit our village was the man who sharpened knives and scissors. His bicycle was both his transportation and his sharpening equipment. He, too, would find a location and holler out his services. It never failed to bring a big group of women out of their houses, as there were always things to be sharpened. The bicycle was placed on a stand that raised the rear off the ground and by turning one of the pedals the man made a grinding stone spin. Another bicyclist making daily rounds through the countryside was Mama's cousin still living on the Herbst estate in Heyerhof. Also named Jean, he made a living as a barber despite his hunchback condition.

Before Hitler labeled them as undesirables, Gypsies also visited Marnheim several times while I lived there. I was told that Gypsies were not German, but came from distant places like Hungary and Romania. I hadn't yet learned exactly where these countries were, but Gypsies intrigued me. They always parked their horse drawn house-wagons at the side of the road, or on a meadow, just outside the village. Gypsy men rarely came into the town. It was mostly the women who walked the streets, offering fine lace and the telling of fortunes. Mama loved buying their laces, and I liked watching them read my mother's palm or lay out the tarot cards.

The colorful dress of Gypsy women fascinated me. The full, many-layered skirts topped off by fancy scarves, shawls, and an abundance of jewelry made me stare. The village men didn't like their wives inviting Gypsies into the house. It was said that they had a thousand secret pockets in their skirts to hide stolen things. Mama once had a Gypsy lady in the kitchen. It was a wonder for my young eyes to watch her reach from pocket to pocket to show Mama different laces. Nothing came up missing after the visit, though Papa later said we should have nailed everything down. He said it with a smile so I knew he really wasn't afraid of Gypsies. Later, there were numerous reports of children being kidnapped and killed. Some people said Gypsies were doing it. Perhaps such scares contributed to the absence of public protest when Nazi persecution of Gypsies began. Papa said Gypsies weren't bad and I believed him.

As early as my third year, Mama began giving me chores to do. Simple things like pulling weeds in the garden, never anything beyond my abilities. It was a good job for me, she said, because I was closer to the ground. The same theory must have been employed when she had me dust under the beds. When she boiled laundry in a big pot over a fire in the wash kitchen, I kept her supplied with firewood. There was one chore I really wanted to do — help mush up the boiled slop for the pigs like she did with her hands. It looked like fun to me and I would beg her to let me do some mushing. Every time the answer was the same. "Nay, Märe. You hold the lantern." I did, but with spirits dampened. Being called 'märe' (girl) by her had that effect on me. Papa always called me Annchen — why couldn't she?

There were tumultuous events occurring in the world outside Marnheim in those years, but Mama and Papa never worried their children about things they couldn't control. Poverty, however, was one condition my parents felt they could overcome. In this struggle, Erich and I were a part, but we never thought of ourselves as being poor. Just looking around us, and at other people, our situation seemed quite normal. And, for the moment, I could still discover pleasant surprises in my world like visiting street musicians, traveling puppet shows, and even an organ grinder with his monkey. They also entertained and diverted attention from our primitive existence. Best of all, my brother and I had a dedicated optimist for a father.

Chapter Two

Cold winter weather always brought with it two plagues on my life — kidney infections and inflamed eyes. The doctor told Mama he believed the eye trouble came from a mold in the old stone interior walls of our home. If mold was the problem, nothing could be done short of moving. That had to wait. In the meantime, winter meant often going to bed feeling fine only to wake up unable to open my eyes. During the night the eye lids would be sealed shut as the infected mucus flowed and dried. It would take Mama several warm water rinses to get my eyes open. One eye was usually so red and painful that the doctor would put a dressing on it and cover it with an eye patch. No sooner had one eye healed than the other eye required the same treatment.

Every winter it was the same. People around the house became accustomed to seeing me with a patch over one eye or the other. One morning, a customer came into Onkel Heinrich's workshop while I watched him stuff kapok into a mattress. The stranger saw me with the black eye patch, and expressed his sympathy that I had lost an eye. Onkel immediately quipped, "Ach, don't feel sorry for the girl. We'll start to worry when she has two eye patches." Then he roared with laughter. That kind of humor always eluded me.

I liked Onkel Heinrich and spent much time with him in the workshop downstairs. He didn't seem to mind my presence as long as my talk stopped during complicated tasks, otherwise he would be sure to growl, "Sei still, Märe!" (Be quiet, girl!) He was another Herbst who rarely used my proper name, but at least he smiled.

One of the few things I liked about the shorter days of winter was that Papa would be home earlier from his work. The first thing he did, after cleaning up, was put me on his lap for a little affectionate review of my day and to make promises about a brighter future. This ritual went on until I was six or seven years of age.

By December, the rain and fog of November had turned into heavy snow, and long icicles hung from the roof eaves. The fire in the kitchen iron cook stove would now be kept alive until April, as it was the only heat for our two rooms. Slow burning coal-dust briquettes kept the fire from completely dying in the night. Mostly, it was Papa who got up very early to get the stove roaring again, with Mama working alongside him preparing breakfast and his lunch pail. He was usually gone before Erich and I crawled out from under thick feather comforters.

My brother always had to rush his breakfast and make a mad dash to school. Our two rooms then quieted down for my day with Mama. As I grew older, the more jealous I became about Erich going to school. Unfortunately, Marnheim had no kindergarten so my wait would be even longer before I could attend.

Still, my life was far from boring. There were errands to be run, and visits made to friends and relatives around the village. Time for socializing was greater in winter with less outside work to do. From the age of four, my memories of places and people visited remain sharp.

Tante Giloy was the first truly eccentric person I encountered in the family. The younger sister of Mama's mother, she lived in her own house just down the street from us. For the longest time I thought Giloy was her first name. Erich soon set me straight on that.

"Dumb girl. Does 'Giloy' sound like a first name? Her name is Katharina, but doesn't want to be called that by anyone."

"No one?"

"Well, I suppose some people call her Frau Giloy, but for sure, nobody ever calls her Katharina."

"She sure isn't very friendly," I said. "Yesterday, coming home from the bakery, Mama wanted to stop by her house. You know how high the snow is, well, Tante Giloy wouldn't let us in until every speck was brushed off our clothes and shoes!"

Erich laughed. "And I'll bet she didn't invite Mama and you to sit the whole time. She never does. Papa is right. Tante Giloy thinks she's the 'Grand Dame' of the Herbst family. It's all her crazy ideas about the Herbsts having royal blood!" My brother had reached an age where he'd heard most of the family stories and rumors. What's more, he'd formed some definite opinions he didn't hesitate to spout off to anyone, except Papa. Erich had learned early on that his father didn't abide his rash opinions.

Talk of 'royal blood' meant little to me, and all I could do is wait to learn more about this woman my mother liked to visit. My impressions from that winter morning never changed. Tante Giloy remained rigidly the same all her life. The image I still see is that of a lady unlike anyone else living in the village. She always wore black frilly Victorian dresses, and her stiff demeanor was perfectly matched by an ever-present stern expression. I did admire what appeared to be a pile of gray hair all puffy on top of her head. And, always by her side, a black and brown German shepherd with 'a drawer full of teeth.' At least, that's what I told Mama.

23

Christmas of 1934 started my understanding of the importance of traditions to my parents, especially Papa. During the first week of December, the aroma of cookie baking filled our small home every evening. Papa's self-appointed job was stoking the fire to keep the oven heat perfectly even. It was my first time to help Erich stamp out favorite cookie shapes for Mama to bake. For several evenings in a row she made a different sweet dough, creating a new aroma to delight the senses. During poor times Mama made only two or three kinds of cookies, but by the mid-thirties life for Germans had improved enough that she was able to bake many more kinds.

Mama always put each type of cookie in large tins, storing them away in a cool place. She said the tins made the cookies nice and soft to eat by Christmas Day. He was told not to, but my brother never failed to test the softening process long before the appointed day came.

As I was four years of age, Mama and Papa thought it was time for me to be introduced to another tradition. I remember it well. On the last evening of cookie baking, Erich was sent off on some unexplained errand. My brother was hardly ever sent out in the dark of night. Worried about him, I begged to go along. My plea was out of the question, naturally, and he was out the door and thundering down the stairs in his clodhopper shoes. Within a few minutes, I heard other shoes hitting the steps, and a clanking noise. Soon a heavy knock landed on the door.

"Annchen, see who's there," Papa said. I rushed from his lap to obey, not knowing in the least that what waited on the other side would give me a terrible shock.

Standing there was a tall hooded creature cloaked from head to foot in black. When the figure stepped up into the kitchen light I could see, under the hood, the face of a very old man with dark eyes, a beak-like nose, and a thick white beard that came to his waist. One bony hand held on to a sack draped across one shoulder, and the other gripped a tall staff. A heavy chain hung from around his waist to the floor. I don't know how I got there, probably in one leap, but I was soon behind Papa and holding on to one of his legs in real fear.

Mama and Papa must have struggled to keep from laughing. I didn't notice. I couldn't remove my gaze from the specter that filled our doorway. My father tried to soothe me. "Annchen, there's nothing to fear. It's only the Pelznickel."

he said. "We've told you how he comes at Christmas time."

They had indeed told me over preceding weeks the story of Pelznickel, and I'd seen drawings of him, but it hadn't prepared me for this.

The old tale had St. Nikolaus visiting the homes of boys and girls, usually on December 6th, to see if they had been behaving all year. If they have, he gives out a small treat and promises to tell the Christ Child, who — according to our custom — actually brings the gifts on Christmas. If they've been bad, he leaves nothing but little sticks. In our dialect we called him Pelznickel, because Pelz is fur, and St. Nikolaus always has fur trim on the collar of his black cloak. He also had a long chain that hung down and clattered along at his feet to scare bad children into being good.

With a slight smile, the Pelznickel lowered the sack and invited me to join him. My parents nodded their approval, and urged me to talk to him. Papa gave me a nudge, and I walked over to him finally. Answering his questions, I assured him I was a good girl.

"How do I know that's true?"

That seemed a strange question. My truthfulness had never been questioned before. Checking the faces of Mama and Papa, I finally answered. "Because I'm not allowed to be a bad girl."

A broad smile spread across his face, and I could see the empty spaces where teeth should have been. Reaching into his sack, he brought out a paper pouch of cookies.

"I'll tell the Christ Child how good you are," he said.

With that, he turned and left, and without clanking the chain as he descended the stairs.

I excitedly told Erich all about the visit of the Pelznickel when he returned later. Of course, he had known all about it — and why Papa had sent him away. He figured the boy wouldn't be able to keep a straight face, ruining everything. The Pelznickel never checked on me again, but the time would come when I would play the bearded one!

That same Christmas when I was four, our parents took Erich and I to Kirchheimbolanden to see the decorated shops. It was a five-kilometer walk, and that's just how we got there, often trudging through heavy snow cover. It should be noted that when I was a very small child, such winter trips outside the village saw me bundled up and pulled on a sled to our destination. Erich never let me forget my pampered treatment.

For a couple of youngsters from a village where few homes had electricity, it was a wonderment to see a place so aglow with light. In the town center of Kirchheim was a huge Christmas tree covered with white lights from top to bottom. Tall as any of the buildings that surrounded it, the tree alone was worth the walk from Marnheim.

Our parents made sure we got a good look in the toy shops, paying close attention to things that excited us. It didn't take long to learn the reason behind their interest. Over the years, Mama and Papa rarely missed the mark with the gifts we received. For Erich, there was a miniature steam engine, a hot lead molding set, and just anything he could tinker with. Naturally, my wishes fell in with the usual girl things like a toy sewing machine or dolls. However, my best gift of all didn't come from a store. In 1934, I was given a doll house hand-made by Papa. It was an exact replica of our own living quarters, and included many pieces of furniture. In the following years, pieces were added, like a floor lamp that really turned on with the help of a battery. Another treasured piece was an iron cook stove, the mirror image in miniature of Mama's stove.

For most of my playmates in Marnheim gift-giving came on Christmas Eve, but for as long as we lived there, Erich and I had to wait until morning. Space was the problem with only two rooms.

Papa would go to a nearby forest late in the afternoon of Christmas Eve day. The tree selected was always quite small, no more than a meter high. While brother and I had an evening bath in the kitchen, Papa would stand the tree, undecorated, on top of a low dresser in the bedroom. Soon we were put to bed, and urged to fall asleep. Of course, this was easier said than done, and we'd whispered to each other in anticipation until dozing off. As we slept, Mama and Papa came in, decorated the little tree with colored balls, tinsel and real candles, then placed our gifts nearby.

Large things like my doll house and Erich's steam engine, put away each year, were brought out from storage and set up in the kitchen. After a year, these almost seemed new again.

It never failed to amaze me how Christmas had an odd effect on the men in the house. I hardly ever got to play or work with my gifts first. Erich just had to try my sewing machine before I could. Then, on top of it, break the crushing news that the machine didn't have a bobbin to lock in the stitches. Even an embroidery kit had Papa and my brother rushing over to try their hands at needlework while I sat and waited. I still hear Mama's irritation: "Ist das Euer Geschenk oder Annchen's??" Her pointed question as to whether the gift was theirs or mine usually put the article back in my hands in seconds.

҈

The twenty-sixth of December is called the Second Christmas Day in Germany, and is also a holiday. It's a day usually spent with members of the extended family. For us, that might mean a quick visit to Mama's relatives at Heyerhof nearby. We would likely also encounter Tante Giloy at the estate, in which case, we wouldn't want to linger. Though Papa was always nice to her, I'm sure he knew that the woman believed Mama had married below her Herbst station. My father's nature allowed him to accept her attitude with a grain of salt and good humor. We all looked forward to a warmer welcome from the Bolanden family. As soon as it was polite, we would be on our way to visit Papa's mother, sisters and brothers.

I loved visiting Oma Klein. She had more than a dozen grand-children, but always treated me as if I was the only one. She was small, energetic, and good-natured — traits passed on to Papa in abundance. Any visit to her always began with a joyful dialect command, "Geb mer ä Schmätz!" I was more than happy to respond with a big kiss on her soft, wrinkled cheek. Erich didn't like 'schmaltzy' stuff and would avoid kissing anyone, if possible. Papa had a special relationship with his mother. No meeting between them ever occurred without warm embraces and kisses. Of all her children, he felt the most responsible to her, and she trusted his advice more than any of the others. Papa had been her husband's right hand.

In time I came to understand that Mama's feelings about Oma were highly erratic. She would never bad-mouth my grandmother, yet she showed little enthusiasm in going to Bolanden, really no farther away than many places we visited frequently. Christmas was one of the few times in the year when she joined in a visit to Oma. She did so, I think, from a feeling of obligation. She wanted harmony with Papa, and after all it was a family tradition to exchange Christmas cookies. I have wondered if my mother never forgave Oma for not keeping a closer watch to prevent Raul's accidental scalding death years before.

27

Chapter Three

1935and 1936 were filled with events that would shape my family's future. Adolf Hitler's position of power was firm, and the trickle-down effects, which seemed mostly positive at the time, became more evident every day throughout Germany. Mama and Papa were beginning to believe that the promise of National Socialism meant economic salvation — plain and simple. Common folk like my parents wanted only to feel good again about themselves and Germany's future.

There were signs that not everyone shared the new optimism. One evening in early 1935, Papa informed us that he'd learned the Stern clothing store in Kirchheim was going out of business. The Sterns had been given a short time to sell out by the authorities. Papa was still driving a delivery truck for a flour mill in Kirchheim owned by the Decker family. Though he always kept a sharp eye for bargains, news of the Sterns didn't set right with him. The Sterns were Jewish, as was his boss Isaak Decker. How soon would it be before Herr Decker was forced out? And would a new Nazi owner keep Papa on?

Papa wanted to help the Sterns for reasons he didn't tell, but he looked very unhappy. By 'help,' he meant that Mama should go with him to buy a few things as soon as it turned dark. Mama said later that they entered the store by the back door. Papa was worried the store was under surveillance to see who was spending money with Stern. Erich and I had to promise not to tell anyone about it.

It would be years before I understood all of Papa's concerns for the Sterns, people he'd known all his life. Kirchheim was home to several Jewish families. Many were life-long natives, and most would eventually disappear — never to return.

It seemed like only days after the night visit to Sterns, Papa's worst fear came true. The Decker family was told to sell the flour mill and leave. Papa took me with him on his bicycle from Marnheim to the Decker villa on the edge of Kirchheim to say his goodbye. The mill had a new owner, and as my father feared, all the old workers were let go. Still Papa wanted to bid farewell to his old boss, and didn't care if he was seen entering the villa. His association with Decker and his mill had been long and friendly.

The maid took us through to the kitchen so quickly that I never got an impression of the rooms or furnishings. The kitchen however, stayed in my mind. There was something discomforting about her behavior, about the way she looked at us, but it didn't seem to bother Papa. She left us in the kitchen while she went to inform Herr Decker. I didn't like the idea of being alone with the maid, but changed my mind when she came back and spoke respectful to Papa. "Would you come with me, Herr Klein?" I stayed behind and took the chance to look over the gleaming white kitchen.

It was a spacious place — bigger than our two rooms at home put together. Cabinets lined the tile-covered walls. The floor was also of tile, with two large work tables standing in the center of the room. I recognized several electrical appliances, but didn't know how they operated. The maid came back, but said nothing to me. I would have liked to ask about the kitchen and all its curiosities, but Papa soon returned and we left for home.

The Stern and Decker families did finally reach the United States. America's doors to fleeing Jews were not exactly wide-open and successful immigration often depended on whether there were sponsoring relatives. Of the original 65 Jews living in Kirchheim in 1933, only 11 remained by 1940.

In my pre-school years, I often tagged along on Papa's bicycle outings. He attached a wooden platform on the cross bar for me to sit on while he pedaled. Like the visit to the villa, our trips together weren't always for happy reasons. Now unemployed, he had to report to the government finance office in Kirchheim once a week to collect a small amount of money used to buy staples like sugar, cooking oil, and bread, but between our garden and previously stored food, starvation wasn't a threat. Unemployment was the big problem in our area, so we often waited in a long, slow line that extended out into the street. Papa knew so many people, and if he wasn't chatting with them, the two of us never lacked for subject matter.

The bicycle rides to Kirchheim continued a few months, until he found a job driving a truck for a flour mill in Morschheim — yet another nearby village. Now, Papa would ride the bicycle alone. It was over ten kilometers each way, and with the colder weather of fall, the trips took a toll on his health. Finally, pneumonia put him in the hospital and the job was lost after just a couple of months.

When he was well again, it was decided that rather than stand in the unemployment line, Papa would seek odd jobs. It turned out to be a wise decision, for the name 'Kleine Seppel' was still respected throughout the area. Scores of villages and farms circled our mountain, and he knew the territory.

For much of 1936, Papa found odd jobs everywhere, and kept busy most of the time. All was not entirely without mishap. One day, as he pedaled toward Bolanden, a threatening German shepherd approached him along the road. The animal didn't bite, but in the process of falling, my father broke his right hand. This, however, was not enough to keep him from working one-handed in the cheerful manner that made him so likable. Getting out nearly every day, he was also able to find out what was happening in the countryside.

In late summer, he began telling Mama that 1937 would bring massive government construction programs for highways and bridges. He felt a good living could be made if he only owned a truck.

Heyerhof, the Herbst ancestral estate east of Marnheim, is a big farm settlement with several houses and barns situated on open rolling land. It was an easy fifteen-minute walk from our house. Mama's Uncle Adam was in control of farming. My mother's Uncle Philip and his wife Sophia also lived there in a separate house. Philip owned parts of the estate, but leased his share to Adam while he worked for the government in Albisheim. From her mother, Mama owned small sections of field in the area as well. These she rented out to a local farmer for extra income. It didn't amount to much and often took the form of a share in the potatoes harvested.

Mama considered a winter supply of potatoes better than money.

She usually took me along on her visits to Heyerhof. It was there, during the occasion of cousin Adam's confirmation party, I stuck my tongue out at the camera. A road from Marnheim passed the entrance to the estate, but our favorite way was on a path along the Pfrimm, a picturesque stream. In all seasons, it was an ideal nature trail bordered by wild flowers, berry bushes, and trees. The water rushing over the rocky stream bed provided all the company a person would need.

Mama was especially fond of her Uncle Philip, and showed it by naming her son Erich Philip, in his honor. The feeling was mutual and it was to him that Mama turned in late 1936 for a great favor. She asked him to co-sign a bank loan so Papa could buy a truck. I went with her on more than one visit to Philip to discuss the question. Onkel wanted to help, but it took weeks to convince Tante Sophie, who apparently didn't trust in my father's 'wild' dreams. She needn't have worried. Papa was right about an upturn in the economy. Government building programs in the new year brought more work than he could handle. The loan was paid off in record time.

❧

In 1936, the Third Reich began to affect my family life in other ways. Erich, at the age of ten, began his mandatory service in Hitler Youth. He was so proud to finally be old enough to wear the uniform — brown shirt, black kerchief with leather knot, and a black leather shoulder strap. Twice a week, he attended meetings at the school, where leaders taught the ideology of the Reich through pep talks and songs. Marching songs replaced older folk songs in public. Even in little Marnheim there seemed to be lots of marching to the new music designed to instill love for the Fatherland and absolute loyalty to the Führer. Both boys and girls in Hitler Jugend, as we called it, frequently marched down my street singing lustily of our new pride. I would soon be leaning out of our window singing along, having quickly memorized many of the songs. I also dreamed of the day when I would be old enough to be in Hitler Jugend.

"Ein frischer Wind kam durch die Gegend!" This was a phrase heard often in this time of rapid change. Everyone around us felt like there really was 'a new wind blowing through our country.' As a young girl, I could hardly know the larger causes behind this renewed spirit. My awareness of it sprang from Erich's Hitler Jugend activities. More so, was my witness to Mama's happier disposition and outlook. It was a side of her I had never known.

Around this time, a new and wonderful sound came into our kitchen. Papa bought or bartered for a record player during one of his trips out in the countryside. It was an old wind-up model with an acoustic speaker that could be placed on top of a side table. Several records came along with it — arias from opera, songs from operettas, and a tune I would soon start humming called "Glühwürmchen." Years later, I'd hear it again, but under the name "Glowworm."

All the records were played repeatedly. I was thrilled by the music of Beethoven and Mozart, scratchy as the old records sounded. Mama especially liked the opera arias sung by Richard Tauber, one of Germany's most famous tenors. Only later I was told he was Jewish and had already fled to England.

I suspect the record player, and the old radio Papa brought home soon after, were both picked up at household sales where the owners had been ordered to leave the country. I have no facts, just a feeling and the knowledge that we didn't have the money for such things at the time. My parents would not pay even 'second-hand' prices charged by stores, but Papa probably could handle a deal offered by someone in a hurry. He did so without pleasure, and often at risk with authorities. They preferred to confiscate the property of the

31

"undesirables" for themselves.

The radio was a strange assortment of three large pieces — a tuner, a horn-shaped speaker, and a battery. It took up a lot of space, but this was overlooked in our excitement of being able to hear the outside world. As we had no electricity, care was taken not to wear down the battery, which limited listening to mostly news programs. Every week or two, Papa had to take the battery elsewhere to be recharged.

❧

Jean, Mama's first cousin and an itinerant barber, was a bitter man. A hunchback, he peddled his bicycle out from Heyerhof to customers far and wide, including stops in Marnheim. Since one of these was Onkel Heinrich in the shop downstairs, I got to see Jean often. It was his habit to make my uncle's haircut the last one of the day, as he worked his way home. Since the two were friends as well as relatives, the arrangement allowed for a bit of relaxing with a glass or two of wine.

On one of these evenings, I made the mistake of going downstairs when they were sitting at a work table drinking wine. Jean acted much friendlier, almost jolly. My uncle was his usual happy self, inviting me to visit. Curiosity got the better of me, and I asked what they were drinking. When I was told wine, I must have thought it strange. They were filling big water glasses, and I knew that you drank wine from wine glasses. Poor as we were Mama and Papa used fancy wine glasses, and I told the two so. Being all of six years old, I was beginning to exert my opinions more freely.

"Here," Onkel Heinrich said. "Take a drink and see for yourself!"

I did — a big swallow. It was my first really good sampling of the famous liquid of the Rheinland-Pfalz, and I liked it.

Pestering for more, even the normally dour Jean decided to share until my initial good feeling turned to sour dizziness. It was time to leave and I started back up the stairs to Mama.

From this point in the story I must rely on my brother's details of the aftermath. He was there to witness it, and I have no personal memory of events. No doubt he may have improved on the tale with much retelling over the years, but knowing Mama, it sounds mostly true.

Hearing a noise on the stairs, Mama opened the door and saw me trying to negotiate the steps on my hands and knees, whimpering. Quickly helping me up the stairs, she immediately recognized my state and sat me down in the kitchen. As there was always barley coffee on the stove, she made me drink some — probably hoping it would sober me. Putting me in Erich's care, she headed for her brother's workshop below. My brother said he had never seen Mama in such a rage. The laughter in the shop ended abruptly as she ripped into both brother and cousin for making her daughter drunk.

Erich said he could hear both of them pleading with Mama not to do anything reckless, and promising never to give Annchen any more wine. He didn't know what the 'reckless' thing was that had Heinrich and Jean pleading, but it sure made him curious. Finally, my brother couldn't resist tiptoeing down the steps to see what Mama was doing to scare the two men. Peeking around the corner he saw that she had picked up a leather strap that Onkel had been working on, and was slamming it repeatedly down on the work table like a whip. Both Onkel Heinrich and cousin Jean were up against the wall, cowering like two trapped rats.

It was all too unreal, Erich would say, with each retelling of the story. Onkel Heinrich was much taller and stronger than our mother, yet he crouched as low as Jean in the face of her fury.

While Mama was understandably protective of me in things like the wine incident, her fears for me went to extremes at times. I'm thinking of such activities as skating, swimming, and hiking. Erich was allowed to do all. I was not. It's true Erich was five years older, but upon reaching the age when my brother did all those things, Mama's answer to me remain the same; "No!" Her reasons always seemed to center on my health, and it didn't help that she could never forget Raul's tragic death. Then, adding to her fears was the drowning death of a neighbor's son, Rudy Frey, who also happened to be Erich's best friend.

Rudy's father was so devastated by the loss of his only son that he tried to hang himself a few weeks later. Fortunately, in answer to Frau Frey's frantic screams, Papa was able to cut the man down in time. Herr Frey lived several more years, finally dying of what Mama called 'heartbreak.'

A Bolanden girl, about my same age of six, drowned in a flooding creek just a year later. Mama knew the family, and took me to the girl's house so I could see her body in the coffin. It was my first experience seeing a dead person, and the scene has never left me. The coffin was placed in the center of a small sitting room. Family members sat on chairs along the walls, but I was most amazed at all the flowers. The room was filled with flowers and their heavy fragrance. Mama walked me to the coffin, where I could just barely see the girl laying. She appeared covered by flowers, even around her head, and only her small, waxen face showed. My mother didn't take me to the cemetery for the burial — I had seen enough to scare me for a lifetime about going into water over my head.

ತಿ

In late spring, for the Pfingsten (Whitsuntide) religious holiday, Germans make a special commune with nature. I first participated when I was four years old. I know that because of a photo taken of the 1934 outing. My parents, Erich and I, and a group of neighbors are shown resting on a grassy embankment that ran along the narrow road half way to the top of our Donnersberg (Thunder Mountain).

The Donnersberg is 687 meters, or 2,273 feet high — the highest elevation in the Pfalz. It's always had a great significance in the lives of our people. One of our Pfälzer writers, Heinrich Weis, once wrote that the mountain reminded him of a god, who in the form of a huge bull, came to rest among the forested hills. Happy there, he stayed and allowed the trees to cover him as well. While small as mountains go, it does obstruct and disperse severe weather coming from the west, but I don't know if the name comes from that or Celtic mythology. Tramping up the mountain each year as a young girl, such things meant little to me. In time I would learn that the Donnersberg had many legends, some that came down through the centuries from Celtic tribes that made the top a fortified home. Much later, Napoleon Bonaparte would be so impressed by the mountain on one of his campaigns into Germany, he designated the region Departement du Mont-Tonnerre. For the moment, however, local history had no place in the excitement of reaching our destination.

We young ones always separated from our elders, upon reaching the peak, to make the more arduous climb to the top of the watchtower. Called the "Ludwigsturm" after one of our old Kaisers, it was higher than any of the tallest trees.

Entering through a door at the base, we'd start up a spiral stone staircase. Except for the occasional small square opening in the outside wall, it was quite dark. Even young legs began to ache before bright daylight greets the climber stepping out on a large platform, enclosed by a meter-high stone wall. The view from the top of Ludwigsturm is breathtaking. Erich took pleasure in showing off his knowledge by pointing out distant big cities like Kaiserslautern far to the south, Mainz in the north, and Worms on the eastern horizon. In between, was the panorama of rolling fields of every hue, deep wooded valleys, and villages spotted here and there. To the west and southwest, the landscape was almost entirely rugged forest, as far as my eyes could see.

Not one of the adults in our group had climbed the tower. By the time we had rejoined them, they had already found seats at one of the long tables in an already crowded outdoor pavilion. Papa and the others were well into their drinks and conversation with other wanderers. Now and then, a band struck up a tune, and that meant schunkeln, the linking arms with your neighbors and rocking back and forth, while singing merrily.

After the tower climb, it always seemed to me, there was barely time for a soft drink before starting the return journey home. Papa would never fail to stop for a short visit with his mother in Bolanden on the way. Any friends along would take their leave of us there, and go on ahead to Marnheim. My father would never pass by Bolanden without stopping at Oma's. Mama often didn't understand his loyalty, but held her tongue.

∿

The annual summer festival in Bolanden can't be compared to Kirchheim, but I liked it better than Marnheim's small carnival because it meant seeing Oma Klein. A few of Papa's brothers and sisters, still living there, were also fun to be around. The rides weren't much to speak of and there were only a few vendor booths to check out. Still, I loved seeing the wares and listening to the ladies gossip, as they searched for bargains. I was only six years old, but that didn't stop me from recognizing a bargain, and I saw one!

At the toy booth, my eyes fell on a tiny tin baby carriage, perfectly proportioned to go with my doll house and one of my clay dolls. Only 99 pfennigs (pennies) and it had little tin wheels that turned. I had no money with me. All my savings were in a child's bank at home. I was left to plead with my parents.

I caught up with them at Tante Gusta's home nearby, which turned out to be the wrong place to ask them. The answer was a stern "Absolutely no." Had I been older and wiser, I would have known Mama wouldn't want her sister-in-law thinking I was spoiled. Heaven forbid!

The little baby carriage stayed on my mind all the way home to Marnheim that evening. I dreamed about it through the night, and woke up thinking about it in the morning. It was a Monday and when Erich came home from school for lunch, I cornered him.

"Would you please walk with me to Bolanden after school?"

"Why would I want to do that," he snorted. I could tell he wasn't having a good day.

"Just do it for me, please." I put lots of sugar on the please part. It made him hesitate; probably trying to think of some job I could do for him in return. While he was thinking, I continued, "The carnival is still on and I want to go back and buy that baby carriage with my own money!"

"How did you get your own money?"

"Just like you showed me one time. I used a knife in the slot on my strawberry bank to make the coins come out."

"Oh, God, girl. Mama will kill us if we go all the way over there without her!"

"She would not," I reasoned. "Papa wouldn't let her."

"Maybe not, but I really don't have time today anyway. You'll just have to forget that toy."

He was gone, running to catch up with one of his friends, before I could think of a new argument. Besides, a new idea was forming. Wernerchen will do it. That's Werner, who was my age, and the son of Mama's best friend Frau Kaufhold, who lived just down the street. We often played together, sometimes for a whole afternoon. I decided to pay Werner a visit.

He didn't disappoint me, though he had some worry his mother wouldn't want us to leave the village. I could see Frau Kaufhold was doing the weekly laundry. That would take most of the afternoon, I was sure.

"She won't even miss us, Wernerchen. I know a shortcut and we'll be back in no time."

We were on our way, leaving Marnheim behind. There were two ways to go — a five-kilometer trek along the main roads, or the more popular pathway my family used. I had been told that people of both Marnheim and Bolanden had used it for hundreds of years. It was a bit shorter and I liked how it coursed through open fields, into stands of poplar trees, dipping into hollows and over gentle hill rises. Reaching the outlying gardens of Bolanden, the path ended at the market square. That's where the carnival was set up, and I was delighted to find it still in business.

Werner and I quickly took care of my purpose, and with baby carriage in hand, I decided to stop at Tante Gusta's house for a drink before heading home. She appeared startled to see me with a strange boy, and immediately asked if my mother was along.

"No, this is the son of Mama's friend. Wernerchen and I came over together. Can we have a drink of water and go to the toilet?"

"Of course, you can. But you must hurry back home. Don't you know how worried your mothers must be?"

"They aren't worried," I said. "They don't know we're here."

We left before she could react to that news. I had wanted to also visit Oma and Tante Lisbeth with my prize purchase, but thought better of it when the village church bell let me know it was already five o'clock. We had to be back before the Marnheim evening bell at six.

We got back to Marnheim with time to spare. I thanked Werner and left him at his house. When I got to my own, and walked through the door into the courtyard, I immediately saw Mama bending over the slop pail. She was up to her elbows in the pigs' evening meal. Holding the baby carriage in one hand behind my back, I wondered what to say.

"Where have you been all afternoon, Märe?"

"I was with Wernerchen," I answered, truthfully.

"You should have told me. I was getting worried about you."

That could have been the end of it. I could have walked by and hidden the baby carriage, to bring out later. But I'd never lied to my parents and I must have sensed that my world was too small to keep any secrets. Mama was still mixing the pig slop when I decided to show her the baby carriage.

"Mama," I started, holding my purchase out front, "Wernerchen and I walked over to Bolanden." I don't know what I expected, probably a spanking, though she had never spanked me. She stood up to look at me speechless. Her arms hung straight down, dripping slop on the ground for what felt like the longest time. Then, nodding her head toward the house, she said. "Go in and get ready for supper."

As I turned to do her bidding, she added, more sharply, "Don't you ever leave this village again without your father or I."

Erich couldn't believe Mama hadn't "killed" me. When Papa learned of my escapade, Mama's warning was repeated, but I could tell he wasn't angry with me. Actually, the threat of discipline had little to do with my usual obedience to rules. I truly wanted to meet my parents' approval at all times.

Daughter Kristina's sketch of my birth home in Marnheim.

In the photo section later you will find a very old photo from the family archives showing the same scene. I find her vision more appealing. I was born July 15, 1930 in a two-room apartment upstairs in the building on the right.

Chapter Four

With my seventh birthday, I was enrolled in school. The first day, Mama accompanied me to be sure the teacher placed me up front in the class. Her fear was showing through again, this time about my 'poor eyesight.' Since I was taller than most of the other kids, her concern bothered me — I didn't want to be so conspicuous in front. As we moved along in a line to meet the teacher, I noticed that a mother in front of us made the same request for her daughter that Mama had in mind for me. I heard the teacher, a man, ask the girl to look across the room at a picture and tell him what it was "Flowers in a pot?" she replied.

"Fine," he said. "You'll do okay in the back. Next."

After Mama had her say, I argued that I really had no problem seeing. "Well then, child," he said. "What do you see on that wall over there?"

"Flowers in a pot," I answered.

It didn't work. Mama insisted that I be placed up front, and that was that. I think the teacher also noticed I hadn't even looked at the picture before answering.

So it goes.

"Wo man singt da laß Dich ruhig nieder, böse Menschen haben keine Lieder."

That was Mama's answer when I once asked her why she sang around the house. My mother loved singing while she worked — it is one of my happiest memories of her. Sometimes I sang along, and came to agree with her folklore message of 'Seek companionship where people sing, for bad people have no song.' Mama had a lovely voice, but only sang when alone or for Papa, Erich and I. She wasn't shy by any measure, but her personality couldn't be called outward in a joyous sense. When it did come out, her humor lacked gaiety. She could be sentimental, though rarely. Mama had to smile or laugh to have a pretty face. A lovely mouth and perfect teeth made it so. Sadly, unlike Erich, I lacked the talent to make her smile or laugh very often.

I admired Mama, despite no hugs and kisses from her. She set the moral standard in our home and, without complaint, she worked hard to keep her family clean, nourished, and clothed. In that, and in her faith in God and the Bible, she couldn't be faulted. As for her inability to give me affection, this didn't bother me as a child. Papa more than filled that need for me.

Mama was trim and petite, and in a nice dress, she really had a nice shape and good posture. Most beautiful of all was her hair. I liked to watch her brush it to a sheen, then make two braids that hung well past her waist. These would be twisted and turned into large circular mounds, pinned behind her ears. It was a hairstyle neither too young nor old for her, and she never changed it. Papa said hair was the only good thing she got from Oma Herbst. Her sisters Anna and Katharina, both much younger, had thin hair that turned gray in their thirties. On the day she died, there was not a gray hair on Mama's head.

While Papa had the loving nature and explosive humor of his mother and father, Mama seemed trapped by a Herbst female tendency toward frequent and unfathomable depressions. These would continue all through our years in Marnheim, despite many efforts to lift her spirits. Among those who tried were two of my Klein uncles. Otto and Rudi adored Mama and came often to the house. Both called her "Mariechen," just like Papa. Coming through the door, either one would likely pick her up, swing her around, and plant a kiss on her cheek. One of their favorite lines while doing so went something like, "Ach, Mariechen, you're as beautiful as ever!" Mama would insist, in mock anger, on being put down. Everyone could see she really liked the attention, but lacked the ease of humor to join in the fun.

As for my uncles' attempts to break through the barrier, their efforts were doomed from the start, but they always had fun trying. That was the Klein way — a positive and affectionate approach, edged with humor. My brother Erich picked up a lot of the Klein genes — more than enough. The truth for me, I came to realize, was that I got far too many genes from Mama's side. Along with her hair, I inherited many of her darker traits to battle as life unfolded.

అ

My school career had been underway a few weeks when I was rescued from the front row. I'd been selected as the only child from the village to attend a children's health retreat in Bad Kissingen, a famous resort city to the north-east and a long way from home. It was one of Hitler's programs for children of working class people. I was chosen as a good candidate because of a govern-ment nurse who knew of my ailments. A member of the Protestant Deaconess sisters in Kirchheim, she made regular rounds in Marnheim.

I'd be gone for seven weeks. Mama wasn't too happy about it, and I didn't help by being uncertain myself. Papa reminded us of Erich's good experience the year before. He had attended a different kind of camp program, and raved for weeks after about the good food and fun.

꙰

Mama had a village dressmaker quickly whip up three dresses for me, one fashioned entirely out of new material. I was feeling special — these were the first new dresses I ever had. Until then, all of my clothes were hand-me-downs from various cousins.

Finally, with one packed suitcase, I was taken to the Marnheim train station. A tag with my name and destination was pinned on my dress by Papa. Aboard the train, I was too excited to be sad, so I happily waved 'auf Wiedersehen' to my parents, who stood on the platform until I was out of sight.

The first stop was the large town of Grünstadt, still on the Pfalz side of the Rhein River. More children, some teary-eyed, joined me. Bad Kissingen was still far away. I'd been on train trips, but never on one that required several hours. Mama had taken me to visit Herbst relatives in nearby villages, and on shopping trips, but I'd never been anywhere out of the Donnersberg's shadow.

The surprise of unexpected tunnels and long bridges excited me, and I found the changing scenery fascinating, especially the flat farmland that looked so unlike my hilly Pfalz. The other children seated nearby must have thought me terribly shy — I didn't speak more than ten words the whole time. Just when my eagerness to arrive was about to reach fever pitch, the conductor came by announcing "Bad Kissingen." My heart suddenly jumped with the realization that I might not like it.

Pulling into the train station, I also worried about my suitcase in the baggage car. It was too heavy for me to carry very far, and I wondered what to do. Stepping down on the platform with the other children, all such worries vanished. A pleasant looking woman appeared and gently guided us to a small bus nearby. It had KINDERHEIM printed in large letters above the windshield. A man was loading our suitcases on the back of the bus, and we were soon on our way to the children's home.

The Kinderheim was located at the edge of the city, yet still within walking distance to the large health resort in the heart of downtown. Groups of children from other parts of Germany had arrived earlier in the day. I was surprised to learn there were no boys in residence. They would join us during the daytime only.

The woman who greeted us at the train had my group follow her to a large open patio behind the main building. She told us that she was one of the nurse's aides who would care for us, all under the guidance of Deaconess Sisters. On the patio, we met more of the other girls who'd just arrived. We were divided into age groups, and following a snack, taken on a tour of the home.

The dining hall seemed huge to me, and it looked out through large windows onto the patio. As it was summer, the long tables would sometimes be set up on the stone patio for meals. The bathroom was also large, with a line of wash basins down one wall. Each had faucets with hot and cold running water. I had heard of hot water from a faucet, but like most of the girls, had never seen it. The toilets in another room were just as amazing. They flushed.

We didn't go into the kitchen area that took up most of a kind of half basement. Later when we went outside, it was easy to see all the white-clad people rushing about the kitchen through a line of windows half above ground level.

And then there were the dormitories. Our suitcases had been brought in, so all that remained was assignment of beds. There were more rules to learn, but nothing very difficult. I was shy and my mother's daughter, so I had few problems with orderly behavior and cleanliness. We had to line up for meals and field trips and such, but the German reputation of doing everything in lock step is really undeserved.

Each of the three dormitory rooms had twenty beds arranged in three rows — a row along each of the two facing walls, and one row down the middle of the room. I got a bed in the middle row. Our suitcases were taken away, as there were no drawers or footlockers for storing clothes in the rooms. All clothes and shoes were kept in a special room in wire baskets on shelves. The garments stayed neatly stacked in the baskets with each child's name and hometown on tags. Once a week, clean clothes were issued and the soiled ones were turned in to be washed. We wore the same socks, dresses, and undergarments for a whole week. We were expected to wash all of our bodies everyday. It was another rule I had no problem with — Mama insisted on the same.

Our first supper was good, though nothing more special than the typical German fare of soup and open-faced sandwiches. Each table seated ten girls, and we learned immediately that we didn't serve ourselves. Teen-aged helpers filled the dishes just prior to our sitting down. Many of the girls had a hard time eating everything on their plates. It was no problem for me. Over the weeks to come, I grew to love the food so much, I was often willing to finish another girl's meal. I should note that no grace or mention of Hitler before eating was required. Instead, we were told to join hands around to wish our tablemates "Good Appetite."

After supper we got to walk outside on the grounds for a while, or we would gather in small groups for introductions and games. Bedtime came as darkness in the summer sky set in. Preparing for bed, I got to know my neighbors on either side. Both were nice, and I would like them a lot before long, but one was an especially beautiful child. Luise was a year younger than I, soft-spoken and very polite. Surrounding an angelic face, was naturally curly, very thick light brown hair that she wore in two heavy braids. My memory of Luise also remains because of what happened the first night.

I'd somehow sensed her unhappiness, but didn't think much of it until after we were under the covers. She started sobbing so softly that, at first, I didn't know exactly what it was. As the room quieted down, the sound of her crying became clear. When I sat up in bed, uncertain what to do, one of the nurses came over. I remember how gentle she was with Luise, stroking her face and whispering with a calm voice. Shortly, she settled down and the nurse came over to tuck me in. I asked her what the matter was with Luise.

"Sie hat Heimweh," she whispered. ("She is homesick.")

"Where does that hurt?"

A silly question, but I simply couldn't imagine such a malady. She smiled at my naiveté. Her name was Frieda, and she quietly tried to explain how it could hurt all over when you miss your home and family. I just shook my head in disbelief. I couldn't see how anyone in such a wonderful place as the Kinderheim could feel bad about not being at home. For many years, 'Heimweh' was for other people. Perhaps I was a very secure child.

❧

The first full day in Bad Kissingen began a well organized routine that would continue through our stay. I was learning how orderly Germans can be — everything done according to some 'master plan.' The Kinderheim was no exception, and as the planners expected, we children went along without complaint.

There were a few activities and rules a young country girl had to get used to, like being dunked naked into a vat of murky green mineral water. It was a major struggle for me, and I made an enemy of Nurse-aide Hedwig when I protested that the wood sides and bottom were slippery and I would drown. In my mind, I saw the Bolanden girl in her coffin. Hedwig, however, didn't understand my fear and forced me to sit in the water, up to my head, many long minutes. I never felt comfortable about the "treatment," but settled into a tolerance of it. We were told the mineral water was healthy. Soaking in it improved circulation, breathing it as a mist healed damaged lungs, and drinking the stuff cleansed and revitalized organs of the body.

Another unpleasant incident with Hedwig came when picture postcards of

Bad Kissingen were passed out to all the girls. We were told to write a short message to our families. We used the tables in the dining room, and as I sat there staring at my card, her form loomed over me.

"Why aren't you writing?" she demanded.

"Ich kann nicht schreiben," I said quietly.

"What," she bellowed. "You can't write? I don't believe it. Lazy, that's what you are!"

Every eye in the room focused on me, of that I was certain. How could I explain that while seven years old, I had only been in school a few weeks. I could count and I knew my letters, but at that point I could only write my name.

One of the older girls came to my rescue. She didn't seem intimidated by my nemesis, and insisted on writing my postcard message for me, letting me sign it. Her name was Karola, a fifteen-year-old helper at the home. I was glad for her kindness, and sorry she couldn't always be around to protect me.

Each week, the aides washed our hair under faucets in the courtyard. My hair, thick and curly, was just starting to reach my shoulders. After a childhood of short bobs, I wanted long hair like my mother's. One week, my hair washer was none other than Hedwig. After a rough shampooing, she rinsed my hair, grabbed it in one hand, squeezed, and jerked upward. Pain shot through me and I surprised both her and myself with a loud scream. There were tears in my eyes, and I was so angered that I could have kicked her. She claimed innocence in wanting to hurt me. I knew otherwise.

There were five Deaconess nurses, a few aides, and several older teenage girl assistants at the Kinderheim. With the exception of Hedwig, all were kind and helpful to me.

꙯

Thinking back on it, I find it amazing that sixty girls lived together for nearly two months in such constant harmony. Being kept busy following a daily program helped, but it's interesting that I never saw anything more serious than a slight verbal disagreement between any of the girls. We felt lucky to be there.

The Kinderheim had a clean and healthy environment. We sensed that those in charge were determined to send us home rosy-cheeked, and probably a lot plumper. The aromas flowing out from the kitchen were enough to build anyone's appetite. The food wasn't more nutritious than we got at home, but the cooks spiced most dishes differently, and I liked the results.

My last day at Bad Kissingen.

The inset has a closer view of me on the left and Luise, the 'homesick girl' on the first night at the right. I can't say I felt healthier, but then I didn't feel sick when I arrived.

(Me)

(Luise)

The daily regimen changed little. Mornings were devoted to health activities, like mineral water baths, exercise, and play. Several drinks of mineral water were also a daily requirement. Weather permitting, field trips were the common afternoon diversion. We always walked to our destinations — mostly the beautiful gardens, pavilions, and large parks that made up the health resort center of Bad Kissingen. I marveled at the acres of roses and other flowers, and sculptured bushes of every shape. There were open-air band concerts attended by hundreds of men and women all dressed up in their finery. The sight of it all left me speechless.

We saw other groups of children just like us being chaperoned around this picture postcard world Germans call "taking the cure." As a child I was not aware of it, but Germany has many health spa cities and towns — meccas for the wealthy and famous. For the rich, there were the fabulous hotels and casinos to pass the time when not bathing in, drinking, or breathing in the vapors of the treasured waters. The spas really came into being in a big way back in the 17th century when royalty ruled the land. Hot mineral water springs had always been known, and someone was bound to get to the idea of selling health to people of power and wealth.

Under Hitler, the spas became more available to even working-class people through government health programs. No doubt, members of the elite class only tolerated our presence. But thanks to National Socialism, children like myself got to take the 'cure' in everything but the gambling and liquor.

We visited the spa almost daily. The long walks to and from were considered healthy for us. A large park setting, with the Saale River running through, surrounded the main building and rose gardens. What I found fascinating, throughout the park area, were big structures called Salinen. Persons passing by these Salinen on the downwind side could find themselves in a fine mist of mineral water. Moisture being wind-driven off soaked branches, stacked fifty feet high and perhaps a hundred meters in length caused this. I don't know how much we benefited, when the nurses had us sit on park benches breathing in the mist, but every bush, flower, and tree nearby appeared very healthy.

The days and weeks went by all too quickly in Bad Kissingen. We must have known the end was upon us when events began to break into our routine. Our visit to the health park was shortened one afternoon, and we were taken into the city's shopping district nearby. All of the girls had been given a small amount of spending money by their parents, but there had been no chance to spend it until this day. Before setting out from the Kinderheim, we were warned by the nurses to take along our money.

We were hurried along in our shopping, so I didn't get into many stores. As I passed by several, I could tell my five Reichmarks wouldn't even buy a

<Upper walkway>

The Salinen that we children passed every day, weather permitting.

46

breath of air on the inside. The group leaders knew this and guided us to the least expensive souvenir shops. I picked up a pin cushion for Mama and a pack of picture postcards for Erich. Papa's gift was a piece of calcified wood I'd picked up previously at one of the park Salinen.

Then, the following morning we were told to shower and pick up our nicest dresses from the storage room. A photograph of our entire group was to be taken. I was excited by the thought I would have a picture of all the girls, and most of the nurses and helpers I liked so much. In the photograph, Luise sits near me in the same row.

I was excited about going home. There had to be all of a million things to tell my family. The Kinderheim experience wouldn't soon be forgotten. It had sparked a new and lasting ache in me. Luise had suffered 'Heimweh.' My 'Weh' would be the opposite. We call it "Fernweh" — a longing to explore faraway places.

At home, everyone thought I looked healthier. The souvenirs I brought seemed to please, even the calcified wood I gave Papa. Not one to hurt anyone's feelings, he looked it over with high interest. Thinking back, I'm sure he didn't consider it the treasure I did. We had many health resorts in our own area, and for all I know he may have even been hired to haul the stuff away by the ton with his truck. He did get around.

I am also certain that both my parents, but especially my mother, wearied of my never-ending praise for the Kinderheim. Mama soon demanded that I not make it sound so wonderful. She worried aloud. "People will think we mistreat you."

I returned from Bad Kissingen just in time to participate in a Marnheim youth tradition.

Just a few steps from the village bell tower and school building was our only church — very small and old, and very Protestant. The Catholics in town had to go over to Bolanden for services in a larger church used by both Protestants and Catholics. Since very young children were rarely taken to church in those days, I saw the inside of our little church just a few times. Seventy-five people would more than fill the old wood pews. The floor was sandstone slabs and it, along with the doorsteps, were well worn by countless feet in more than a century's use.

The infrequent weddings conducted in the small church always took place on Saturday afternoons. Word would spread fast when one was to happen and village children, though not invited, got ready to attend just the same. It didn't matter if the prospective bride and groom were known. On the wedding day children lingered about the narrow streets in small groups, waiting for the wedding party to settle inside the church. We then gathered quickly in front of the church, perhaps thirty strong, aware that there was no other exit. Older boys, including my brother, had borrowed a heavy rope from a local farmer, the most important part of the plans. With three boys on each end, the rope was stretched across the doorway.

The ceremony inside was never long, so the wait soon ended with the doors popping open and the bride and groom being stopped in their tracks, barred from going through the doorway. If the groom was a good sort, there would be a great show of mock horror and concern. He might try to lift a leg over, and the boys would jerk the rope higher. A willing groom could make several more comical attempts to escape, but it always ended the same. He had, as expected, come to the church fully aware and prepared to honor local tradition. Reaching into his pockets, he brought out handfuls of Pfennigs to toss out to the rope holders and the assembled children, and naturally, the rope was lowered to release the laughing prisoners. The following moments were filled with the scramble of children trying to find all the Pfennigs. Sometimes, we'd catch up to the wedding party as it marched along toward the place of celebration. Mostly we dropped out to spend the money.

The Marnheim Photo Collection

(left to right) Mama and Papa at age 18.

They were not yet married. In fact, they did not know each at this time.

Looking from Marnheim toward the rising fields and the Donnersberg.

Spanning the wide Pfrimm River valley was an iron bridge with a single set of tracks connecting Kirchheim with Marnheim.

The Herbst family homestead in Marnheim. On the left, the big house where Mama and her siblings were raised. The smaller building on the right was where Opa had his saddler's business. The upstairs was two storage rooms. Later I was born upstairs front.

Oma and Opa with all eleven offspring.

Papa with his truck, thanks to Mama's Onkel Phillip at the Heyerhof farm estate. The truck vastly improved Papa's chances to again get a hold of the 'green twig.'

Cousin Edith, daughter of Tante Gusta and the same age as Erich, shown here with the Oma to the Klein side.

Three of Onkel Adam's seven children: Hans in back, with Martha and Ernst in front. I knew each one very well through their lives. As a young man, Ernst wanted the artist's life. He took his own life when his father denied him the chance.

A familiar street scene growing up in Marnheim. Here, one of our neighbors, Frau Franzreb is at one of two public wells available. The water was intended for horses and passing live-stock, but some folks also got water for clothes washing. It was a good place for neighborly gossiping too.

52

Back in the time when television and other diversions didn't exist, leaning out on windows to chat with passersby was popular. Here, Opa Herbst listens to the ladies.

In fall it was common to see licensed traveling hog butchers busy at work in the many farm villages in the area. Here it is Herr Steinbrecher, who would become Erich's father-in-law.

My family always joined with some neighbors and hiked to the top of the Donnersberg each spring. Here we are taking a much needed rest stop on a road side embankment.

One of the first things a child learns upon entering school is that most teachers love taking children on what were called 'outings.' This would be the case throughout my school years. These are first graders. I am sitting dead center. Marnheim did not have a Kindergarten, so I was seven when I was enrolled.

Erich's first day at school, a traditional photo. He was five years ahead of me. Sadly, I lost my own '1st day' picture.

I was missing two front teeth, but that didn't seem to bother me. Only weeks later I was taken out of school to spend seven weeks at one of Hitler's Health Spa programs for children.

My Onkel Robert Klein became a chef in one of München's five-star restaurants. Being the oldest of Papa's siblings, he could have become the next 'Seppel' after Opa Peter. He didn't want to stay in the Donnersberg area and passed the honor over to brother Fritz, my Papa.

Marnheim's Grey Tower with the 'talking bells.' The highest structure in the village, it was not attached to any building. Some folks believed it was a part of a church in centuries past. My elementary school stood nearby across a play area. A small old church was located close by.

A road construction crew building one of Hitler's new roads in our area. The mid-1930's saw the start of Germany's turn around economically. With great relief, Papa, on extreme right, was ready to once again grab on to 'the green twig.' This time he had his own truck.

Marnheim train station. For such a small village this rail point was the gateway to the world. From this place a person could easily travel to most any direction, including the bigger city of Kirchheim.

A rapid stream, the Pfrimm River passes through Marnheim and eventually empties into the Rhein. Along one side in my youth was a well worn path that ran for at least three to four kilometers. The pretty path made a fine 20 minute hike, safely away from road traffic, to Heyerhof. The vast estate was still under the control of Mama's Herbst family, mostly her uncles, aunts and cousins.

Even in small villages like Marnheim our growing army was becoming more evident long before it entered war with frequent displays of soldiers 'on parade.' An appearance of the troops in your village, town or city, led to greater belief in Hitler and nationalism.

Chapter Five

By the middle of 1937, I was seeing less of Papa. Our family had experienced an upturn in finances. New building projects of every kind kept him on the road from dawn to dark. The Daimler truck with its hard rubber tires — the one Onkel Philip helped in financing — was quickly paid off, and Papa soon convinced Mama that he could handle even more work with a new and better truck. The Daimler was old to begin with, and all materials hauled had to be off-loaded by hand. He'd seen other truckers pull up to a construction job, and with a touch to a lever, make their truck beds tilt up in three directions. I learned a new word for this magic — "hydraulisch." Unloading with hydraulic help would speed it up and allow him to carry more loads and increase his pay. Mama agreed with his reasoning, and we had a new Opel truck before the end of the year.

My father was a self-taught mechanic, and could handle most any needed truck repairs in short order. He strictly adhered to daily maintenance to prevent breakdowns. I remember that hardly a night or weekend passed without Papa spending time fine-tuning his truck. Erich was soon brought into the maintenance work; learning for the future.

Brother and I didn't recognize the early signs, but our parents were cautiously working toward a dream. They had long wanted out of the cramped quarters and the rent they had to pay to the absent and unpleasant Onkel Wilhelm. The previous state of the economy had kept the dream on hold. Now, good jobs were plentiful. People could begin planning for a brighter future. Hitler's economic programs were working, bringing believers by the millions into National Socialism. In early 1938, my parents started looking for a new home.

Despite all the home construction for middle-class families in progress, properties that suited our needs weren't all that abundant. Months passed before the break came. Papa's constant mingling with folks had paid off again. The perfect new homestead for his family came on the market. He said nothing to Erich or me about it, but took Mama to inspect the Kirchheimbolanden property. It was her dream come true, a property big enough for home, garden, and business.

For Erich and I, our acquaintance with Kirchheim was mostly limited to the old city business district. Though we liked what we knew, it was still a bit of a shock when told it was to be our new home. My brother was especially upset — not about moving — but over leaving friends before completing the eighth grade.

My own objection was minor in comparison. My best friend, Hänschen, had already moved away with his parents to Worms. Still, I did love visiting my Uncle Adam and his family near the Marnheim train station, where they lived and worked in cramped quarters. There were six children, with number seven on the way. Onkel Adam, like his father and brother Heinrich, was a saddler, but unlike them, he made only saddles and harnesses. The small workspace by a window in the kitchen didn't allow room to compete with Heinrich in the upholstery trade.

Mama promised that after our move to Kirchheim, I could still visit Onkel Adam. It was a short and inexpensive train ride to Marnheim. All in all, moving to a new home in a new town was fine with me. One prospect had me downright excited. I'd just started second grade, and I couldn't wait to see if a new school and teacher would see things my way in the seating arrangement.

The property Papa found belonged to a blacksmith who had recently died. It was his widow who agreed to sell in late summer. The actual move was delayed until November, however, for several reasons. The widow asked for time to find another home, and Papa wanted to make a few changes in the living quarters. Mama also insisted on having the rooms freshly painted. While we waited, I dreamed of having electricity, a water faucet in the kitchen, a living room, an attic, a basement, and space — lots of space. Best of all, we would no longer have to sleep together in one bedroom.

For reasons I can't recall, the first time Erich and I saw the house at Breitstraße One was the night we moved there.

It was a September evening after supper a few weeks later, when Papa suddenly announced that it was time for the four of us to have a day of frolic. It was his idea to celebrate the pending move to the new home.

"Fritz, we don't have the time or money to spend foolishly," Mama responded. "There'll be a chance after we move."

"No, there won't be," he replied. "You know we'll be busier than ever with the new house, and the children with the new schools. We should take the time now." Then, before she could bring up the matter again, he continued. "And we don't have to spend a lot of money. I've already looked into it."

Stopping her dish washing, she turned around to face Papa. "Just what do you have in that head of yours?"

"The Dürkheimer Wurstmarkt!" Erich and I were stunned. The Dürkheimer Wurstmarkt was one of the biggest fall carnivals in the whole Pfalz, and maybe the whole of Germany, so we had heard. Both of us had been to Bad Dürkheim, but never to the Wurstmarkt. It was an exciting proposition. We pleaded with Mama to say yes, but she said nothing, waiting for Papa to say more about what he had arranged.

"Tomorrow is Sunday," he started to say, holding up his hand to stop Mama. "Ja, ja, I know. We can't take the truck, so I've arranged to rent a car from another trucker who doesn't need it."

Mama didn't look happy. "Rent! You arranged to rent a car!"

"It's nothing for you to worry about," Papa insisted. I made a good deal with the guy, and we can have the car the entire day!

My mother turned her back to finish the dishes. "We'll talk some more about this."

"Of course," Papa replied. He looked at us. "You two should be getting ready for bed. It'll be a big day tomorrow." With that, he smiled and winked.

Erich and I had a hard time getting to sleep. He whispered from his bed about all the wonderful things he had seen two years earlier when he had stayed at a Kinderheim in Bad Dürkheim. He imagined, he said, that a million people must go every year to the Wurstmarkt, because the city was so big and beautiful. I remembered his stay in Bad Dürkheim very well, since I missed him so much.

While we lay there talking about the next day's outing, our parents continued talking in the kitchen. We couldn't make out the words through the thick door separating us. Erich didn't seem worried though — he thought Mama would give in.

The next morning was sunny and beautiful. Mama had breakfast ready, and Papa was in his Sunday suit. He had picked up the car earlier, and it sat waiting in the courtyard.

We ate quickly and dressed in our best clothes. Erich noticed that Mama was still in her house dress, and making no move to change. "Mama, why don't you have your pretty dress on?"

"I'm not going. Someone has to stay and feed the pigs."

"Feed the pigs!" Erich echoed her in disbelief. "They're only fed in the evening. We'll be back before — —"

"You heard your mother," Papa interrupted. "Now, let's get a move on.

The day is waiting."

I looked at Mama, but she had turned away to busy herself at the wash bowl. Heading down the stairs, I heard Papa. "We'll see you tonight, Marie."

He hardly ever called her anything but the endearing "Mariechen," Never just "Marie." I suddenly felt sad. As we began our forty-five-minute drive to Bad Dürkheim in the borrowed black Opel, I'm sure Papa sensed that Erich and I had lost some of our appetite for a 'fun day.' Something was missing, and we didn't understand why. My 'Seppel' father, however, wasn't about to have our day dampened. With all of his humor and affection, he turned our mood into one of great expectations, giving us a running, colorful description of all the marvels of the Dürkheimer Wurstmarkt.

The festival is called a Wurstmarkt because Bad Dürkheim sausage makers were renown for their endeavors. Combined with the famous wines and beers of the area, there couldn't be better reasons for a celebration. Over the centuries, the original event had grown into hundreds of food booths and tents, carnival attractions of every sort, and vendors selling anything from plastic toys and dishes to fine table linens and traditional German costumes. And everywhere, music filled the air — from the single accordion player wandering the food tents, to small brass ensembles tooting away in the beer gardens. My favorite was music from the various carnival calliopes. Entering the Bad Dürkheim carnival grounds, and to my delight Papa immediately headed through the mass of people straight for a calliope. I held tight to his hand, as there really seemed to be a million people moving about the festival. My father wanted to look up friends from Marnheim who operated one of the colorful merry-go-rounds.

With Erich staying at his side, Papa had his chat, while I nearly got dizzy on the merry-go-round. The friends conveniently forgot to charge for all the times I went around.

Leaving the ride behind, we slowly made our way through throngs of people crowding narrow passageways. I couldn't have imagined so many vendor booths and food stands all in one place. For sure, I took in more sights and sounds than an eight-year-old should in one afternoon.

The entire carnival arena surrounded a huge permanent building — a restaurant in the shape of a wine barrel lying on its side. Half way up the front of the famous structure was the legend "Inhalt - 1,700,000 liters." Erich said that meant that if the building could be filled up entirely with wine, it would hold that much.

Papa led us straight toward the building. Erich and I had been nagging

Papa to buy us a famous Dürkheimer sausage from one of the many vendors around the carnival grounds, but he wouldn't.

"You should be patient for the best."

The best, we learned, came from a vendor inside the restaurant. We had to wait outside while he went in. He thought it was too rowdy for children. Our patience was soon rewarded when Papa re-appeared balancing three orders of Dürkheimer wurst. He was right. We'd never tasted sausage so delicious. I was convinced Papa was a very smart man about all things.

It was a long walk back to the parked car, and I was ready to sit quietly in the back seat for the ride home. The closer we got to Marnheim, I thought more about how stubborn Mama was for not joining our fun. I finally decided to ask Papa why she had acted that way.

Papa said nothing, but Erich turned around and snickered. "Ha, if Mama is stubborn, she got it from you!"

"I am not stubborn. I'm not, isn't that right, Papa?"

Clearing his throat, "Well, I do seem to remember a carnival in Bolanden when you wouldn't take no for an answer."

"That's not fair," I retorted. "It's not the same!"

"Ja, I suppose it's not exactly, but you were quite bull-headed."

"Ja, Papa," I admitted, weakly.

I sat back knowing I may never understand Mama.

෨

We moved on November 17, 1938, a date easily recalled — exactly one week earlier the Jewish synagogue in Kirchheim was destroyed. A long time passed before I learned that hundreds of synagogues across Germany were also ruined in a lunacy to be forever known as Kristall Nacht (Crystal Night). The name derives from all the broken glass in the destruction of Jewish property.

In the excitement of moving, and living in a new house, my brother and I paid little attention to the 'Crystal Night.' A short-cut street to my new school and the downtown area, a route that passed the synagogue ruins, was blocked for several weeks. And, I am certain that my parents, like most adults, used caution in publicly referring to events on the night of November 10th.

The weather on that long ago Saturday night was dreary, cold, and rainy, with the usual late autumn fog. None of it dampened our enthusiasm as we all worked to load Papa's new truck. Some of the neighbor men helped with the heavier furniture, though we didn't have all that much in the two rooms. It was mostly personal belongings such as clothes, dishes and kitchen utensils, lots of canned and preserved foods, and even the firewood and coal. Darkness came early on that evening, and oil lamps and flashlights were brought out to help guide the way as we went back and forth from house to truck. Even an eight-year-old girl was expected to do her share.

With so many helping hands, the loading was done quickly. While my father checked to make sure it was all tied securely onto the truck, Erich and I went with Mama for one last look around our old two rooms. I don't know if she was taking a look for nostalgic reasons, but it was I who saw what everyone had overlooked. There on the wall in the bedroom were two large pictures. All of my young life I had stared at and loved those pictures. One had an angel carrying a baby toward a village below, and written across the bottom were the words Von Gott (From God). The second picture was similar — two angels taking a small child toward heaven. The legend on it said Zu Gott (To God). I always knew they had special meaning to Mama because of Raul.

Erich reached up, handed 'Von Gott' to me, and took down the other. As I turned to carry my picture down to the truck, Erich grabbed it back, saying, "Nay, you're too small to carry such a large picture." It was just like him to exaggerate and be bossy. I tried to get the picture back, but he wouldn't let go. So, I tried what had always worked in the past — I aimed a swift kick at his shins. He put 'Von Gott' in front of my target, with shattering results.

&

The cold fog and drizzle enveloped us as we slowly drove away from a life in Marnheim to a new home in Kirchheimbolanden. With Mama, Erich and I beside him, Papa proceeded cautiously, adding long minutes to the time normally needed for the trip. The windshield wipers worked overtime, but did little good against the thick fog. He couldn't see the road at all and seemed to drive by instinct. None of us were really worried. That was the effect Papa had when he took charge of a situation. Finally, he made a slow, sharp turn off the main road onto a wide cobblestone street leading into a part of Kirchheim I'd never seen. The fog cloaked everything as we began to follow the street ever higher. As though knowing the question on the minds of his children, Papa suddenly informed us that our house was near the top of the highest elevation in Kirchheim. For Erich and I, the new information only added to our anticipation. Alas, the fog and late hour made exploring the new surroundings impossible.

However, Papa knew exactly where he was and soon pulled up in front of two large doors facing the street. Before I could blink, my father was out of the truck to open the doors. Just as quick, he was back to drive family and household belongings through the passageway into the courtyard. Only the cab of the truck was exposed to the continuing drizzle in the open yard, the loaded bed remained protected by an extension of the second floor over the driveway.

The first item to be unloaded and moved in was the iron cook stove. It had been dismantled into many sections for easy carrying, but the remaining large stove frame was still heavy for Papa and Erich. It had to go to our kitchen on the second floor. My mother and I carried up smaller sections, and then I was sent to bring firewood from the truck. Mama wanted to start a fire as soon as the stove was back together, and the stove pipe installed. The house was damp and cold, but that didn't stop me from inspecting some of the rooms, and trying out the electric light switches. I couldn't believe that with just a flick of my finger, there was light. The light fixtures weren't fancy, but for me each one was beautiful.

My parent's bedroom already had furniture in it. They had bought a second-hand bedroom set, including a double bed, nightstands, a dresser and a huge wardrobe. It all had been delivered and set up the day before. Erich's bedroom was off the center hall. While I had to pass through my parent's bedroom to reach my room, I was still delighted to have my own private place.

After the cook stove was set up and blazing, the rest of the kitchen was put in place. The beds were made up, and Mama urged me to bed. I doubted sleep would be easy at the end of the most wonderful day of my life. Before crawling under covers, I looked at the door and decided to leave it open.

Suddenly, it was morning and the first day of a new life.

The Kirchheimbolanden Years

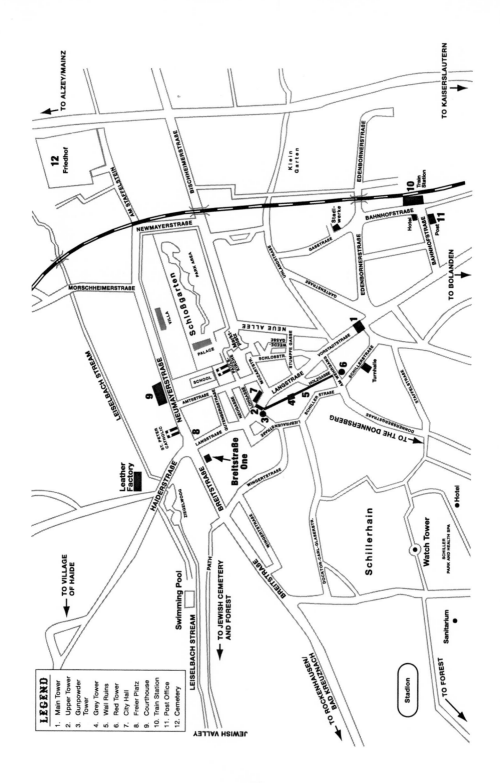

Chapter Six

Having my own bedroom had one drawback. I overslept. When I finally awoke, the others had already eaten and unloaded the remaining items from the truck. We didn't have much for the living room — just a table and chairs and a small buffet. When I came out, Mama was in the midst of directing her men on how she wanted things arranged. It would take several days before she was completely satisfied. After my own breakfast, I gave the new home a close inspection.

Almost the entire second floor was set aside for our living quarters. There was a kitchen, three bedrooms, a living room, and a couple of other rooms that would later be rented. All were reached from a center hallway running from front to back. Across from the kitchen was the door and stairway leading up to a full storage attic. Nearby, an open half-spiral staircase of highly polished wood went down to the hallway on the first floor. It also divided the house, running from the front door to a back door that opened to the courtyard. Entering through the front door, on the immediate right, was a large room rented by a shoemaker. I didn't meet the young Herr Kasper until the next day. On the left, across from the shoemaker, was another large room with stocks of motor oil and other automotive supplies. This room was part of a new side business for the Klein family — serving the motoring public. A large gasoline pump stood half-embedded in the front outside wall near the big double doors.

Toward the back of the house, on the ground floor, was the wash kitchen opposite another room used as a pantry. The laundry room, white washed and clean, was in one way just like a kitchen in that it had a wood burning stove. Here, however, the stove was built-in, and had a surface with two large holes into which round-bottomed copper kettles fit. In these kettles my mother, and later I, would boil and wash laundry. The same boiling kettles came into service in the hard work of making sugar syrup from beets, and the cooking of fruit preserves. Nearby were rinsing tubs and a sink with running cold water.

The pantry room, at the other end of the hall, was entered from the courtyard. It was never heated, and because of the very thick stone walls, always had an even cool temperature — an ideal place for storing canned goods and large quantities of flour, salt and sugar. Huge wide-mouthed crocks for making sauerkraut and pickles stood on the floor near one wall.

The hallway and all ground floor rooms had odd-shaped stone slab floors. I marveled at how each stone was cut to fit perfectly with all adjacent slabs.

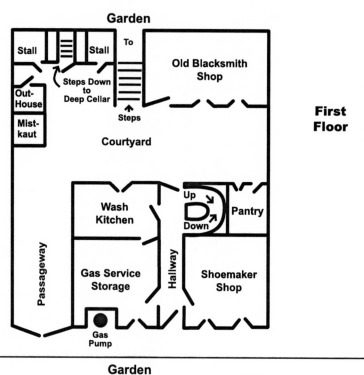

Garden

Stall

Stall

To

Old Blacksmith Shop

Steps Down to Deep Cellar

Out-House

Mist-kaut

Steps

Courtyard

First Floor

Wash Kitchen

Up

Down

Pantry

Passageway

Gas Service Storage

Hallway

Shoemaker Shop

Gas Pump

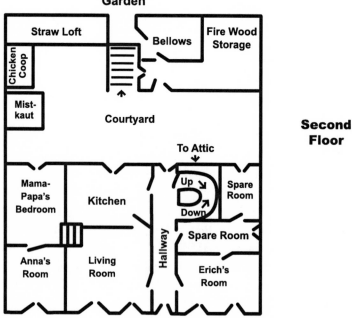

Garden

Straw Loft

Bellows

Fire Wood Storage

Chicken Coop

Mist-kaut

Courtyard

Second Floor

To Attic

Mama-Papa's Bedroom

Kitchen

Up

Down

Spare Room

Anna's Room

Living Room

Hallway

Spare Room

Erich's Room

Breitstraße One Floor Plan and Courtyard

Upstairs, the floors were all polished hard wood, my mother's pride and joy.

It would take plenty of hard wax to keep them shining.

In the courtyard, growing up the rear wall of the house, I discovered a very old grapevine. A single thick trunk grew out of the ground and up to just below the second floor windows, where many vines sprouted from the main stem and were attached to wires running the entire length of the building. In November the vines were bare, but I could imagine how nice it would be in summer to just reach out of the kitchen window to pick plump grapes. There were also grapevines in the garden.

There was one other door off the hallway opening to a stone stairway going into a dirt cellar under the house. It was only partially dug out and had only one small room.

As with the property in Marnheim, the courtyard was completely enclosed by buildings and walls. But instead of a barn directly across the courtyard from the house, there was the two-story blacksmith shop. When we moved in, the shop appeared as though the old blacksmith was still in business. The anvil, tools, scrap iron, a pile of coal, and even ashes in the hearth, all suggested he would soon be there to start work. In a loft above the hearth, a large bellow was ready to be pumped again. My father couldn't have been happier about the shop. He saw a great opportunity in using the facility for his trucking business. He did all his own repair work, and could make good use of the space and equipment.

Near the shop, in the open courtyard, was a huge grinding stone with a big crank handle. We soon learned that the blacksmith allowed local farmers to come and sharpen tools for a few pfennigs, and we continued the service.

Another reminder that a blacksmith once operated at Breitstraße One, was a beautiful wrought iron sign that hung from the second level over the street. Made by the blacksmith, the design was a large horseshoe with a horse's head and an anvil in the middle. We left it hanging.

Center steps next to the shop went up into a higher level, long plot of ground used as a garden. To the left of the steps was another useful two-story building. At ground level, on each end, were stalls for hogs to be raised and butchered. Above was a roofed area for storing straw and feed. Turning the corner, the structure had two more uses. Off the courtyard, a door opened into the outhouse, with a chicken coop overhead. Indoor toilets were still not common in working-class homes, and outhouses weren't so bad when you didn't know anything else — not even when it's located below roosting chickens. One of my more chilling discoveries was what lay behind a door between the pig stalls. When I pushed the creaking door open and saw old stone steps going straight down into darkness, my heart leapt with curiosity and fear. There was no light switch to be found, so I went off to get both a flashlight and Erich to help me investigate an ancient entry into the earth. My brother hadn't had a chance to look over the property, and was glad to leave our parents and their planning to join me. With a light, we could see that the steep stairway had stone walls and a curved ceiling constructed with un-mortared stone. From the top, our light still didn't allow us a view to the bottom. It was with a shiver, I followed as Erich began slowly down. Moving deeper, the walls became slippery to the touch, the air increasingly warm and moist. Ever deeper the steps took us under the garden, and we began seeing salamanders and other creatures scamper over wet surfaces.

Finally reaching bottom, we suddenly found ourselves in a large room, the walls and high-arched ceiling again covered with tight, un-mortared stone. "Ha! I can't wait to tell my friends about this." Erich was almost jumping up and down with excitement at our find. "You know what this is? Nay, you wouldn't." I confirmed it by shaking my head.

"I learned about it in school," he continued. "This has to be a remnant of an extinct tunnel system." He paused to shine the light around. "It makes sense — this property is on the path from the old walled city straight up to the forest. It's how people could escape when an enemy broke through the gates."

Not that we needed more room for storage, but Mama found the even year-round temperature in the deep underground room useful to keep some foods. As for the salamanders, Papa said these animals were helpful in keeping after harmful bugs, but that hardly calmed my nerves whenever I had to go down. I'd always whistle loudly. I'd do the same going down into the partial dirt basement under the house with its low tunnel and hard packed dirt walls winding back to a small storage room. Taking up a small area in the courtyard was a shallow open pit we call a "Mistkaut" bordered all around by a low wall. Since we would no longer have animals except for chickens, there was no need for a place to turn manure and soiled straw into fertilizer for the garden. We used it instead for composting other materials.

Our "new" home dated well back into the 17th century, and like most structures built in times of constant turmoil, the exterior walls were very thick and constructed of stone and mortar. As time passed, a stucco finish was applied to the outside. Later, when water and electricity were brought into the house, the lines were installed full view on the inside walls. Delighted as we were to have water and electric, the few visible pipes bothered no one and were simply painted to match the walls. Coming from the tight Marnheim quarters, I could see that Breitstraße One had wonderful, endless space. Through the eyes of an eight-year-old, it was truly the 'green twig' Papa always talked about.

It would be several days before Erich and I could begin to fully explore Papa's hometown of Kirchheim, and to start our education of its historical significance. Our new home had always been at the center of historical events in the region. There was much to learn. Breitstraße was aptly named, being

Kirchheimbolanden landmarks as they appeared in my youth.

This is the main tower entrance into the old town.
The view is that of approaching to enter the oldest part of Kirchheim.

quite broad (breit) compared to most Kirchheim streets. Homes and businesses up and down were built in the typical fashion of earlier centuries, right at the street edge and without break along the entire block. The walk area was nothing more than a cobblestone strip between the house fronts and the asphalt paved street. At the time, Breitstraße was one of a few so paved. Most streets were still entirely cobblestones.

Walking uphill on Breitstraße from our house, it's possible to be out of town and into deep forest within fifteen minutes. The street became the main road to Rockenhausen and Bad Kreuznach. Just beyond the last houses, another road swings off to the left and goes to Schillerhain — a beautiful park, and a major way into dense forest.

Going down Breitstraße, it's only a few steps to Bossung's Inn next door and to where Breitstraße turns into Neumayerstraße, and the way to join the highway to Worms on the Rhein. The cross street also changes names at the intersection. To the right, the Langstraße winds its way down cobblestones through the old walled town, past the main tower, and out toward Kaiserslautern. Turning left at the crossroads, the Langstraße became Haiderstraße. This took you past the small Ziegelwoog lake and out of Kirchheim, and on to the Haide village, toward the cities of Alzey and Mainz. It was easy to see how this intersection always played a big role in the movement of armies during times of war.

Going almost anywhere into the old Kirchheim, the Langstraße became my route of choice for school and errands. The way was rich with side streets, passageways and quick short cuts. Whatever the way, buildings, centuries old, plain and fancy, greeted my intrusion stoically. By instinct I knew they had already witnessed more than a young girl's creative mind could conceive, but for me that was stimulating. On the first Monday after we moved

This "Red Tower" stood at one end of the wall.

74

Papa took Erich and I on a short walk to the Amtsstraße and the elementary school to enroll. We were in the middle of our school year, Erich into grade 7, and I into the second grade. On arrival, my father was told the school had a student over-flow problem, and that some of the classes, including all of mine, had been moved to yet another building several blocks away. The only excitement was that it was by the Schloßgarten. (Palace and Gardens). It also meant that until Easter, when I could return to the Amtsstraße to enter the third grade, my walk would be four times longer than Erich's. Before I could get too upset about that prospect I heard the school official tell my father that he should take me to the "Herrengarten." I thought that sounded fancy and, as we walked, I chattered on about having my class in the 'Lord's garden,' making Papa laugh.

The wall ruins from the outside, with the Grey Tower at mid-point. The steeple left of the tower is the Upper Tower. To the right is the steeple of the Protestant St. Peter's Church. At the southern end of the wall ruins is the Red Tower entrance.

"Ach, Annchen," he smiled, "the Herrengarten is just the name for some apartment buildings old Prince Karl put up near his palace for royal officials and families."

I wanted to know more about the old royalty in Kirchheim, but something more important was on my mind.

"Please Papa, don't let the teacher put me in the front row. I didn't like it in Marnheim. I'm much too tall and the other kids will make fun." He nodded and smiled. Short as he was, I was shorter still, at least for the moment. Time would soon have me a head taller. He simply said, "We'll see."

Arriving at Herrengarten, the teacher, a woman, immediately came up and offered her hand to my father. "Guten tag, my name is Hilde Klein."

That made Papa and I smile. "And I'm Fritz Klein. This is my daughter, Annchen — I mean Anna."

Fräulein Klein now smiled over our common name. "That's alright, Herr Klein. 'Annchen' fits her very well."

The two of them briefly discussed a possible family relationship, but found

Old St. Peter's church. A round the corner to the left is a bigger Protestant church across the Amtsstraße. It is where Mozart played his organ concerts.

none. Somehow though, I felt sharing the name got me off to a good start. Besides, she could have been one of us with her dark hair and brown eyes.

Papa then asked in a rather casual manner, "Fräulein Klein, don't you think Annchen here would do better seated more to the back of the class? She is a bit tall for a second grade girl, wouldn't you agree?"

I could have kissed him. He hadn't forgotten my wish. I was glad that Mama hadn't brought me to school. Looking at Fräulein Klein, I knew my wish was granted. I was ushered toward the last row to an empty desk next to another girl who turned out to be quite friendly. Her name was Renate Walter. Because she was also well liked by many of the students, my entry into the classroom was that much easier.

At the end of the short school day, Fräulein Klein approached me. "I understand you live on the upper side of town. I'll get someone to walk with you."

I tried to explain that my father had already told me of the best route home. She wouldn't hear of it, and called over a girl in the class named Rosalinde Rösel. I recognized her right away. She had been in the window of the house across the street from us on Sunday, and had stared in our direction for a long time. Walking home I found her a bit shy, and I did most of the talking. We became friends, but I enjoyed her mother and siblings even more. Frau Rösel was a pretty woman, and had the most wonderful soprano singing voice. She would answer my requests with one song after the other whenever I visited.

I would still walk home with Rosalinde, but more often I'd go with Renate to her house after school. I was never invited inside for some unexplained reason, but I liked talking to her even if it was only to her front door. I discovered we had many mutual interests. Both of us collected picture cards of elves from a certain company's oatmeal boxes. One afternoon, Renate decided to ask her mother if she might come home with me to look over my card collection. Standing on the entrance step of her house, Renate and I didn't have to wait long for the answer. To my surprise, Frau Walter refused.

"Renate is not allowed to roam around town." Her warning came at me as chilly as the late November wind, but I wasn't old enough to take the hint and tried a different tack. "I'd be glad to walk her home from my house."

"I think not," she replied, impatiently.

"Then can Annchen bring her cards to our house?"

Frau Walter's answer was to pull Renate through the doorway and give me a look of disfavor, as the door slammed shut.

This was my first taste of a trait I would learn is strongly embedded in the minds of many in German Society — class-distinction. There aren't many places in the world free of it, but uppity Germans seemed to have it down to a fine point. I was very troubled by Frau Walter's attitude toward me, and that evening, at supper, I brought the class prejudice episode up to Mama. When I finished my tale, she looked at Papa. "Isn't this the same Herr Walter who is vice-president of the Volksbank, and gave us our house and business loans?"

"Ja, ja," my father said, "but he's quite a nice, considerate fellow. Too bad his wife thinks she's better than anyone else is. Herr Walter's got himself a real prize in her!" He then shook his head and chuckled before turning serious again, and nodding toward Erich and me. "You two must never forget the Kleins and Herbsts are hard-working, respectable folks — and honest too. When you run into such people, keep in mind their outhouses stink the same as ours!"

"Ja, Papa." We answered almost in unison. Our father's tone of voice had given his words the status of marching orders for the rest of our lives. "How are the two of you getting along in my Kerchem otherwise? The 'big city' treating you alright?"

Papa's half-humorous reference to Kirchheim's size didn't dampen our responses. We knew he loved his birthplace, and were beginning to understand why.

"It's big enough for me," Erich replied, beating me to it. "I still miss my friends in Marnheim, still there's much more to do here."

With enthusiasm came my answer. "I could never be sorry we moved to Kirchheim, Papa! Everyday I see something I want to know more about."

The Upper Tower inside. City Hall is on the right. On the left, abutting the landmark tower is the Schwan Apothecary. Once upon a time, only royalty could enter to seek a cure.

At center, the same Upper Tower from outside the wall. On the right is what remains of the Gunpowder Tower, an important structure at one time long ago. Kirchheim did play a role in the famed "30 Years War" between Catholics and the Protestants.

"That's your daughter, Fritz. The girl has more curiosity than a barn cat." Mama's comment only made our father smile broader at my brother and I.

"Ach, Mariechen, I want my children to learn all they can about Kirchheim. It will help them understand their Papa better. Old Seppel used to say, 'To know me, you must know the place and people of my roots.'"

Sister and brother had not, in fact, wasted any spare time in acquainting ourselves with Kirchheim the first weeks after the move. Our explorations were greatly aided by Erich's studies in school and the local boys becoming his friends. At the age of thirteen, he liked to share his growing knowledge with me, when in the mood.

Lucky for me, my position as 'dumb little sister' was temporarily forgotten in the excitement of learning about our new hometown.

Some things were easy to discover. The narrow one-way Langstraße gently curved down from our place on the hill and past dwellings and small shops. About halfway along, the first tower entrance into the old town came in view.

Next to it, a smaller rough-stone structure Erich called the "Pulverturm." I guess 'Gunpowder Tower' says it all. A nicer looking taller tower was named 'Upper Tower' and was part of the large city hall, just inside the entrance passage. Above the main door, my brother pointed out the Coat of Arms for Kirchheim — a wild boar in a green field with a checker-board design above. Across the street from the city hall was the Schwan Apothecary. My learned companion revealed that the still operating pharmacy once served only the royal family.

❧

Just past the city hall, a small street branched off to the left and down a steep incline to the Amtsstraße, and on into a business district of larger stores, many cafes and restaurants. Continuing along the Langstraße, the main tower, came into view surrounded by some of the oldest businesses in the city. At this spot, two other towers can be seen with a long section of wall ruins in between.

Unlike the stucco-finished main and upper towers, the old stone-work of the 'Red' and 'Gray' Towers lay bare, giving them an ancient look.

In the seventh grade, Erich's class was then learning about local history. It was one of his favorite subjects and often shared his growing knowledge over the supper table. Even Mama would stop what she was doing to listen sometimes. She had lived in the area all of her life, but hadn't been very interested in history when she went to school. Her son was beginning to change her opinion on the matter.

There had been no formal housewarming after

The White Horse Inn remains much like it did in my youth. It was used in many ways under French and American occupations. Later we Germans reclaimed it for food and dance. I danced away many a Saturday night in the upper floor ballroom. My addiction to dancing left no room for wine and smoking cigarettes.

we'd settled in at Breitstraße One. But that didn't keep the relatives, near and far, from dropping in, usually on weekends. Hardly anyone came to visit us in Marnheim. That had changed. Our relatives were curious about our new situation, and we were happy to show them. Among the more frequent visitors were my father's sister Lina, her husband Willi, and their two children, Helmi and Fritz. Having a car helped, as they had to come all the way from Monsheim near the Rhein river.

Helmi and Fritz were slightly older than Erich and I, but fun to be with. They liked coming to our place because of the hills and forest, something they didn't have at home. Their visits always included a tramp through the forest. Being older, they apparently gave comfort to Mama about our safety. She would've been unhappy to know that Erich and I had already been exploring some parts of the forest. We had discovered, like children of every generation, that what Mama didn't know wouldn't hurt her.

Closer to Christmas time, the increasing snowfall made trips into the forest more special. For the first time, I experienced the beauty of a still forest dressed in white. Only the occasional scampering of an animal through the thick stands of snow-laden trees and underbrush broke the silence.

Erich showed me how it was nearly impossible to get lost, if I stayed on the trails. Pointing to the trunk of a tree near a trail separation. "See all the symbols painted there. Each one identifies a different pathway. It's that way throughout the forest around Donnersberg."

"But how do you know where the trails go?"

"Dumb girl! Didn't you see that big map by the tree where we started? You'd better learn that map if you don't want to get lost. There are some places in here where nobody could find you, not to mention the chance of you stumbling into a wild boar wallow."

My brother was always such a comfort.

The weeks before our first Christmas in Kirchheimbolanden were hectic for Mama. She handled all the bookkeeping for the trucking business, pumped gasoline for motorists, did the banking, and dealt with the constant government red tape. Her duties as housewife and mother went right on, as did her loyal attendance in church. Weekly hospitality to visiting relatives was probably too much, but she loved it all. Mama blossomed as a businesswoman and, as her faith in Hitler grew, she believed again that hard work would bring prosperity.

One more burden of preparing for our traditional Christmas celebration didn't faze Mama either. The Christmas tree was now set up in the living room and Erich and I were allowed to help decorate it. Also, we were not taken to the stores. After an expensive move we couldn't expect much. It was no problem for us, as we both felt our new home was the best present of all.

The cookie baking didn't change, except that I helped more. Mama still believed storing cookies in tightly covered tins in a cool room helped to make them soft. Waiting for the cookies to soften was something Erich had difficulty doing. Many times I heard Mama exclaim, "Gott im Himmel, what's happened to all the cookies I put in this tin yesterday?" Erich's capacity for sweets never failed to shock.

I liked cakes and candy as well as anyone, but my brother's appetite in this regard was ridiculous. If he had any money earned from running errands and the like, it never went into his pocket. The nearest bakery or sweet shop got it.

After being bawled out by Mama for shamelessly raiding the sugar bowl, Erich responded with a new ploy to satisfy his sugar habit. I'd just walked into the kitchen where Mama, doing her pre-Christmas cleaning, had just discovered his latest sneaky plot. She had pulled the radio and the small table it sat on away from the wall to clean. Glancing into the open back of the radio, she found a small sack of sugar cubes. Holding the sack up for me to see, and rolling her eyes toward heaven, she declared, "Ach, that boy! Someday all his teeth will fall out." We both had to laugh then, as it reminded us of the last Easter spent in Marnheim.

Erich had eaten all of his chocolate Easter rabbit and while no one was looking, started in on mine. I had wanted to save my rabbit for a while, and Papa put it on top of the wardrobe in the bedroom. That's where Mama found it a few days later, the bottom half gone. Seeing the damage for myself, she and I waited in anger for my brother to return from an errand. There followed such a woeful tale of mishap, he almost had us believing it was the rabbit's fault for tempting him.

Erich and I were stuck as to what we could buy our parents for Christmas. We'd decided it was time they received a little something from us. Finally, we approached Papa, since he would have to give us the money anyway. He confirmed what we already thought he'd like, and then suggested that Mama would probably like a nice bottle of some fancy dessert liqueur. It wasn't something she'd buy for herself, but someone had given her a bottle years before and she enjoyed a small glass during Sunday coffee. He was sure she would like the chocolate-flavored kind. As instructed, Erich and I went to a wine store and bought a bottle of local wine for Papa and a bottle of Creme de Cacao for Mama. It was possible in those days for youngsters to buy alcoholic beverages, as long you were known.

On Christmas, Mama was quite pleased with our gift and enjoyed a small glass of liqueur with the afternoon cake and coffee. Erich received a much wanted tool kit that included a hand jigsaw and a drill. I was happy of course, to see my dollhouse again. To my amazement, Erich had bought a gift for me. It was a miniature floor lamp that lit when hooked to a battery. The bad news was he would no longer play with me. He was just too old, he said.

All too soon, our childhood times were ending.

The remaining useful part of what was the home of an early Prince. A nearly identical wing as shown was destroyed in one of the many battles fought by the French and Germans long ago. That half of the palace was never rebuilt.

Chapter Seven

I started attending church with Mama after our move. At the time, it wasn't customary to take children until they could comfortably sit through a service. We went to the smaller St. Peter's, a charming yet plain church with well-worn pews on the ground floor facing a simple altar and pulpit. A curved balcony covering the back half held a pipe organ and extra seating. I found the church experience a little surprising. Except for singing, people kept quiet and paid close attention to the Pfarrer (pastor).

St. Peter's Kirche was located behind the city hall on Langstraße, but faced the Amtsstraße. Back when it was built in the year 1200, and for centuries after, it was Catholic and called St. Remigius Kirche. The Reformation in the Fifteenth century, led by Martin Luther, changed all that. Later, as Kirchheim became primarily Protestant, it was decided by the ruling Prince to build a church five times bigger, across and just up the Amtsstraße next to the old palace grounds. The new one was named St. Paul's. It was too big to heat in winter, except for special occasions, and the smaller St. Peter's would come back into use for the cold months.

Most memorable was my first Christmas service held in St. Paul's, especially heated for the occasion. December 25th fell on Sunday that year, a fact that enabled Erich to come along. Sunday meetings of the Hitler Jugend usually kept him from attending. With Papa, it made for a rare appearance of our whole family seated in the pews. My father went to church once a year — on Christmas.

On Christmas, I heard for the first time the grand "Mozart" pipe organ, so named because Wolfgang Amadeus performed concerts on it. The congregation area, both on the ground floor and upstairs, struck me as rather plain. The sidewalls and rear area were also without embellishment, except for the lovely stained glass windows, still in place at the time. All the glory was concentrated in the front altar area, and in the pulpit at the second level. Here was all the grandeur of the woodcarver's art. The railings, tables, chairs, lecterns, pulpit, and even the wall behind the altar were all beautifully hand-carved. At the third level above, was the famous pipe organ created by master craftsman Michael Stumm. When it's glorious roar reached out to me on Christmas day 1938, there was no doubt of my new addiction.

In many ways, St. Paul's didn't appear like a church at all on the outside. No fancy steeple reaches for heaven, no bell tower of any kind — just a huge block of a building with only stained windows to indicate it's religious purpose. Even these beautiful works of art were later removed, leaving only the altar and pipe organ as the center of beauty and religion.

Mozart, on his first visit in January 1778, was also confused about St. Paul's lack of religious appearance, asking his hosts if it was the Royal Theater. Mozart would learn that it was the Schloßkirche (Palace church), as it was called in those days. The church was built next to the Schloßgarten (Palace garden) wall, which allowed the royal family private access to it. It was Princess Caroline, wife of Prince Carl Christian, who asked that Mozart performed an evening concert at the church's massive pipe organ. He apparently entertained well enough to be invited back two more times. All this, I read in a pamphlet from a holder by the front door.

I have no idea as to the truth of it, but folklore says that Prince Carl August von Nassau-Weilburg, father of Carl Christian, had the church built in the 1740's from ill-gotten money.

Seems that Carl A. loved to gamble, and he especially liked to go to France and wager against King Louis. According to the story, the last time he traveled to Paris was in 1741 when he promptly got into a high stakes game with the king, losing all his money. Apparently, in the heat of the moment, the Prince became a bit rash and bet all his lands, including Kirchheimbolanden, against the King's hand in the next game. Agreeing with the bet, this Louis — the fifteenth in a long line — is said to have taken the time to figure the worth of the lands in question. Once settled, the bet went forward. Luckily, for us, Carl August won and Louis XV graciously paid off in gold!

Supposedly the gold was used to build St. Paul's later on. It did not include a bell tower, according to legend, because the new church was already higher than the Prince's palace. Besides, he thought the bell tower of St. Peter's, just across the street could be used. And so it was as I settled into Kirchheim life.

❧

The heavy winter snowfall offered breathtaking excitement for children in the hilly neighborhoods of Kirchheim. We'd all manage to get a hold of some kind of sled, and spend hours whizzing down the snow-covered streets. From the house, our street went steeply up for about three blocks, and the danger of it was absolutely ideal. Sledding on city streets was strictly prohibited, or so we were told. The city fathers did provide a Rodelbahn, a sledding run in the forest, but most of us were too lazy or scared to go there.

The policeman who walked a beat by our house seemed to stay away on purpose in the early evening hours. We took advantage of his absence. There were hardly any vehicles using Breitstraße, it being so steep and slippery. Even without the occasional threat of a car or truck running us over, I was amazed the most we suffered from was frostbite. Reaching the bottom of the hill, our only brakes were the shoes on our feet. That meant quickly soaked shoes, and sometimes, frostbitten feet.

Of course, during Christmas break from school, there was always someone zipping down Breitstraße all day, when they could get away with it. That included Erich and I, but we had to have our chores done. Mama was strict about that. I liked to fly down the hill alone, but as there were more kids than sleds, I usually had company.

The winter of 1938–39 sticks in my mind as the last time Breitstraße witnessed this kind of carefree fun in the snow. Such simple pleasures would soon be only in our memories.

❧

The Sylvester celebration (New Year's Eve) in 1938 was a special one for me — I was allowed to stay up. Erich was also permitted for the first time to invite his friends for the occasion. My brother, like Papa, made friends quickly and several showed up. To give the boys something to work on, Papa demonstrated a way to make an old-fashioned noisemaker. He'd earlier gotten salt-

85

peter from the pharmacy. Now, using an empty can with a push-down lid, he put a little saltpeter inside, spat on it, and closed the lid. A small hole had been punched in the bottom. Waiting a moment, and moving back, he put a lighted match to the hole. To everybody's surprise, except my father, the lid blew off with a loud bang. The can didn't go anywhere because he kept his foot on it. He explained that spit on a small amount of saltpeter creates gas, and warned that too much of both might blow the whole can apart. His last warning was for them to wait until midnight. "We're just testing it!"

That was Erich's excuse when a louder than normal explosion caused Mama and I to throw open the kitchen window to remind my brother and his friends that it was not yet midnight. I think Papa was jolted by the noise, too, because we heard his voice from across the courtyard telling the boys not to put so much spit in the can. With only moonlight visibility, it was hard to see clearly the courtyard activities. A dim light coming through the open door of the old blacksmith shop was of no help. Papa was doing something in the shop most of his spare time. 'Fiddling,' he called it. On this night, he was staying around to keep a close eye on the young rascals. Closing the window, I heard one of them complaining that he still couldn't find the lid. It would be fun out there with them, but I knew they'd just call me a nuisance. Contenting myself to stay awake in the kitchen, I listened to music on the radio and watched Mama prepare our special meal. For us, this consisted of hot spiced wine, bratwurst with mustard, and rye bread. Our own tradition was to serve this right after the midnight hour struck, and everyone had finished with handshaking and 'good wishes.' Other families we knew had wurst and wine too, though not everyone. Whatever the menu, even small children had to shake hands with everyone on New Year's.

When Erich learned I'd be staying up, he bet Mama I wouldn't be able to keep awake. That made me more determined to prove him wrong. To do it, I walked around a lot and stuck my head out the window into the cold air, when my eyelids grew heavy.

When the New Year arrived, there wasn't any question about it. The boys in the courtyard joined the other neighborhood noisemakers, making loud bangs just as fast as they could retrieve the can lid. But most memorable to me, were all the church bells in town ringing out a joyful noise that lasted several minutes. The sound is unforgettable.

Papa and I stepped out into the snowy street while the bells rang out. It surprised me to see many of our neighbors doing the same. "Frohes Neues Jahr!" Papa shouted it to anyone looking his way. The closest neighbors returned his

'Happy New Year' greeting, and stepped over to shake hands.

I remember being very tired and happy as Papa and I rejoined Mama in the kitchen for the Sylvester meal. Papa had allowed Erich to build a fire in the old blacksmith hearth so he and his friends could have their food and drinks in privacy, away from parents and a little sister. Altogether, it was a happy celebration as we welcomed 1939 into our lives. Mama prayed, but I know Papa believed that a new green twig had been found for Seppel's family.

New Year's Day had its surprises. After more than an hour of sledding, I was glad to be in our warm kitchen again, stripped of wet clothes and shoes, my frozen feet propped up on the open oven door. A wonderful thing about a wood and coal burning stove, the oven is usually warm. Erich was still at the top of the hill with some of his friends, but I was sure he wouldn't forget we'd be having afternoon coffee and cake. I saw that Mama had three cakes sitting out on the cupboard shelf already, but she was not around when I came in. I was just thinking about sneaking a sample from a plum cake when Mama came through the door, closing it behind her.

"Märe."

"Ja, Mama?" I could tell by her tone something serious was up.

"Do you know where I keep my Christmas present?"

I wasn't expecting that question. "If you mean that bottle of chocolate liqueur, I have no idea where you put it. It was your present."

She stepped out of the way as the door opened. I noticed then that she held the bottle in one hand behind her.

"Well, Mariechen, I can see you like that stuff more than you told me." It was Papa. I knew he was joking when he said her name endearingly, but Mama never seemed to understand this.

Angrily, she held the bottle high in the air so even I could plainly see that it was half-empty. "Fritz, you know I had just one tiny glass of this on Christmas, and no more!"

"Well, you know I don't like sweet liqueur," He said, trying to calm her. "Are you thinking Annchen here drank it?"

"Nay, I didn't say that. But it means there's only one left who could."

At that moment, Erich came in from the cold to find the kitchen hotter than expected. Mama was still holding the bottle high in the air, and my brother's stare shifted cautiously from the half-full container to her face. Without a word, she lowered the bottle to the table. Papa stepped over and quietly closed the door Erich had forgotten to shut behind him. The effect, though unintentional, must have made my brother feel that there was no escape.

A long sigh from Mama carried the sharp and unmistakable sound of regret. She truly loved the boy. I came to believe that Erich gave her more pleasure than either Papa or I did. Still, she had high moral standards. Her son's craving for sweet things had gone too far.

Directing a dark look at him, she asked, "Can you explain to me how so much of my Christmas gift has disappeared?"

"Mama, I — "

"And what were you doing in my wardrobe?"

"Mama," he started again, "I was just looking for something when I saw the bottle behind some stuff." There was an uncomfortable pause. "I really only had a swallow!" No one said anything, but we all looked at the fancy bottle now sitting on the table. With much of the contents missing, and liqueur so much stronger than even wine or beer, we all knew that one big swallow would do Erich in. He saw that they weren't swallowing his claim, and admitted, reluctantly, "It may have been more than one swallow. I like the taste and went back a couple of times."

"Why didn't you say so in the first place?" my father demanded. "At thirteen years, you're too young to handle alcohol!"

Papa didn't often raise his voice. Erich looked to Mama for support, and she responded to his silent plea. "Fritz, I think we've made our point. It's time for coffee."

"It is for us," he answered, looking at her and I. "Erich needs to wait a while for his sweets." With that, he ordered my brother to go and straighten up the work area in the old blacksmith shop and in the courtyard. "You and your friends made a good mess of it last night."

❧

I was sweeping the first floor hallway when the shoemaker came in to open shop the following day. My family and I had liked Christian Kasper right away. A young single man, thin and not very tall, he had been renting space from the previous owner. My parents saw no reason to change the arrangement. It was extra income, and we really had no need for his workshop area. I especially liked him because, even more than Onkel Heinrich in Marnheim, he tolerated my presence and terrible curiosity. Over time, whenever I popped in, he'd often say, "Ach, Annchen, come in and sit a minute."

Herr Kasper usually had a young boy apprentice fresh from eighth grade, but their relationship was always that of teacher and student. It was like that between us, only on a more social level. Still, he didn't hesitate to scold me when he thought some criticism was in order.

It wasn't long after our becoming acquainted that I got an example of his expectations of me. One afternoon, after finishing my homework and most of my house chores, I told Mama I was going down to visit Herr Kasper.

"First, get me the eggs from the chicken coop." Obeying, I ran down to the courtyard and back. Before she could think of a new errand, I skipped down the stairs again to the shoemaker.

Coming through his door, I was greeted with a pointed question, asked without the usual smile. "Annchen, was that you on the stairway?" Sophistication was still years away for me, but I could tell it was not a question requiring an answer. Herr Kasper and his apprentice knew I had just used the stairs!

"Come in and sit down. I want you to hear something." He then turned to his young helper, "Go and do what I said."

The boy left the room and disappeared down the hallway. Even then, I wasn't quite sure why the apprentice went out. After a moment, there came a noisy rumble of hard-soled shoes crashing up and down the stairs. I was horrified and embarrassed, and even more so when the boy, only slightly older than my brother, walked back into the shop with a smirk on his lips.

But the smug apprentice got his own rebuke from Herr Kasper, "I give you a small role to play and you overact. Go and see if you can do any better with Frau Usner's new heels." The boy rushed to a rack of shoes needing repairs, but I could see he still wore a faint smile. Without another word about my not-lady-like use of the stairs, Herr Kasper gave his attention again to a boot heel. "Did I tell you, I'll be seeing my sister in Heidelberg on the weekend and we're going to the theater, of course."

"What will you see? Is it an operetta? Have I heard of it?"

"Ach, Annchen," he laughed, "You ask questions just like you run the stairs!" He saw my cheeks turn pink and quickly softened the point, "But I can live with the questions. At least, I know the house isn't falling on my head." A shy grin was all I could manage.

From the start, it was clear the shoemaker had his mind on a greater love — live musical theater, especially opera and operetta. He would come back from one of those frequent visits to his sister in Heidelberg, filled with word pictures about the theater, and whether the production and singers had been up to his standards.

Until Herr Kasper, my music knowledge had been limited to the folk songs of Mama, church music, and the new songs extolling the glories of National Socialism. The few scratchy records we had were rarely played anymore on the wind-up machine. Our radio was still the old battery-operated unit with a speaker horn, and not very good for listening to music programs. This was about to change.

Many of Papa's hauling jobs took him to Worms on the Rhein to transport materials back to various building sites around Kirchheim. On one such mission, he found a lost and abandoned box. A careful driver, always scanning the road ahead, he suddenly caught sight of a snow-covered square object down the embankment where the road curved sharply. It was late January, and the last snowfall had been days before. My father was tempted to stop and investigate, but drove on with a nagging thought of something being amiss. The road to Worms was as familiar to him as his own feet, and that box didn't belong in the passing scene.

On the return trip, he braked to a halt near the object spotted earlier. Papa made his way down the snowy embankment on foot and saw that it was a large wood box lying up against a tree. He hoped that it might be a wood container he could use at home, but even damaged there was always a need for kindling. In any case, he was bound to check it out.

Brushing the snow off revealed a wooden crate, as he had expected. One of the corners was smashed and splintered, apparently from the impact of falling off a passing truck. It had to have happened during the recent snowstorm. Thinking Erich could make a good job of cutting it up for firewood, Papa turned the crate over to carry it up the slope. He immediately discovered that, packed and undamaged inside, was what appeared to be a large tabletop radio. After some thought, he put the crate on the truck and drove home to store it until a decision was made on what to do with it.

At supper, Papa explained the situation to us. The crate sat out in the workshop, still unpacked. Since he knew most of the truckers who worked in the territory, it was decided he would check around for a few days. "If there's no word on a missing radio in a crate," he explained, "we'll keep it." He smiled, and added, "Don't get your hopes up. It's just a guess about it being a radio. I'm only going by the name and number printed on one side of the container." The name was Mende, a brand of radio known to be of excellent quality and very expensive to buy.

After a week of discreet but fruitless inquiries, and daily check of area newspapers, we gathered in the workshop to watch Papa dismantle the crate.

All of us then helped to undo the heavy packing. What was revealed made our eyes pop — a large Mende radio with a big four-band dial in a beautiful wood cabinet much too big for me to lift.

The Mende, with its many bands, was about to give us an ear to the world, including forbidden foreign broadcasts. It is from the Mende that we would hear news of the pact between Hitler and Stalin of Russia, about the fate of Czechoslovakia, and the Blitzkrieg attack on Poland — all events leading to a new world war.

Chapter Eight

The voices coming from the old radio receiver had seemed so tinny and remote, and it was almost a shock to hear the clear quality of the new radio. Now the words of Hitler and Joseph Göbbels came to our ears with more impact and meaning. The Führer's voice and powerful rhetoric could mesmerize listeners. His propaganda minister, Göbbels, was also a good speaker, but his voice lacked the tone and force of Hitler's.

My family's evening listening habits changed with the arrival of the Mende. Radio had never been a part of daytime activity and, for the time being, it remained that way. However, starting with supper hour and into the night, the radio became our regular company for news and music programs. And, woe to the child talking or making a disturbance during newscasts or speeches from our leaders.

The dour and sometimes bitter demeanor that best described Mama during the Marnheim years started giving way to a new positive outlook after the move to Kirchheim. Her behavior in early 1939 surprised me at times. A near radical fervor for National Socialism grew stronger in her with each passing day. And, it worried Papa.

"Mariechen, he is not a god," He said, following another speech by Hitler. "He's only a man, and can make wrong decisions too. It's not good for you to have total faith in a politician!"

Papa wasn't all that concerned about the excitement his children had for all the radio talk of 'a new and greater German Reich.' We were young and needed a feeling of pride in our country. He believed most people of his generation and older weren't completely taken in by Nazism, and would go along without complaint only as long as the programs of the government continued restoring financial security. As for the more radical elements — those who espoused complete loyalty to one man and his ideas, my father looked on them with suspicion.

With Mama, he worried that she was the perfect target for the Nazi message. Since the collapse of Seppel's empire, forcing them back to Marnheim, Papa had lived patiently with her despondency and absence of faith in anything but the Bible. For years, he lost every effort to make his wife believe that success would come again. Adolf Hitler had succeeded where he'd failed.

Hitler was very clever in winning the loyalty of the common people through the kitchen door. His speeches constantly extolled the virtues of the "Deutsche Frau" and "Deutsche Mutter," as guardians of the home and the nation. And, we all heard when the Führer repeatedly used phrases like "Gott ist mein Zeuge!" (God is my witness!). God and the 'German mother' references always had a special appeal to religious women like my mother.

ɸ

I learned early on that it doesn't take much of an excuse for German people to hold a celebration. I've heard it said that a break in bad weather is sufficient reason to have a parade and carnival at the same time. When the festivities are connected with a religious event, the time and money spent is even greater.

Fasching is the longest and most popular carnival time in Germany, particularly in the Rheinland-Pfalz. Officially it begins on the eleventh day of the eleventh month, and builds in intensity until Shrove Tuesday in February. Nearly every village, town and city joins in the fun. The bigger the town, the more of things to do, from special children's events to fancy masquerade balls for the adults.

Having come from a village that put on only a small Fasching parade, I was delighted to hear Kirchheim had programs for children at the White Horse Inn on the Schloßstraße. It was only a short distance from our house. The very thought of participating must have been too much, as a serious bout of illness put me in bed the entire last week of the celebrations.

Sudden attacks of sickness had put me down before, but never as serious as that year. At one point, Mama feared I would die because the high fever refused to go down for more than two days. Erich later told me I hallucinated constantly — scaring everyone. Antibiotics weren't available, and aspirin for fever and aches was still not widely known or used. Old-fashioned herbal medicines and personal care were all Mama had in the battle against death.

The closest brush with the grim reaper came during the high fever stage, when my tonsils became so swollen I wasn't getting air. Mama tried to ease the swelling by using the old remedy Krumbeerwickel. It's dialect name for putting hot potatoes in an old sock, mashing them down, and wrapping the result around my throat. Momentarily, she'd forgotten that what worked on the pain of a sore throat didn't help in reducing severe swelling and fever. It was a near fatal mistake. Finally, Papa tried cold compresses on my head and throat. Cold, not hot, reduces swelling, and I was soon able to breathe easily again.

Only much later did I learn how Mama and Papa stayed with me, taking turns applying the compresses. At one point, they even sponged my entire body with icy water. Erich was kept home from school to handle phone calls for the business, and any customers pulling up to the gas pump. He later told me Herr Kasper downstairs asked about me every few hours. And, a Deaconess nurse came once, but she left saying it was in the Lord's hands.

The fever finally broke on the third day. Papa put my mother in bed for needed rest while he stayed with me. Mama found him asleep on the floor next to my bed when she awoke.

My few memories from the early days of recuperation include chicken broth and herbal teas. When I could sit up, Erich brought me books to read, but better still, played cards with me a couple of afternoons. Teasingly, I reminded him of his Christmas declaration, the one about being too old to play with a little sister.

I remember one more incident about my illness. After I was up and around again, I asked Mama why she never got sick — or even a cold.

Her reply was a sharp, "God help us if I come down sick!"

Again, the health department took an interest in my well being, and when Easter break came, I was sent to another children's home operated by the Deaconess Sisters. Unlike the seven weeks in Bad Kissingen, my stay would be only four weeks in a place called Völkersweiler near the better-known city of Annweiler, deep in the Pfälzerwald. And it wouldn't be as far from home — just two hours by train, but in a new part of the Pfalz for me.

Approaching Annweiler by train or car, one travels through heavily wooded valleys, some quite deep and narrow. Suddenly, the last narrow valley widens into a broad panoramic view of rolling hills and forest, dominated by three steep, high peaks named Trifels. Very much in view at the top of one was what remained of an old fortress castle, said to have been the favorite place of Barbarossa. Legend also tells of King Richard, the Lionhearted of England, being held for ransom there at a later period in history.

During my four weeks at Völkersweiler, we hiked many kilometers through the forest when weather permitted. At least twice, we tramped up steep and winding paths to the old fortress ruins. The field trips were the best part of my stay. I was among forty-five girls lining up first thing every morning in military fashion on an open meadow for exercises. It wasn't that hard or strict, and most of us made it fun. After an hour, we certainly had healthy appetites for the breakfast that followed.

Because I was to be away over Easter, Mama sent me a package filled with chocolate eggs, each wrapped in colorful foil. As it was my habit to conserve on sweets, I had some left over for bribery purposes. An occasion was on one of our forest hikes the second week. Halfway through the afternoon trek, we stopped to rest and have a snack. Where I sat with some girls, a nurse came along handing out apples to all except me. I was given a tomato. The red object in my hand immediately brought on the frightening thought that the nurse wanted me dead. Mama had said tomatoes were poisonous and refused to grow them. I tried exchanging the tomato for an apple, but no takers, not even when I threw some of my chocolate eggs into the deal. Failing a trade, I began looking for a bush to throw the terrible thing behind. A nurse appeared and ordered me to eat it. Not about to die willingly, I turned stubborn. "My family doesn't eat poison!"

"Come with me," she said, reaching out to take my hand. "Come, I want to show you something important." I took her hand and followed, finally stopped in front of two girls who were eating tomatoes. My guide asked them, "How long have you been eating tomatoes?"

"For years and years," said the one girl, and the other nodded in agreement.

"You see," the nurse said to me, smiling. "That's an old wife's tale that tomatoes are poisonous. Now, would we really give you anything harmful?"

"I hope not," I replied.

At that, she laughed outright, then repeated her order that I eat the tomato. "Hold it away from you to keep the juice off that pretty smock!"

I did, and loved every bite. I would later trade apples for this new treat called a tomato. Erich had once asked Mama why we didn't have tomato plants in our garden.

"Tomatoes are poisonous because they're from the nightshade plant family. You can't be too careful about eating them. Your grandmother told me so and besides, we have enough other vegetables in the garden." Mama would never be convinced that she was wrong about tomatoes.

My four weeks at Völkersweiler flew by. It was totally different than at Bad Kissingen where everything centered on strange tasting mineral water. That had been a new and interesting experience, but it couldn't match the rejuvenation powers found in the sparkling clean air of my Pfälzerwald. A popular dialect song of the time boasted that the Pfalz was "earth's paradise." My short time at the Trifels had me convinced of it.

Arriving back home, I found that everyone had missed me. Mama said she missed not having me to run errands. Papa said he missed hugging me, and Erich admitted he missed hitting me on the arm. For the first time, I realized I had missed them too.

Easter marked the end of the school year, and not long after my return from Völkersweiler I began the third grade and had my ninth birthday at about the same time. German schools go all year round, with short breaks — the longest being for about a month in summer. I also attended school six days a week, but only half days on Wednesday and Saturday. It was good that I enjoyed school, even though it required a big chunk of my time in and out the classroom. We always had homework. My routine was to attack the homework immediately after I got home. Erich, who had entered eighth grade, usually put it off until late at night, and sometimes, minutes before rushing to morning class. Because he put socializing with friends first, he was ever in a panic about homework.

I found it interesting that in Erich's class the boys and girls were segregated. Since the boys were being directed toward the male-dominated work world and the girls geared toward homemaking skills, eighth grade meant separation of the sexes. I believe that for us, in that time, it was more comfortable not sharing the classroom. I never heard Erich complain about the situation, though he did have his eye on a girl in the same grade. He must have fueled his passion after school.

My brother also believed my education should include the art of self-defense, or at least that's what he called it. I suppose it's typical for an older brother to wrestle around with a younger sibling on such childish pretexts, but in surviving the initial pains and occasional tears, I did learn how to handle him. The truth is, I loved Erich's attentions most all the time. He was the only person in my life I could love and hate with equal passion.

At fourteen years of age, my brother was spending more of his free time outside of school with his friends. From the immediate neighborhood, that was Franz Wilz, Ernst Gass, and a couple of others. They'd take over the old blacksmith shop with their schemes, and would only let me in when it suited their purpose. One time, they figured I'd be useful in pulling the bar handle that made the big bellow on the second floor open and close. Done correctly, the hearth fire got hotter. I had to stand on a barrel to reach and operate the bar, and my labors seemed to do no good at all. The bar of scrap iron held in the fire refused to turn red. In frustration, Ernst and Franz began a verbal attack on me that went beyond friendly chiding. They were instantly shocked into silence by the slamming of heavy tongs on the anvil.

"That's enough!" All eyes, including my own, flashed to the source of the angry warning. "You heard me. Leave her alone." The murderous glare Erich gave my tormentors, left no doubt as to their choice.

From that day, my brother's friends limited any harassment toward me to the mild-teasing sort. They'd come to understand that Erich, good friend that he was, still put family first. It was a lesson I was grateful to learn as well.

༄

Days later, Erich found me in the kitchen doing homework. "There's a witch living down at Bender's shop."

"Come on," I snickered. 'You're just teasing me. There's no such thing as a witch!"

"Ah, but there is," he insisted. "I just went in there today and this stringy-haired witch popped her head out of a doorway and told me to wait. She had the strangest voice. Sort of eerie."

"So," I laughed. "What did you do — run?"

"No, I waited. And then this skinny man came out; all dressed up like something in old postcards, high stiff collar and all. No one wears clothes like that anymore."

Bender's was one of Kirchheim's shops along the curving Langstraße that I still hadn't visited. Mama never asked me to go, and I wasn't sure what was sold there. The front window display had some very old posters, and from the outside, the interior appeared dark and unfriendly.

With that picture in my mind, I could almost swallow Erich's witch tale. And what about the man in the strange clothes? As I thought about it, I couldn't recall having seen anyone go in or come out of Bender's. Now, if I was to believe my brother, he had gone in and survived the visit. I decided to ask Papa about it.

While the Klein ancestral village was Bolanden, my father was born in Kirchheim during the period his parents were temporary residents. Sixteen when the family moved back to Bolanden, Kirchheim remained the place he knew best his whole life. I could rely on Papa for the truth about Bender's.

When I told my father what Erich had said, I thought he would fall on the floor, he laughed so hard. Mama heard his howling, and rushed into the kitchen from elsewhere to also hear the story. She wasn't one for laughter, but she shook her head and smiled.

"Ja, ja," Papa added, breathing easier after his laughing fit. "You know he just likes to fool you."

"Oh, I know that, Papa," I said firmly, "but what can you tell me about Herr Bender and the stringy-haired woman."

97

Again he chuckled. "The stringy-haired woman is the old maid sister to the tall skinny guy who happens to be an old bachelor. You could well say they're stuck with each other."

Mama chided him, "Fritz, you stop that. Tell the girl what she needs to know and no more."

I learned that my father had known the Bender family for many years. The parents had died, leaving the property to the surviving son and daughter. This included the once busy shop and two apartments upstairs. They lived together in one apartment and rented out the other. For reasons not known or talked about, neither one ever married, and were now past middle age. Papa added that both had always acted a bit strangely growing up, as though they lived in a separate world. And they were rarely seen in public outside the shop, just the opposite of the parents who had been very social.

Erich was surprised when later I asked if he had any money.

"Nay, not even a Pfennig."

"Well, I have some pfennigs, and I want to go to Bender's."

"So you want to see the witch."

"There's no witch. Papa told me all about the Bender family."

"Ja, Papa would know, but she still looks like a witch to me."

On the way, I asked what Bender's had that I would like. "Ah, he doesn't have much in the way of treats," Erich replied. "Mostly, it's sugar, flour, herbs and spices. Mama doesn't send us there because she thinks all the stuff is old and stale."

A bell at the top of the door jingled when we entered the dark interior of the shop. Not a soul was in sight, as Erich had described. We waited by the door, peering down the poorly lit, narrow shop. There were showcases and counters all along both sides of a center aisle, and behind the counters were the strangest cabinets I had ever seen. Instead of glass doors and shelves, each cabinet had drawers of all sizes running from the floor to the high ceiling, and the drawers all had a little glass window and brass plate. On closer inspection, I saw that the plates were inscribed with the names of herbs, spices and coffee beans. The larger drawers near the bottom were for dried beans, sugars and flour. And, being all dark wood, it gave a gloomy impression.

Along one wall, there was a door that went to some other part of the building. After a few minutes of waiting, a head with tangled hair popped through the door and looked our way. "Wait a moment, please. Someone will be here to help you." Her voice wasn't harsh or particularly strange, like I had imagined a witch would sound, but in that empty place it reached my ears with an eerie echo that was enough to weaken my knees.

The witch was right. In less than a moment, a tall man, straight out of a Dickens novel, came through the door and approached the two of us. Herr Robert Bender could not be called unfriendly, but he was so formal in manner that he was the first person I had ever heard speak the dialect and make it sound like High German, the rigid form of our language.

Bender's was not the kind of place that invited browsing, so when we went in we had to think of something specific to buy. Half the time, we hoped he wouldn't be available and the sister would have to show more than her head, but it never happened. After a while, my brother and I began thinking up exotic things to buy, usually spices and herbs, in hopes of stumping the shopkeeper. One day we asked Mama for help in our game of making Herr Bender scratch his head. She didn't know this, thinking that our questions amounted to no more than childish curiosity.

Taking a causal approach, Erich said, "Mama, what's the rarest herb in Germany?"

I think she was pleased that Erich would expect her to know, so she paused in her baking and gave it some serious thought. "I do believe," she said, after a minute, "there is an herb from the mountains of Bavaria they say is almost impossible to find. Let me think — ja, it's called Tausendguldenkraut."

"What's it good for?" I wanted to know, in case Bender tested me.

"Well, they say it works wonders on stomach ailments and fevers. Lots of things."

A short time later we were back at Bender's, standing at the front and waiting to hear the old bachelor say, "I don't have Tausendguldenkraut." It was to be the same routine. The disheveled head telling us to wait followed by the approach of our intended victim. Screwing up his courage, Erich looked up. "If you please, Herr Bender, we're in need of a few grams of Tausendguldenkraut."

The response wasn't exactly as expected, but familiar. He scratched his head with one hand while massaging his chin with the other. He turned and walked down the aisle a few steps, muttering "Tausendguldenkraut" over and over. He stopped to sweep his eyes across the dozens of drawers, then moved again toward the back. We followed along behind listening to his, "Tausendguldenkraut…Tausendgul — ach, ja! Now I know."

Never had we seen him so excited. He quickly went behind the counter and headed back toward the front, rolling a ladder hanging from a ceiling track to the rear wall. "Ja, ja, I'm certain." He nearly shouted it, climbing up the ladder in spurts, checking plates on rows of drawers as he went.

Erich put his mouth to my ear. "You'd better have some money," he whispered. My hand was already on my coin purse, and I could see Herr Bender pull a cloth sack from a small drawer near the top.

As he descended the ladder, we were cheerfully told what a lucky day it was for us. At home, Mama was very surprised to learn that Tausendguldenkraut was not so hard to find after all.

&

That first summer in my new hometown was all I could have wished. I was making good friends and along the way, exploring every square centimeter of the place. I couldn't get over the hustle and bustle of what was really a small city. As it was both a government and market center for a wide area, not a day went by without hundreds of people coming in and going out by train, bus, bicycle or on foot. A few cars and horse-drawn wagons were part of the mix too. It was also a time when housewives food shopped nearly everyday. To me, it seemed that all the ladies left their houses at about the same time. Down the street they'd come, like a parade of clean aprons. Most women kept a clean apron, like a sleeveless housecoat, hanging by the door. Changing their soiled, everyday working version for the public one, the shopping trip could commence.

Mama was an exception to this parade of Hausfrauen. She never wore an apron for any activity outside the home. Usually Erich or I were sent to bring back the daily bread, milk, or meat, so shopping for food was not a common task for her. When she left the house several days a week, it was for reasons connected with the business, and she was dressed accordingly. The bank and tax office would never see Frau Klein in anything but a conservative suit. The same can be said for any shop she did business with. Mama enjoyed her role as a businessperson, and she played the part almost too well. She wasn't a cold woman, as some thought, she was merely demanding respect.

Her grim demeanor in public was in sharp contrast to Papa's wide-open approach to people. He felt bad about being pulled out of school in sixth grade to help his father, but he recognized and gave credit to Opa Peter for an education not found in books. What he learned from Opa, prepared him well. He was street smart, and quickly sized up people and situations. His was the most important contribution to the trucking business. But all would have failed without Mama. She alone understood the bookkeeping and banking. On Sunday afternoons, she would sit Papa down for debriefing of the previous week. Knowing how intolerant Mama was of Papa's record-keeping, I always tried to escape

100

the room.

"Fritz, where did you go Monday?"

"Let me think. Monday, you want? I'm sure it was sand over in Albisheim."

"Fritz! You delivered five loads of sand in Albisheim on Wednesday. I found the note in your pants pocket. Now think about Monday. How am I supposed to send out bills? You don't even make notes most of the time. Now think!"

It all made Papa look foolish and I didn't like it. My mother was right, of course, but I avoided these weekly confrontations.

All around us during the summer of 1939, we saw evidence of Hitler's promises coming true. New homes for working-class people suddenly appeared at the south edge of Kirchheim. Papa helped haul materials to the sites and said the homes were of a good solid brick construction. He also worked on road improvement projects in the region, and talked of a new super-highway called an "Autobahn" being built from Kaiserslautern to Frankfurt. The local finance office was no longer a place to collect subsistence for the unemployed. No able-bodied worker was without some kind of paying labor. The impact of the economic upswing was felt by everyone at some level, and gave rise to ever more faith in National Socialism.

Our trucking business reached the point where Papa had to hire his younger brother Ludwig from Bolanden to help with the work. Of all his brothers and sisters, Ludwig had always been a special responsibility for my father. Only a lad when Seppel Peter died in 1932, Oma Klein relied on her Fritz to help guide Ludwig into manhood. Now that he was a young man of seventeen, Papa thought he'd be just the reliable help he needed — especially with his plan to add a second truck.

During my month-long school vacation in late summer, Kirchheim held its Jahrmarkt, an annual market festival (Kerwe). At night, the town center is bathed in colorful lighting. The air was filled with sounds of the excited babble of children mixed with the shouts of the hawkers, all blended into the carnival music and voices of beer garden singers. Some nights, if the wind was right, I could go to sleep listening to all the sounds of Kerwe through my open bedroom window high on the hill.

Around this time, Mama did something that shocked all of us — she began going out in the evening. She'd made friends with an older woman just four doors up from us, Frau Usner. She was the grandmother of Henriette, a new friend of mine. Henny, as I called her, became my closest buddy. It was with Frau Usner that Mama decided to join the Nazi Frauenschaft, an organization for older women with chapters in every town. There was nothing evil about the group, the ladies mostly worked on welfare kinds of projects, but her willingness to join reinforced Papa's worry over her near fanatical belief in Hitler and the Nazi Party. My father was just as strongly anti-politics, saying he had little time for foolishness. He wasn't happy about his wife's new evening occupation of attending meetings once and twice a week, but said little. Papa knew better than to fight it head on.

This is what is called the "Four Corners" intersection. Here Breitstraße (where you see a motorcyclist with a Volkswagon behind) meets and becomes Neumayerstraße. On the right is the doorway into St. Peter's Catholic Church. To the left, with the monument, is Freierplatz. The large building behind is Bossung's Inn. Starting here to the left, is the beginning of Langstraße, which takes you into the old walled town. To the right is Haiderstraße, which takes you to the village of Haide and all points north and west. The intersection became very important to the American occupation.

Chapter Nine

My summer vacation gave Papa a chance to satisfy the only complaint I really had about his heavy workload — I didn't see enough of him. Over breakfast one day, he surprised me. "How would you like to go with me while I make deliveries around the area?"

When no objection came from Mama, I jumped at the chance to go. I loved riding high up in the truck cab with my father. He'd point out landmarks and other places of interest wherever the journey took us. And there were always family stories to tell — mostly about the Kleins, but also the Herbsts. It's how I learned more about Mama's Tante Giloy in Marnheim.

"Ach, look, Annchen. There walks your mother's royal aunt."

We were passing along the main street of Marnheim, and I had to quickly look to catch sight of her. "Why do you say 'royal'? She looks and acts like some grand lady, but Mama never said Tante Giloy has royal blood."

That brought a chuckle from Papa. "Maybe I should let your mother tell you about her aunt's eccentric attachment to the past."

"Please, you tell me. You know she hardly speaks of the past."

"Ja, ja. My Mariechen isn't quite sure how she should feel about the Herbst connection to royalty. It was a long time ago and, except for old Tante Giloy, few in the family care about it."

"You mean it's really true? The Herbsts once were kings and princes?"

"Nay, Märe, not that high up!" Papa roared with laughter and shifted gears to pick up speed leaving the village. I watched and waited for him to go on with the story as we passed below the high iron railroad bridge that stretched a thousand-feet across the wide Pfrimm valley. Glancing over at me, he smiled. "I suppose you won't be happy until you hear it all. Alright then, maybe hearing the truth of it will open your eyes to the foolishness of some people. Listen and keep what I say to yourself. I don't want to hear of you telling fancy stories to your friends. And, please don't talk about the Herbst family to the folks in Bolanden. They long ago decided your mother's relatives were a little strange."

"I won't say a word, Papa."

Our destination was Oberwiesen to pick up a load of stone. In the twenty minutes it took to get there, Papa had told me everything about Mama's link to a 'royal' house. Though only nine years of age, I could see that any link was a mere thread leading to a wealthy property owner, not a real baron or prince. Katharina Junker, Papa added, was to blame for the high-minded notions of Tante Giloy and my grandmother Herbst. She was their mother, and had come from Kriegsheim to marry Philip Herbst, owner of the Heyerhof estate. Katharina was said to be the great-granddaughter of a squire who owned a castle and much land in the Odenwald, east of the Rhein. In German, a Junker is often the title of a rich squire whose power came from land holdings, not royal blood. Land was usually awarded by royalty for services rendered, like fighting in the Crusades for the King.

Papa said Katharina probably made everyone in the Herbst family believe her ancestor was royal because he lived in Rodenstein castle. "But living in such a place doesn't make it so. Any fool can live in a fortress castle, if he has the power to rob the people. Don't be impressed with castles, Annchen. Most of them were not pleasant places for the people who lived in them."

After a pause, Papa decided to change the subject. "Tomorrow I have business in Worms. Why don't you come along and I'll drop you off for the day at Lina's."

Papa's sister was married to a man who managed the government electric utility in Monsheim, not far from Worms and the Rhein river. Along with their older children Fritz and Helmi, they often visited us since our move to Kirchheim. Tante Lina had named her son after my father, and both he and Helmi loved tramping through the forest with Erich and me.

"Ja, Papa, I want to. Maybe Helmi will be there." We'd already heard that Fritz was away at a preparatory school leading to pilot's training in the Luftwaffe.

The twenty-kilometer drive to Monsheim the next morning was over all too quickly. Papa barely had time to assure me that he'd be by later in the evening to pick me up.

Tante Lina's family lived in a rather grand apartment on the top floor of the same building that housed the main offices of the utility. Behind, and walled off from public view, was a bountiful garden with just about everything in the way of fruits, vegetables and flowers. There were also fruit trees surrounding a garden house. On the other side of one wall, passenger trains pulled in and out of a nearby station, but it was all that disturbed the tranquil setting of the garden. My aunt had made a great success in creating a touch of rural beauty in an otherwise drab place.

Tante Lina, with her uppity ways, was not my favorite aunt. During visits to her house as a very young child I found her quite intimidating. Instead of a hug and warm words, she insisted on shaking hands, saying something like:

"What's the matter with your tongue? Did you leave it at home in a drawer?"

Still, she was my father's sister. I liked the apartment, and enjoyed looking at all the beautiful things. And cousins Fritz and Helmi were always nice to me. I had figured a day there would be fun, and it was. That evening, after supper, I helped with the dishes and then prepared myself for Papa's arrival.

"Helmi, why don't you show Annchen some books? She might find a nice one to read."

"Nay, Tante. I don't think I should start reading. Papa will be here any minute."

Tante Lina cautiously cleared her throat. "I don't know. It may be that his business will be very late. Perhaps you should plan on staying here tonight."

I thought that was ridiculous. My father's word had always been absolute. "Tante, I can't stay. I brought nothing to sleep in, not even a comb for my hair."

"That's not a problem. You can wear one of Helmi's old night-shirts. And we certainly have enough combs in the house."

I smelled a trick, but I decided to play the game and not spoil my visit. I couldn't imagine why anyone thought I wouldn't like staying at Tante Lina's for a couple of days.

It turned out to be three days and two nights before my father returned, looking very sheepish. There followed some straight talk on the trip home. He told me that Tante Lina had it in her head that I was too shy, and needed to be with other people.

"Papa, you know I'm not shy with family! It's just Tante Lina's way of talking that bothers me sometimes. She acts so stuck up!"

He chuckled. "Ja, ja. She can be a real queen at times, but you must admit she's not as bad as Tante Giloy." Then, looking over and seeing me smile. "Well, my Märe, I think you're getting too old for me to fool. From now on, I'll ask if you want to stay."

The travels with Papa ended when school resumed, but only a month later he looked across the breakfast table at me, a mischievous twinkle in his eyes. Turning to Mama he said, "I have to haul stone over to Bad Kreuznach tomorrow. Annchen has just a half-day of school and I'd like her to meet my cousin Hilde. Write a note to her teacher excusing her from classes."

I was so excited about meeting my father's blind cousin I could only think to ask, "Should I take my night clothes along?" I smiled.

He laughed. "Nay, Annchen," he said with a wink. "I'll bring you home in the evening. But, if you like it there, you can go with me again. I have lots of jobs taking me to Bad Kreuznach."

The forty-five minute drive from Kirchheim to Bad Kreuznach the next morning was a beautiful journey. The forested hills and deep valleys found at the edge of our town became denser the farther west we traveled. There were a few open meadows used for hay or grazing, and now and then a cultivated field, but mostly our road curved, climbed and dropped down through heavy forest. I sometimes felt like we were traveling in a dark tunnel, with only splashes of sunlight coming through the high tree canopy.

We were on the road very early in the morning, so Papa stopped at a bakery in one of the first villages. He bought two piping hot hard-crusted rolls, fresh from the oven, and a small chocolate bar. We each took a roll, literally cracking them open to reveal the steaming soft interior. Quickly popping chunks of sweet chocolate into the center, we closed them again to await the delicious result.

All along our route, we drove through inhabited places of varying size. Tiny villages like Marienthal, the castle ruins of Falkenstein, the larger market town of Rockenhausen, and a big wine-producing monastery overlooking the quiet Nahe river, were all part of the passing scene. I felt like a tourist, for much of what I saw was new to me.

Bad Kreuznach reminded me of Bad Kissingen, with all of its fancy resort hotels and gardens, mineral-water Salinen and lovely open parks. I would have liked to see more, but Papa drove into the city center to a row of high apartment buildings right on the Nahe river's edge.

Hilde lived in one of the buildings with her husband Walter and twelve-year-old son Horst. Both were already gone for the day when we arrived, so it was Hilde herself who answered the door. She didn't know we were coming, but that seemed to make no difference at all. In our family, people always 'dropped in.' Papa greeted Hilde warmly. "Here, Hilde, I've brought you company for the day. My Annchen!"

She immediately reached out, hugging me and drawing me through the doorway. My father had said she could only sense light and dark, so it surprised me that she knew where I stood. Her soft hand explored my face, head and long braids, as her kind voice welcomed us. Shyness wasn't my problem as I tried to respond to the tiny lady — it was more like being overwhelmed that someone, who obviously couldn't see, accepted me nonetheless.

Papa briefly explained that he would come in the evening, giving me a smile as he said it. Then he was gone. I was left to face a new challenge of being with a blind person, and for a whole day. I'd been told Hilde was born blind, but not much more. My head was filled with questions for her that I couldn't ask. Something inside told me to watch and listen.

As we walked through the small apartment to the living room, I could see that Hilde moved with grace and ease. Everything was sparkling clean and neatly arranged. The temptation to ask how she kept the place so nice was strong, but I resisted.

"Come, child. Sit by me and tell me all about yourself." She then reached to a side table, picked up a knitting project, and quickly started working the needles. "I'll knit while you talk."

I was amazed as I watched her fingers expertly purl and knit the yarn. I had gotten to be a pretty fair knitter, but in no way could I match Hilde's skill. She obviously knew what I was thinking. "I knit all our sweaters. The only difficulty is putting together all the finished pieces. Walter's mother lives near by, and helps me do that part." She changed the subject back to me. "Tell me now about school and that rascal Erich, and dear Marie too."

In no time, her interest and attention to me had my mouth going non-stop. Because she always turned her face my way when I spoke, and by witnessing all her abilities, Hilde's blindness was nearly forgotten. When I discovered that she also knitted garments for regular customers to bring in extra income, I knew what Papa meant when he called her a special person.

After the noon meal, she showed me around the apartment. Its neatness and order told me the old saying, 'A place for everything and everything in its place,' was especially important to someone who couldn't see. I was also shown the balcony projecting out over the Nahe river. At one end was a small enclosure which I learned was the toilet. The inside of Hilde's balcony out-house looked just like mine at home, except our waste went into an under-ground storage to be emptied several times a year for eventual use as garden fertilizer. For Hilde, and others living along the river, waste disposal was less of a problem. I was not exactly comfortable with the idea of dirtying the river, but that's the way it was.

Hilde had flower boxes along the balcony rail that were filled with showy red Geraniums. Most of the balconies I could see had similar displays, and it made me sad that she couldn't see them. From my balcony vantage point, I could also see one of the landmarks of Bad Kreuznach. Just downstream, the river swirled beneath a group of large houses built across a bridge.

Later, when Hilde and I walked to the town center to shop, we had to cross the famous stone bridge that had been built several hundred years before. Going along the inhabited side, there was no sense of being on a bridge. All of the buildings, arranged in a solid line, appeared like the usual apartment houses, with businesses at the ground level. The realization of being on a bridge came only by looking across the street. There, beyond a low wall, was a view of the Nahe flowing away. I had to wonder what it would be like to live on a bridge.

As we went from shop to shop buying for the evening meal, she took my arm and hardly used her walking stick. Normally, she said, the stick was used to warn her of obstacles, but she had the exact steps to each turning point and store put to memory. "It's nice," she laughed, "to not have to count today."

I smiled, studying this person who was only as tall as me. "I just hope I don't get us lost."

"Don't you fret about that," she chuckled. "I'll say something when the sidewalk doesn't feel right under my feet."

It was to Oma Klein's side of the family that she belonged. That explained a lot about her sweet nature, but more than that, I learned disabled people could be productive and happy.

In the evening, I met Walter and Horst. Hilde already had the potatoes peeled and the other ingredients prepared. Her husband did the actual cooking. How I expected Walter to look didn't match reality. Slightly taller than Hilde, he was a pleasant-looking man, one that any woman with sight may have been pleased to have. It was another lesson — jumping to conclusions was a bad habit.

Driving home and talking with Papa about Hilde and others in the family, I began to realize what he wanted for me. Over the summer, he'd been using our travels together as a main chance for me to know and understand his love of family. I never doubted that he loved his wife and children, and I'd seen his great affection for his mother, but until that day I'd never fully known the true size of his heart.

❧

Mama hardly ever talked about the 'old times' in her family, but if I pushed hard enough, she would tell me about herself and Papa before Erich or I came into the picture. As I have said, my mother wasn't filled with humor, though some of her stories were outlandish, or so they seemed to me.

When they were first married, Papa would take her to as many Kerwe as he could talk her into. With most every village around having a carnival time, the occasions must have been frequent. I could just hear him. "Ach, Mariechen,

108

let's walk over to Bischheim. I hear they have a good band."

Any of a dozen village names could be substituted for Bischheim. Mama claimed she always argued against it. "Fritz, we have no money to waste on food and drink," she'd say.

"We don't need to eat. And as for drink, I have enough in my pocket for two glasses of wine. What more do we need? The rest will come."

Reluctantly, she agreed to go but only, she told me, because Papa needed "looking after." I asked why this was so.

"Because he would end up singing and dancing on top of the table, that's why!"

"Mama, I can't believe that! My Papa dancing on a table?"

"Ja, ja. Always on top of the table. Oh, everything started out just fine. One glass of wine and we would dance maybe once or twice. Then someone, who knew him, perhaps a relative or a person he delivered for, would come over and your Papa's wine glass would never be empty again. Soon he would sing and dance on the table."

"But what did you do then?"

"What did I do? When everyone stopped applauding, I hauled him down from the table top to walk me home."

"Was he sorry? I mean, were you embarrassed?"

"Ach, nay," she answered. "I'm just glad he doesn't do it now."

"So, your mother has been telling secrets from my youth."

I'd gone down to Papa, repairing some problem on his truck in the passageway. When he wasn't driving, there seemed to be endless maintenance work.

"Ja, I'll admit to doing a jig or two on a table here and there. Today, I'm much too old to tap dance."

I knew he was born in January of 1901, which made him thirty-eight years old. In my young eyes he was old, but I didn't like him saying it.

"You're not old, Papa!" I insisted. "Someday we'll go over to Fretz's and you'll dance for me."

"Nay, nay! I don't think so." Then he roared with laughter.

I had to laugh too. At that moment, Papa had grease smears on his face, hands and work clothes. In my mind's eye, I could see him happily singing and dancing on a table just for me, dirty face and all.

᪥

The beginning of September was around the corner, and I looked forward to a beautiful fall season in my Pfälzisch home. I felt truly blessed in all things.

Chapter Ten

When Papa hired Ludwig in the spring to help in the business, he bought a used truck for him to drive. It proved to be a right decision for meeting the hauling demand, but Ludwig was a bit erratic at times. He was just eighteen, handsome in a tall skinny way, and still lived at home with his mother in Bolanden. My young uncle was responsible about work, but like my father, he had a social nature that had to be kept in control. Mama now had two Seppels to keep an eye on.

Erich and I liked Ludwig very much. He seemed like an older brother, and hated being called 'Onkel.' Many were the times I'd be sitting at my little table in the kitchen doing my homework, when Ludwig popped in to check with Mama on hauling jobs. In the process of checking, he never failed to give my long braids a pull and say something cute. Often, after a long day, Ludwig joined us for supper before going on home. At first, his truck remained with us in Kirchheim and he walked home. It was a big day indeed when Papa allowed Ludwig to take the truck and keep it in Bolanden overnight.

We really didn't have room for two trucks anyway, so letting his brother keep one in Bolanden was convenient for everyone. Having Ludwig in the business was a great help to my father, who would send him out on evening hauls. It freed up time for Papa to pursue one of his passions — gardening. Working in the garden had always been a family affair under his strict guidance.

Besides hoeing and pulling weeds constantly, Erich and I were in charge of watering. Papa was a stickler on how the garden was watered. We knew about hoses and begged him to buy one. A hose could be connected at the house and would cut out all the hauling of heavy sprinkling cans back and forth to the rain water barrel in the courtyard. The answer was a firm refusal. "Water from a hose is too cold for the plants."

Whatever his hauling schedule, it was rare when the rest of us sat down to supper before my father could join us. Mama believed a family should have at least one unhurried meal together each day. At the evening meal, the slower pace of eating came with a demand for quiet during the radio newscasts. I wanted to talk about my day, but Papa always forbade it until after the news program.

The evening of September 1, 1939 began like all before it as we sat down to eat. Turning on the radio, Papa warned my brother and I to be quiet. Both he and Mama seemed on edge as they waited for the news program to begin. I looked at Erich whose expression matched my own feeling of curiosity about our parents' behavior. We didn't have long to wait for the answer.

An announcer's voice, more strident than I'd ever heard, seemed to erupt from the Mende's speaker. "Early this morning, in response to a sneak attack on one of our radio transmitters, heroic Wehrmacht crossed into Poland in retaliation!"

In shock, we listened to a further description of our army's advance on the ground, supported by Luftwaffe air raids. Papa finally broke his silence. "This is bad. It means war!"

My father sensed that he had frightened me. I had heard many horror stories from World War I, about family members that had been lost in the slaughter. "Don't worry, Märe," he said to me in a calmer voice. "It's just a little squabble. It'll be over in a few weeks."

Erich spoke, influenced by three years in Nazi Jugend. "I think it's time we Germans showed the world they can't look down their noses at us! The Poles have been giving us trouble for a long time. We need to slap them down!"

Mama feared her husband, and possibly Erich, would be taken away to fight. "I don't want you talking like that, Erich. We will not talk of war!"

"I'm still sorry I'm not old enough to go into the Wehrmacht."

That reality actually gave Mama some comfort. Ignoring my brother's outburst, she turned to Papa. "Fritz, do you think they will draft you?"

The very idea of my father going into the army, into war, sent a shudder through all of us. My parents had worked hard to build a new and prosperous life for us, and a few words from the radio suddenly put a dark cloud on everything. However, Papa wouldn't be defeated so easily. "I doubt it. I'm almost forty, and I have a business that's important. Besides, this mess won't last long. Not if England and France stay out of it."

We stayed in the kitchen a long time that evening listening to news reports. In only hours, we knew that England and France were mobilizing and war was certain.

Papa tried to reassure me again. "Don't worry. It can't last long. A few weeks." He smiled, but I knew he didn't believe his own words.

"Who cares," Erich said, "whether it's few weeks or four years. In school I'm reading about a war that lasted thirty years!"

"Where was that?" I asked, mouth agape.

"Right here in the Pfalz."

I then learned he was talking about the religious wars that had happened hundreds of years before, but that didn't make me feel any better.

In the days that followed, there was a lot of talk in the shops, in school, and on every street corner. Just talk, and nothing more. Life seemed to go on undisturbed. I don't know what I thought would happen. Perhaps I had expected bombs to fall from the sky, or soldiers to be marching in the street. Our teacher didn't say much to us, except that we all had to wait. The Führer would lead the nation in the right direction, he said. Many of the boys in my class felt like my brother, while most girls worried about losing fathers and older brothers to war.

෴

There was a lot of activity on the corner down from our house in front of the Bossung Inn. On a normal evening, it was common for a small group of men to stand on the corner, smoking and debating politics. Now the group was larger, and the talk much louder. In my doorway, I could hear the men, some as young as my brother, speaking out for war, while the older men urged caution. Some of them had been in war, and carried the scars. A missing leg or arm was their proof that war wasn't a game of cards, but they were shouted down. Erich, though only fourteen, was fired up, and wanted to join the debates in front of Bossung. Papa absolutely forbade it. His order didn't stop him from debating the issue at home, and upsetting Mama.

There were many changes in the days after the first of September, though the significance of some were not clear at the time. One that I didn't give importance to was in the new way of greeting people outside of home and family. In school, when the teacher entered the classroom, we all rose as one with our right arms extended to shout "Heil Hitler." Everyone did the same in public places like offices and shops. Oddly, I can't recall being trained about the 'Heil Hitler' rule. Along with large pictures of the Führer showing up on the walls of classrooms, offices, stores, and in everyone's living room, it all seemed to happen overnight.

Mama had been ahead of the crowd in regards to Hitler's picture. Months before, she had replaced our fancy one of the Kaiser with a plainer framing of the Führer, his pose just as serious. None of us used the living room very much, but he was there to gaze down on any visitors who dropped in.

In mid-September, upsetting news hit the family. Ludwig came by to report that he was being drafted. Papa immediately went with him to see their mother in Bolanden. He later told us how she cried and cried, but nothing could be done. Mama and I cried too. We were very fond of Ludwig, and he

113

had become valuable to Papa. Erich's response was to repeat his tiresome wish to be old enough to go.

Each new day now brought news of more family members on both sides being drafted or enlisting. Onkel Heinrich's son Friederich enlisted in the cavalry. In the beginning, horses were still a part of army operations. Because so many of my relatives worked with horses in civilian life, it seemed a logical choice.

In the neighborhood, Frau Usner's son-in-law, the father of my new friend Henny, soon joined the ranks of the infantry. He was shipped almost right away to Poland. Henny, already a member of Hitler Jugend, was proud her father would be fighting for the Nazi cause. Being two years younger, I was not yet in the youth group, but she made sure I was informed about the program in advance.

My music teacher Herr Keidel was called in, leaving me stranded. I'd been learning to play the Handharmonika and continued to practice as best I could. Mama promised, "If you keep playing, I'll find you another teacher." Papa told me my playing perked up a Sunday afternoon, something he wanted with all the gloom in the air.

I had taken up the instrument after our move from Marnheim. It was originally intended that Erich learn to play, but he tired of it quickly. I began lugging the heavy thing to lessons with Herr Keidel soon after. From the start, I loved the Handharmonika, our name for an instrument that looks and operates like an accordion, but has buttons instead of a piano-type keyboard. And, unlike the accordion, the right-hand buttons sound different notes when opening and closing the bellows. Despite that difficulty, I learned to play it very fast.

Two months passed, and the military draft still ignored my father, though other older men began to go. His business was flourishing, war or no war, and he was tempted to find a replacement for Ludwig. But in the end, it was decided to store the second truck in the garage of a friend in Worms.

"If only Erich was out of school," he often lamented.

Papa had allowed Erich to drive on isolated back roads, and was pleased with his natural ability. But Erich had to finish eighth grade and have confirmation in the church. This was a few months off and desperate as he was for help, my father would not pull his son from the classroom. It was all too vivid in his mind how his father had taken him out of school. The same had been done with all of Papa's brothers. School wasn't important to Opa 'Seppel,' except for reading and writing. Not even the war mobilization could keep Papa from dreaming aloud about the future he wanted for his son and daughter. It included no less than an eighth grade education, and he hoped much more.

æ

As winter came, and still no overt reaction from Germany's enemies, we all began to relax a little as Christmas approached. This period would later be called the "Phony War." The first days of war fever that had followed the invasion of Poland diminished with each passing week. England and France didn't move against us militarily, and some people began to believe Hitler had succeeded again in restoring German pride and power in the eyes of the world.

Words like unschlagbar (invincible) were used to describe our armed forces. My father fluctuated between hope the war alert would soon end and declaring, "England will not hold back much longer."

While the war scare seemed to slowly die, and life appeared normal again, there were signs that it was only quiet on the surface. Mama's Frauenschaft meetings had increased from once to twice a week. The ladies knitted scarves and mittens for the soldiers, and prepared gift boxes for Christmas. A lot of Kirchheim men and boys weren't expected home for the holidays, though a few got furloughed. Henny's father made it home and brought gifts for his family from Poland. Most of it was gold jewelry. Henny said it was beschlagnahmt (confiscated) from the Polish people. It was a new word for me, but I didn't want to ask her what it meant. I went home and asked Mama.

"It means to take over someone's property," she explained.

"Ha!" My brother laughed as he sat at the kitchen table. "It means stealing. Don't you know the victors in battle always loot and steal? Even honest people do it, according to my history book."

I was appalled. Erich's bluntness made my mother shake her head, but she didn't contradict him. He was, after all, studying history in school, and she figured he must be right. As for his strong opinions, that was a trait inherited from the Klein side. At least, that's what Mama thought.

The Christmas season was no different for me than before, except that our tree in the living room now had the portrait of Hitler gazing down on it. Mama baked the usual cookies and cakes. What we didn't know was Hitler's planned invasions of neighboring countries would soon begin. Denmark, Norway, Belgium, Holland and Luxembourg were the first, with France following in June. We knew none of this as the new year began — our first family news of 1940 was entirely happy.

Late in January, Tante Lisbeth and her husband began building a new house at the edge of Bolanden. My aunt and uncle had been married several years and had children, but until then had only lived in rented quarters. The fact that they could now own their own place was significant to all of us, because it meant another member of the family was doing well. Best of all, the house would have plenty of room for Oma Klein. Oma was getting on in age, and her children didn't want her living alone. She was still active and quite independent, so she insisted on the right to maintain her own quarters in the arrangement.

I was very pleased to hear of the news. Tante Lisbeth and my father were very much alike, and in nature and looks both followed in their mother's footsteps.

Oma had been especially lonely and worried with three of her sons now serving in the army. Otto and Rudi were drafted soon after Ludwig. The fate of young Ludwig was of special concern. She read the letters he sent whenever we stopped by. She confided all her worries to Papa. As with many old people, family losses in the First World War were as fresh in her mind as yesterday. My father did his best to reassure her of a happier outcome. "This mess will end before you know it," he'd tell her.

Now almost ten years old, I was as tall as Oma. Her small bony frame was always dressed in dark clothing, and her thinning gray hair was combed straight back and twisted into a knot at the nape of her neck. Tante Lisbeth took up the same hairstyle for all her life as well. Despite the severe appearances, both were affectionate and gentle. While my grandmother was ever an old person to me, she had the most remarkable dark brown eyes that shone and sparkled with pure joy whenever family came around. I was the only female grandchild with the Klein name, so she paid special attention to Seppel's daughter.

"Come, child. Sit by me and tell me all about your mother," she'd say to me, usually adding, "I haven't seen her lately, and I do so miss her visits."

"I know Mama would like it if you came to visit us."

"Ach, my poor legs won't carry me to Kirchheim anymore. So I sit here and wait for people to come and visit me!" Oma would laugh, her dark eyes sparkling. "Today I am lucky. You're my visitor!"

Lisbeth was the same. She never failed to extend her embrace in greeting, though we might have seen each other only two days previous. It was the same for Erich and Mama, but it was for Papa that she had the most affection. One facet of my aunt's love for him I witnessed many times when I was along.

"Fritz, come in and sit a spell. I'm just getting ready to fry up some of your favorite potatoes. It won't take a minute."

Of course, I was invited to sit and eat with Papa, but the invitation confused me in the beginning. We rarely visited at mealtime and she had not been preparing to cook. I learned it was just her way of showing concern that her hard-working brother was getting enough to eat.

Whatever the workload, Papa made every effort to keep a close check on his mother. Any problems or questions regarding family were left to him to solve. Sometimes his attentions to Oma made my mother mad, but her jealousy couldn't diminish his sense of responsibility to his Bolanden family.

Mama's occasional rages about his family and friends only baffled my father. This would never change.

Chapter Eleven

Starting a week before Palm Sunday, the house at Breitstraße One was turned upside down in preparation for Erich's confirmation celebration. The formal religious service not only signified his acceptance into the church, it also meant the end of full-time academic studies. At the time, only a few classmates went on to high school, and fewer still considered university study. Most followed the course Erich chose by entering an apprenticeship program. For him, Papa made arrangements for training in a local machine shop.

It was Mama's intention to make her son's confirmation an event he wouldn't forget. Tante Anna came by train from Kriegsheim to help her clean the house from top to bottom. Her husband had been killed in an accident, and she was a young widow with two small girls. My namesake never had much money, but she declined all offers to marry again. Somehow, I admired her even more for that.

Cousin Helmi came from Monsheim to stay with us for the week and help Mama with the cleaning and food preparation. I don't remember how many cakes were baked, but they were beginning to fill up all available storage space, and I began imagining the size of the crowd descending on the house Sunday afternoon to devour every morsel. Mama took the attitude that my ten years were insufficient for, as she put it, "serious cleaning and cooking." I did, however, come in handy for running errands and keeping an eye on Tante Anna's Margot and Elfriede.

Seeing all that was going into Erich's confirmation, I began to dream about my own, still five years away. It wasn't my desire to become an apprentice. My dream was to continue school and become a teacher.

The confirmation service was held in the big church, and would last about two hours. As we prepared to walk down to the church, a young neighbor girl from a few doors up the street joined our party. Ida Steinbrecher was also having her confirmation. We suspected that Erich was smitten with the slim and pretty girl with dark curls.

There were some fifty students making confirmation, and it was quite a sight to see them all standing up front facing the congregation, nervously awaiting the questioning. The boys were dressed in dark suits, white dress shirt, and black ties, and the girls were all in black dresses, black stockings and black shoes. Any other attire was prohibited.

As for the Bible quiz that took up most of the first half-hour, Erich did well the two times he was called on. I thought of all the evenings since Christmas Mama made him review his lessons over and over.

Another family member, and one of my favorite people, was also being confirmed that day — my cousin Elsbeth from Bolanden. The only daughter of Tante Lisbeth, she had all of the gentleness and loving traits of her mother. Following the church services, we invited her to join us later. My aunt agreed to let her leave the Bolanden party early, and she came by bicycle to our house at mid-afternoon. It was a bittersweet visit, because everyone knew Elsbeth was leaving for years of nursing school in far away Speyer. The ancient city on the Rhein river was not all that 'far away' — it just seemed like it was to me.

Since the days when my parents lived in the same house in the Kloster Hane with Tante Lisbeth and Onkel Jakob, the slim, black-haired Elsbeth had always been Mama's favorite niece from the Klein side. After we moved to Kirchheim, she was a regular visitor. Quiet and mature beyond her years, Elsbeth, unlike my brother and his friends, never treated me as some sort of nuisance.

Though only fourteen, and not much more than a child herself, Elsbeth had long talked of her dreams of what she would do after confirmation. When the day came, we knew she had been accepted by the Deaconess nurses in Speyer, for studies to become a nurse.

So, Elsbeth's eminent departure to Speyer was the only sour note to Erich's confirmation party — we would miss her. I admired my cousin's determination to be a nurse for children, but I knew it was something I wouldn't want. Older children were alright, but I didn't like babies at all.

Our house was packed with friends and relatives all day. Many were there for a sit-down dinner at noon, and even more came and went during the two hours that Mama served coffee and cake later. Some stayed for a light supper. All in all, she was pleased with the turnout, and seemed to appreciate all the helpers. Of course, I visited with cousins more than I worked — one of the few privileges of being ten years old.

During the course of the day, I heard the adults worrying over the war that to me didn't seem like a war. Some of the speakers came close to calling Hitler foolish, but avoided direct criticism of the course he was taking the country. Among the friends and relatives present, there were many Nazi loyalists, and already people were learning to be careful about public statements that may come back to haunt them. It wasn't easy. Germans had become accustomed to spouting off their opinions. Slowly, almost without a sense of when or how it happened, the right to speak openly had disappeared like the Gypsies and Jews.

Even the previous evening ritual of loud voices on Bossung's street corner had quieted. The male gatherings still took place, but they now spoke in the low tones of a private conversation.

Papa tried to keep all table talk neutral, constantly pointing to Erich's opportunities for learning at the machine shop, and other non-controversial subjects. It was supposed to be a celebration of his son's entry into adulthood, not a forum for debate on Hitler's policies.

❧

"Don't you think I'm a little too old for this?"

One more time I had coaxed my brother into helping me build an Easter nest in the garden. "No, let's do it just once more, please! If you do, I'll let you eat some of my Easter rabbit."

That's all I had to say to get Erich to give in to my plea. He agreed to go up into the forest and bring back some soft, fresh moss to use for the nest. By bending twigs and using the moss for both the roof and the floor, my brother again built a lovely nest for the expected Easter eggs — all the while muttering that it was beneath his dignity.

I don't know why it was important to me. Perhaps at heart I knew that this was the last time we would be children together. Papa came into the garden as we were putting the finishing touches on the nest. He watched but said nothing. He knew that after Easter, Erich would be starting his work life at Hirschbiel's machine shop. Perhaps he too understood the need to be a kid at Easter one last time.

Erich's apprenticeship at the machine shop wasn't intended to make him a machinist, but to better enable him to join Papa in the trucking business. My father had often said his son had diesel in his blood — he just needed to know how machines were put together.

❧

During the Easter break, target shooting with the new air gun Erich received for Christmas became another activity he sometimes invited me to join. Mama had forbidden him to shoot at the pigeons in the neighborhood, so he confined himself to the garden area to shoot at tin cans. I became his partner whenever his friends failed to show. I was pleased with his attention, and surprised at his patience in teaching me how to shoot. I was proud when, after a few practice sessions, he told me I was as good a shot as any of his friends.

Mama wasn't enthusiastic about Erich teaching me to shoot, but refrained from saying too much. She didn't go against my brother's wishes often, especially after he had entered his teens, and it was not a matter of good manners or morals. In my case, my brother thought Mama was too protective in not allowing me to swim, ice skate, or have a bicycle. As soon as he had worked a short time in the machine shop, Erich set out to do something about it.

One evening after Erich had washed off a day's accumulation of shop grime, he pulled me aside as we waited for Papa to come home for supper.

"I don't want you making a peep to Mama yet, but I've been talking to Herr Hirschbiel at the shop. Promise? Not a word!"

Obviously my silence was important to him, so I promised.

"Here's the deal. I noticed that there's a pile of old bicycle parts laying in the back of the shop, so I asked old Hirschbiel if he would let me try to make one usable bike from the mess."

My eyes grew wide and my mouth fell open at the prospect.

"Quiet!" He put a hand over my mouth. "It's not done yet, and I'm not sure it's possible. I looked the parts over, and there's a girl's frame and a lot of other junk. What I want to do is talk to Papa, and if he says I can try, we'll let him convince Mama!"

Later, we got Papa alone in his workshop and Erich explained the plan. Being a tinkerer himself, our father agreed, figuring that it would be a good learning experience. As for Mama, that was something he would figure out.

Two weeks of waiting for my brother to come home every night kept me in a nervous state, especially since he usually acted less than optimistic. Erich hadn't given up. His behavior was intended to keep me guessing. He succeeded right up to the moment I caught sight of him coming home on his own bicycle, towing alongside him the most wonderful but strange two-wheeled creation imaginable.

I was so happy it took me several minutes to notice that, from front to back, many unrelated colors clearly told the story of my bicycle's difficult birth. No matter, to me it was gold-plated. I used the bicycle Erich created — out of many — for several years.

❧

A company of German soldiers came into our midst not long after Easter, and they boarded at the White Horse Inn very near my school. The 'phony war' had ended with Hitler's move on the Low Countries of Holland, Belgium, and Luxembourg. In April and May came Nazi rule in Denmark and Norway. When the small troop of soldiers appeared in Kirchheim, there was already talk of a German military build-up to the west of us, toward France.

Suddenly the tranquil mood of our community had ended. Every man, woman and child was issued a gas mask and instructed on its use. I feared the strange looking rubber helmet and felt claustrophobic when I tried it on. We were told to keep the masks with us at all times, in case of gas attacks by the French or British. Older people, remembering the last war, didn't need to be convinced. Fortunately, the fear of gas weapons lessened in a few months. After that, only a handful of people continued to carry the masks. I threw mine up in the attic with pleasure.

One evening, Papa brought one of the sergeants from the contingent at the inn home to dinner. My father had struck up an acquaintance with the man, and wanted him to enjoy one of Mama's good Sunday dinners, though it wasn't Sunday. I recall that the sergeant came from a far off part of Germany, and he missed his two little boys. He cleaned his plate twice, which made my mother happy.

There was careful talk with my parents about the new war developments. The man didn't seem very happy, telling Papa that his group would soon be leaving Kirchheim, orders had come to move west and join the main army command. When the sergeant left us he gave Mama a large can of army ration corned beef in appreciation for the home cooked meal.

❧

Two coming events had me simultaneously excited and concerned. My tenth birthday meant entry into Hitler Jugend. I could hardly wait, but was also somewhat anxious about the twice-a-week meetings. I didn't like the idea that one of the meetings was on Sunday at the same time as church services. I liked going to church with Mama, but she didn't seem too bothered about the conflict.

Erich was in his fourth year in Hitler Jugend, and had lost some of his enthusiasm. His true feelings had become noticeable a few months after moving to Kirchheim. Surprised, I asked why.

"In Marnheim, most all the boys were my friends," he answered. "We were all the same, with the same kind of interests. No one got away with thinking he was better than anyone else. Here in Kirchheim, we have a bunch of snobs who think they're better. I can't wait until I'm old enough to go into the army with real men."

Such talk about going into the army made me sad. I'd be lonely without him. But I could sympathize with his dislike for snobs. "Remember what Papa said, 'Don't pay any attention to snooty people.' And don't talk about leaving. You're not old enough."

He laughed loudly. "You forget that in a year I go into the Arbeits Dienst."

He was right. I'd forgotten about mandatory 'Labor Service' for young men and women from sixteen to eighteen years of age. If physically able, all were expected to give community service for the country for up to two years. The next step for the men was military duty.

The German attack on France struck like lightning, and one immediate loss to the family was contact with Tante Dina, sister of my mother. I never met my aunt, but Mama talked about her quite a lot, especially when a letter came or when she had one of her black moods when we still lived in Marnheim. I remember becoming very upset when she'd say things like, "How I wish I'd gone with Dina to France. She wanted me to go with her, long before I met your father. I should have." I pleaded with her not to talk that way. Now, there was no mail service between the two countries. Mama had lost even that link with Dina.

Slightly older than Mama, Dina had married one of the French soldiers occupying our area after 1918. For a few years, my aunt had come back to visit, but as time passed, contact was reduced to letters. With the ban on mail, Mama fretted over her sister's fate when our army entered France. How were Dina's French neighbors treating her?

Chapter Twelve

All the news on the radio was about Germany's "righteous cause" in bringing France to heel. For my family, and many others I knew, Hitler's ambitions were a source of concern. We wondered which male members would be drafted next. Mama thought Onkel Adolf, another of Papa's younger brothers, was certain to be called.

To me, Onkel Adolf was a character straight out of a comic fairy tale. Short and thin like my father, he had a head and face that appeared overly large and oddly long. He had no lips, just a slit that seemed to extend from ear to ear. When he opened his mouth to laugh, which happened often, he looked as though he could swallow a chicken whole. His gregarious nature perfectly matched his looks. He remained a bachelor, which seemed odd to me at the time.

My uncle continued to live in Bolanden, but spent most of his time in Kirchheim working for the post office delivering parcels with a stagecoach. It was quite a vision when he and his rig rattled along the cobblestone streets. I was so proud to see him coming, high on his seat, greeting everyone. Naturally, he never failed to hail his brother's daughter with a happy "Guten tag, Annchen!"

In the winter, Adolf had a second job for the city driving the same team of horses. But, instead of a coach, they pulled a V-shaped plow to clear the streets of snow. He stood on a kind of sled behind the plow, and I thought it looked like a fun job. Of course, with so many hills to go up and down, I felt sorry for the horses.

Onkel Adolf was never drafted into the army, and no one ever said why. He was physically able, quick-witted, and could read and write. I once heard a neighbor joke that his name may have kept him out. I believe Papa knew the reason, but he said nothing.

Even with the anxieties of our uncertain times, some things never changed. The many beautiful barn swallows came back to us just as they did every spring. Most of them found places to build mud nests along the crossbeams supporting the house over the driveway into the courtyard. It amazed me that all the human activity in the passageway below didn't scare them away. When my father made too much of a clatter working on his truck in the evening, the swallows would stick their heads out of the nests and scold the little man. They seemed to say, "Don't you know its time for bed!" Papa would laugh and say back, "Es tut mir leid, Schwälbchen." ('I'm sorry, my little swallows.')

During the daytime, when the birds weren't flying in and out, feeding themselves and their little ones, they often came to rest as a group on the power line that stretched from near the kitchen window across the courtyard to the old blacksmith shop. There, the little blue and white birds sang for each other and the world. Our kitchen window was always open in nice weather, and with no screen, it was easy to lean out on the sill and listen. Mama often sang their song with them. "Als wir fort zogen, als wir fort zogen waren Kisten und Kasten leer, doch als wir wieder kamen war alles wieder vooooll!" ('When we flew away last fall, our food supply had diminished, but when we came back, everything was replenished.') Now and then, a swallow came in through the window to perch on top of the kitchen cupboard. Acting as though it had every right to be there, the bird might sing a short tune, cock his head around to see if all was in order. Then it would fly back to the group waiting outside on the line.

As my mid-July birthday approached, I began to pressure Mama for permission to get my ears pierced for earrings. My cousin Helmi's ears were pierced, and I thought she looked wonderful with her sparkling earrings. My mother, whose ears weren't pierced, answered my pleas with a shake of her head. "Don't you have enough holes in your head? Why do you want to change yourself?" She would say.

A battle of words went on for a good two weeks before I wore her out. The day before my birthday, she gave in. "Fritz, take Anna down to Schnabel's tomorrow and get her ears pierced. I have no interest in watching or hearing her scream when Schnabel punches holes in her ears."

Papa defended me. "Ach, she's a braver girl than that. But I'll take her and help pick out the prettiest earrings in the shop." He made no further attempt to have her come along — he knew his wife too well.

The visit to jeweler Schnabel took no time at all. We picked gold wire earrings that circled the ear lobe and closed in the back. Dangling just below each wire was a small amber stone, and I agreed with Papa that they were the prettiest in the display case. As for the actual piercing, I didn't holler. I had gritted my teeth too hard to scream. Besides, it really didn't hurt, and I couldn't imagine why Mama had made such a fuss.

Shortly after my birthday, as expected, I was asked to join Jungmädel, the

After receiving their uniforms a lot of girls went right out and had their pictures taken, either by family or a professional. We did not have a camera, and Mama thought it was a foolish waste of money. Here is my daughter Kristina's view.

young girls' section of Hitler Youth. The invitation in no way seemed mandatory. All my friends, like myself, were anxious to be a part of the Jungmädel. What made it even more of an honor to be accepted into the group was that each of us had to pass physical and mental tests. These were conducted not far from my house at the ancient Liebfrauenkirche and cemetery grounds.

It seems an odd place for gymnastics, but the church building was no longer used for worship or the cemetery for burials. These purposes had long been abandoned. Most of the old tombstones had been removed from their original locations and placed along the walls surrounding the grounds.

For the physical tests, we had to run and jump, and do pull-ups and somersaults. The latter was not my favorite, as I always lost my perspective of what was up and down.

Later, at a building near my school, we were put through mental tests to show our reading and writing skills, and were told to talk about our families and ourselves. Afterward, we all stood with right arms raised, to pledge our loyalty and lives to Hitler and to the Fatherland. The indoctrination included songs. First, we sang "Die Fahne Hoch," which told of holding the flag high, then the national anthem, "Deutschland, Deutschland Über Alles."

Within days of the testing, we got uniforms of navy blue wool skirts, white blouses with the Hitler Jugend emblem on one sleeve, and a black neck scarf, folded and worn so as to lie in a triangular shape on the back. A black leather knotted ring held the scarf together in front. Naturally, I was proud of the uniform and the way I looked in it. I could not have known then that Hitler's intention of eliminating class distinction by having everyone wear the same uniform wouldn't succeed. The uniform didn't disguise the true identity of anyone in a community as small as ours. This would become for me the biggest sore spot when attending my group's weekly meetings.

Erich had warned me of his experience in the boys' organization, and now it was my turn to learn first hand how girls from certain families isolated themselves from the rest of us who couldn't claim a politically powerful father or old wealth. Of course, having the status of "new rich" with solid political connections served just as well. The few girls who did make such claims made life miserable at times.

Our first meeting of the week came on Sunday morning, and the second was on Wednesday evening. The Sunday affairs often took the form of outdoor rallies when weather permitted. Both girls and boys participated, though segregated, and our activities usually included a march through the town in military formations while lustily singing patriotic songs. I hated the fact that I could no longer go to church with Mama, but a sharp reminder was given to my class one Monday morning. I remember being surprised at the teacher's tone when he questioned a couple of the girls as to why they had not been to the rally the previous day. He ended by warning them not to let it happen again. Our schools and the youth organizations worked hand in glove.

Aside from missing church and having to deal with snooty girls, I enjoyed my group. We did a lot of exercising, played games, learned new songs, and made crafts. I wanted to be the best and most loyal German girl possible, and the Jungmädel, I thought, was going to help me make it come true.

All this put my daily activities on an even tighter schedule, but I could never turn down Erich. He was ever my weakness and I always catered to his whims. He wasn't always satisfied with my efforts, but he couldn't say I didn't try. After Erich began his apprenticeship at the machine shop and had put together the bicycle for me, I felt even more indebted to him. How could I refuse his demands on my time?

At fifteen, my brother had entered a stage of life we called Halbstarker, which literally means "half-strong one," or more directly — trying to be an adult without the necessary experience. For Erich, it meant that after a day in the shop, if he didn't have to help Papa, he liked to put on his better clothes and stand around on the corner with his friends debating life — and watch the girls go by. It was for such an occasion that Erich asked me if I would press his good pants. He knew Mama would be out all day, and I'd be home from school early.

"I've never pressed out pants."

127

"Ach, you can do it," he said, heading out the door that morning. "The pants are on my bed. Just lay them out flat, like you've seen Mama do, and press out the wrinkles."

He was gone before I could protest more about the job. When I later got home from school, I went to find Erich's pants. He'd left them all crumpled up in a pile on his bed. As I picked them up, his billfold fell out, and from it another object dropped to the floor. It was a square, flat foil package unlike anything I'd ever seen. I could feel through the foil something round inside. The foil itself was quite worn, and one corner had completely worn through, allowing me to see just a bit of what looked like a balloon.

The faded wording on the outside meant nothing to me, but it made me think of a conversation I'd had with Henny once about a subject she'd discussed with other girls in her class. Since she and the others were two years older than I, they liked talking about boys. I couldn't care less about boys, but I did find it both interesting and disgusting when she said they use a kind of balloon when kissing girls.

"Yuck," I had said. "Why would they do something like that?"

"It has something to do with babies," Henny replied. "If a boy puts on a balloon when he's kissing you, there won't be a baby."

It had sounded crazy to me at the time, but as I stood in Erich's bedroom holding the little package that looked like it had a balloon inside, I made the connection. I quickly put the silver thing back into his billfold, knowing that my brother wouldn't want his family to know he was kissing girls. Mama would surely be upset.

Back in the kitchen, I plugged in the iron, and put an ironing mat on the table. Thinking about how Mama laid each leg out, I did the same, and began to work diligently to smooth out every wrinkle. And, just like Mama, I used a damp cloth to steam and press. All I needed was facing my brother's wrath for scorching his pants.

Finally the job was finished, and I inspected the trousers for the slightest wrinkle before laying them neatly on his bed. I then did my regular chores and started on school homework. Mama soon returned from her downtown business trip and began supper.

I was about to tell Mama about the ironing project when a roar made us jump. It came from Erich's room across the hall, and through a closed kitchen door, to our ears. It was followed immediately by him slamming through the doorway, shouting and holding up for us to see his neatly ironed trousers. I still had no idea what the problem could be, but I was wishing Papa were at home. Erich wouldn't dare shout in anger if Papa were there. Unfortunately, my father was not expected for another half-hour. In the meantime, my brother raged on like a wounded wild boar, and we began to understand that I, a stupid girl, had done something terrible to his trousers. "Look at this! Where is the crease? The stupid girl has ironed away the crease!"

That made me mad, and I shouted back, "You told me to iron the trousers just like Mama does, and I did! I've watched Mama iron pants a hundred times and she irons them just like that!"

I looked to Mama for support and discovered that she was beginning to laugh out loud. Erich, too, was taken aback by his mother's behavior, for Mama hardly ever laughed so as to hear her. But he soon started up again. "You dummy, this is how you iron work pants, not dress trousers. The crease goes down the front and back, not down the sides!"

Suddenly I knew he was right. I had seen Mama iron work pants. Papa's Sunday pants had a sharp edge down the front and back.

Mama finally quit laughing and reassured her son that the world had not ended. The mistake was easily corrected, she said, walking to the cupboard where the iron was kept. Still, I felt so stupid and tried to think of some way to retaliate. I thought about the balloon I found. That would shut up his 'stupid girl' talk. Then again, he might kill me. I wisely decided not to further test his sensitive nature.

By mid-1940, there weren't many Jews left in Kirchheim. Perhaps four or five in our immediate neighborhood, and I occasionally saw someone with the yellow star in other parts of the town. The yellow star confused me. I thought it was crazy that someone had to wear a Jewish symbol when everyone knew who was or wasn't a Jew. The yellow star made no sense to me, but I couldn't get anything out of Mama. "It's just politics. Don't worry about it. Someday it will end."

I remembered that Papa hadn't been happy when Herr Decker sold the flour mill and went to America. Many other Jews had packed up before and after Kristall Nacht, their destination unknown to us. Papa thought the whole Jewish question would blow over. He was wrong.

Of those Jews who remained, all were elderly. One evening, after clearing away the supper dishes, Mama finally broke her gloomy silence. She asked Papa, who had been hauling out of town that day, if he'd heard about the Hausmann couple and the Scholem brother and sister. He hadn't. Both families lived nearby.

"The Hausmanns were taken away in the middle of the night," she said. And the Scholems are gone too. What's happening?"

My father was stunned. He hadn't been close to either family, but he knew they were good people, all natives of Kirchheim. "I don't know, and I don't see any reason for it," he finally replied. "Old Decker must have been right about getting out. I thought he was panicky, but it seems he was right to go. Instead of getting rid of Gypsies and Jews, the man in Berlin should be thinking more about peace!" Papa looked worried.

"Where have they taken the old people?" My parents had forgotten I was there listening, and my question seemed to shake them.

Papa looked at me. "I hear there is a labor camp down south. They will probably stay there until the end of the war."

"But how can they make old people work?" I said, in disbelief.

"Child, we talk too much about these things. We can't know all the answers. And please don't ask questions outside this house." Mama, who had started the discussion, now wanted it ended, at least with me around. Normally I would have obeyed her warning not to speak of the matter elsewhere, but I knew I could talk to Henny. Her house was next door to the Scholems, and I was sure she had better information. I approached Henny the following day.

"What can I say," she began. "No one I know saw the old sister and brother taken away. And it wasn't just them. The boarder Isidor Schwarz was taken as well. The Knoblauchs, who own the house and live upstairs, told my mother they heard something, but didn't dare look out to the street. In the morning, they checked the apartment and all the furniture remained, but most of the clothes were gone."

"Will the Knoblauchs keep the furniture until they return?"

"Frau Knoblauch said they are going to burn it, or haul it away. They want the rooms for themselves."

"I don't understand why the Jews have to leave. Papa says they are being taken to a labor camp down south. What good is that?"

"We're told in Hitler Jugend that the Führer doesn't trust the Jews. Haven't you seen the posters around town? He wants them all in big labor camps where he can keep an eye on them."

Henny did seem more knowledgeable, so I let the matter go for the time being. I had seen the posters warning not to trust the Jews, but they didn't say why. I figured I would learn more about it the longer I stayed in Hitler Jugend.

Chapter Thirteen

Henny Hemm was my closest friend during those early years in Kirchheim. We delighted in a mutual interest in music, books, and nature, and we had an intense curiosity about the immediate world around us. Our age difference mattered little to us and never caused friction.

Frau Usner, Henny's grandmother and Mama's new friend, was a happy person, always full of vitality. Henny's mother was another case. Earlier on, I worried that she didn't like me. It was her ever-present grim expression that had me convinced. One day, I told Henny about my fear.

"Ach, Mama likes you," she replied. "She has this problem with migraine headaches. That's what makes her look that way."

Her father had been one of the caretakers at the still inhabited Schloß and gardens, a place forbidden to most people in Kirchheimbolanden. With his help, Henny could unlock the huge ornate wrought iron gates that kept me, and other uninvited people, out of the former palace gardens. Henny and I visited her father in the Schloßgarten many times before he was drafted by the army.

There I discovered not only acres of vineyards, orchards and vegetable gardens, but also a villa and a number of greenhouses. Once the property of Prince Carl August, and others that followed, it had since come into the hands of the Heinrich von Brunk family. Von Brunk was connected with the big BASF chemical firm in Ludwigshafen on the Rhein.

Henny's father allowed her to take me anywhere on the immense property, except near the villa, separate and distant from the palace. He feared we might disturb the family and get him into trouble. I'd heard many tales about Schloßgarten, but to see it up close was amazing. Our school building abutted on one corner of the gardens, but little was visible from classroom windows.

In the fruit and vegetable areas every tree, grapevine, bush, flower, and vegetable plant was placed precisely, then nurtured for beauty and maximum bounty. Everything was kept from the sight of passersby with a high thick stone wall.

Henny guided me over neatly laid-out pathways, through cultivated sections, and around fruit trees of every kind until we finally reached a low wall. The wall wasn't high on the garden side, but looking over, we could see that there was a drop of at least ten feet. Later we found a gate that allowed us down into a new part of the old palace grounds.

I was simply overwhelmed by what we found waiting. In front of us was a forest of trees on a sea of manicured lawn, dotted with lily ponds. There were statues, large and small, and gazebos, and in a complete circle around the wide expanse of green was a well-kept carriage path with a fine pebble surface. Part of the old palace stood in the distance, but too far for us to see clearly.

You can bet Henny and I kept a low profile while exploring any part of the grounds. The closest we got to an encounter was on our third visit. We had gone to the gate opening to the park area with the intention of a closer inspection.

We both saw her at the same moment, and ducked back through the wall opening. Not a hundred meters from us, strolling along the carriage drive, was an elegantly dressed woman. She was walking away from us, which helped to keep our presence secret, but it also kept us from seeing her better. With a stylish hat and dark tailored dress reaching to her ankles, an umbrella hung from the crook of her arm. The lady appeared quite at home in the private sanctuary.

We waited and watched until our mysterious woman disappeared through another wrought iron gate at the far end of the park. Later we saw that the gate leads to the remaining, usable part of the old palace. Only a wing of the larger royal home survived a fire set by the French during a past war.

When we felt that it was safe to enter the park, it was to follow the circular drive to the gate where the woman left the park. We had no business entering a courtyard there, so we continued following the curving drive until we came upon a long stone carriage house. It also looked to have horse stables and a small apartment. We hurried by, though no one seemed to be around. On this side of the park there was another long low wall. Peering over the top, we saw another sharp drop to the Allee, a street that bordered the park near the city market square.

Henny and I managed a few more visits before her father went into the army. After it was no longer possible, she introduced me to another remarkable and tranquil place a short distance from the Breitstraße. Considering the political climate at the time, it shouldn't have been a surprise that a new person in town hadn't heard of the Judenthal (Jewish valley). Henny had the advantage of having been born and raised in Kirchheim. Actually, the name 'Judenthal' was strictly local usage. The real name for the nearly hidden and heavily wooded valley was Birkenthal, but it was the site of a big cemetery for Kirchheim's once thriving Jewish community. Few people visited the small-secluded valley, reached by following an over-grown path that branched off an alley from Breitstraße. The alley abruptly ends after a hundred feet. A pathway going to the right led down to the Ziegelwoog, a small lake that acted as a catch basin for the small valley we intended to explore. Henny guided me to the left on a path that sloped gently higher into a forested area.

Leaving the bright sunlight behind, I found wild blackberry and raspberry bushes in abundance along one side of the path, and on the other side, hazelnut bushes nearly as tall as small trees. The underbrush forced us to walk single file, and it was clear that way was hardly used. After a short distance, the area widened into a sanctuary of old forest so dense shrubs could no longer succeed. The broader path also allowed Henny and I to link arms as we walked. For some reason we started singing, but that lasted only a few minutes — we were beginning to feel the solemnity of our surroundings.

The path continued gradually upward along the left slope. Soon we could see the right slope coming nearer as the valley closed in near the top. Below the path, a small stream hurried down to the lake, making a delightful sound as the water splashed over rocks.

I didn't know what to expect at the Jewish cemetery. Henny attempted a description, but her words didn't really prepare me. After another ten minutes, I could begin to see it. The moss covered stone walls almost blended into the setting as the side embankments of the valley came together and met on the backside of the cemetery to form a cul-de-sac. There were so many trees around and in the cemetery itself that the illusion of oneness was startling.

The path became wider as we neared, and led right up to a rusted wrought iron double gate. It was open. There was no hesitation on Henny's part — she walked right in. I followed, shivering as I went. I wasn't afraid, but chilled by the notion that sunlight had rarely entered the place.

The cemetery wasn't that small. Counting the tombstones, I lost track after fifty or so. Some of the fancier stones were inscribed with three and four names, so I figured that well over a hundred Jews had been buried there. That seemed about right, since Kirchheim had up to two hundred Jewish residents as far back as the early 1800's. Walking around the narrow pathways separating the tight rows of burial plots, it was clear the place hadn't been maintained. Everything was just moss-covered and dreary. I was grateful that despite common knowledge of the Judenthal locally, no one had ever come to destroy the sanctity of this final resting-place for the Jews of Kirchheim in the past. In the years to come, I would wander among the tombstones, speculating about the names of the deceased and the Hebrew writings. The Judenthal became a kind of holy place where I could take a troubled mind. It was there I found momentary peace in a warring world.

A path near the backside of the cemetery went straight up the embankment. It brought us out onto the highway to Rockenhausen, about a kilometer outside Kirchheim. Walking across the road, another path led into a part of the Pfälzer forest that borders Kirchheim on the west and north.

Following the new path up a slope to an open meadow, the first landmark is the Schillerhain (Schiller's Grove). It was Kirchheim's most popular park area. Here were found the town's old lookout tower, a large outdoor pavilion, a sanitarium-spa complex, and a soccer field. All was surrounded by beautiful park grounds used by the town's people and by patients with lung diseases. Kirchheim had long been designated a Luftkurort, a place where doctors believed the air was pure enough to help in the treatment of respiratory problems. The park was named after Friedrich von Schiller, a beloved German poet of the 18th century. I could never find a record of him ever having come to Kirchheimbolanden, but he had been enormously popular through time. The Schillerhain also provided a major entry point into the forest.

Kirchheim's "fresh, clean air" health spa at the forest edge near Schillerhain park.

❧

Henny and I were often mistaken for sisters. While we both wore long braids, my hair was almost black and hers was light brown. The similarity in appearance ended there. The misleading impression really happened because we acted like sisters, but without the usual sibling bickering — we never disagreed to the point of anger. We liked each other's company so much that we even had a seamstress make identical dresses for us. I know we silently found faults in each other, yet these feelings never came to open criticism. There were other girlfriends, but none were as close to me as Henny.

When Henny got her small Handharmonika, I had already lost my music teacher and was looking for another. For several weeks, she came to my house to pick up what I knew. In no time, we could play simple duets, but what we needed was a teacher. We got lucky. Karola Kiefer was about to enter our lives.

Henny's grandmother was a cleaning woman at the city hall in the evening after office hours. Since Frau Usner was Mama's friend, there was no problem when Henny asked if I could come along sometimes to help carry brooms and mops from office to office, floor to floor.

Tagging along one evening to help Frau Usner, we discovered that the city library was open. The library was located in the city hall building. Reading was one of Frau Usner's loves, and she knew we girls felt the same. After a while, she took a break from cleaning and led us into the library for an introduction to Fräulein Karola Kiefer. In her mid-twenties and unmarried, we learned that she carried much responsibility in Kirchheimbolanden. Along with being a librarian, she also worked in the city's records office, and was the principal leader of the older girls in the Bund Deutscher Mädchen (German Girls Alliance).

The BDM was a Nazi youth organization not quite as sinister as some have suggested. Unlike the boy's group, which had military overtones, the girls' activities could only be called wholesome. The girls primarily learned physical fitness, handicrafts, singing and dancing, and performed community service. I would never have Fräulein Kiefer for my BDM leader, but she did involve Henny and I with her group.

Fräulein Kiefer wasn't especially pretty. Her brown hair was cut too short, and she wore glasses that made her appear at first glance to be quite severe. This feeling vanished in a hurry once we began talking to her. She smiled easily and was soft spoken, and her immediate interest in us was pleasing.

It was during that first meeting that we happened to complain of our problem in finding a music teacher. I can still recall the sudden pause in the conversation and the look on her face, as though she was about to make some serious decision. She looked at each of us in turn, then made her judgment.

"As it happens I play both piano and the Handharmonika. I sometimes give lessons. If you really want to advance with your instruments, we can see how it goes." She gave us a stern look. "But I tell you now, I'll expect you to study and practice hard."

Henny and I danced, sang and laughed all the way home that night, glad that we had met our new music teacher! Even Frau Usner had to chuckle over the coincidence. She had known quite a bit about the Kiefer family, but was unaware the daughter gave music lessons.

We'd arranged to begin with our new teacher the following week at her home. We learned it was one of the nicer homes built in more recent times at the edge of the forest near Schillerhain park.

Fräulein Kiefer's late father, Ernst Kiefer, had been a well-known author, and much beloved writer of Pfälzisch dialect poetry. Karola was herself a university graduate, and had a younger brother away at school. Her mother was the one who answered our knock.

Upon entering the house, Henny and I saw the presence of both father and son throughout. Their pictures were everywhere. The piano and our lessons were in the library, and as one might expect in an author's home, it was an immense library. After a while, when Fräulein Kiefer felt she could trust us, we were permitted to peruse the books as long as we returned each one to its proper place.

Karola Kiefer was a wonderful musician, able to play the clarinet as well as piano and Handharmonika. I found her an excellent teacher, and we slaved over our lessons to please. I was in such awe of her that, even when invited, I couldn't stop addressing her in the formal speech mode — "Sie" instead of "Du."

"Why don't you call me Karola instead of Fräulein Kiefer."

"I can't do that."

"That's nonsense. Why can't you?"

I wanted to say it wouldn't be respectful, but I didn't. Instead, "It just wouldn't sound right."

With that she laughed, and laughed even louder when Henny chimed in that she would call her Karola. I can understand how it must have seemed very humorous teaching two students at the same time, and each conversing with her in very different forms of German.

She was our teacher and friend from 1940 to 1944, and I thought of her as a godsend. She helped to expand our awareness of culture, of German music and art, and the world of books. Few of our peers had the opportunity to receive the personal attention of someone like Fräulein Kiefer. And, with her influence, we were given the chance to participate in activities not usually available to girls so young.

Because Henny and I worked so hard to meet her expectations, we rapidly became proficient enough to perform in public. Over the years, she several times had us provide the music for folk dances performed by BDM girls. Her talents extended to writing original music and choreographing for the dances. I fondly remember a May Day dance performed around the May Pole in the market square. Girls of all ages in pretty costumes designed by Fräulein Kiefer danced while we played her music.

In 1942, we gained a new audience when Arbeitsdienstlager XVIII (Labor Camp 18) was built on the south edge of Kirchheim. The wooden buildings were much like army barracks, the type built above ground on piers. The new camp was all the way across the town from our neighborhood, but that didn't keep Fräulein Kiefer from getting us invited to play for the girls living there. Two of the bigger girls from the camp escorted us to and from the Breitstraße. One of them carried my instrument case, as it was much too big and heavy for me to lug all through town.

It was the first of many visits we made to the camp. The girls liked our playing, and afterwards invited us to visit awhile. It was an education to find out firsthand what Arbeitsdienst was all about. Being members of Hitler Jugend,

Some of the girls of Arbeitsdienst Henny and I played for. I am sorry not to remember all of their names, except the first girl — Marie. She most often carried my heavy instrument from my house to their encampment.

both Henny and I showed up in our simple uniforms. The girls we performed for were also in uniform, a different but attractive brown outfit with a long, belted jacket over a skirt. The girls were all seventeen or eighteen years old and only a few were from the Donnersberg region.

They came from all socio-economic backgrounds, but in their uniforms, girls from wealthy homes looked the same as those from the working class. If there was a class distinction problem between some of the girls, I saw none of it. It all made me look forward to when I could be a member of the Arbeitsdienst. The girls might work a week in a butcher shop, switch to a shoe store or dress shop, then move on to help a mother with many children — greeting each task gladly in the name of National Socialism.

For many months, we were asked to return every week, often to eat supper as well as play music. Girls came and went as terms of service expired. On most visits we could meet someone new from another part of Germany. It was a good learning experience, a fun time for a couple of wide-eyed girls, and owed it all to Karola Kiefer.

❧

Several months after our music lessons had begun, we got word from our teachers that Fräulein Kiefer wanted to see us after classes. When we arrived at the front door of her house with our instruments in hand, the warm September sun was beginning its descent in the west. There would soon be a chill in the air, and we were glad to have brought along sweaters for the walk home.

The Kiefer home was not the kind of place one walked into unannounced, so after ringing the doorbell, we waited to be received. The door was opened by Frau Kiefer, her mother, a person we didn't often see on lesson days. Like so many widows in town, she had worn a black dress from the time of her husband's death. She was pleasant, as usual, explaining that her daughter was late and we should go right into the library. Stepping into the now familiar room, we turned to thank her, but all we saw was her graceful form already moving quickly up the stairway across the hall.

Setting our instrument cases on the floor, Henny and I once again slowly wandered around the room, careful not to touch anything that appeared valuable. It all looked valuable. We never tired of perusing the Kiefer bookshelves that covered two walls. A piano stood on the wall next to the French doors that opened to a patio. A Persian rug covered the middle of the hard wood floor. Most of the chairs were covered in soft leather, including a chaise lounge against one wall with a large picture of the late Ernst Kiefer hanging above it. Two chairs, separated by a small fancy table, were arranged on the ornate rug in the center. Some of the bookshelves and all of the various side tables around the room held framed pictures or lovely porcelain figurines of men and women dressed in 18th century finery. There were also hand-carved wood statues of old-time hunters and peasants. These we left untouched, but the books were fair game.

"Someday, Henny, I want to have this many books, and more."

"Ja, for sure. Here, look at this one. It shows all the trails through the forest, starting at the Donnersberg and leading to villages in every direction."

"So! I thought you girls could entertain yourselves with Papa's books." Fräulein Kiefer had startled us, slipping through the door quietly to witness our interest in the books. She laughed and added, "You know I don't mind, as long as your hands are clean and you put the books back."

After apologizing for being late, she continued on with the reason for her summons. "I've just finished a new folk dance duet for your instruments, and I want you to get started on it. You'll play it at the next Sportsfest in a week!"

We practiced for nearly an hour on the new piece before she was satisfied we could go practice the number at home. Fräulein Kiefer was both fun and strict in her teaching. She could take either one of our instruments or sit at the piano, to demonstrate exactly what was wanted, and never belittled a sour note. Whenever I hit one, she simply raised an eyebrow. "Again," she would say politely.

❧

It was almost suppertime when we packed and said good bye to our teacher. We were pleased that she had trusted us to play one of her new compositions at a Hitler Jugend Sportsfest. We whistled the new tune all the way down to the Breitstraße, and after we parted, I continued to whistle and hum the melody all the way through my front door.

As soon as I climbed the stairs and entered the kitchen, I knew something wasn't right. Papa was busy shining his work shoes. Mama stood at the stove stirring something in a pot, and Erich sat staring at the pattern on the table's oil-cloth covering. Nothing unusual really, except I could tell my happiness wasn't matched.

It was Erich who broke the silence. "Papa has been called into the air force. He's leaving in a few days."

I ran to Papa, who opened his arms to me. Perhaps my mother wondered why I didn't run to her — she was the one the load would fall on. But I could only think of losing Papa, my best friend.

Chapter Fourteen

Papa had been drafted. I had almost forgotten that such a threat still hung over us.

"Ja, Annchen, the order came today in the mail. I must report to Wiesbaden by the end of the week. What's worse, they want my truck too."

Crying was never easy for me, but I did now wholeheartedly, holding him tight around the neck. He didn't push me away. The tears soaked into his shirt as he continued talking to Mama about informing the customers, all the while patting me on the back with hands stained from the shoe polish. He said nothing directly to stop my tears or to loosen my grip on him. He just went on talking about things needing to be done, seemingly undisturbed by my behavior.

Gradually, I released my hold and stopped my crying to ask a logical question. "Why would the air force want you? You can't fly."

"That's for certain," he chuckled. "No, I think it's because the Luftwaffe also wants my truck. I'll probably be driving supplies. So, you see, it won't be dangerous. No more than what I'm doing now."

His words were reassuring, but I was not patriotic enough to happily wave my father off to war.

Nonetheless, on the following Sunday we gathered in the courtyard to watch Papa drive his new truck into the street and off to Wiesbaden. I cried again, and it didn't help seeing Erich's mournful expression. For the first time, my brother had nothing to say, and I then knew how much he too needed Papa.

Almost immediately, Mama set about to bring her husband home — to have him released from the air force. The plan included regular visits to the local government transportation office and Herr Klag, the man in charge. He may have been distantly related to the Klags of Bolanden with whom we were connected, but not enough to give much weight to Mama's arguments. Herr Klag knew my father well, and had warned him many times that things could get bad unless he joined the party. Papa hadn't, and Herr Klag's predictions had come true.

I went with Mama a few times to the transportation office, in the weeks after Papa left. It was always the same: "Frau Klein, you know this matter would be so easy to solve if Fritz was a party member." Herr Klag then repeated his claim that he liked my father and was doing his best. "But I can make no promises," he always added. "We'll just have to wait."

Papa had to take basic training during the first weeks, and when that was completed, Mama and I took a train to Wiesbaden to visit. For reasons I can't recall, Erich didn't come along. We didn't get to see any of the beautiful parts of the famous spa city — the entire visit took place in the train station. But I was so happy to see Papa that I didn't care. The day was cold and rainy.

Papa gave me a present, a small braided jute purse with a little bottle of violet cologne tucked inside. It was my first purse, and I was thrilled with the gift.

"You're spoiling the girl," Mama said.

Papa laughed and changed the subject to matters of home, school, and Christmas plans. All too soon the visit was over, and we climbed aboard the train for the return trip. Mama promised she'd keep working on his release, a goal that was never far from her mind.

The growing numbers of local men leaving for army and air force service drove home the reality of war on us, but it was a series of regulations for civilian behavior that really changed daily life.

Neighborhoods were divided into bomb shelter districts. Most houses and buildings had basements, but many weren't deep or large enough to suit authorities. Our handy deep storage cellar across the courtyard, the one with the salamanders, was more than deep enough. The inspector ruled it out, saying it was too small and damp. I hoped Mama would argue that it was big enough for our family, but she didn't. We were given the choice of two shelters. One was two doors up Breitstraße at Herr Lander's, and one was across the intersection below a large apartment building next to the Catholic Church. After a few air raids, we settled on the latter as being safer.

The fear of air raids brought darkness everywhere after sunset. No light was permitted to show through windows and doors to the outside. Erich and I helped put up black roller blinds on all windows, which could be pulled up during the day. Going in and out of house doors at night meant turning off any lights that might shine into the street or courtyard. Until we got used to the blackout rules there were mishaps. One evening I slipped into the kitchen from the hall and snapped on the light, not realizing Erich was sitting at the open window staring out into the night sky. The resulting beacon of light sent out over the courtyard and garden created a moment of panic.

"Damn! You stupid girl! Turn off that light. Hurry!"

I was dumbstruck by his anger, and must have hesitated reaching for the switch again. At the same moment my fingers returned us to darkness, Erich had grabbed and pulled the blackout blind so hard that the entire roller crashed to the floor. My wits told me it would be wise to exit while my brother was still thrashing about in the dark, trying to find his bearings. I didn't like the words he was using, and the time seemed right to visit Mama in the wash kitchen downstairs.

Block wardens constantly patrolled the neighborhoods, issuing tickets to violators of the blackout rules. After the initial so-called warning tickets, fines were levied.

Except for cloudy, rainy nights, when it was truly pitch black, I didn't mind finding my way around outside at night. The moon and stars provided more than enough light. Later, when the bombers passed overhead, toward the Rhein, I wished the moon was not so bright. I was convinced the pilots could see us below.

૎

Alarm over bombing attacks was heightened by public meetings conducted for every resident on the use of air raid shelters and the kinds of bombs expected to be dropped by the enemy. There was talk about phosphorus and gas bombs. At first, I didn't take the air raid scare serious, remembering my father's optimism that the war wouldn't last. It seemed true. Our army was winning everywhere, and the latest news was of a great victory in France. The one worry that remained was Great Britain, but we fully expected to win in the end.

Air raids had increased sharply just weeks after Papa was drafted. Kirchheim was too unimportant to be a target, but we were on the flight path, forcing all of us to scurry into shelters at the approach of every bomber formation. All of the raids occurred at night in the early days, but school children had many practice drills during classes. A low, mournful siren brought us quickly into columns for a fast march to a shelter below what had been a seminary nearby. Authorities had found the deep cavernous basement ideal for hundreds of students.

I hated the sound of the raid alert siren, and the high pitched all-clear siren didn't settle any better on the nerves.

When the alert sounded for real, usually close to midnight, we could be out of our beds and on our way in minutes. Both Mama and I had our clothes laid out next to our beds, and she had a flashlight to help guide our steps. Erich, however, often refused to leave his bed for a shelter, or refused to join us, going instead to another shelter where he expected to find one of his male friends.

Not long after visiting Papa in Wiesbaden, the midnight bombing runs over Kirchheim took on a more serious meaning for me. I had arranged with Erich to stay with him, letting Mama think that we would go to another shelter. The siren wailed its warning and we all rushed from the house, Mama going one way and we the other. When she turned the corner, we went back into the house. Erich had told me earlier that when he stayed home, he sat and watched out the window toward the Rhein target areas, and described how searchlights criss-crossed the night skies trying to find the flying invaders. At times, he said, flak sent up by German gunners on the ground could be seen, as could the beams of light — despite the many kilometers between us and the cities under attack.

We barely had time to open a window facing toward the east when the throbbing rumble of many bombers could be heard, first from the northwest and growing louder as they passed over. We couldn't speak until the roar faded into a drone. Off in the distance, we counted several beams of light moving back and forth, desperately seeking out the planes. There was no moon, and from our window, we didn't see any of the bombers — not when they were directly above or in the reflected flak and bomb explosions. A fire glow from north to south on the horizon grew from individual flare-ups that had come together into almost one line of hazy orange and red.

Once or twice, we saw what appeared as a fiery burst in the sky. It was all Erich could do to contain himself. "We got one of them," he whispered excitedly, slapping the windowsill with delight. I didn't know what to say. I just shivered in the cool night air coming through the window. "They'll be coming back over us soon now," Erich said, again whispering loudly. "I don't think we knocked down many English tonight. I hope I'm wrong."

Minutes passed. "Listen. The planes are getting close." The throb of engines and rumble of air being disturbed made me cover my ears and in doing so, another sound and shock hit my whole body. A terrible blast was closely followed by a second, and we fell back from the window and onto the floor. As we lay there, I was certain we would die. "Damn," Erich shouted, "they never got that close before!"

There were no more explosions and the noise of the planes receded, followed by the all-clear signal. I promised myself to always go to the bomb shelter in the future. Erich grabbed my arm. "Hurry! Let's get this window closed and wait for Mama in the street." I never told anyone about our little adventure.

The next morning brought reports of many bomb craters in the fields outside of town. Most still had bombs in them that needed to be disarmed. Someone said that even the unexploded bombs made holes big enough for a house. Two larger craters were found very near houses on the edge of Kirchheim. These may have been from the exploding bombs that gave Erich and I a scare.

Mama was distraught. "Why do they bomb Kirchheim? This is just a small place with innocent people!"

Naturally, Mama had heard and felt the two explosions, and like everyone, had feared the worst. In the town, no houses or persons were harmed, but it seemed like a warning that the British didn't care where their deadly loads were dropped. On the street and in the shops, people talked about "ein Terrorakt," an act of terror on the innocent. Most of the kids in my neighborhood wanted to go into the fields to inspect the crater damage. It was forbidden.

In the following days, rare daylight bombers unloaded on us with greater accuracy, but not with exploding bombs. Three times in a row, thousands of propaganda leaflets had covered the town and countryside when we emerged from the shelters. This enraged local authorities. Orders came for all children to pick up and turn in every leaflet. Perhaps they didn't want anyone reading them. It was a ridiculous reason. We children couldn't possibly find every leaflet. And those of us who could read, would talk to parents and friends about the printed messages anyway. Weathered leaflets continued to be found in the weeks ahead as the dirty pieces of paper fluttered down from a roof or high tree branch.

"Quatsch, nix wie Quatsch!" That's what Mama called the messages printed in the leaflets. Our word 'Quatsch' in this instance means rubbish, in the strongest sense. Most people felt exactly as my mother. The British, in perfect German, were urging us not to support Hitler, and to refuse to serve in the army. Another one had the dire warning that, "This war will not end well for Germany," along with more anti-Hitler comments. The timing was bad — the German reaction was one of anger, not fear. There was yet a long road ahead before the leaflets had the effect intended.

By Christmas of 1940, in spite of every effort to keep our lives normal, Hitler's war became a daily unwelcome companion. Few people still talked of a quick solution or the early return of prosperous and happy times. The mail-man became a very important person as most everyone was looking for a letter from a loved one in uniform. Papa didn't write long letters, but did send postcards with brief messages. He would say he was fine, and little else. Of course, he couldn't talk about what he was doing, but we already knew. He delivered supplies, mostly to our army and air force in France.

Mama kept her word, constantly pressuring Herr Klag, and any other government official she could corner, on the matter of releasing Fritz Klein from the military. She insisted he would be of greater good to his family and country at home. All of them must have hated to see her coming, but remained respectful. Mama's rigorous appearance and manner didn't allow for anything less. While all Kirchheim officials gave allegiance to Hitler and the Party, if a well-liked fellow "Kerchemer" could be helped, it had been known to happen.

In the meantime, Papa was driving materials into the newly occupied areas of France. We knew that because he sometimes made a little detour to stop at home, if only for a few minutes. The Rheinland/Pfalz shares a border with France, so it was a simple matter, though strictly unauthorized, to shift his route slightly.

We never knew when Papa might stop in, and sometimes he was there and gone before Erich and I came home from work and school. When this happened, Mama reported little to us about what he had said. I believe it was because he said negative things about the war and politics. His opinions made Mama angry. I once witnessed it.

"Fritz, don't you dare talk like that outside this house. We both know what has happened to people who've been reported. Here I'm trying so hard for your release, and you risk going to prison."

"Why do you fret so?" Papa used his soft approach in calming her. He hated arguments. "You know I don't speak of politics outside these walls. But I must be able to tell you what I see and what I think!"

"Ja, ja," she retorted. "And I also know how a glass of wine can loosen you up!"

"Mariechen," he replied, standing at the door to leave. "Will you never learn to trust me?"

He quietly closed the door behind him, and was gone. I looked at Mama with hurt and disgust and ran after him. Catching up as he reached the front door, I threw my arms around him.

"Papa, she didn't mean it! Please don't go yet. We haven't talked, and you promised to tell me what you see and do in France."

"Ach, my Annchen," he laughed, hugging me back. "Du bist mein Schatz, immer mein Schatz! But I must go now. You wouldn't want the authorities arresting me for being AWOL."

It had been a long time since he had called me his 'treasure.' I let him go on his promise the next stopover would be longer. As usual, he asked me to always obey Mama and help her with the house.

My mother wasn't happy with me when I returned upstairs. She didn't say anything, but her attitude expressed her thoughts better than spoken words. She knew whose side I was on, and I didn't try to dissuade her.

"Märe, haven't you been paying attention to all the posters around town, and the warnings on the radio about loose talk?"

"Ja, Mama." Whenever she started off calling me 'girl' in harsh tones, I knew a lecture was coming. I didn't mind being called "Märe" by my Herbst uncles and aunts — they were mostly friendly about it. Not Mama. This time, however, she said no more about the daily reminders that "Feind hört mit." (The enemy hears too.) The warning had become part of German life.

We weren't supposed to listen to foreign radio stations, and we were warned anyone caught would be severely punished. That didn't keep Erich and I from trying — whenever Mama wasn't around. German programming could be quite boring most of the time, and it was hard resisting the temptation to flip the dial around. There was no sinister motive, just a curiosity to hear other languages and music. Erich was a born mimic, and could make both Mama and I laugh ourselves to tears with his versions of Arabic, French, and English. He would say, "All you have to do to speak English is put a hot potato in your mouth." Mama wasn't too pleased to learn where Erich had picked up his talent with language, but urged him to be careful listening to the radio. And never was the dial to be left set to anything except a German station.

After Papa was called into the air force, and while the outcome of Hitler's move into France was still uncertain, some people living in the Saarland, another German state bordering the fighting area, were offered the chance to temporarily move farther away from the conflict. In short, they would take up residence in the Pfalz. It was how we were assigned a family from the Saar.

I wasn't at home when a city housing inspector came around seeking space for these German Flüchtlinge (refugees). He and Mama determined that by putting me in the bedroom with her and moving Erich from across the hall to my bedroom, his bedroom and two adjoining storage rooms would be just fine for the Presser family. Erich and I weren't happy about giving up our private space, but were very curious about having someone in the house from a different part of Germany, specially a place so close to the fighting.

We learned that the Presser family consisted of a father and mother, a four-year-old daughter Gisela, and Herr Presser's mother. We liked them right away, and they were obviously grateful that we had opened our home to them. Young Frau Presser was seven months pregnant, but I didn't know it until almost before the baby was born. In my ignorance, I had thought she was just naturally chubby.

The Pressers brought some furnishings, including a small cook stove that was easily connected with pipe to a chimney serving what had been Erich's room. It would be their kitchen. Herr Presser was in the poultry business, and he quickly went about renting another section of ground in the neighborhood for his trade. That taken care of, he drove back to his home near Saarbrücken to gather his stock for the truck ride to Kirchheim.

"First, its displaced people, now its displaced chickens!"

Leave it to Erich to come up with that opinion when Herr Presser returned with crates of the birds. We were sitting in our kitchen. "Hush!" Mama said. "Herr Presser can't be blamed if he doesn't want to sit around doing nothing until it's safe to go home."

I looked after and played with little Gisela as much as I could. Her mother seemed to appreciate it, as she wanted to rest more and more. She was young, and I couldn't figure out why she needed to lie down so much. Oma Presser reminded me of my own Oma Klein in Bolanden, her white hair combed back and twisted into a knot.

The old woman did the cooking, and one afternoon, while visiting in the Presser kitchen, I watched her prepare a yeast dough recipe for cake. My mouth dropped when she started to flatten the dough with an empty wine bottle. "Wait," I said. "I'll go get Mama's rolling pin."

"Nay, nay, child," she laughed. "This bottle will do just as well as your rolling pin." With those words and a sprinkle of flour on the bottle, she rolled out the dough with amazing skill.

As the weeks passed, it finally dawned on me that the Pressers were expecting a baby, a fact I found exciting and frightening. When the event occurred, it was another girl, and my feelings about babies hadn't changed. I didn't like babies, and believed nothing about them was appealing until they grew old enough to talk. The new little girl in the house didn't change my mind.

A month or so after the baby's arrival, the Pressers prepared to leave, feeling it safe to return to the Saar and their own home. The fighting was over, and Hitler had won again. Still, we all had grown to like the family and it was with some sadness that we bid them farewell. They were only the first of the refugees still to come.

On another afternoon, sitting in the kitchen doing schoolwork, I heard the familiar honk of my father's truck. He had a special way of honking when he wanted someone to open the big doors into the courtyard.

Racing down the stairs, I thanked God shoemaker Kasper wasn't in the shop to hear my noise. Papa hadn't stopped to see us for a month, and it was a wonderful surprise!

Passing into the yard and parking, he quickly joined me in closing the doors again. Holding me at arms length, he said, "So, you're growing taller and your hair longer. I like that," My braids were getting quite long down my back, and I was happy he noticed.

When I ran from the kitchen, I had left Mama standing at the stove preparing supper. Now we would have a special guest. Passing by the truck to go in the house, Papa reached into the cab and pulled out a box. It appeared used, so I guessed it couldn't be a gift. Papa didn't say as I followed him up to the kitchen. Setting the box on the table, he turned to offer his wife a kiss on the cheek. Then, while I waited anxiously, eyeing the box, my parents stood and talked for several minutes. Finally, Papa turned his attention to the box.

"I've got something here I believe our girl can put to good use in the months to come."

Looking in the box, I saw dozens of skeins of fine wool yarns in different colors. Such beautiful yarns were no longer seen in our shops. Most wool, even fine quality wool, was going to the war effort. Mama and I just stared at it and cautiously touched its softness.

Papa laughed. "Well, I agree it's good quality knitting yarn, but nothing to make you both speechless!"

"Fritz, these all say that they were made in France. How did you get them?" Mama had been reading the paper band circling each skein.

"I'm going to tell you all about that. But, first, you must know I didn't loot some poor yarn shop in France."

He went on to explain that just two days before, while driving supplies to our troops in Verdun, a major city well inside France, he had to pass through many villages. Most appeared deserted, but at about noon he was getting hungry, and so decided to stop at one of the farmhouses to ask for something to eat. This is not at all hard to believe, as my father was known to do the same in his home territory. A friendly sort, Papa must have assumed he would find a similar welcome in a French village.

He pulled up to a house, and seeing the front door open, figured someone was home. "I left my rifle in the truck and approached the house slowly. I didn't want to surprise anyone and get shot."

At the door, he knocked and shouted what little he knew in French, but got no response. Walking down a hallway, he found each room virtually empty. The furnishings had been moved out in a hurry, though a few pieces remained. Working his way to the kitchen at the rear of the house, he hoped to find something to eat. There wasn't a crumb to be found. The kitchen had a door leading to the outside, and he stepped through it onto a small stone porch. There, on a step beginning to get wet in a rain that had been threatening, was the box now before us. Thinking there might be some food inside, my father lifted the top. What he found was the yarn, a pair of small ladies shoes, and two small plaster busts of an old peasant couple.

Papa reached into the box, brought the pair out, and handed them to me. ""You can care for them. As long as they were left to fate, it might as well be with us. I'm sure they aren't valuable, just nicely painted plaster."

Perhaps the little busts weren't valuable, but I was instantly struck by the familiar appearance of the two, especially the woman. "Papa! She looks just like —"

"Just like my mother."

The old peasant woman wore a head scarf like Oma Klein often put on her head. And the face — it was Oma's thin, wrinkled, sweet face to the last detail. The man with his beret wasn't at all like my late Opa Klein, but that didn't matter.

"Shouldn't you have just left the box there?" Mama said.

"I thought about that while I was standing in the kitchen of the house. As you can see, the box had been in the weather for many days. Luckily, it's made of heavy paper board, or the contents would've been ruined before I found it."

"You could've put it in the house on a table for the owners to find when they came back."

"Ja, that's true. But I knew our soldiers are still roaming through the countryside there, and what they do, at times, is not nice. Many are foolish young men who loot and vandalize. If one of them found this box, it's not likely he would care about knitting, or find beauty in those busts."

Clearly, Papa had given the matter some serious thought, and Mama said no more. Besides, the box was for me, and if there was to be any guilt, it was his and mine. As we prepared to eat, I asked Papa if he ever did find food. "Ah, naturally," he laughed. "At another farmhouse nearby, I found an old man who hadn't deserted his property sitting at his kitchen table. He got scared when I walked in, but when I smiled and said 'Bonjour,' he became easier."

"But, Papa, how could you tell him what you wanted?"

"When your Papa is hungry, he can remember the few French words in his head. I simply pointed to my mouth and said, 'manger, manger.' He knew I wanted to eat."

"And?"

"My girl, you know I wouldn't harm him. He kindly got up and made me the best sandwiches I've eaten in ages. And before you ask, I did thank him very much."

The fine yarn Papa brought took about two years to use up. Mama could knit, she just didn't. Since I was still limited to simple knitting techniques, she agreed I should find instruction to broaden my knowledge. Asking around, we learned that two of the Sisters in the Catholic convent near my school taught advanced knitting and needlework. Mama and I approached the convent about taking non-Catholic students. Sisters Renate and Wilfortis greeted us.

"Naturally, Frau Klein. We have many Protestant young people who come to learn. It's never a problem," assured Sister Renate.

"And adult Protestants, too!" Said Sister Wilfortis. "We just ask a small donation."

"A small donation is all." It was Sister Renate's turn to repeat or embellish what the other just said — a quirk I'd have to become accustomed to in the following weeks.

It was arranged that I would go to the Sisters twice a week after school. I found the convent and its occupants very interesting, and I was glad my mother allowed me to attend. Strictly conservative on most matters, Mama had an open mind when it came to religion. She judged people solely on behavior and cleanliness, and in her mind the work done by the Catholic sisters was as admirable as that of the Protestant Deaconess sisters.

Even before the sisters began tutoring me, I had begun an ambitious project — a cardigan sweater for myself. I picked from the box Papa brought a gray yarn with speckles of red and green. I wanted to make a fancy pattern on the two front panels. Renate and Wilfortis thought I wasn't ready, and went into one of their echo routines to change my mind. I met the double-barrel argument with an equally determined reasoning in favor of the complicated task. Surprisingly, they gave in, and over the next weeks directed my efforts with patience and humor. My stubborn nature often proved to be my undoing, but this time, with guidance from the sisters, I managed to finish a sweater even they were proud of. I was so pleased, I immediately started a similar cardigan for Mama.

The room where the sisters worked with students was actually the convent's large dining hall. The door into it was just a few steps from the front door, so I rarely had a chance to investigate any of the other rooms. A beautiful open stairway with hand-carved wood railings led to the second floor from the main hall, but I didn't have the nerve to go up even one step. The room where we worked was light and airy, especially in summer when the large windows were opened, allowing a breeze to join our company. Two pictures decorated one wall — Jesus and Mary.

There was singing almost every time I went. The songs were not particularly Catholic, just folk tunes, happy and sad. As time went on, more songs about war were added to our entertainment. One that I've often thought about almost made me cry every time we sang it. It told the story of a mother searching a battlefield for her son. Finally, she came to a small chapel, and upon entering, sees a body on the floor covered by a black shroud. Lifting the shroud, she discovers the body has both legs missing, and that it is her son.

By that point in the song, most of us were in tears. I liked it only because of the lovely melody. Oddly, such songs went counter to the daily radio news of the glorious German victories by our Wehrmacht everywhere. At the time, radio commentators almost always spoke of German losses in terms of the 'brutal murder of innocent civilians' by the British bombers. Soldier casualties in battle were either not reported publicly or made to appear insignificant. Only families and friends were beginning to know the real story from black-bordered letters from the Wehrmacht. The black border always meant death.

Chapter Fifteen

With Papa away in the air force, Erich was noticeably less enthusiastic about his apprenticeship at the machine shop and staying around home. Before, he could share his experiences at the shop with Papa almost every night at the supper table. No doubt, he thought his mother and sister wouldn't understand. Instead, Erich began leaving the house after eating to spend the evenings with friends Ernst, Helmut, and Franz.

I missed Erich's feistiness. He seemed to lose interest in our normal sibling battles, and wouldn't even give me a surprise punch on my arm, one of his favorite tricks. The new somberness made me think he was sick, and maybe he was — sick of being the only man in the house.

Thursdays were a little better for him. It was the one day of the week spent entirely at the Fortbildungsschule, a kind of academic school. All his friends did the same — it was required of everyone in apprenticeship programs. Working on the family farm wasn't considered being an apprentice, so Ernst didn't attend the school. But his other friends still made Thursday one of his better days of the week. It was through the school that my brother made a discovery that brought him out of the doldrums and back to me.

One afternoon, after his classes, he came home excited. "You've got to come with me right now," he said, having caught up with me at the chicken coop collecting eggs for Mama. "I've found just what we've been looking for when I went to buy school supplies today!"

"I don't need any school supplies. Besides, I've been in Gau's many times. I know what they have."

"I'm not talking about Gau. This place is called Kasper's Office Supplies. It's in a regular house on the Neugasse, not in the old business district."

I had never heard of Kasper's, though I knew the Neugasse. If a 'straße' is a street, a 'gasse' is usually a short narrow side lane, barely wide enough for horse and carriage in olden times. "I still don't need anything for school," I said, finally. "What else is there?"

"Books! They have a private lending library, and it doesn't cost as much as the one at city hall."

That was all it took. I grabbed my coin purse and we ran to the Neugasse.

My brother's accidental discovery was a gold mine for readers. The owners had set aside three rooms behind their shop just for lending books. Most were organized by type and author, and many still had their original dust covers. At the city library, every book was wrapped in a green cover, with just a number — no title or author — printed on the binding.

Kasper's allowed browsing, and gave advice on stories I might find interesting. This was not the case in the city library. There, a clerk removed books from the shelves, but only if an author or title was given and the book's number was found in a card file. Whenever Fräulein Kiefer was on duty, she'd help in my choices, but that wasn't often enough.

Kasper's was user friendly, and they charged under the official rate. We were also allowed to take more than the usual one or two books. On our first visit, my brother picked out several books he thought we should read. I paid the rental happily, for I couldn't believe we had eight whole books to take home. At the time, Erich was interested in stories about the old American West. I soon followed his lead, reading both American and German authors on the subject. One of my favorites was the story of Indian chief Winnetou by Karl May, who wrote many authentic tales about the American West. I later heard May had never been in America.

Frau Kasper was very much like Fräulein Kiefer in urging me to read classic literature, but I was also fascinated with books somewhat less than 'classic.' Kasper's had a number of illustrated books for young girls about life in Victorian England, and the setting of the books intrigued me. Images of pretty girls dressed in elegant finery at a tea party or under a beautiful willow tree etched themselves in my mind.

It was all of five blocks home from Kasper's, and as the eight-book haul got heavier, reality dawned on me. There was no way either one of us could possibly read eight books in the allotted two weeks. Erich corrected me in a hurry.

"Don't worry about that," Erich said, grinning. "I'm sure this sore throat I feel coming on will lay me up in bed a few days."

I knew my brother was capable of putting on a good show as a sick patient. "You look fine to me. How is anyone going to believe you're sick?"

"Ach," he laughed, "by the time I get upstairs to the kitchen I'll have to ask Mama to let me go to bed right after supper. It will be worse in the morning, and she'll have to call Hirschbiel's with the bad news. It may be Monday before I'm able to go back to the shop."

I don't think Mama was fooled by his 'illness,' but I knew I could never get away with the same stunt. With more than enough time for reading, Erich returned the books without penalty. I had to borrow most of them again — two were all I could manage.

The only book we owned was my mother's Bible. To my knowledge, it was all she read as an adult. I often wondered why.

My household chores increased after Papa went into the military. Mama was firm in what a young girl's role should be in life. I was encouraged to be good at all household chores, and frugal in shopping. She thought I needed to spend less time playing games with friends, and a new push to keep me busy followed an incident in our courtyard.

Henny and other neighborhood kids came over after school to spend the remainder of the afternoon. As there was only one boy in the group, someone said, "Let's play Chimney Sweep." It was a silly game based on our belief that a chimney sweep is good luck, so a girl selected to be his wife would be lucky all her life. The game rules call for all the girls to line up and sing a childish ditty about wanting to be the sweep's wife — all while the boy marches up and down the line looking them over. At a certain point in the song, the sweep stops to pick his bride. He offers his arm, and the couple skips off to a lucky future. My mother must have heard the singing and looked out the kitchen window in time to see me and the boy skipping away from the unlucky wailing girls.

Her voice cut through our noisy activity, asking sternly that I join her upstairs. I promptly obeyed, expecting to run some errand.

"You're getting too old for those games. I want it stopped."

Her logic baffled me. "I know it's a silly game, but Henny is two years older, and she's playing. Why can't I?"

"Because. Now tell your friends you're through for the day, and come back and help me." The look on her face let me know that I would get no reason. I had seen it before.

❧

Papa was released from the air force just in time for Mama's birthday in the first week of December. It was the best gift ever, she said. All the visits Mama had made to Herr Klag since September had paid off. Mama had probably gotten word from the Nazi official beforehand, but said nothing to us. I learned about it when I met Erich on my way home from school.

"Papa's home for good," he shouted as we passed on the steps. He was on his way to buy some wine. My braids must have stood straight out as I flew the rest of the way up the stairs and into the kitchen. In one leap, I landed on Papa's lap, my arms tight around his neck.

"Ach, my Märe," he laughed, trying to keep us from toppling over. "I came home to be safe from attack and injury!"

154

Despite his teasing, I hung on tighter and begged him to say he really was home for good.

"I guess you're not very happy, Annchen. A flea squeezes harder."

My father had been saying those words to me for as long as I could remember. No matter how hard I hugged, it was never hard enough. This time, my older and stronger arms tightened around his neck, making his face red and his voice squeak. The sound made me release my hold in laughter. Watching all this, Mama just shook her head.

"You two are a pair for the circus. Märe, get on with your chores. Your father and I have things to talk about while I fix a supper."

The meal she prepared was everyone's favorite, but especially Papa's — boiled beef, potatoes, green beans, and lots of a very special Herbst-recipe horseradish sauce. Erich and I were even allowed wine, heavily diluted with mineral water. It has the fancy name of "Schorli."

During dinner we learned that while Papa was released, his new truck had not been. Some compensation was paid, but not enough for a new truck, and it was impossible to buy one anyway because of the war. The old truck stored in Worms had been destroyed in a bombing raid, and he'd have to find another used truck.

Buying a truck was undoubtedly the subject of my parent's talk after I had left to do chores. My mother wasn't in favor, considering the uncertain times. Papa was optimistic as usual, saying he couldn't just sit around picking up odd jobs. He wanted his business back and prospering again. Within a week a truck was found, and Kleine Seppel was on the road once more.

Erich was as delighted as I about Papa being at home. The machine shop training had lost its appeal for him, but he couldn't leave it without his father's approval. A chance was at hand to use all of his persuasive powers to convince Papa. I could tell how nervous my brother was when he brought up the subject just before Christmas.

"Papa, I want to leave Hirschbiel's. Machine work is alright, and I've learned a lot, but it's not what I like."

In the past, my father might have treated such a proposition with a humorous comeback. On this occasion his response was serious and calm. "What do you have in mind? You know solid work training is needed to make it in this world."

"I know, Papa, and I think I'm old enough at fifteen to begin training with you. I want to be a trucker!"

Mama, who had been rolling out dough for Christmas cookies, found her voice. "I can't believe what I'm hearing. Driving a truck is hard, stressful work, and financially uncertain. Stay in a job where you'll always have steady work and pay."

Erich had listened respectfully to his mother, but had a quick, determined reply. "I know I can help Papa make a good living for our family. Let me do it."

A twinkle came into Papa's eyes as he studied his son. Shifting his gaze to Mama, it disappeared. "Marie, I'm sorry you think driving a truck is poor work. Must I remind you we've done very well in this business, when politics and war don't interfere." His voice had begun to grow louder, and he glanced at Erich. "I think our son is right. A person should be happy in work, and he'll be just the help I need. I'll arrange that we can start after the New Year." He then chuckled, "You may yet become a true 'Kleine Seppel.'"

Mama silently returned to the cookie dough rolled out before her.

She wouldn't make as many cookies, everyone was cutting back on flour, sugar and butter. Erich and I were warned to stay out of the cookie tins. "You can do with less so that we can send a nice full package to Ludwig," she said.

Lots of people were sending packages that Christmas to husbands, fathers and sons in the service. Uncle Ludwig would be sure to receive something from Oma in Bolanden, but Papa's youngest brother had worked for us, and was like a son and brother in our family circle.

In October, I had begun knitting a pair of Pulswarmers for Ludwig. The woolen tubes, wrist warmers, would be useful in the winter cold of Poland.

From the first week of 1941, customer orders for my father's trucking services rolled in, and Erich had joined the family business. That alone made Papa proud and happy, but being busy with work made him cheerful — he seemed to always be whistling happy tunes the whole day. I know he dreamed of no more war, and of a father and son building a prosperous business. Maybe with hard work and some luck, he said, even his daughter would be needed to help run the office. I didn't have the heart to tell him it was not my dream.

"Mama," my brother began, walking through the kitchen door, "here is your Fips!" Under one arm he was holding on tightly to a wriggling, panting, tail-whipping young fox terrier.

When Mama turned from the stove to see this latest effort to win her over, I was more than sure she'd point to the door and issue marching orders. I didn't even bother to get up from my school work. There'd be no need to put my hands on the squirming black and brown spotted fur bundle. To my surprise, she took the animal from Erich and held him up to her face with both hands like a baby. This sent the young dog into vain attempts to lick my mother's face. Failing that, the animal peed on her apron smock. I let out a loud groan, certain that the terrier had sealed his fate.

But the surprised look on Mama's face turned to laughter as she handed the dog back to Erich. Papa walked in just in time to see the wet spots spreading down her front. He laughed, too, "Well, I see you've become acquainted with — what shall we call him — Fips?"

"Ja, he can be called Fips." She looked down at her spotted smock. "Watch the food on the stove while I change." Walking through the door toward the bedroom, she turned. "My old Fips used to squirt me, too. It meant that he liked me."

Leave it to my father to understand that the only dog Mama would want around had to be just like her "old Fips." Our new fox terrier liked my father and brother, too, but he never tried to squirt them. It was Mama and I who had to be alert at all times. We learned that his loving ways were fully matched by a devilish nature. Taking on a dog in such troubling times had to be an attempt to bring us some sense of normalcy.

My cousin Fritz of Monsheim was accepted into the Luftwaffe academy for pilot training. Tante Lina and husband Willi were so proud of the honor, they took the occasion of the boy's first furlough to see us. As an official of the big Rhein Electric utility, Onkel Willi had no problem obtaining gas for his car, a big four-door sedan.

Cousin Helmi, soon to be a member of the young women's labor corps, came with them. I had to admit Fritz looked impressive in his Luftwaffe uniform. It'd been quite a while since their last visit to Kirchheim and I was surprised both cousins remained so friendly and open to me, a much younger person. They were down-to-earth and not at all like their mother. Tante Lina was the only member of an otherwise warm, outgoing Klein family who began and ended each visit with a formal handshake, including with her own mother. I never saw her embrace Oma, that dearest heart of all.

Helmi, the same age as Erich, but only my height, loved art and drawing, but could also play the Handharmonika very well. Whenever she came with Fritz to visit, I could always count on good advice for improving my playing technique. Later, when I showed an interest in sketching, Helmi was generous with encouragement and tips. And so it was that Sunday, as Erich and Fritz were forced to sit all afternoon with the parents in the living room while they visited. 'Forced' is perhaps a bit strong. They stayed because it was family custom for males as they enter adulthood. Helmi and I stayed in the kitchen and kept the door open to eavesdrop on the conversation, all the time drawing people's heads and faces, animals, and roses. Naturally, Fritz talked about the growing strength of the Luftwaffe. Erich didn't want to disagree with his cousin, but he promoted the Kriegsmarine. Lately, he had become interested in the German navy.

Following coffee and cake, Papa looked to change the topic. "Let's get out the Handharmonika and cheer the place up!"

Helmi didn't have her Handharmonika, so we took turns using mine and everyone joined in to sing along. Even Tante Lina moved her lips now and then. After awhile, Papa insisted on playing the instrument. The idea tickled Helmi and me, though I was reluctant to be a party to embarrassment. My father's acquaintance with the keyboard hardly went beyond knowing the center button in the middle row was middle-C. It's the only note that plays true, when opening or closing the bellow. All the other buttons sound different notes, unlike the accordion. It makes noodling around on the Handharmonika more difficult for a novice to get a recognizable tune from it.

My father wasn't above making a fool of himself, if it was for the sake of having fun. Helmi and I adjusted the straps on his shoulders, all the while attempting a quick lesson about the thirty buttons under his right hand and the eight bass buttons on the left. We then sat down with the others to await disaster. After a few test openings and closings, and pushing down most of the buttons, Papa proceeded right into his favorite tune, "Waldeslust" (Forest Joy). Wonder of wonders, he was doing very well finding the correct notes and we should have been able to sing along. Instead, we all fell apart laughing at all his facial and body contortions, as he struggled to make the instrument do his bidding.

I doubt Mama had ever seen such an array of expressions on her husband's face. Maybe only in their younger days, when Papa tap-danced on table tops. All I know is, on a lovely spring day in 1941, he helped create true Gemütlichkeit within the walls of Breitstraße One.

We all had to believe there would be many more happy days like it. Little did we know.

Chapter Sixteen

Papa kept on the move from dawn until late at night. Trucking in those days was plain hard physical labor, but the perfect job for Papa in that it allowed daily travel somewhere in the Donnersberg region. My father had an obsessive need to stay in touch with people. There was a crowd of extended family members he liked to visit scattered all around in nearby towns and villages, but he was just as apt to drop in anytime on friends and past customers. He could hardly pass through a village without popping into the local bakery where he had delivered flour years before. Always, it'd be under the guise of having "a terrible hunger for one of your hard-crusted rolls." Words any baker loves to hear. Then, he would add, "No one makes rolls as fine!" I know this approach to be true, because I've been with him.

Without question, Papa was fully at ease passing the time of day with anyone — banker or beggar, male or female. My mother restricted her contacts to a handful of people up and down the street, and made no close friends at all. It was not my father's style. In the true 'Seppel' manner, he was friendly to all and won many friends in the process.

It was during my eleventh year, and for reasons I didn't understand at the time, Papa's open banter with some of the neighborhood women began to put a cloud over his relations with Mama. Her sudden black moods after seeing him in a happy chat with a woman on the street baffled him, but didn't change his ways.

Erich quickly picked up on many of Papa's traits. Any past shyness he had dealing with people outside the family was nearly gone by his sixteenth birthday. Working with his father everyday, Erich got a steady dose of Papa's way with people. And, while he had a model to emulate, Erich began to show signs of developing his own brand of 'Seppel' ambition and wit. The girls began to notice Erich's youthful good looks, though the matter was one I paid little attention to. I did notice that like Papa, he was not against chatting it up with the ladies, even while his eye remained on just one — Ida Steinbrecher.

Life may have been changing for Erich outside our home, but our brother-sister relationship stayed the same. He continued to either look down his nose and boss me around or switch on the charm to entice me into another favor. I liked the attention in either case, so my responses were usually limited to a few choice words. I was a sucker for his charming ways.

As with most siblings, it was always trouble when our encounters ended in physical pain. I didn't realize he wasn't mature enough to control his streak of youthful cruelty. He'd say that he was only trying to teach me how to protect myself. Then came the arm twist, finger bending, and choke holds. The outcome rarely changed in the early years — screams of pain and tears, and usually a sharp rebuke by our parents.

By the time I was eleven, my defenses against Erich's tricks were vastly improved. I had discovered, thanks to his tutelage, that a sharp blow to the stomach, an elbow in the ribs, or a swift kick on the shin, worked miracles in breaking a painful hold. If that didn't do it, I added anything throwable to my defense.

Considering my lack of talent in throwing anything straight, it seemed at first to be a poor defensive choice. On the contrary, Erich knew that any broken dishes or dented pans would end in a more severe punishment. And, it was more likely that I would get off completely, since he was older and held to a higher standard. If I could manage to get hold of anything after breaking one of his strangle holds, that often ended the tussle.

As fate would have it, a Saturday afternoon came when Erich decided I needed more self-defense lessons. Doing my homework, for once I was in no mood. Besides, I knew my brother was under orders to clean the truck while our parents were off on an errand. All my pleas to leave me alone, and get on with obeying Papa, fell on deaf ears. Grabbing my arm to pull me off my chair, I saw what was coming — the old arm twist behind the back routine. Before he could flip me around, my right foot kicked out hard and high. He must have thought the kick was intended for a shin and he jerked his legs apart, insuring that my foot impacted on a tenderer target. With a howl he released me, moving backward doubled over. For a moment, I was sorry since I didn't want to hurt him that badly. My sorrow was cut short though, when he slowly began raising up like an enraged bull.

I had moved back up against the cupboard. Desperately, my hand searched behind me all across the shelf surface for a pot or pan. With a quick glance to the top of the cupboard, my eyes found but one object and I grabbed and threw it just as Erich started toward me. The effort was useless I thought, but to our mutual surprise, the shiny steel ball-bearing struck him dead center on the forehead. I'd marveled over the golf ball-size bearing when Papa brought it in the house the night before. Now it had been used to kill my beloved brother. I was absolutely certain of it.

The heavy steel ball had no sooner hit the floor, rolling under the kitchen cabinet, that I saw blood begin to flow from the bright red spot on his forehead.

Momentarily stunned and stopped in his tracks, Erich slowly put a hand to the wound. I thought he was going to keel over and I wanted to run to him, but lucky for me my legs wouldn't answer the urge. Erich had brought his hand down, seeing for himself the bloody result of my counter-attack. The look on his face said it all as he lunged at me. The legs that wouldn't serve me seconds before suddenly allowed me to jump away from his grasp and run out into the hallway, slamming the kitchen door behind me. I didn't stop running until I reached the safety of the street. Even then, I wasn't sure I wouldn't have to run all the way to Bolanden for protection from Oma. Fips ran out of the house to dance and yip around my feet. At least, I had company while waiting for Mama and Papa.

With their return, it was discovered that the damage was far less than all the blood made it seem at first. The bleeding had stopped, revealing a tiny cut and a growing bump. I was given a stern lecture about throwing objects. Erich didn't get off completely — not when it was found that the truck was still dirty. From that time on, my brother kept his efforts to toughen his sister limited to the occasional punch on the arm.

๛

Papa liked taking me along on his trips when Erich wasn't available. On an early spring day in 1941, a chance came to go with him on an errand to Ludwigshafen on the Rhein river. Erich had his Thursday academic classes and I was free to go. It would take only forty-five minutes to drive there, but the purpose of the trip would take the whole day. Papa was going to what we called an Autofriedhof (auto cemetery), a name even Germans chuckle about. Being nothing more than an auto salvage yard, Papa was going there to find usable parts. The war had made finding and buying new truck and car parts near impossible.

"Fritz, I'll have supper waiting," Mama said. "So don't dawdle along the way. And that girl can't be getting to bed late. She has school in the morning."

"Don't worry," he replied, smiling. "But don't forget I'm giving your brother a lift into the city. How quick he is will determine when we return." With that said, he kissed Mama's cheek, and we were off to pick up Onkel Heinrich at his home in Gauersheim. My uncle still operated his upholstery shop in Marnheim below what had been my first home, and he needed new raw materials for the business. These too were becoming ever harder to find.

"Ach, Märe, you've grown so much since I last saw you. And look how long your braids are!" With those words, my uncle climbed into the truck cab,

161

sliding me over closer to Papa. "What do you think? Will we be home for supper? I told Sannchen we would be back."

"Ja, of course, we'll try. Your sister wants us home for supper, too. I'm sure if you're successful, and I have luck, we won't be late."

Tante Sannchen was one of my favorite aunts, though not blood-related. I liked her better than some who were. 'Sannchen' was what everyone called her instead of Susanne. She was a kind-hearted soul who invited affection. I know Heinrich loved her dearly and wouldn't want to disappoint her. I should mention that my uncle also loved a good time and being with Papa.

The city we were heading toward was a major industrial center and a dangerous place to be during the night bombing raids by the English. The large manufacturing city of Mannheim across the river made the area a doubly important target for the bombers.

"Papa, are we going to see any of the bomb damage?" Now and then, I managed to squeeze in a comment or question in the stream of conversation between the men on either side of me. I'd been thinking about the almost nightly bombing raids on the Rhein cities.

"Nay, Annchen, I think not. The junkyard is out of the area the English have bombed."

"But we hear in school most of the bombs don't really hit the factories, just fall on innocent people for kilometers around."

"That's true," Onkel Heinrich put in. "It may be worse than we know. Still I have to find some kapok and leather, even if the bombers pay another visit while I'm looking."

"Not today." Papa was looking intently through the windshield at the sky, which was a leaden gray. "They won't come today. We're in for a long cold rain by noon. Poor weather for bombing."

I don't know how he knew that, but it was comforting all the same. Just to sit next to Papa provided all the security I needed as the road now rapidly dropped into the flat approach to Ludwigshafen, and its sister city. We stopped talking as the cities come into view.

There were no bombed areas to be seen as we drove into a section of factories, and working-class homes dirty with soot nearby.

Soon we came to a place where trolley cars made a turn on street tracks to begin return runs back into the city. There were two waiting, and a third coming into the turnabout. My uncle left us to go on by trolley, and it was agreed that we'd pick him up by four o'clock.

Driving on, Papa soon turned onto a road that seemed to skirt the main factory and apartment areas. Rolling down my window I was greeted by smells ranging from strange to awful, and not at all like the wonderful smells around my Donnersberg home. A manure pile gave off better aromas. I was soon wishing that it were four o'clock. Papa told me quite a few people in Kirchheim came by train everyday to work in the factories off in the distance, and I didn't envy them.

"Look over there, child." My father pointed to the far horizon on his left. "Beyond that line of smokestacks, see the fires?"

I couldn't actually see any fires, but along the distant skyline I could make out a series of black smudges rising into the darkening sky.

"Fires still burning from the bombing yesterday, or possibly the day before," he explained. "The rains coming in will help put them out."

Big drops of rain hit the windshield before Papa finished speaking, and I wished hard that what he said was true. "It should rain everyday," I said, feeling angry. "Then the enemy couldn't find us and drop his bombs."

A serious expression spread across Papa's face. "Ja, and I imagine some little English girl has made the same wish."

It was a mild rebuke, and a needed reminder that such matters usually had two sides to consider. I was doing just that as we came to a place completely surrounded by a high wood fence. I had been with Papa to an Autofriedhof in Worms, but this place was much bigger. Turning off the road, we drove through the open gate without slowing, as though it was something we did everyday. We followed a dirt track not much wider than the truck. On either side, neat rows of every type of vehicle could be seen, including a couple of battered trolley cars. I couldn't help but think we had entered a kind of huge automotive museum, and told Papa so. We finally pulled into an open area with a good-sized shack standing in the center.

Coming to a halt in front of the shack, he laughed. "Let's hope this museum has what I need, or our truck will end up in a place just like it. Come along now, and don't forget your sandwich."

With the onset of cold rain, it was decided I would remain inside where it was warm and dry. Papa said the owner of the salvage operation would be driving him around the big property in the parts search. When we entered the smoky office, it was plain my father had been to the place more than once. He was greeted by name and a hearty handshake. The man even offered me a greasy hand, which I took out of politeness. We were introduced to a second man in the room who looked to me to be much older than the first. The owner pulled a stool over by the little potbellied wood burner and invited me to sit. He said the "alt Vater" would keep me company. People call most any elderly man 'old father,' so I couldn't be sure if the gray-haired fellow with the walrus mustache was really the man's father.

Left alone with the old man, I unwrapped and began eating my sandwich. I didn't have anything to say, so I made an effort to chew each bite slowly while eyeing the dingy room. It smelled of fuel oil and gasoline, odors I'd been around all my life and didn't mind, but I would have liked to open at least one of the two dirty windows for fresh air. Though it had a swept look, the wood floor was rough and stained. On one wall, fan belts and other car parts hung from hooks. An old crank telephone graced the wall near a scarred wood filing cabinet. The only other chair stood by a marred and dirty wood desk.

As I sat chewing, my host had to answer the telephone several times. The connections never seemed very good, and he had to shout constantly. Every so often a person in grimy clothes stuck a dripping wet head around the door to show recovered parts and strike a deal. One time the part was the whole hood from a big sedan, much too large to bring in the office for appraisal. I think the buyer was lucky the old man had no longing to stand in the rain haggling price. He just stood in the doorway, glanced at the hood, gave a figure he knew would be paid, and quickly closed the door.

My companion appeared to be cold, because it seemed every few minutes he threw wood and coal in the little stove. I had to remove my coat and pull the stool farther from the heat. Somehow I hadn't expected the trip to Ludwigshafen to mean sitting and waiting for hours in a shack. Getting restless, I wished for a book to read. Every ten minutes I peered through the nearest window for any activity in the yard, but there was nothing but rain and a blackening sky. The room was becoming so dark that the old man lit an oil lamp and covered the windows with blackout curtains. It was twenty minutes past four, he said.

I wondered what could possibly be keeping Papa so long. I was sure Onkel Heinrich would be waiting already, cursing his brother-in-law and the rain. I began staring at the door, willing that my father would come through it. The old man got up from his chair. "Ah, I hear something. I think they are finally here child."

A truck had driven up and I heard doors slamming, and the shifting of parts to the bed of our truck. By the time the old man had opened the door to look out, Papa and the other man rushed through the opening and went directly to the hot stove.

"I'm sorry it took so long, but we found the parts." My father's words came out with a shiver, and he rubbed his hands together over the warmth of the little round stove. The owner handed him a clean rag to dry his hands and face. Papa then paid the man, and we rushed out to find Onkel Heinrich, who had wisely brought along an umbrella and was standing under it, when we got to the trolley turnabout. He didn't appear upset over our tardiness. Maybe he had expected it.

The rain had slowed to a foggy drizzle as we moved farther from the city. No light showed from any building we passed because of the blackout rules, and the light fog added to the eerie sensation of traveling past seemingly deserted homes and businesses. Seeing the road itself was difficult — the truck's headlights were covered except for a small slit, another blackout rule. The slits provided little illumination of the roadway. The amount of light emitted was mostly intended to warn oncoming traffic. I had faith in the driver, but my uncle seemed glad to stop for a drink when Papa offered.

"We'll stop in Zell," Papa said absently. "No doubt we're all ready for a drink."

We were running late, and Zell was slightly out of our path to Gauersheim and Kirchheim, but just hearing Papa say Zell excited me. It was the home of one of my Godmothers, Tante Katharina.

"Can we visit Tante Katche?" After all, she was the sister of Heinrich, sitting next to me.

"Nay, Annchen, we don't have time. We'll just stop in for a quick drink at the inn. I once delivered flour to the bakery across the street and they know me."

It was pitch black as we entered Zell. "I don't know, Papa. Maybe we should drive on home. Mama has supper waiting."

Onkel Heinrich shouted over the roar of tires on cobblestones, "Ach, Märe, your Papa and I need a quick drink after such a long day. We won't stay but a few minutes."

"Onkel, don't you want to say hello to your sister?" Katche was someone he didn't see often. I couldn't understand why he didn't tell Papa to stop at her house.

"I know you'd like to see Katche," he replied, "but I happen to know she likes to go to bed early. It wouldn't be nice to keep her up."

I couldn't see it in the darkness of the truck, but I knew my uncle winked in the direction of Papa. I remembered that peculiar chuckle that came with a wink when he had teased me as a child.

જ

The front door of the inn opened right into the small public room, which was typical of village inns everywhere. At the far end of the room was a small serving bar and in the center a large round table, where most of the locals gathered. A few smaller tables were scattered around the remaining space. A door near the bar went back to a kitchen. The inn served a few food dishes to the public. Very likely it was the same kitchen used to fix meals for the owner and his family since they also lived on the premises — a common practice.

A haze of tobacco smoke drifted near the ceiling of the room, lending a strange glow to the few hanging light fixtures. Perhaps ten or eleven people were already settled around the room, and all stopped talking at once to look over the new guests. All were men, ranging in age from three young ones in army uniforms to one old, toothless Opa. Most of the older ones nodded or mumbled a greeting toward us, to which my father responded with a loud and happy, "Guten abend."

Suddenly the three soldiers shouted, "Heil Hitler!" — staring hard at us. I found my right arm and hand coming up in a kind of half-Nazi salute, my mouth softly repeating their words. Papa just continued to smile at the young men. The proprietor quickly emerged from behind the bar. The small round man with a glistening red face smiled broadly as he rushed forward.

"Seppel! I can't believe it. What a surprise! How long has it been? Three or four years, I know." His words came out in a nervous stream, while guiding us to a corner table not far from the soldiers. I got the feeling he was trying to assure them that we could be trusted.

"Nay, it hasn't been that long," Papa said. "Don't you remember? I stopped in about a year ago."

"Ja, much has happened this past year. It's easy to lose track of — "

"Gastwirt! Get Seppel and his friends something to drink before they die of thirst!" 'Gastwirt' means innkeeper, and he quickly moved to bring us two wines and a Sprudel. The man who shouted at him was seated two tables away. When the drinks came, my father and uncle raised their glasses at the man.

"Prosit, Jakob!" Papa gave a toast to the heavy-set man, adding loudly after a long sip, "I'm sure my brother-in-law agrees you have again vinted a wonderful wine." My uncle nodded his head and raised his glass for another 'prosit.' The jovial man with the Bismarck haircut was a local winemaker in a village totally devoted to the art. My father apparently knew him well.

166

I was both fascinated and worried by a large cuckoo clock hanging on the wall by the bar. Darkened with age, the wood front was carved into images of grape clusters on either side and below the clock face. Just above, a door for the cuckoo to appear was located under the bearded chin of a carved ram's head adorning the top. Looking at the time, I pulled on Papa's sleeve. He leaned his head over.

"Papa, it's long after supper. Mama will be upset!"

It was as though he didn't really hear. He waved his hand for the innkeeper. "Some pretzels won't hurt your appetite for supper. I'll get you some." Since I liked pretzels and didn't get them often, and because he had said in his off-handed way that supper would come soon, I sat back in silence.

New people came into the inn, and not surprisingly, many of them knew my father and uncle from years past. Naturally, a drink was in order. Seeing the fuss people made over 'Seppel,' even the soldiers warmed up and started chatting. They were on a brief furlough, but unfortunately wanted to talk about only war and politics. Both my father and uncle were feeling happy, and I had to think of Mama's warning about discussing politics in public. I again pulled his sleeve and he leaned over. I put my mouth to his ear. "Papa, please, no politics! Can't we go home? It's going on nine!"

He patted my hand. "We will, Ännchen. Don't worry. As soon as I'm finished talking to my old friend Hannes we'll go. Your mother will understand." I didn't agree that Mama would understand at all. His friendships weren't that important to her.

The three soldiers were quickly interested when they learned my father had been drafted into the Luftwaffe and only recently released.

"I can't believe it," one of them said. "It had to be a mistake. You are almost as old as my father!"

"And mine, too," offered another, probably trying to envision my little father filled out a glorious air force uniform.

The third spoke up. "Naturally, it's the reason you were released so soon. Reichsmarschall Herman Göring himself ordered the release when he learned of the mistake!"

Everyone laughed uproariously, including Papa, but I didn't. Papa wasn't old. He was just needed at home.

The laughter was still in the air when he seemed to see the clock for the first time. "Ach, look at the time! Come," he said, grabbing my hand, "we must take your uncle home. Sannchen will be worried sick."

His sudden burst of determination to leave caught me by surprise. He had nearly jumped up from his chair, one hand already under an arm of Heinrich, who did not have so easy a time standing up. My uncle had drunk the same as Papa, but was obviously much worse off.

Heinrich took a deep breath. "I've been sitting much too long," he mumbled.

"Annchen, let Heinrich rest his other arm on you until we reach the truck."

Stepping into the cold night air seemed to help Onkel Heinrich wake up a bit, but he still wobbled getting to the truck. Papa did most of the work getting him settled in the cab. This time I sat on the outside.

"Roll down your window some, Annchen. The cool air will do us all good." Papa began a stream of happy talk that didn't end until we reached Gauersheim and the door leading into my uncle's courtyard. Papa said later that he kept up the chatter to keep Heinrich from falling into a deep sleep.

"But you had as much to drink and you don't act funny or sleepy."

"Everyone has a limit and you must be careful not to go beyond. Your uncle just doesn't know when to stop filling his glass."

"But how do you know?"

"Luckily I was born with a button right here." He pointed to the side of his neck. "When it pops, I know it's time to put my hand over the glass."

I had to laugh at his way of describing it. He was right, though, about knowing when to cork the bottle — to that time I'd never seen him drunk.

We had wanted to accompany Heinrich to the house door, but he insisted on going it alone from the courtyard entrance. We did wait until he got inside the door, then drove on to Kirchheim. By that time it was after ten o'clock, and I was getting tired and anxious to get to bed. Supper was out of the question anyway for Papa and I.

The last few kilometers to Kirchheim passed in silence and, after pulling into our dark courtyard, we managed to climb out of the truck and move over to the back door without any noise. Papa then startled me by whistling one of his loud, happy tunes, keeping it up along the dark hallway and up the stairs to our quarters. I had hoped Mama was already in bed.

Apparently, he knew differently, and was preparing to face the music with some of his own.

"You fool! Stop that racket. Erich's asleep, as should your daughter be at this hour." Mama was sitting at the kitchen table mending clothes when we came through the door. She stood up and stared at us, but said nothing further after her initial outburst.

Papa smiled. "We're later than I said, but I hadn't counted on it taking so much time to find the parts. Luckily, I found everything."

When she still remained quiet, he attempted another tack. "I'm sorry we're late, but don't forget, I was also looking after your brother. He got home empty handed after looking all day. With such bad luck, I thought it only right to stop for a drink. Heinrich — "

"Heinrich what?" She exploded. "Heinrich wouldn't keep his daughter from her supper. He wouldn't keep her up late watching two old fools drink on a school night. That he went along with your selfishness doesn't surprise me. He's just as weak as you!"

"Marie, you have no reason to —" My father wearily seated himself on a chair, suddenly too tired to cope as she pressed her attack.

"No reason? You show no responsibility to your family," she screamed, waving her arms and moving closer. "Friends mean more to you than any family and home obligations!"

I couldn't believe what was happening as I watched Papa with his head bowed, and my mother losing all control. As she raved and shouted a litany of past sins down on his hunched form, I began to fear she would hit him. Both of them seemed to have forgotten that they weren't alone. It wasn't as though my parents had always displayed perfect harmony in front of their children. They would disagree on occasion, but this was a one-sided vicious assault that seemed to crumble all the security I'd ever known. I knew Erich could hear through the stone walls, and I wanted him there to stop her. I waited for the door to open, sure that only her son could make her stop lashing out at Papa.

"Mama! Stop it! Stop! Stop!" In hysteria, I had thrown myself between them, my arms around Papa. I was hurt and angry, and at that moment, I hated her. "He did nothing wrong. Stop it!"

"In all my life, I'd never shouted at Mama. The tears flooding my face in fear and anger must have shocked her. The bitter accusations ended in mid-sentence. Struggling for control, she stared at me before finally turning away, a hand over her eyes.

I clung to Papa to comfort him, not knowing if my mother would renew the attack. It was clear after a few minutes that the storm was over. She remained standing with her back toward us with one hand to her face and the other holding on the edge of the sink. In another moment, my father eased me away gently from him and wiped his tear stained face with the back of his hand. "Go to bed," he said quietly. "I've kept you up far too long."

Mama turned and calmly added, "Ja, Märe, go now. Tomorrow and school will be here soon."

I adored my father completely, but I wasn't blind to what others considered to be his faults. He didn't go to church as often as he should, and I also thought he was wrong not to join the Nazi party. But, I felt that Mama was wrong to accuse him of being irresponsible and lazy. Vacations were for other people, and it was a rare day when he was not found working in the business, in the house and shop, or in the garden. Most days he stopped work only to eat and sleep. It should be forgiven if once in a while Papa allowed himself some fun socializing among his friends for a few hours. Mama no longer forgave him. That much was obvious.

The ugly kitchen scene stayed with me all night, but I was up early and ready for school in plenty of time. The morning kitchen I entered seemed oddly normal. Mama scurried about preparing lunch pails for Erich and Papa, who were busy planning their workday. All normal. But something had changed in our little family, and everyone knew it.

Chapter Seventeen

For several days following the incident in our kitchen, I rushed through my homework and house chores after school to be able to leave and visit with Henny. Mama's display of rage in attacking Papa had put a strain on my love for her, and had dampened my normal desire to make small talk with her until the men returned from work.

She didn't seem to mind that I hurried my work in silence or that I spent more time away from home. I was always back early enough for the evening meal.

With Henny, the process of ridding my mind of the horrible kitchen scene could begin. I revealed nothing of it to Henny and her mother, but threw myself wholeheartedly into some of my friend's fun ideas. We might practice our instruments for awhile or visit the growing animal menagerie in the courtyard — usually new goat offspring. Once or twice we did the girl-thing of combing each other's hair into various styles, then laugh ourselves silly over some of the more crazy results.

One afternoon, I was greeted at Henny's front door by the sight of her in the hallway, putting a harness and leash on a sheep. The big woolly ewe wasn't protesting the idea, though she appeared nervous about her footing on the slick stone floor. I had to laugh.

"What are you doing with that poor animal? She can hardly stay on her feet."

"Ja, but between the two of us, we can get her out the door to the street. I want to take her to the meadow by the Ziegelwoog lake."

I'd never heard of anyone taking a sheep for a walk, but it sounded like great fun. We proceeded to push and pull the animal along the highly polished and slippery hallway floor and down three untried steps to the street. The fun part was fading fast.

Neither Henny nor I had given a thought as to how all this would appear to a watchful neighborhood. Two young girls with a reluctant sheep on a leash — out for a stroll — had to be a rare sight along Breitstraße. As it happened, the day of our sheep outing was one of pleasant sunshine. Those people on the street were soon joined by a growing number of window gawkers of all ages, smiling and laughing at the sight passing before them. As we struggled to keep the ewe moving past my own house, I prayed Mama wouldn't look out to see the spectacle.

Henny and I continued, with some embarrassment, our tug of war around the corner onto the Haiderstraße to our destination by the lake. Suddenly our battle with the beast was reversed. Smelling a fresh meal, the ewe raced ahead, dragging the two of us behind. Since I had been tugging the leash, it was no match when the ewe decided to do the pulling. Henny had to grab me around the waist.

"Hang on," she screamed. "Don't let go. If she gets away, we'll never catch her!"

☙

The spring of 1941 brought news of the war against the British in far off Africa. Hitler's interest in conquering their North Africa colonies was nearly as high as his wish to crush the island nation with Luftwaffe might.

Rommel's Afrika Korps victories made him a Reich hero. For months, the name of Rommel was heard constantly on our radio and on any street corner. Places like Tobruk and Tripoli became a part of our vocabulary.

"The war is getting too big for us," Papa declared one evening. He was looking at Erich's atlas for the newest places just mentioned on the radio report. My brother and I were enthusiastic about defeating our enemies, so it was hard to understand his negative comments. Respect for our father was all that prevented an argument with him. Naturally we didn't dare repeat his words outside our four walls.

The mounting military and political events caused a higher need to plan around news broadcasts. A news flash would abruptly halt any activity. People no longer enjoyed family talk in the evening until after newscasts. Family matters and decisions were rescheduled. At the time, all the radio reports were entirely favorable to the German side. This would never really change, not even when most Germans only had to look around to see that the situation wasn't as it had been described on the radio.

One of the realities was the continuing exodus of our male relatives and friends to military service. The Wehrmacht drafted most. The Luftwaffe and Kriegsmarine (navy) drafted a few recruits, but preferred volunteers. We knew none that refused to serve. Fear of reprisal by authorities may have been one reason, however I must say that young Germans overwhelmingly believed in the aims of the Third Reich at the start. Disillusionment had plenty of time yet to set in.

One evening after closing his shop downstairs, shoemaker Kasper appeared at our kitchen door. Supper was not yet on the table when he stepped in. Papa looked up from tuning the radio. We all looked at our visitor, half knowing his news.

"Herr Klein," he began, then nodded to Mama. "Frau Klein. Guten abend. I'm sorry to bother you at this hour, but I have very little time to make arrangements."

"Please, come in and sit. What arrangements?" My mother pulled out a chair from the table.

"Of course," Papa added. "Sit and tell us what you need."

"I am to report immediately to the Wehrmacht. I don't think they'll need me for long, and I don't want to lose my location here."

The idea of losing a mentor and friend hit me hard, harder than when I heard about some relative in a distant village being drafted. I wanted to tell Herr Kasper how much I'd miss our talks about music and theater, but was afraid I'd cry.

He went on to explain that he would simply lock up the shop temporarily and his parents would continue to pay us the rent, if that was alright. It was, and with that settled, he prepared to leave by coming to each of us for a handshake. I was the last, and he must have seen how my eyes glistened with tears.

"Ja, and you," he said. "Watch out running those stairs. I want you in one piece on my return. We still have lots to talk about."

Nodding to my parents again, he turned and left.

The shoe repair shop had been closed just a few days when we learned of another man drafted. This time the man was not all that young. Heinrich Andres, our next-door neighbor and good friend of Papa, was the father of two small girls, with another baby on the way.

Heiner, as everyone called him, worked at a nearby stone quarry, and he often helped my father on the truck after his own work day had ended. Papa and Herr Andres also shared the love of playing cards and their favorite place to play was at our kitchen table. Actually, they had to play in our kitchen, because Herr Andres had a bad habit of shouting when the cards weren't going his way. Frau Andres simply refused to let him disturb the young children with his yells of displeasure over losing a single pfennig. Papa was more tolerant, but insisted on playing a hand for no more than a pfennig. He figured if Heiner yelled about losing the smallest coin in our currency, what would happen if he lost a whole Reichmark? Many times, when Herr Andres slammed his cards on the table and began screaming, Papa would calm him. "Heiner! It's only a pfennig. You couldn't buy a whiff of Limburger with a pfennig." More often than not, Papa could turn Herr Andres' anger into laughter. All of which wouldn't have helped the Andres' children sleep. His laughter was just as loud.

The birth of the third Andres child was expected just weeks later and he was worried. "Please keep an eye on my Frau when she's ready to deliver," he said to Mama. "I won't rest easy about her and the girls." He had come over to say goodbye and shake hands all around. He needn't have been so concerned. Most everyone on the street kept an eye on his wife's needs, before and after the birth.

Frau Andres was one of the few women on my block who worked outside the home. She cleaned houses and shops three days a week, and her services were in demand. Having been in the Andres home, I questioned her reputation. She kept herself and the two little girls clean and neat, but her own house always looked neglected. I also thought Herr Andres was far more attractive than his wife. With his black hair, dark complexion, and flashing brown eyes, all made me question again Hitler's preference for blue-eyed, blonde people.

❧

Most of the housewives along the Breitstraße stayed at home every day. Their work day usually began with the airing of bedding in open windows, a ritual disrupted only in extremely foul weather. On nice days, the ladies liked to take a break from their labors to check on street activity by leaning out of the open windows for a bit of gossip with neighbors and passersby. Since few people had telephones, it was the quickest way of passing along town news.

Mama was an exception in this scene. She leaned out the window solely to check the weather or find one of her family. But, on another matter, Mama was no different than most of the women in believing all of the Führer's rhetoric about German mothers holding home and hearth together, and bearing children for the Third Reich. She had no plans to further increase the German race, but she loved hearing Hitler say it.

When my fourth grade ended in late spring of 1941, Papa was ordered back into the Luftwaffe, this time without his truck. He had just a few days to find and hire a driver to work with Erich to keep the business going. The young man taken on was recommended by a friend, and had been spared from military service by a crippled leg. Mama didn't agree with the hiring, but finally saw that it was the only way to keep Erich busy.

The day before my father had to report for duty for the second time, we all piled into the truck for the short ride over to Bolanden to visit Oma Klein, who was now living with Tante Lisbeth. It was hard for my grandmother to hold back tears, despite Papa's cheerfulness. "I have known too much grief from war," she said, referring again to the many relatives and friends she had lost in the 'Great War.' Now four of her sons — Ludwig, Otto, Rudy, my father and three grandsons — were now facing the dangers of a new war. Papa devoted almost all our visit comforting his mother and promising to return.

Back home later in the evening, we sat around the kitchen table talking about the future. I did more listening when talk turned to running the business in Papa's absence.

"Do as much of the minor repairs to the truck as you can, Erich. Going to a garage will take away the profit," my father warned. My brother promised to do his best. Mama was happy that Erich was taking everything so seriously. It made her less anxious about the new arrangement with a hired driver.

Papa, too, seemed more serious about being called back into the Luftwaffe. He had words of advice for each of us this time. The first call-up by the Luftwaffe had been treated like some kind of mistake that had quickly been made right. We all knew that wasn't the case now. Papa's manner told us that he didn't expect to be home again to stay until the trouble was finished.

As we prepared to turn in for the night, Papa pulled me to his side. "Sei brav, Märe, sei brav."

In the village culture of the Pfalz, to be told 'sei brav' means far more than the ordinary dictionary definition of 'be good' or 'be brave.' Papa rarely said 'Sei brav' to me and it made a great impact. He was commanding me to live by a code of behavior that would never bring shame on the family. I fully intended to obey.

In the morning, with Erich already off on the first run with the new driver, it was left to Mama and I to walk Papa to the train station. Early morning shoppers crowded the town center, and as usual, many people hailed the little man with his suitcase. "Seppel! Where are you off to now?"

With a laugh, Papa shouted, "I'm off to fight Hitler's war!"

Such a remark, made in public in the coming months, could have brought punishment down on Papa's head. Fortunately, anywhere in the shadow of our Donnersberg, 'Kleine Seppel' and his friendly humor were widely known. Still, such comments were becoming increasingly dangerous.

Papa in the dress uniform he usually wore, except when driving a truck. I thought he looked nice. From the beginning to the end of the war, he never rose above the rank of private.

Chapter Eighteen

Near the end of the fourth grade, my regular teacher, Herr Schardt, came down ill and had to be replaced for a day. I knew his substitute, a much older Herr Lawaldt, only by reputation. I had heard he was very strict, which didn't bother me, since I believed all teachers were strict. In the few hours he had charge of my class, we were awakened to a new degree of strictness.

Herr Lawaldt didn't know our routine. Usually, Herr Schardt showed up well after we did, giving us a chance to visit. Someone always kept an eye on the hallway to warn of our young teacher's approach. One word from the lookout caused a mad scramble back to our desks to sit quiet and erect for Schardt's entry.

The routine never varied. All eyes would watch as he crossed from the door to his desk carrying a fat briefcase. The instant that case hit the top of the desk, we stood up sharply with right arms extended in the Nazi salute, and shouted "Heil Hitler." The seats of our wood desks were the folding types and my class took special pride in making the seats pop up with our legs for one loud clap of wood on wood.

Finding Herr Lawaldt already seated at Schardt's desk, all thought of precision went out the window. We didn't all arrive at the same time. A few of us managed to mumble "Heil Hitler" as we passed by to find our seats. His response was barely audible. "Heil Hitler, move along to your seats."

I went to my desk in the back and waited with seatmates Else and Renate for the others to straggle in. In those few minutes, I tried to size up the man, all the while hushing the talkative Renate. Much as I liked the girl, she could be a nuisance with her non-stop chatter.

With the last student accounted for, Herr Lawaldt stood up next to his desk. The room was still. Introducing himself, I noted he was shorter and heavier than Herr Schardt was, though not fat. Unlike so many of the younger teachers, his voice wasn't strident. It landed on the ears with a pleasant resonance, though still firm enough to keep me riveted to his words. His round face seemed to have a fixed serious expression. His head was topped off with thin, receding gray hair, and combed straight back. His dark pinstriped suit, vest, and black bow tie made him look more like a businessman than a teacher.

After asking each of us to stand and give our names, we were told to "line up." There was no mistake in the meaning of the order. Students knew from first grade that to 'line up' meant sitting very erect with hands resting flat on the edge of the desk top, with only eight fingers showing. The thumbs were curved around and below the edge. It was all to be accomplished in absolute silence. We did the same thing at the beginning of the Hitler Jugend meetings, whenever they were held at school.

It was at that moment of lining up for Herr Lawaldt that Renate decided to tell me something, reaching over to tap me on the arm. I couldn't believe she would do such a thing, and I hissed a warning to stop. My angry words must have come too late and too loud because the teacher's eyes were instantly on the back row.

"You in the back. State your name again!"

I glanced over to Renate, fully expecting her to stand, but she sat staring straight ahead, her hands resting neatly on the desktop.

"You on the aisle in the back. Stand and give me your name. Now!"

I stood. "Klein," I said, quickly adding, "I didn't start this." I glared at Renate for embarrassing me not only in front of the class, but a strange teacher. She refused to look back at me.

"Klein, you will remain after school two hours so that you may learn that lining up also means silence. Do you understand?"

"Ja, Herr Lawaldt!" It was all I could do to keep from choking on the words. I had never been disciplined by a teacher.

The rest of the school day passed quickly. I supposed that Herr Lawaldt now thought of me as a troublemaker, so I refrained from my usual active participation. I refused to speak to Renate, even when she got up to leave at the end of classes and gave me a sorrowful look. If she had anything to say, my expression shut her up. What would Mama think when I didn't show up at the normal time?

Without a word, teacher and student sat, waiting out the next two hours with work. Homework never took two hours for me to complete, so after an hour and fifteen minutes, I finally closed my workbook. Folding my hands, I studied Herr Lawaldt. He must have sensed my gaze, and he, too, started packing papers into his briefcase.

"You may leave now, Klein."

I expected that he might let me go, but was still surprised and relieved when permission came so softly spoken and with no further reprimand. I wanted badly to try to explain that I was not a troublemaker, but decided against it. Still, I had to say something. He had turned his back when I reached the door. "Danke, Herr Lawaldt."

He was surprised, and turned and looked up at me before waving a dismissive hand. "Schon gut, Klein." (Very well, Klein.)

Walking home, I thought of how the day's events could be explained to Mama. Turning onto a side street that would take me to the Breitstraße, I heard a familiar voice call my name, and the sound of footsteps behind me. Ready to let loose a barrage of angry words, I turned to find a breathless Renate. On the verge of tears, she told me how she had gotten away from her mother with a lie. She was supposed to be at the library, not waiting for me outside the school.

The sad look on her face quickly softened my resolve to end our friendship, but I couldn't let her off the hook entirely. "What you did wasn't right. How am I to explain being kept after school to my mother?"

"It was because of my mother that I couldn't stand up and take the blame," she pleaded. "You know she would have killed me, or worse. If she found out you were involved in my punishment, she would never let me speak to you again. I'm really sorry. You know I wouldn't have done it otherwise."

It was true. Renate's mother was a snob, and didn't allow her to socialize with any classmates out of school.

"I know from how you talk, your mother isn't that way," she continued. "Just tell her that it was my fault, and why I didn't take the blame."

Before I could answer, she turned and rushed off, shouting back that she had to hurry home.

As it turned out, I didn't have to explain anything to Mama. She'd been so busy, she hadn't noticed the hour. I decided not to tell her about it, but I was still bothered, and needed to talk to someone. A few days later, I discovered that Herr Lawaldt was to be my teacher in fifth, sixth, and seventh grades. I turned to Erich with my fears that I had ruined the next three years of my life, and for once, my brother didn't laugh about my latest dilemma.

"Listen," he said. "I know Lawaldt. He can be tough, but he's usually fair. Besides, in two months when you start fifth grade, he won't even remember it."

"How can that be?" I said. "He must think I'm a bad student!"

"Anna, haven't you heard that Lawaldt's only son was killed at the front just weeks ago? He's not going to remember you or anything about the affair."

I was stunned, and realized that Herr Lawaldt wasn't mean, just very sad.

"I'll tell you one thing for sure," Erich added. "I wouldn't be a friend to that Renate girl. She will end up just like her mother, thinking she's too good for you."

I'd been wondering about that myself, but didn't say anything to my brother. The relationship with my school chum had already returned to normal. It wasn't hard to forgive Renate, knowing the risk she had taken returning to school to wait and apologize.

❧

The days flew by during the brief summer vacation between fourth and fifth grade. Papa had come home from the air base in Gießen for my July birthday. I was happy about that, but the visit was too short to suit me and I began to pester Mama about going to see him.

During the school break, Hitler made a military move that would eventually bring grief to almost every German family. On June twenty-second, the German Wehrmacht attacked Russia. Nothing that the Führer had previously done caused as much talk among the people as this latest military decision. There was no joy in the streets. With centuries of history to recall, many Germans believed the attack on Russia was very dangerous, but no one dared to speak of their doubts publicly.

The Russian campaign, still young and without disaster, remained the major topic through the summer, but as I approached my first day of fifth grade, it was the least of my concerns. Would Herr Lawaldt remember our encounter just weeks before?

I decided to get to school early to stake out my usual seat in the back row. I figured a change in appearance might also help, so I styled and braided my hair differently. Like me, my classmates also made a point of being early. Else found her seat next to me, but the third place at our three-seat desk remained vacant. Where, we wondered aloud, was Renate? Since her mother didn't allow us to visit her at home over summer break, we could only speculate that she must be sick, and we decided to keep the seat reserved for her return.

Just as the final class bell rang, Herr Lawaldt entered, moving in a slow and courtly stride across to his desk by the window. We rose as one for a snappy "Heil Hitler." The single loud clap of our folding seats seemed to awaken him to our presence for the first time. Jerking his head around, he stared at his new students for what had to be a full minute. We remained standing at attention with right arms raised. Finally, and with just a twitch of a smile passing over his lips, he mumbled "Heil Hitler" without returning the hand salute. I barely heard his response, but followed the lead of others and sat down.

We were asked to stand and recite our names. When my turn came, he didn't seem to recognize me, but the glimmer of a smile came to his face when I said, "Klein, Annchen." I knew the reason for his reaction, and could

180

have kicked myself. An eleven-year-old should know the proper form. Persons shouldn't introduce themselves using the endearing form of their names.

"Is 'Annchen' your given name, or could it be Anna?"

My face had to be beet red, as a collective chuckle passed through the class. "I'm sorry, Herr Lehrer (teacher). I meant to say Anna. It's just that no one calls me that."

"Well, we'll have to see when I think 'Annchen' fits you best."

If it was a rebuke, he said it so gently that I no longer felt embarrassed. As the last students were giving their names, it occurred to me that I had been challenged to make my new teacher want to call me Annchen. It wouldn't be easy. Our teachers followed a strict protocol — addressing students only by their last names. The only exceptions were favored students. I intended to be one.

"Order, please." Herr Lawaldt was about to make an announcement, and it seemed directed to the back row. "I see that most of you have found the seats you find most comfortable. Today I have no problem with your choice, but be forewarned. Our journey together will be for three years." Pausing to scan the room, he added, "Except for a few of you who may not be able to keep up."

Being forced back to a lower grade was not unheard of, and I looked around wondering who it might be.

"I expect your undivided attention to class work," he continued. "Those of you in the back rows will find yourselves under closer observation in the front, should you fail your duty."

I was happy his eyes hadn't fallen on me when he said it. Maybe Erich had been right about Lehrer Lawaldt.

❧

Renate didn't come back to take her place with Else and me. At the end of the first week, Lawaldt announced to the class that she was very ill.

"She'll get well again, won't she?" A boy in the front asked.

It had been a blurted interruption, and such a violation at another time would have resulted in a swift penalty. Lawaldt overlooked it, perhaps relieved that he could reveal the worst by having been asked.

"By a miracle only," he replied, somberly. "Over summer vacation, it was discovered that Renate has a terrible illness called leukemia. It came on rapidly, and today after just weeks, she can't leave her bed. I would encourage all of you to say a prayer for her."

Herr Lawaldt had picked the end of the class day to break the news. He'd learned that Renate was well liked in our class. She had been a gentle, sweet-natured girl and, I thought, one of the prettiest girls I knew who wasn't vain about it.

I tried to see Renate, even stopping her mother on the street with my appeal. The encounter brought only a sharp refusal.

Just a week later, Herr Lawaldt informed the class of her death, adding that we shouldn't think of attending the funeral procession and burial. The family had requested privacy. We knew the truth behind the request. The mother was still trying to protect Renate, even in death, from her working-class friends.

At about the time we lost one friend, Else and I found a new deskmate. Elfriede Schwab, I was delighted to learn, lived not far from my house. Else was a good school friend, but lived too far from my neighborhood to be a part of after-class activities. Elfriede, and soon another girl named Hannelore, joined Henny in a tighter circle of friends living close by.

Hannelore Rihlmann didn't sit in the back row with us. Herr Lawaldt wouldn't allow her be anywhere but in front near his desk. He, along with the rest of us, had discovered early that Hannelore had a gregarious nature that knew no bounds. Elfriede and I were shy and reserved in comparison, but for some reason we liked her. She provided the needed spice in our existence.

Hannelore was a favorite with the boys in class, something that puzzled me at the time. Her face and long blondish hair were pretty, but she had a body that was all wrong. She reminded me of a newborn foal, all spindly legs and not much else. Though only eleven, I was already aware and often critical of physical appearance, both my own and that of others. But the boys didn't care if Hannelore was all arms and legs. Her lack of guile and love of fun were the attraction, especially after her body filled out.

Elfriede was actually a native of Kirchheim, the daughter of a farmer who lived near the Ziegelwoog lake, around the corner from the Breitstraße. We hadn't met sooner because the family had gone to the Saar region just after our move from Marnheim. For more than two years, her father had farmed in the Saar near the French border. It was one of Hitler's programs that replaced Saar refugees like the Presser family that stayed with us during the war to defeat France.

In 1941, the Schwab family had come back to Kirchheim, and I found a new friend. I knew instantly that we could be best friends, but I was also envious of her. She was the perfect blue-eyed Aryan type so desired by the Nazis — even to the long blonde hair, braided and pinned up on her head. With my dark hair and brown eyes, it occurred to me more than once as a child that I might be cast out of the German race. "Look at me," Mama would say. "If they throw you out, I'll have to go too. This Aryan stuff is all talk."

That 'Aryan stuff' actually went far back in our history, long before Hitler and National Socialism. Frederick, a Prussian king and father of Frederick the Great, loved to surround himself with tall blonde men. He even sent out scouting parties over the land to search for such men. When found, and if they wouldn't come to serve in the king's court willingly, kidnapping was not unheard of. Frederick thought they best represented his idea of a super German race. Obviously, the Führer agreed. Service in the SS (Schutzstaffel), Hitler's personal military organization, was mostly limited to tall blonde recruits.

One concern Elfriede and I never had was boys. There were too many other interests and things to do during our three years with Herr Lawaldt. We both enjoyed school, and generally got excellent grades. She was especially good in math — my weak subject — but I was stronger in writing. We devoted much time to our progress, and got all of the young male attention we could endure from our older brothers. By the time any hormonal changes occurred, sometime around eighth grade, the school wisely put boys and girls into separate classes. In any case, by my eighth year of school, there would be no time for romantic notions.

The war had taken away several teachers in my school, so it fell to Herr Lawaldt to teach all classes except three. Two days a week, while the boys had shop crafts, the girls studied needlework. Together, we had religion twice a week, and on Saturday mornings, physical education. We look to Herr Lawaldt for math, history, grammar, social studies, writing, literature, ecology, music and art. He readily admitted lacking expertise in art or knowledge of a music instrument, but he tackled both subjects head on. For music class, he usually led us in singing folk songs, both in the classroom and while marching out to the countryside on field trips for ecology classes. It was one of my favorite classes. As for art, Herr Lawaldt had no special talents, but knew what he liked.

Herr Lawaldt was as much a father figure to us, as he was our teacher. Very few of us still had our fathers at home, not to mention older brothers, uncles, or male cousins. He seemed unaware of this role, but I liked to think that we helped him by filling the void left by his son's sacrifice to the Fatherland.

Aside from my parents and close friends, there is no one I tried harder to please than Lehrer Lawaldt. My homework was always in on time, in the best penmanship I could muster, and I participated in most subjects — not so easy for a shy girl. If he asked for three pages on Celtic tribes, I struggled to make it five with one or more illustrations. Adding pictures to writing assignments was not requested, so my first efforts were somewhat risky. Some teachers might consider the added 'art' a deviation from their instructions and would give a penalty, but Lawaldt didn't to my great relief. He wouldn't say anything directly when handing back my workbook in the first weeks. I had to flip quickly to the last assignment where he had written "Good!" or best of all: "Very industrious!"

It was a few months into the school year, when embarrassment and pleasure reached out to strike me in the back row. Lehrer Lawaldt had only begun the morning session.

"Annchen, come up front, please."

I was dumbstruck and rooted to my seat. In spite of all my efforts to please him, I never expected that he'd ever call me anything but my last name. To that day, the only exceptions he had made were for a couple of boys who often carried student workbooks and papers to his house for grading.

"Come, come, Märe," he urged, "I need you to put some work on the blackboard."

Shaking off my paralysis, I quickly moved toward the front, hardly believing what he continued to say to the class.

"I'm sure you've noticed that I've written very little on the blackboard. Until now, there hasn't been a need and, in any case, it's my practice with a new class to discover who is best suited to assist me at the blackboard. Several of you have good hand-writing skills and I will be calling on you from time to time." Turning and nodding to me, now standing at the board, he added, "However, Annchen here will probably have the most burden, since she is taller than most and has a knack for drawing.

One Wednesday noon, when I returned home from the half-day school session, I found that my older cousin Martha had just walked over from Marnheim. Her news was upsetting, especially to Mama. Her brother Adam had just received a Wehrmacht draft notice. Martha's usual smiling round face was stained from crying, and she had come to look for comfort from her Tante Marie. The draft order had come as a shock for many reasons. Adam was in his early fifties, with seven children, and had already served Germany in World War I.

Mama was beside herself with anger; more so, it seemed to me, than when

Papa was called in. "How can this be? Adam served in the last war. He's too old to go again," she said, spitting the words out. "It has to be a mistake. He should appeal."

My uncle had been in the cavalry in the war of 1914. It was the best duty, he often said, since he got along so well with horses. His contact with the animals continued over the years by way of his profession of crafting harness and saddles. It was no longer a prosperous trade, but it provided a fair living for Tante Elise and seven children. All but one of my cousins were still at home. Hans was already taken into the army.

"Come, Märe, let's walk back to Marnheim with Martha. I need to speak with my brother. I must tell him to appeal!"

Since it appeared my lunch was forgotten, I reached to slice off bread to nibble on the way. It was a five-kilometer walk, and I had a habit of getting faint on an empty stomach.

"Ach, mein Gott," Mama exclaimed. "I have soup on the stove we haven't eaten. Come, Martha, you must be hungry, too. We'll eat before our hike to Marnheim."

On our arrival in Marnheim, I was surprised to find my uncle sitting in his usual place at the corner workbench in the kitchen, still working on a harness. His eyes lit up at our approach, and he shouted a happy greeting through the open window. "How nice of you to come over for a farewell, Mariechen." Spotting me, he added in typical Herbst fashion, "And you. It's been a while since you visited. Come, turn around and let me see how much longer your braids are!"

The Herbst and Klein men were just alike in loving long hair on the women folk.

Telling Martha to put on water for coffee, Onkel Adam told Mama he wouldn't appeal his call up, because he knew why the army wanted him. "You know, our army still uses horses to pull many of the guns and wagons at the front. They'll just put me to repairing harness. It won't be dangerous. Besides, all the horses will soon be replaced by motor trucks, and I can come home."

"How can you be so sure?"

"My dear sister, this new war can't be fought for long with horses! The Luftwaffe was smart. You notice they drafted both your husband and his truck. Machines have to replace horses in the army soon, or we'll lose this war. That is certain."

Chapter Nineteen

In October, I had a short school holiday, and Mama said we could visit Papa in Gießen. My pestering had paid off, or so I thought. I soon learned that our trip had more to do with Hans, the hired driver, not working out. Erich still had to meet his once-a-week academic requirement, and couldn't always keep a sharp eye on Hans. My brother was still not a "full-fledged Kleine Seppel," or so Papa said. With only the occasional call from an old customer and other chance orders, business had dropped by half.

A few incidents had my mother questioning Hans' honesty. There was the mysterious disappearance of a good sum of money that had been intended to buy diesel fuel for the truck. Hans claimed he didn't know about it, but Mama knew better — she just couldn't prove it. She kept the anger inside until she could see Papa. Erich was told to stay. Mama wanted him to keep an eye on things, though he didn't know it at the time.

"I don't think the house should be left empty for two days," she told him. "There's Fips and the chickens to feed. Someone may call with a job, and you need to be here to help Hans anyway."

Erich liked being on his own, so there wasn't a peep of protest. He was fast taking on a manly attitude. I was torn about leaving him at home. The bright side of my dilemma was that I'd be having Papa mostly to myself.

It was mid-morning when our train left the Kirchheimbolanden station. Mama said it would probably take at least three hours to reach Gießen, and we would have to change trains in Frankfurt. I didn't mind. Riding in trains was one of my favorite things to do. Mostly, my trips had been short hops to nearby villages and cities to visit relatives or to shop. Only my journey to the Kinderheim in Bad Kissingen had been farther than Gießen.

The first leg of our ride toward Gießen was on a local train that stopped at the smallest villages on the way. From my window seat, I got the chance to take a longer look at places I'd never seen. This would change at Frankfurt, where Mama said we'd catch a fast train. I remembered that Erich had once said that all the small places are just a blur on a fast train.

Gazing at the changing scenery, my mind wandered. I thought of all the changes that seemed to threaten my stable and protected existence. For the moment, I still remained quite happy and secure in my world. All was well with school. I had my friends, old and new. I loved my family, my home, my town. I had my music, a dog, and a bicycle. But, even with all of that, I recognized that things had somehow become unnatural. No one should have to keep a gas mask, have black-out curtains on the windows, or go to a bomb shelter every-day. Was it possible to become used to living under a daily threat of violent death? The worse thing of all was having loved ones sent to fight in a war that I didn't understand. It all seemed too much for a young girl to think about.

There was, however, a positive side to Papa's absence — it forced my mother to give me some responsibilities sooner than she would have. I'd re-cently taken on more important errands like picking up the monthly allowance at the government finance office. The money came from Papa being in the Luftwaffe. He was just a second level private, and the pay didn't amount to much, but Mama made it last a month, and saved some too. My father loved saying that his wife turned over a pfennig ten times before spending it.

Watching out of the train window, I had to smile thinking about the first time I went to pick up 'Fritz Kleins sei Geld.' The official just stared in disbelief hearing the purpose of my visit. He wasn't about to hand over a fistful of money to a pig-tailed child. Then I remembered I had a note from Mama. He read it and counted out the money.

"Hold on to that money tight and don't dawdle on the way home."

"Is that what my mother said in the note to tell me?" I didn't think she had, and his remark upset me. "She already told me not to 'dawdle' when I left home!"

I didn't wait to hear his reply to my fresh mouth. I was out the door in a flash, my fingers clamped around the Reichmarks in a vice-grip as I ran all the way home.

My reverie on the changes in my life was interrupted as I noticed a very different view through the window. We were no longer running through rural countryside — the fields, trees, and livestock were gone. Our train had entered a congested area of dingy buildings. The wheels beneath us clattered and our car swayed as the train seemed to pitch itself from one set of tracks to another. Soon, all I could see were tracks and other trains of every sort.

I looked at Mama to see her reaction to the passing scene, a jumble of freight and passenger trains, some moving, but many standing still. Across the wide rail yard small work crews were moving around, seemingly uncon-cerned about the heavy traffic of smoke-belching locomotives. They appeared to be struggling to repair bomb damage. Big holes and twisted track could be seen here and there. I heard another passenger say that not all the bombs had exploded, and that it was hazardous work. I marveled at the workers' fearless-ness.

"Good," Mama said, her first utterance in awhile. She usually didn't talk much in the midst of strangers. "We're coming into the Frankfurt Hauptbahnhof, and not a moment too soon. We will have to hurry to make our other train."

"Haven't you been here before?" I hadn't thought to ask her before, and I began to worry. "How will we find the right train?" We were coming to a halt, and from what I could see through the window, it was overwhelming.

"Nay, Märe. I've never been to Frankfurt, but they do speak German here." A couple seated across from us smiled at her reply. Mama did have a way with words, when she wanted. Getting up to move toward the exit, she warned me not to leave her side. I had no plans to do otherwise.

We stepped down to the platform, and began our hike to the main station and assembly area. Weaving our way through the crowd of travelers, Mama held her purse close, and grabbed my hand.

With so many people swirling around me, it was hard to take everything in. The Frankfurt Hauptbahnhof was a major rail junction, and for the uninitiated, changing trains was a challenge. As I looked around, I saw people in uniforms of all kinds. It was exciting to recognize members of the Hitler Jugend and BDM girls, serving drinks and sandwiches to men in uniform. Suddenly I noticed that wounded soldiers were being brought through on stretchers and in wheelchairs. A trainload of wounded must have just arrived, and I saw many of them being taken outside to waiting ambulances in the street. Crowds blocking their way through the huge lobby instantly parted to let them pass. I hadn't expected to see war casualties, and asked Mama about it.

"Hush, Märe," she replied, guiding me toward a stairway going down into a tunnel. "We mustn't talk about it here."

As usual, she never explained why. I was too fascinated by our scramble to catch a train to press the issue. We hurried along the tunnel, passing many other stairways going up to train platforms.

"It's a good thing everything is marked so well," Mama said, shouting and pointing to signs and arrows along the way. "We can't possibly lose our way."

I heard a brass band playing, and its off-key rendering made me think it had to be another Hitler Jugend group. They often played for soldiers returning from the war front.

We took the next stairs up to our waiting train. I had hoped to see the youth band one platform over from ours, but as luck would have it, the train we boarded blocked the view. Germans love their march music, so it was no surprise to see that many of the other passengers had windows lowered to listen. Despite the clamor and hissing of nearby locomotives, I recognized every tune played.

The third-class car we got on was already full, as was the next, and after searching through four cars, we finally found facing window seats. Soon after we settled in, the sensation of released brakes and the inevitable jerk signaled our departure. I noticed when getting on the so-called 'fast train,' it was much different from our first train.

"That's because this train has dining cars and several sleepers with private compartments," Mama explained. "It costs a lot of money to travel that way."

I would have liked exploring the first-class accommodations, but I knew she'd say no. I'd seen how rich people traveled in the movies, and the excitement of soon seeing Papa kept me glued to the seat as I watched the world fly by my window. Erich had been right. Everything close by, was a blur on a fast train.

Mama unwrapped the sandwiches and gave me one. "Watch you don't soil your new cardigan."

"I'll be careful." I was anxious to show Papa the new sweater made with the yarn he had brought from France. Mama had seemed pleased with my first big knitting project, especially the little flowers I embroidered on it.

We were among the few civilians in the train car. Almost all of the passengers were men in uniforms very much like my father's. I told Mama they must all be going to Gießen, and on our arrival, it proved to be true. Getting up from our seats to leave, it brought a smile and a "Danke" from Mama when the soldiers allowed us to go first.

I think we were both relieved to find the Gießen station not nearly so big as the station at Frankfurt, but again we had to make our way through crowds of soldiers. Happily, none were wounded. I didn't see him right away, but Papa was there, patiently waiting by the platform gate. When I finally spotted him, a grin and waving hand made me want to run to his embrace, but Mama held my hand tight. That served to remind me that I was now "a big girl, and should act like one." This had become one of her pet admonitions. Papa was of a different mind, as he grabbed me in one of his super hugs the moment we came through the gate. "How is my Märe?" He laughed, squeezing so hard I couldn't breathe. Turning to Mama, he patted her cheek. "How was the trip?" That was all the affection she would allow in public.

Walking toward the streetcar stop, he told Mama and I he had arranged for us to stay overnight in the nearby village of Daubringen. "Gießen is no place for us. Too much military." He said, looking at me. "But first, I'll show you where I live." We climbed onto a streetcar that took us out of the town center to the outskirts of the city, and to the entrance of an enormous air base. I was surprised by how boring it all looked.

"Where are the airplanes and hangers and runways??"

"What?" Papa said, laughing. "Ach, Annchen, all that is on the other side of the base and I can't take you there. Believe me, it's nothing so wonderful."

Later, I learned Gießen could be a dangerous place when the British made it a target. For the moment, I satisfied my curiosity by looking around Papa's barracks, where he slept in a big open room with his comrades. Mama and I met some of his friends, and one of them joined us outside the barracks and took a photograph showing me standing between my parents.

I noticed that wherever we walked around outside, Papa saluted other men in uniform when they came near us. He said they were officers, and lowly privates like him had to salute them. "That's why I want us to get away from here until tomorrow," he said, after saluting another young man. "I'm tired of this game of saluting officers barely old enough to vote!" He laughed, adding, "I have an overnight pass. Let's leave this place and get on to Daubringen!"

With that, the three of us marched out of the main gate to a bus stop and took a short ride to the small quiet village. Papa had already made reservations for our stay at a Gasthaus, a new experience for me. The room had two single beds. My parents would sleep in one and I in the other. I was reminded of the Marnheim days.

Following supper downstairs in the dining room, Papa thought we'd enjoy a walk around the village, as we still had early evening light. The only interesting thing I saw as we walked was a dome-shaped brick oven in the village square. I'd read about the community ovens in my history class, but it was Mama who got the most excited as we all took a closer look.

"Would you look at this. It's just like the old village ovens we used to have in the Pfalz. Feel the side, it's still warm!"

"Ja, Frau. Too bad it's Sunday tomorrow and no baking. You'd probably find it interesting how the village ladies bring bread dough to the oven."

It made me think that the aroma wafting through the village had to be wonderful on baking days. The very idea of it almost made me hungry again.

Back in our room, I was more than willing to turn in for the night. The excitement of a full day of train travel and seeing Papa had made me bone-weary. Under my down-filled comforter, it was only seconds before my mind and body drifted toward sleep while Mama continued talking to Papa about business at home. Their voices and pieces of conversation came to me in waves, and the sound provided a sense of comfort in the strange bed.

"Come, sleepy head, you can't be wasting away these few hours with me!"

Papa's hand had found my cheek half-hidden by the thick comforter. It all fell into my dream of being in my bed at home. There was no war, just happy times and Papa patting my cheek to wake me before heading out to work.

"Yesterday must have worn her out," a voice said. "These days she's often out of bed before me!"

(In my dream state I wanted to say, "That's true. Mama has a harder time getting out of bed lately.") Suddenly my eyes snapped open to see Papa's smiling face. Across the room, my mother stood in front of the mirror, pinning a coil of braided hair behind an ear. In that instant, I knew where I was and how little time remained with Papa. No further prodding was needed to get me up.

We went again to the dining room for breakfast where, for the first time in my life, I had a fried egg on top of ham. The slice of bread with it was so big, it had to be cut in two for me to handle. Papa then took us for another stroll, saying we'd enjoy seeing a different kind of Sunday scene in that part of Germany.

Leaving the Gasthaus, we discovered numerous people making their way along narrow cobbled streets into and out of the village square. The one large church situated there seemed to be the main reason. As in Kirchheim, there were almost no young men to be seen except those in uniform who served at the nearby air base. The rest were women of all ages, some children, and a few very old men. The men seemed to all have big walrus mustaches. What fascinated me, and Mama too, were the costumes worn by the women and many of the young girls.

We knew that all regions of Germany had costumes particular to the area. Aside from different color patterns and combinations found elsewhere, the Pfälzer costume also had heavily gathered skirts, decorative tight vests over white puffy-sleeved blouses, all topped off by large colorful shawls. But ours was worn only for celebrations. In Daubringen and surrounding villages, Papa said, women could be seen wearing the local costume even during the week, with a nicer version worn on Sundays.

The three of us found a bench under a linden tree facing the open market square to take in the curious sight of so many women dressed in the same fashion. Something else separated the Daubringen scene from any I ever had seen at home. All the women, from the youngest to the grayest, had combed their hair straight up and twisted it, creating a single knob that was pinned on top of the head. Many had a tight black cap over the round knob, securing it with long bands hanging down and tied under the chin.

Mama was the first to react. "Fritz, do you think the ones with the black caps belong to a religious sect?"

Papa laughed. "Ach, how should I know. Do you think I asked any of them?" He looked from Mama to a group of women nearby. "Just don't you get any ideas. I like your hair the way it is."

He knew his wife was becoming more religious everyday. I don't think it was a big problem for him — he was simply concerned about her getting radical. My father believed that the radicals of the world caused the most problems.

Leaving the bench, the three of us left the village, walking into the countryside a short distance. It was clear my parents hadn't reached a decision about the trucking business after I had fallen asleep. Turning into a quieter farm lane, my mother insisted on having a decision before boarding the late afternoon train back to Kirchheim.

I was sandwiched between them as we strolled, Papa's arm around my shoulders. "Couldn't we stay another night, please?" The question came from a surge of hope that Papa might need more time to mull the problem over. He squeezed me closer.

"My dear daughter," he said finally, a sad smile on his face. "How I wish you could stay another day. The problem is, I won't be here myself. I have orders to drive supplies into France."

For once I was silent — some things can't be protested. We walked a short distance to a clump of trees, all that broke the line of an otherwise flat plain. It was a good place to rest a few minutes in the crisp air and warm autumn sun. Soon it would be time to head back to Daubringen for lunch, and back to the Gießen train station. Papa appeared to be deep in thought, commenting only now and then about things like the "tasty" Gasthaus food, my "very pretty" new cardigan, and the flat and nearly treeless landscape around Gießen. "Flat and boring," he said, "but a good place for an air base!"

As we approached the train station, he finally revealed his decision. Mama's patience had been diminishing by the minute.

"Say nothing to Hans, now. It's best that I handle the matter. Try to keep the young man busy until I can arrange to come. That way, I'll be able to help him find a position with someone else. Erich will have to return to his apprenticeship at Hirschbiel's. I should be there to break that news too, in case he makes a fuss. Afterwards, we'll store the truck. You're right that we can't afford to run it, make repairs, and pay wages under the present conditions. It's this war. Who knows when it will end? I don't think it will be soon."

It was strange to speak of war on that day of sunshine and quiet. But for all the uniforms in view, our brief visit to Gießen was undisturbed by any blatant signs of hostility. I had expected Luftwaffe planes to be constantly flying overhead, but I saw nothing, either in the air or on the ground. My father explained the unreal setting.

"Ja, the peace here is ironic. The fighting and killing doesn't stop for Sunday in Russia and Africa. Everywhere in this war, death cares not at all about the name of the day. Everywhere, but in the Reich. Here, for most ordinary people, Sunday remains a day of rest. I believe our Führer wants it that way."

I knew that Papa was speaking in general terms. Whatever the day, Germany still flew bombing raids from isolated locations to England and elsewhere. Troops and supplies were still on the move to and from battle zones. A visit to any major rail center was witness to that reality, but it was also true that in the early war years, a strong effort was made to make life within the Reich normal. That the effort succeeded on many levels is astonishing. By late 1941, though, few Germans anywhere in the country could ignore the conditions of war inside or outside our borders.

At the train station, Papa hugged and kissed us both. For once, Mama's reluctance to show affection in public didn't make her push him away. In fact, as we passed through the gate, I was surprised at the warmth of her farewell, "Take care, Fritz."

He stood by the gate until the train began moving. I watched and waved at him, wishing he were coming home with us.

Chapter Twenty

"It's all for the best."

Papa came home in late October to close the business, and during every step of the process, Mama repeated the words to cover up the blow to her pride.

"Ja, ja, Mariechen." It was Papa's answer each time.

As on the previous occasions when the future of the Klein family was at stake, we all sat around the kitchen table discussing the options. Of course, Mama and Papa did most of the talking and deciding, though Erich was allowed more say. I had my own thoughts, but hardly spoke unless I was personally affected. In a matter like this, I was more than happy to let older and wiser heads prevail.

It had been a busy day for Papa after arriving home late the night before. Hans was let go, but not without my father's help in locating another job.

It was also arranged for Erich to return to Hirschbiel's machine shop, and remarkably, he put up little protest. "It'll only be for a few months before I'm drafted into the R.A.D. Helmut and Franz are already gone, and I hear they like it.

"Mama and Papa looked at each other, but said nothing. They knew the next step after the Reich Arbeits Dienst was military service. Erich couldn't wait to go. I always felt lonely thinking about Erich leaving home, and my mood didn't improve with Papa's words. "We won't be storing the truck. I found a buyer while helping Hans find a new position. The offer was good, since new trucks are no longer available. They'll pick it up tomorrow."

The Luftwaffe confiscation of our new truck, the loss of another in the Rhein bombing, and now the forced sale were all a hard blow after so many years of struggle to make a better life.

"Come now," Papa said, trying to be cheerful. "Turn up the radio. Maybe there's good news about our boys in Russia."

"How could there be bad news?" my brother said. "We've been beating the ragtag Russian army every step of the way!"

An evening music program had ended, followed by several seconds of silence. As usual, the heroic passage from Franz Liszt's "Les Prelude" introduced a series of reports on the latest successes in Germany's great crusade against our enemies on the eastern front and elsewhere.

Erich brought his big atlas book to the table so we could find the places the announcer talked about. Studying the Russian map, it seemed that our armies were attacking everywhere unimpeded.

"It may all be going too fast," Papa murmured.

"But that's how you're supposed to hit the enemy," Erich boasted. "The Blitzkrieg worked in Poland, and it'll work again."

"You have to listen between the lines." Papa's voice was stern with warning. "Winter is already on the Wehrmacht's heels. We'll see if Hitler and all his generals can do better than Napoleon with the Russian winter. I think they've forgotten Russia isn't only very big, it's also very poor. There are few hard surface roads for our soldiers and machines to travel on."

Mama was getting visibly upset with Papa. "I don't want you talking like that. We must believe in our leaders. I'm sure the Führer has everything planned."

My brother and I both believed in Hitler and the army, but I also sensed that Mama had great fear about Russia, despite efforts to conceal it with angry words. The Hitler Jugend had done a good job of making me believe in the Führer, but I didn't want to think my father was wrong.

Papa had one more full day with us. The truck was driven away in the morning, so he borrowed Erich's bicycle to visit Bolanden in the afternoon. There were brothers and sisters to visit, but most important was his mother. Skipping school was forbidden, and that was all that prevented me from tagging along. During supper later that evening, he told us of Oma Klein's worry. Not a word had come from her youngest son, Ludwig, in many weeks. Papa promised to get news about Ludwig from the Wehrmacht, but doubted success.

Following supper clean up, we again sat around the table to talk. This time, Papa didn't want to dwell on war or politics, and kept the conversation focused on home and family. While asking me about school and music lessons, Erich stood to leave.

"Sit down, Erich."

My brother was surprised by Papa's stern order, having become independent in his father's absence. He sat.

"I'm told you spend many evenings debating on Bossung's corner with your friends. If your tasks are finished I can't object, but tonight I want us together. Who knows when we'll all be at this table again. This war is bound to get worse before the end. Now there's talk of America coming in on the side of England, like in the past. If that happens, only God can save Germany."

For once there was no protest to his words. Mama's hands kept brushing away crumbs from the tabletop, and Erich stared blankly at the motion of her hands. I couldn't take my eyes from Papa's face.

"Surely you'll be home for Christmas, Papa!" It was I who asked.

"With the way things are, I can't promise. Of course, I'll try to come, but don't expect it. We all must sacrifice."

These were hard words to hear. Christmas was just weeks away and I believed Papa could do anything he set his mind to. I also knew that the subject was closed when Papa slapped the tabletop and smiled brightly.

"Erich, go down to the cellar and bring up a bottle of red wine for your mother to make Glühwein. On such a chilly evening, I think we can all stand a tasty hot drink."

My brother was out the door in a flash. It wasn't often we got in on hot spiced wine. My intake of wine had been restricted to sips from another person's glass. As if reading my mind, Papa smiled at me, and spoke to Mama. "I don't think you need to dilute Annchen's portion with mineral water this time. She's old enough to taste real Glühwein. Besides, the heating up takes out most of the alcohol." Mama gave a look I couldn't quite read, but she may have been planning to water down the entire batch. Erich returned, uncorked the bottle, and handed it to her. Perhaps it occurred to her that it wasn't a good time to haggle. The Glühwein was served full strength.

Thus began an evening of family celebration, despite what was happening in the world outside Breitstraße One. We spoke only of happy memories and future hopes and my progress in school. It was just like Papa to demand to know what I was doing in school. Our learning was always of interest to him. Mama's big concern was that we not misbehave. I told Papa of how I liked my new teacher.

"Ja, I know of Lehrer Lawaldt. Erich had him for a while. He's a good man. The Lawaldt family has been in Kirchheim many generations. I'm not surprised he knows so much about this area."

We also talked a lot about what would happen after the war. Papa talked most, and we listened. Dreaming and scheming about the future was all part of being a true 'Seppel' in search of a green twig.

"Erich will be older and a real help in building our business again when this mess is over. We'll start out right away with two trucks and go from there, hiring more drivers as we grow."

Erich agreed with Papa's plans wholeheartedly, saying that it was just what he wanted.

Turning to me, my father's enthusiasm grew. "And you! You can learn bookkeeping and run the office. Your mother can ease up and devote more time to home and other things."

While I didn't answer, my face must have said it all. Being a bookkeeper was definitely not my dream.

He reacted to my look, but guessed wrong. "Of course, I could probably get you a job in one of the banks, if you'd like that better. I just thought you should be a part of our business."

I looked at Mama's absolute blank expression. Papa clearly didn't understand how much she enjoyed being a business person. The role of a housekeeper who socialized with neighbor ladies over coffee every afternoon wasn't her goal. I knew it, but for different reasons, neither of us protested. She was disappointed in him, and I didn't want him to be disappointed in me.

"That's fine, Papa. If you want me in the office, I'll be glad to help."

Papa didn't warn us that he'd be on his way back to Gießen before we awoke in the morning. I'm not even sure Mama knew his plans when we all turned in for the night. Perhaps he wanted to avoid any emotional farewells.

❧

The fall of 1941 saw my mother wanting to expand her spiritual life. Her need affected me as well. After going by herself once or twice, Mama began taking me along to Wednesday evening prayer meetings in a nearby house. She said I needed to go because of my mandatory Hitler Jugend rallies on Sunday mornings.

My classmates and I weren't completely deprived of religion. Both Protestant and Catholic children had two hours each week of required religious studies in school. A pastor and a priest came twice a week to train their respective young flocks. Protestants far outnumbered Catholics, so the latter had to leave their usual classrooms to meet elsewhere in the building. I remember one aspect of the religion classes that had little to do with the students. Because the class was the last in the school day, and my usual route home passed by the White Horse Inn, I commonly saw the priest and the pastor entering the inn together for ecumenical glasses of wine.

Wednesday evenings now saw us going to the family Webers house on the Schillerstraße near us. Mama called the Webers "Missionaries." To me

197

Papa at the time he was called back to war for the second time by the Luftwaffe. I am glad I saved it.

'Missionaries' were people who took religion to primitive lands. The Webers were German, or at least he was. Frau Weber's darker complexion and an odd accent made me think she was not born in Germany. She played the Harmonium whenever we sang hymns. The meeting room was reached by walking down a long hall, past the Weber's living quarters. About thirty people gathered for Bible study, prayer and songs. I was the youngest in the group, but I liked the feeling of togetherness and the chance to pray for our leaders and soldiers. Mostly, I prayed for Papa's safety. Weber never prayed directly about Hitler, but I did, to myself. After the meetings, Mama always liked to stay several minutes talking to the Webers. Since I never knew her to have long conversations with anyone, these private chats surprised me. It was as if she needed a special outlet.

Around Erich's sixteenth birthday, another prayer meeting was added on Saturday evenings. It was during this time that Papa's worst fear became reality. Japan's December seventh attack on Pearl Harbor brought America into the war against us. Lehrer Lawaldt talked to us briefly about it the next school day. His expression was grim, and I wondered if he was thinking about his son. Whatever his thoughts, he quickly diverted our attention, and our day of studies went on with no further discussion on the matter.

In the following days, the tension and gloom were evident everywhere in Kirchheim. For me, the news simply added to my worry that Papa might not be home for Christmas.

December also brought unusual heavy snowfall and bitter cold. Talk was that it was the worst winter weather in memory, and many people compared it to the harsh Russian winter hammering our soldiers. Onkel Adolf's job of delivering packages with the postal carriage was near impossible, and his other task of trying to keep the streets open for traffic became a dawn to dusk effort. The big wooden plow pushed the snow into towering barriers along both sides of the street. It wasn't unusual in my youth to see snow cover on the ground all winter, but continuing snow and extreme cold was a new experience. Daily, I had to shovel a path from the front door to the plowed street, only to have my uncle and his plow make a mess of my work.

Another worry was the build up of snow against basement windows. Erich got bales of straw to cover our two windows to keep the basement dry, and he wrapped straw around the exposed water lines on the ground floor to prevent freezing. And just like Papa, he sat before the iron cook stove feeding in the right amount of wood and coal to keep the oven going for Mama's Christmas cookies. Clearly, my brother was taking his role of man of the house very serious.

"Your Papa taught you well," Mama told him.

Terrible weather or not, Mama kept to her preferred places to buy bread and milk. We had a bakery and a dairy within a block distance, but her choices were five and six blocks away. Since I always treated errands with speed, I nearly killed myself for a liter can of milk one early evening.

"Märe, go down to Baum's. I need milk for supper."

"Mama, its bitter cold out and my winter coat is too small!"

"My boots will fit you even if my coat is still too large. Just put on two or three heavy sweaters. You'll stay warm. Here's the milk can, now go!"

I piled on the sweaters and climbed into boots a bit big for me. Rushing down the steps, I thought Mama hollered something after me. I didn't stop. Making my way through the snow piles to the street, a blast of wind-driven flakes hit my face like needles. It was then that I realized Mama had tried to remind me to wear a scarf. The house was only a few steps back, but I wasn't about to ruin my reputation for speedy errands. As best as I could in oversized boots, I continued to run down to the Langstraße. Turning the corner, I was stunned to find that Onkel Adolf had missed plowing the Langstraße that day.

"Onkel!" I shouted out in anger and frustration.

Foot deep snow covered the street from one side to the other, for as far as I could see. No one had even tried to walk that way for there wasn't a single footstep to follow. The dairy store was four long blocks away. Stepping gingerly, I prayed the snow stayed below the boot tops and discovered again that such prayers are useless. Changing to a run, or at least an attempt at it, I carved a cold path down the winding street.

Fräulein Baum was startled by the miserable vision coming through the shop door. Without a scarf, the snow had turned my hair white, and as it melted, water ran down and off the ends of my braids — making puddles on the floor. Filling the milk can, she looked at me as if to say "so little milk wasn't worth the effort."

It was easier going back along my own trail, though still a struggle going uphill, facing the wind and beating snow. I think the only dry parts of my body were those covered by sweater layers, but despite the sweaters and all the energy being put into the climb, I began shaking with a terrible chill. I knew I shouldn't breathe through my mouth, but I had to. The freezing air made my nostrils hurt terribly.

Finally getting inside our front door, I had to sit a while on the bottom step before going up. It was all I could do to keep from dropping the milk can, I was shaking so violently from the chill. Then my hands started burning, a weird sensation in the unheated hall and stairway.

After a few minutes, my shivering had subsided enough to carry the milk on up to Mama. Stepping into the hot kitchen, my legs gave way. Fortunately, she had turned toward the door and was able to reach out and grab both the can and me. "Gott im Himmel! Märe, you're white as a sheet. Sit and bend your head down."

Since I was getting ready to both faint and vomit, and maybe die all at the same time, I gladly did her bidding.

In no time, she had me stripped of wet clothes and wrapped in a warm blanket. She toweled my hair dry and combed it out as I sat in front of the stove, my feet propped up on the open oven door. There was no scolding. Perhaps she realized a scarf wouldn't have been much protection in the severe weather. Her caring touch almost made risking my health worthwhile. Only in sickness was Mama able to show me an open loving concern.

Hot chamomile tea to sip, constituted the rest of my care to ward off illness. By some miracle, I didn't come down with pneumonia — not even a cold — on that day or any of the terrible winter days ahead.

December twenty-third was our last day of school, and there still had been no word from Papa about coming home for Christmas. I tried not to be selfish, reminding myself that few families in Kirchheim would have their men in uniform home to celebrate.

During my school years, for the Christmas season, the matter of classroom decorations and activities was a personal decision of each teacher. Since it was to be our first Christmas with Lehrer Lawaldt, we didn't know what to expect until the last day. We learned that he had created his own tradition for the last day — reading aloud stories by the author Peter Rosegger. I'd never heard of Rosegger, and his tales of life in the Austrian Alps, but after Lawaldt's introduction I became a loyal fan.

Ending a brief period of singing Christmas carols, Lawaldt asked us to sit and settle down. He then retrieved a book from a high shelf in the case by the window. All the books on the lower shelves we knew about. These we could browse on inclement weather days during recess. The highest shelf held some of his personal books, taken down at special times.

"I want you to become acquainted with a favorite writer of mine," he began, taking his own seat. "Peter Rosegger was born in the nineteenth century in the high mountains of Austria, spending most of his life writing about the land and people, and his own life. For today, a Christmas story from his collection of tales about being the young son of a poor mountain farmer. The book is called, "Als ich noch ein Waldbauernbub war." (When I Was Still a Forest Farmer's Son.)

Lawaldt turned to the chapter he wanted and began to read. First sitting at his desk, then moving slowly among us, he turned Rosegger's words into a spellbinding tale of a desperate struggle against winter elements in the Alps on Christmas Eve.

It was no stretch of the truth to say that not a breath could be heard in our classroom. Lawaldt, a wonderful reader, made the first-person account of a long ago Christmas Eve so real, I was right there on the mountain with the book's hero. Following an exciting ending, one that brought an audible sigh of relief from my part of the room, our teacher told us more about Rosegger.

"Peter Rosegger wrote many books and went on to great success in his lifetime. He spent much of his income from writing toward improving public education and establishing libraries in his region. If any of you wish, I can give you titles of Rosegger books. Perhaps you can find one to read over the holiday."

We were released early from school, and on the way home I ran into Erich. Mama had sent him to buy a Christmas tree in the marketplace. "Mama says we can't wait for Papa to come home to cut a tree in the forest. It's for sure Papa won't be home."

That made me angry. "He will come. I know he will!"

"There you go again," Erich replied, turning to be on his way.

I couldn't believe what he'd said, and was so furious I didn't even want to ask him if I could help pick out a tree. Instead I went home and helped Mama as she scurried about cleaning before the short day turned dark. My last chore was going around closing the window shutters and pulling down the blackout blinds.

Before closing the front shutters, I looked out and saw that Frau Rösel's house across the street was already dark. I knew that she must be having a tough time keeping the thoughts of four children off of their Papa. Next door, Frau Andres had to be lonely for her husband Heiner. After leaving for the army, a third daughter had arrived.

Back in the kitchen, I found Mama preparing food and Erich listening to the radio with his nose in a book. Fips lay at his feet, but scooted over to me when I sat down. Reaching down to scratch his chin, one of his ears perked up, followed by the other. Normally, I would have caught on, but in my melancholy his signal went unnoticed until we all heard Papa's boots on the stairs.

Christmas 1941 saw the Kleins decorate the tree one more time as a family.

Chapter Twenty-One

The start of 1942 brought with it an awful truth — the Blitzkrieg tactics that had been so successful in Poland were failing in Russia. No indication of this came our way 'officially.' The radio reports still portrayed German military progress in the east with glory. The weekly Wochenschau (newsreels) at the local theater only supported the upbeat messages from Berlin heard on the radio. The Wochenschau wasn't a regular part of my week, but you can be sure Erich happily provided vivid accounts of what he saw. Nowhere was there a public expression over the course of the war, but the worry was there, growing slowly with every bombing, with every life lost on faraway battlefields.

St. Paul's Kirche — The ancient and smaller St. Peter's across the Amtsstraße was not considered suitable for a royal family and so, adjacent to the palace property, a much larger St. Paul's was built. A special entrance was created to allow private access to the newer church from the Palace garden. Common folk were allowed to attend and did, but only on the ground floor well below the royal family. Mozart at 15 years was already well known. In 1778 he was invited by Princess Caroline to play the massive pipe organ. Ever afterward it would be called the "Mozart – orgel."

Approaching my twelfth birthday, I still couldn't face the thought of disaster for my country. Like many other people, I was learning to shut out fear by refusing to doubt Germany's invincibility and just purpose. In my small world, there was plenty to be upset about already. With Papa gone, Mama had to be the family's bulwark against the larger world closing in. As long as her faith in Hitler remained total, my brother and I had to believe also.

꙰

On my way to school one day, I saw workmen gathered at the base of the Catholic church tower just down and across from my house. Farther along down the Amtsstraße, scaffolding had been built next to the steeple of my church, St. Peter's.

The purpose of all this was a mystery to me, until after classes when I was stunned to see that the great bells of both churches were being crated and loaded onto trucks. I ran up to one worker leaning against a bell not yet encased in wood. I had never seen any church bell up close, but having listened to them nearly all my life, and loving the sound, I was on the verge of tears fearing the worst.

"What are you doing with my bells?" I demanded.

"Your bells? I'm afraid the Führer needs to borrow them to make more cannon for his war!"

That shut me up. If Hitler ordered it, what good were protests. The worker must have felt my pain as I stood there.

"Here take a look before we crate her up."

The raised letters and the few Roman numerals circled the top and bottom. Moving my hand over the Latin words I had to worry aloud "You're not taking all the bells?"

"Nay, Märe." He paused and added, "Not now, anyway."

I walked home in sadness. For many months the government had called on all Germans to collect and turn in scrap metals — even the foil from cigarette packages — but taking our bells was much too great a sacrifice. Sunday mornings, New Year's Eve, weddings and funerals in Kirchheim would never ring out in quite the same way again. As I entered my house, it occurred to me that maybe there would never be another reason to ring the bells.

꙰

While I knew nothing of concentration camps, everyone in town was aware of the prisoner-of-war camps operating in the Kirchheim area. Since the invasion of Poland in 1939, war prisoners had been brought into various locations

204

in Kirchheim and the neighboring villages. They were mostly Polish men, and while they were called 'laborers,' all were, in fact, prisoners. The local camps were controlled by the Arbeits Kommando 1028 (Work Command). In 1940, after Hitler's victory in France, the number of prisoners in our midst increased dramatically, filling twenty-nine "Stalags," the name we gave to the camps set up in the Kirchheim district. In 1942, there were added many French prisoners, and some Russian prisoners were to follow.

The Hollywood depiction of a 'Stalag' is one of wood barracks surrounded by strong fences, barbed wire, and high guard towers. This wasn't the case where I lived. By the year's end, some 976 French, 333 Poles, 5 Belgians, and 35 Russians were being held in the district, mostly in former dance halls. The numbers come from the city archives.

Kirchheim had three of these Stalags in the town proper, one just a block up Breitstraße from my house. There, the authorities had taken over the Schilling Inn ballroom for about thirty prisoners. They were mainly Polish and Russian, with just a few French. No American was ever kept there, though later there was opportunity to do so when pilots were captured in the area. The prisoners slept in the ballroom under guard and were fed by Ernst Schilling, the inn's owner. (Actually, it was Shilling's wife and daughter Anneliese preparing food, because Ernst had been drafted.) During the day, many captives were marched out of town to work in stone quarries, small factories, and on farms. Of the other two Stalags in the town, one was in another inn on the Amtsstraße near my school. We were told that all prisoners had to work to help in the war effort. Our Hitler Jugend leader said this was because so many German men were in uniform, and Hitler would never ask German wives and mothers to do war work. Their place was in the home, nurturing the next generation.

The reality never came close to the ideal promoted by our Führer, even with prisoners of war labor. Everywhere in German factories, women worked in jobs previously filled by men. It was in larger cities where most German women joined the war effort. Forced labor from many thousands of foreign prisoners couldn't alter that outcome. In truth, many German women welcomed an escape from their labors in the home, others came to see it as another lost promise of National Socialism.

My own contact with prisoners held in Kirchheim was limited to that of an observer. Germans, especially women, were forbidden any kind of verbal or physical interaction with the prisoners and the penalty for any prisoner and woman caught together in a sexual situation was severe. I heard of girls who had been stripped naked, tarred and feathered, and paraded through their home villages. The offending prisoners had been hanged. Incidents in nearby Harxheim and in my birthplace of Marnheim were widely publicized. I knew of no such case occurring in Kirchheim, but we did have a well-kept secret romance or two at Schilling Inn.

Every day, except Sunday, the prisoners at Schilling's were marched past my house, down in the morning, up in the evening. I often stood behind the window curtain and gazed down on them as they went by, always in three columns, and usually with two guards almost casually trailing behind. At first, the Polish, Russian and French uniforms they wore helped identify the wearer, but the faces of nearly all of the Russians and some of the Poles left no doubt about their Slavic origins. Even when their uniforms took on a similar tattered appearance, it was said that most prisoners could never be mistaken for German, even if they got their hands on civilian clothes.

"I wouldn't worry about any of them escaping," Erich said. "That's why the guards are so lax. It's a long way from here to Russia and Poland. They'd be spotted in a minute. Besides, none of them care to go home and be worse off. The French? I hear they're content to sit out the rest of the war, even though the border is not that far."

I didn't know where my brother got his information, but figured it was probably on Bossung's corner, from the "experts" who gathered there every night. The prisoner group at Schilling's did appear well fed and healthy, only the uniforms deteriorated.

The prisoners were generally silent, keeping their eyes forward as they went to and from their work places, such as the Ebert Tile and Brick factory outside of Kirchheim. In one of our youth meetings, we were told not to stare at any prisoner, and never to make eye contact. One evening, I opened a front window to shake out a dust cloth, and looked down just as some prisoners passed. A Russian in his heavy quilt coat jerked his eyes up, looked at me, and smiled. Jumping back from the window, I dropped the cloth and it fell to the street. I was certain that trouble was coming in the form of a guard pounding on our front door, accusing me of flirting with the enemy. I waited, hardly breathing, but minutes passed and nothing happened. I inched back to the window and peered out on an empty street. Down on our front step lay the cloth, neatly folded.

≈

I learned later that prisoners held in the Kirchheim district were paid for their work. It wasn't a large amount, just thirty-three Pfennigs an hour, and food and lodging costs were deducted. The pay came in special Stalag currency, since having real Reichmarks was forbidden. No prisoner could have in his possession money valued greater than twenty Reichmarks. The money was to be used to buy personal toiletries and whatever else was permitted.

Despite strict bans on fraternizing with prisoners, love did find a way not discovered until after the threat of harsh punishment ended.

In the group at Schilling Inn, the only daughter Anneliese fell in love with a French prisoner Luis. Though she was a few years older than Erich, I knew her well. I can't say the same about her future husband. I believe he was a French settler from one of the colonies in North Africa. When their secret was revealed at war's end, they were married and she returned with him to Africa. After her father's death, both returned to the Breitstraße to help her mother run the inn.

Luis and Anneliese weren't the only successful secret lovers on Breitstraße. Josef from Poland was one of the few prisoners who did not work at the brick factory. Instead, he was put to work helping the farmer Wilz across the street from Schilling's. The Wilz family included two daughters and a son Franz, one of my brother's best friends. The daughters were Elizabeth and Sophie. By the time Josef came to Schilling's as a prisoner, Franz and Erich were both off in the military. After his release, Josef stayed and married daughter Elizabeth, and helped run the farm.

There had to have been many stories like these wherever prisoners were kept in towns across Germany.

Some people in my small world didn't expect any immediate effect from America entering the war against us, but the British bombing of cities along the Rhein seemed to intensify with the New Year. Because we lived in the pathway to the targets, our daytime practice drills at school increased, along with the nighttime dashes to shelters. Bombing attacks could occur anytime between eleven p.m. and two a.m., and more upsetting than ever. We were told the enemy dropped vast numbers of phosphorus bombs to destroy by fire the innocent people hiding in shelters. There were also rumors of bombs that released deadly germs on the populace, or pests such as potato bugs to kill our crops.

But Kirchheim, and all the villages around, remained unscathed for the most part, despite the stepped-up air raids. "There's nothing to bomb here," Mama said, repeating her son's words. She grieved for people living in the target areas. "It's just awful what's happening."

My mother and I began to see for ourselves just how terrible the devastation was during our infrequent train trips into places like Worms and Kaiserslautern. The train rides took us right through both industrial and residential sections that had been damaged. Main rail stations were crippled, but still operating. Walking to a doctor's office or any other destination, it was common to discover whole sections of downtown business buildings turned to rubble. A greater phenomenon to me was the sight of just one building in ruins, while structures on either side were still intact, occupied by workers and shoppers.

One of the more minor worries resulting from the nightly attacks, was the hazard of bumping into people on the street after dark. The blackout conditions caused a number of mishaps with minor injuries or embarrassments, especially when overcast skies blocked even the moonlight. The solution was a new clothing accessory — pins that glowed in the dark.

With reports of all the firebombing attacks not far to the east, Mama had become more and more concerned. What could we do if a firebomb fell on our house? She had us stack sandbags in the attic, along the stairways, on the landings, and in the halls. I had no idea what protection sand would afford us, and prayed we'd never find out.

Erich, tired of answering the almost nightly call of the air raid siren, still refused to leave his bed, and if he did, he went to the basement in the Gass family's big farmhouse down the street to be with his buddy Ernst, who we called "Enne." Neither of them actually went into the shelter half the time, preferring to sit out in the garden, when the weather permitted. Despite the close call we had the night he and I watched out a front window, he preferred the outdoors over a shelter. More bombs were falling in the nearby unoccupied fields and forest, as bomber crews released the last of their deadly loads while returning from the real targets.

It was a miracle, people said. No bomb had come down on any village around the Donnersberg, and no one had been killed, at least not yet.

&

Like any child in a fairly stable family environment, I took my mother for granted. She was always there preparing meals, working in the house or garden, taking care of business. She was moral, hard working, clean, and smart about most things. She could be caring and affectionate in a restrained sort of way. Not one for idle gossip, Mama didn't talk at length with me, accept when I pressed her or she had something specific to say. Papa could hug her, even adding a kiss on the cheek. Erich could, too. I couldn't.

"What's the matter?" She'd say. "Are you sick?" Those kinds of responses taught me early to hold back any desire to touch her. Papa more than filled my need for affection, yet I did long at times for the same from Mama — without having to be sick.

As for her own health, Mama was not one to complain about tolerable aches and pains, but the time came in 1942 when she could no longer ignore an alarming condition.

One afternoon, she was going about her usual tasks while I finished up homework at my small table by the kitchen window. A deep groan made me look up, Mama was bent over, her one hand holding the edge of the supper table — the other hand grasping her abdomen. The sight of her contorted face made me freeze in place. No further sound came out to match the pain so clearly shown in her tightly shut eyes and twisted mouth.

"Mama!" I finally jumped up and went to put my arms around her, fearing she was about to collapse. But as rapidly as it had come on, the worst of the pain subsided, and she pushed me away.

"Don't. It's alright. It's going away now." The words came haltingly, in between deep breaths. After another moment, she looked almost sorry about pushing me away. "Don't worry about it. It's just a female problem. Your Tante Lina gave me the name of a doctor over in Pfeddersheim she says can help. I want you to go with me."

≈

So began a series of many train rides, both long and short, to seek help for Mama's unexplained ailment. The doctors were all old — most of the young doctors were in uniform, taking care of our soldiers. I would take along a book or school papers, as the waiting in doctors' offices was often long and tedious.

The Pfeddersheim doctor recommended by my aunt gave Mama some drops, and for a while the medicine seemed to help, but not enough to confirm his guess at a diagnosis. Not then, or any time after, did she elaborate on her problem to me. All my efforts to convince her of my adequate maturity to discuss 'problems' of the female body failed. She wouldn't let me into her confidence. After a while, I stopped asking. Erich wasn't any better informed, and Papa, I came to learn, knew nothing of his wife's illness until much later. He wasn't home to see the signs.

Along with all the doctor visits, Mama started more frequent day trips to see her sisters Anna in Kriegsheim and Katharina in Zell. Both had been widowed young, and each had two children. Their villages were in the wine country, and my aunts scratched out a living working in the vineyards.

I liked visiting my aunts, since they had always been nice to me, but Mama had a different reason for going. She needed their ear and sympathy for her health problems, but didn't speak of it in my presence. She only needed my company for the train rides, but once we arrived, I was sent out of earshot to deal with my cousins. In the end, my mother got little sympathy or advice from her sisters.

In time, I would know that while her sisters loved her, they didn't believe she was really ill. Their understanding was hampered by a sort of ignorant jealousy. How much comfort does our older sister deserve? It's a question they must have asked because in their minds, 'Mariechen always had life so much easier.' To my aunts, a mysterious pain sounded more like a problem in their sister's head. As time passed, Mama felt betrayed by the very two she had favored and had helped with gifts of money and clothes through the years. We soon stopped visiting.

When Papa finally learned of his wife's problem, he wasted no time urging her to come to a hospital in Gießen near the air base. I stayed home, sleeping over each night at Henny's. Erich got his wish to stay alone with Fips and the chickens. In a few days, Mama came home with some new medicines, but no real answers as to the cause. Only with each round of new drops or tablets, could she find enough relief to again give attention to family matters.

After Easter, my classmates and I would be elevated to sixth grade, still under Lehrer Lawaldt. And because I continued to do so well, Mama again brought up what we call "Gymnasium," a kind of high school devoted to academic studies that led to university admission. She first broached the subject of switching schools when I finished fourth grade, which was the usual time to make a change. Only students who were capable of more difficult studies were accepted. Fourth graders who were interested, had to pass an exam. I didn't take it. At the time, none of my friends had wanted to go to Gymnasium. Besides, I knew there would be another chance to tackle the tests at the end of fifth grade.

"Don't you want to transfer over to the Gymnasium?"

Mama's question forced the issue upon me again, but the passing of another year had given me two new reasons not to switch. After a year under Lawaldt, I didn't want to leave him. Even more exciting was a prospect that Henny had mentioned. She was entering eighth grade, and upon completion, she planned to attend a new Nazi program called L.B.A (Lehrerbildungsanstalt). A teacher training school had opened in Kaiserslautern, a forty-five minute train ride away. Applicants were tested from the area's sixth, seventh and eighth grades. I wanted to follow Henny to the L.B.A. after eighth grade.

I explained all this to Mama, adding that my wish was to be a home economics teacher, since I had enjoyed my classes with Fräulein Kuhn.

Mama nodded. "Why haven't you mentioned being a teacher before?"

"Because I didn't want to disappoint Papa. You know how he talks about me doing his office work, or worse, being a bank clerk. How can I tell him that's not for me?"

"Ach, Märe, don't fret about your father. He'll get used to it and be just as happy!" Mama's eyes were on me as she spoke, but the expression in them was one of a happy memory. "Young as you are, I've seen how good you're getting at sewing and needlework. You remind me of my sister Elizabeth. Now if you learn to cook just as well, you'll make a fine teacher."

"Cooking comes in eighth grade," I said. "And I watch you, though I don't expect to ever become as good."

She seemed to appreciate the compliment. Mama firmly believed that women should learn home skills. She reminisced at length about Elizabeth, her humpbacked sister. It was a familiar story to me — an imperfect young girl who devoted her short years on earth to achieving perfection in needlework of every sort. She died long before I was born, but Mama thought and talked about her often.

Our conversation that day stays with me because we had never talked at length about my future hopes in such a mature fashion. Mama heard me out, asked many questions, and not only agreed with my thinking, but also offered encouragement. I suppose she recognized that I really had given my future serious thought.

After the start of sixth grade, our school principal, Herr Gutensohn tested me for the teacher training school. I wasn't surprised to learn I'd passed the exam — if Henny could pass, I could pass. Herr Gutensohn said I would start in the summer of 1945 if my schoolwork remained excellent through the eighth grade.

June brought terrible news. Young Ludwig was dead. Oma Klein had received official notice of her youngest son's fate in a black-edged envelope handed to her by the postman. In no time, the news spread to every relative in the district. Tante Lisbeth sent word to Mama, who immediately set out walking to Bolanden. She asked Erich and I to help attend Oma. Erich hated sad or sentimental scenes, but readily agreed. For me, there was no question — I was already crying and wanting to be with Oma.

Lisbeth met us at the door, and we found Oma sitting on a kitchen chair, more frail than I had ever seen her. Now and then she sobbed, but like a well gone dry, no tears came from her red and swollen eyes. Mama and I embraced and kissed her, and Erich stood back, mumbling his regrets. Mama could often be jealous of Papa's close attention to his mother, but in her heart, she was fond of the tiny woman. She didn't hesitate to kiss and caress Oma's grief-stricken face. We all wished that Papa could be there. He alone could best comfort his mother.

Finally, after the sobs subsided, Oma handed my mother the form letter. She'd been holding the paper tightly to her bosom, as though it gave her some physical link to her dead son. I moved behind to look over Mama's shoulder as she read it. Curious, my brother also stepped over to look down at the letter.

At the top was the familiar eagle and Swastika insignia, followed by Oma's name and address. It went on with words about "loyalty, duty, and brave service to the Fatherland" and how we could all be "proud of the sacrifice" Ludwig had made. His unit and date of death were noted, along with the place — Russia. Another brief paragraph stated that Ludwig's remains would not be returned to the family, just his personal belongings.

Tante Lisbeth had already decorated a large picture of Ludwig with flowers and placed it on a nearby shelf. He looked so young and handsome in his uniform. Now, he was one of the thousands who were dead and buried in unmarked Russian soil.

We would mourn Ludwig, but with no body to bury, there was no way to bid him farewell properly. That bothered Oma greatly.

In the meantime, a new scare was sweeping the region — potato bugs. We heard that enemy bombers had dropped the pests to destroy our most important food crop and create famine. If it was just a rumor, it was one sanctioned by the government, because all classes in my school were sent into the fields to find and kill the bugs. I saw many old people from town as well, bent over and moving along the rows of plants searching the leaves and blooms. Not many of the pests were found in the fields where my class worked.

Erich later said that he was skeptical about planes dropping potato bugs on us. He thought it was a great way for the farmers to get some free help in ridding the potato fields of the usual infestation. In any case, our town's health officials took rumors of germ warfare even more seriously. Earlier in May, I found myself standing in a long line of children waiting for a repeat emergency inoculation for smallpox. No glad occasion, especially the painful injection into the chest, not the upper arm. I had been vaccinated as a child, but a new and stronger plague from the enemy was feared.

But it wasn't all sadness and fear that summer of '42. A circus came to Kirchheimbolanden. A big tent was set up for business at the top of the Breitstraße. It was an open area we called "Sheep house," though no house was there. The large corral-like area had been used to keep sheep overnight in the days when flocks regularly moved through to new pastures. The peaceful setting was transformed overnight by clowns and trained animals, including one elephant.

Posters advertising the circus went up all over town a week before the event, right next to those that warned about 'The enemy is listening.' When the circus wagons finally rolled in, the excitement among my peer group was intense. None of us could remember a circus coming to town. But, if my mother was any gauge, many adults were wondering if the world had gone crazy. A circus in the midst of a horrible war seemed preposterous. Berlin was obviously trying to cheer up the hinterlands of Germany.

I was excited about going to a performance. Tony, a boy who had joined our class for the week of the circus shows, was a Negro, and cuter than most of the other boys in the room. Our male classmates at first were a bit put off, but he had a smile that put everyone instantly at ease. Lehrer Lawaldt was happy to introduce him to us, noting that he and his parents traveled with the circus. Wherever it went, Tony kept up his education at a local school.

I felt the luckiest in the whole class, because Tony was placed across the aisle from me in the next bench row. I was able to study his every feature, and hoped to get to talk to him. He spoke perfect formal German, without accent or dialect words. He'd been born and raised in Hamburg, home of the circus. He said his family had been with the circus for three generations, and that his grandfather came from Africa. I learned that the circus in Kirchheim was just a small unit of a bigger circus company that had previously traveled all over Europe. With the war, it was no longer possible to move such a huge operation by rail, so only small units went out to perform within the country.

Herr Lawaldt was eager to draw Tony into our lessons, saying he had much to offer, having traveled so widely. When asked what he did in the circus, the boy flashed a bright, mischievous smile.

"Ah, you must come and see me. I do many things."

My friends and I must have stared and smiled like idiots at him — his blackness was so new to us. The second day, at recess, I got up the nerve to ask what all the girls were aching to ask. "Can I touch your hair?"

"Natürlich!" Was his cheerful reply in high German, leaning his head over.

He must have been asked that all the time, and wasn't the least surprised at my request. With his permission, I put my hand on the tight cushion of tiny black curls, pulling some out to watch them spring back.

"I wish I had curls like that!" (It's certain he had also heard that before!)

After school that day, I went to see 'Tony's Circus,' as I called it, and enjoyed it very much. Tony was at the tent ready to show everyone to his or her seats. He looked beautiful in his colorful uniform, topped off with a shiny red satin turban. Later, he stood by to open the curtain where the acts came out, then helped his father with the elephant. My classmates and I were sad when Tony left a few days after. We had learned something about another race of people, and it would be important to remember.

Chapter Twenty-Two

The North Pfalz Bergland, where the Donnersberg mountain dominates, is a rugged highland range running north and south. The forested hills hold special sway over the seasons on the eastern slopes region, all the way to the Rhein river. The temperatures of summer and winter tended to be moderated by the high Bergland, though there were exceptions — the winter of 1941/42 being one. The spring and early summer that followed were normal though, with just enough rain and bright cool sunshine to make our world beautiful to see and feel.

In the mornings, I always liked throwing open every window to breathe deeply all the fragrances, pushed along by breezes off the Donnersberg. From the kitchen window, even before the last of winter snow had melted, the first blossoms of the crocus and "Schneeglöckchen" brighten the edge of our garden. 'Snow bells' showed themselves through the snow even sooner than the early crocus. And, soon after, the swallows returned to flit about and sing through the summer in the courtyard.

In the autumn fast approaching, the Donnersberg could be expected to block an early onslaught of winter, and allow nature to cool gently on our side. The process always brought a new set of treats for the senses, and made the first hard winter freeze less of a shock. In Kirchheim, autumn could linger on for weeks with sunshine that warmed the skin, but never the air. The pleasant cool breezes of daytime turned cold at night, perfect for sleeping under comforters.

A new day's sun would promptly chase away the cold and frost of night. Rainy days only sharpened the aroma of newly harvested crops, while providing moisture to aid the decay of things finished with summer life. The fragrance of ripe grapes and fall apples was heavenly, rain or shine. Walking past houses, I could smell the aroma of prune plums being cooked down into a winter supply of prune jam.

Around Donnersberg, the forest changed with the seasons. Erich and I still tramped through it, mesmerized by its beauty. We loved the Pfälzerwald in any season, but autumn was special. He knew just where to find the Steinpilz, a large and delicious fall mushroom. Having done a lot of exploring on his own, he liked showing me new discoveries. It's how I learned about an abandoned copper mine hidden deep in a forest valley. And he also guided me to flowing springs where we could get our fill of cold, delicious water. The wild boar wallows and their established pathways had the hair on the back of my neck standing on end. Erich had no fear, but I kept looking about nervously, imagining a raging boar attacking us. He just laughed at me.

With his seventeenth birthday drawing near, he expected to be called into the labor force soon. Perhaps that was the reason he suddenly allowed me to be with him more often. For another autumn ritual, Erich invited me along when he helped Enne and his parents harvest their potato crop. Digging up and loading potatoes isn't fun, but I did discover it had some rewards. We got a small share to take home, and I got to be with my brother.

Starting in 1942, our fourth year of war, fall activities like canning foods had to be drastically cut back. More stringent rationing of sugar and other ingredients made the practice difficult. Mama stopped canning entirely because Papa was away, and she didn't feel up to it.

The rationing of foods started with the issuing of small coupon sheets once a month, early in the war. At first, the limiting of purchases to the exact gram applied to items like meats, fats, and flour. This short list was soon expanded to take in almost all foodstuffs, shoes and clothing. It meant more packets of sheets with little coupons to keep track of and present to shopkeepers, when and if something was available. The first hurdle was availability. Next came waiting in block-long lines of hopeful customers — all after the same dab of butter, pound of bread or pair of shoes. Mama left no doubt about me being old enough to do most of the shopping.

"Standing in all those lines, I'll never get my work done."

After a store or government office had posted notice that something was in stock on a certain day, I'd hurriedly arranged to have Henny, or another friend, stand in line with me. It helped to pass the time, up to three and four hours, and also aided in protecting our place in line. A young person was no obstacle to an adult wanting to crowd in ahead, but the protests of two or three young people gave most intruders pause.

❧

By late October, chilling rains and fog abruptly announced that winter would soon win the battle to surmount the Bergland barrier. In a matter of weeks snow and cold would again be our companions.

The coming of winter in 1942 brought another shock to our family. Onkel Heinrich had died. My mother's brother, my childhood friend below our tiny apartment in Marnheim, had left us too soon. Mama and I had been very fond of him, and we liked his wife Sannchen, almost as much.

Heinrich had served in the first world war with his brother Adam, but unlike Adam's fate, he hadn't been called back in this time around. Mama thought the war killed him anyway. Two years before, Heinrich had said that he wanted to retire, and began teaching his son Friederich the saddler trade. But retirement went out the window when the boy was drafted. Pedaling a bike from Gauersheim to Marnheim every day had begun to take its toll. First it was just a head cold, something he'd had many times from riding in the rain, my aunt said. Stubborn, my uncle continued the daily trips, and his cold turned into pneumonia. Sannchen sent word about his illness to Mama, and she walked the eight kilometers to Gauersheim to offer assistance.

"Your uncle is improving," she told me, on returning.

A week later, Sannchen again sent word: "Heinrich is dead." He wasn't quite fifty years old.

Tante Anna came by train from Kriegsheim to accompany Mama as she walked the long way to her brother's village for his funeral. Much as I wanted to go, she thought I shouldn't miss school.

Going to school didn't help. Most of the time I just sat there, unable to get my mind off the slender, black-haired man, with his trim mustache, and twinkling eyes.

A few weeks after the funeral we heard again from Tante Sannchen. Her teen-age daughter Hilde also traveled to work by bicycle, but to Kirchheim — about the same distance as my uncle bicycled to Marnheim. The death of Heinrich shook my aunt so badly, she asked if my cousin could stay overnight with us during inclement weather. Naturally, Mama agreed. Erich was soon leaving for the young men's labor service and there would be room.

November twelfth arrived and I had reason to again dread the efficient nature of Germans. Erich's seventeenth birthday had just passed when the summons came from the Arbeitsdienst. (Labor Service) My brother was the only one who was happy about it. "Finally," he shouted, "a real uniform, in real service to the Reich!"

His orders were to report to the R.A.D. camp in St. Ingbert, near the French border. After training, he was scheduled to be sent into France to work on projects along the coast. Before I could blink, Erich had a bag packed and was saying goodbye. He didn't want company to the train station — there would be no tearful goodbyes for him in public.

"You won't have me here to keep you tough," he said to me as I hugged him tightly. "Don't turn soft on me."

"Don't you worry," I replied. "I'll be tough." I laughed and punched him on the arm like he'd done to me so many times, but I cried when the door closed behind him. Mama was visibly shaken, but no tears came.

∻

In the following weeks, I worried over not hearing a word from Erich. Then a postcard arrived. There was no 'I miss you,' just a warning that he'd soon be going to his work station on the Brittany coast. As Christmas came nearer, Papa took a brief leave and decided we should visit Erich before his transfer, especially since it was not likely he could come home for Christmas. For once, Mama didn't protest when Papa borrowed a car to make the trip to St. Ingbert. She took along some Christmas cookies, which pleased Erich — sweet treats seemed to be nonexistent in the labor force. Just as obvious was Erich's excitement being a step closer to military service. In a way, he already felt himself a real part of the military effort. In France, his assignment had him working on reinforcing what we came to call the "Atlantic Wall," an effort to block an invasion from England.

Christmas at home was a strange affair. I missed Erich, but Papa managed a visit. We went to Oma Klein and Tante Lisbeth in Bolanden, but there was no joy in it. Not only was Oma still mourning the loss of Ludwig, there was another dark cloud hanging low over Germany. Our Sixth Army was surrounded at Stalingrad.

Papa had some possible good news about being transferred from Gießen to a post closer to home. He could make no promises, but felt the chances were good. His young commanding officer had become like a son, and had taken a liking to him.

"My lieutenant thinks I'm too old and will just be in the way when the enemy arrives." Papa laughed like he'd come up with a new joke, he then grew more serious. "Actually, the young fellow told me privately he'd like to see me closer to home as things aren't looking too good."

Papa was referring to the latest news from Russia about our army trapped at Stalingrad. On January 31, the bad news turned worse — what was left of the Sixth Army surrendered. For the days that followed, the radio had little else than mournful music and bold promises from commentators that Germany would still crush the enemy. Hints of "new, powerful secret weapons" were mentioned. I don't know how many other people believed in the new 'secret weapons' or other promised miracles, but I did.

∻

As winter turned into spring, a postcard from Papa announced the welcome news — he would soon be on "special assignment" just outside of Guntersblum, a village near the city of Oppenheim on the Rhein river. I couldn't imagine what kind of special work my father was doing. Mama and I decided to visit him. He was barely an hour's train ride from Kirchheim. We took an early Sunday morning train.

Papa met us with a small military truck and whisked us out to his new duty station about five kilometers away from the village. My father said little on the short drive about what we could expect, wanting to see our reaction upon arrival. He turned off the road onto a grassy path that wound through a small stand of trees, and came to a halt in front of one of three barracks built just where the trees gave way to a great meadow. The wooden buildings were only one story high. Just beyond them, the meadow opened out into what appeared to be a gently rolling green carpet flat and large enough for an airfield. A princely estate would have looked nice sitting in the middle. Instead, several airplanes dotted one side of the field.

But they weren't airplanes at all, not real ones. Papa was assigned to a fake air base.

As soon as the truck came to a stop, a handful of men came out of the barracks to greet us. All were in work uniforms, some not even fully covered, having just an undershirt, pants and boots on. Even the sergeant, the unit's commander, didn't appear all that sharp in his uniform. Papa was not intimidated by the sergeant, saying, "He keeps his shirt on in case one of the higher-ups makes a surprise visit."

It was clear our visit wasn't a surprise. The sergeant told Mama and I something else my grinning father had failed to tell us — Papa's duties mainly entailed cooking for the small crew and driving the truck for supplies. I was relieved. I didn't want him to have a thing to do with the targets that sat there on the meadow. They were supposed to fool the enemy airplanes into wasting ammunition and bombs on nothing more than paper and wood.

All of Papa's comrades showed us every courtesy, including a large meal prepared by three of them. The sergeant said it took that many to replace him in the kitchen. After eating, Papa and another man took Mama and I on a fast tour of the facility. We heard how the men moved the fake planes around on the field from time to time to make it appear like an active air base. And whenever they were shot up, some new wood and paint made them ready for another day. We were also shown something that was real under some trees — a large anti-aircraft gun to fire at enemy planes passing overhead.

As it was still early afternoon, Papa wanted to spend the rest of the day in Oppenheim, where we had gotten off the train. Having satisfied our curiosity about his new post, he was ready to take us away from the war for a better look at the ancient city on the Rhein where we'd catch the train home. Oppenheim had a magnificent Gothic cathedral and I hoped aloud that the massive Katharinenkirche would not be destroyed in the frequent bombing raids.

Weeks later, Erich finished his R.A.D. service and came home. He'd spent the entire time in the Brittany coastal area of France helping erect barbed-wire barriers.

Mama and I thought Erich would stay at home until his eighteenth birthday, the age at which young men were usually drafted into the regular military. We were wrong. He was home just a few days before enlisting in the navy. Mama and I were furious.

"Why are you doing this?" Mama's voice wailed at him across the kitchen. "Isn't it enough that your father's gone. The war could be over by November, and you won't have to go at all. Please wait!"

"Mama, I can't wait." Erich would never shout at his mother, but his voice was firm and he was clearly determined. "This war is going to drag on, and I don't want to end up in the army. You know they'll put me in that grinding machine if I wait to be drafted. Besides, I like the idea of serving on a ship better."

"If you think that would be better." Mama's voice had taken a sudden turn. Her tone was softer — she had caved to her son's wishes with what I thought was surprising speed. My own feeble protests ended abruptly as well. The navy did, for some reason, sound safer. Of course, none of us knew that Erich would be serving on a submarine.

"It'll be a few days before I have to report to Kiel on the North Sea," he continued, in a voice tinged with sadness. Having won the big battle with his mother, there was no longer reason to act tough. "I'm going over to Guntersblum tomorrow to visit Papa, then I'll be back for a day or so before leaving. Don't worry about me. I know it will be better for me in the navy."

❧

The nicer weather of spring and summer 1943 was accompanied by a sharp increase in air raids, which had worsened with the Americans flying day attacks to match the British nighttime raids. In the Kirchheim area, we learned that daylight bombers were less likely to toss any extra bombs our way. On the other hand, the strafing of road traffic and trains became common, causing panic for travelers.

Again, nothing official was reported about the awful death and destruction in the bigger industrial cities from the bombings. Berlin didn't have to tell us the news on the radio — we could learn about it from the children sent out to find safety in places like Kirchheim. Many worried parents had relatives or friends living away from target areas, and who would give haven to the children for the duration. Several enrolled in my school and one in particular, was taken in by her grandparents just up the street from me. Both Henny and I would become friends with Margot.

Rumors flew fast in town, and one afternoon Henny told me of hearing about an enemy plane that had come down in the forest not far from the Schillerhain. We decided to find the wreckage. It took us all of two hours before we finally stumbled across the crash site. I don't know what I expected to see, but having found it, the urge to leave was strong.

"It's amazing the forest didn't catch fire," Henny said. "The plane looks like it exploded." Henny wasn't at all uneasy moving about the pieces of aircraft scattered over the area. I worried about the pilots.

"I wonder what happened to the pilots, Henny."

She had picked up a piece of metal to look at. "Why are you so concerned about that? The plane crashed two nights ago. I'm sure they've been taken care of, dead or alive."

"I heard that another British plane came down in the forest a couple of weeks ago, and the injured pilots were taken to our hospital, but nothing has been said this time about the pilots."

"Ja, Annchen, I heard about that, too. Later, the Gestapo came and took them away. My mother said she heard the police hollered at the doctor and nurses for taking such good care of their wounds."

"Is that true?"

"I don't know. She heard it around town. Come on, let's see what we can find!" Henny continued picking things up and inspecting the insides of the larger sections of the plane that were still intact. I just stood there, taking in the whole scene. Sun rays filtered through the tree branches, and the birds sang and flew about as always, undisturbed by the broken plane on the forest floor. Anyone interested in the scene had apparently already come and gone. We were absolutely alone, but I couldn't be certain.

"This place gives me the creeps," I said. "Let's go back now. We've been gone very long. Mama will be upset as it is."

As I could never lie to my mother, she was told everything. With a sharp look, the lecture began over her concern for my safety.

"Mama, you know I wouldn't go far into the forest alone. Henny was with me, and we didn't see another soul the entire time."

"Ja, and Henny should know better. She's confirmed now, and should start acting like a responsible young woman, not prancing around the forest on a lark!"

My mother's reference to Henny being recently confirmed stung a little. Her remark bothered me in that I was reminded Henny was soon leaving for Kaiserslautern and teacher training, while my own confirmation was still two years off. Since I couldn't argue Mama's point, I changed the subject.

"Mama, how did you learn about everything? I mean, when you were my age."

"What kinds of things are you talking about?"

"I want to know about me. Look! My breasts are beginning to grow, and they sometimes hurt." It had been a mistake for her to leave the door wide open and I think she knew it. Her face was beginning to turn pink as I jumped through the opening. "Does that mean something bad? Henny says I should soon start having a monthly period. My whole body seems to be changing, and I have no answers!"

Mama had turned her back to me and was fidgeting at the cook stove. I waited, wondering if I'd gone too far. Finally, she turned slightly back to me, but didn't look me squarely in the face.

She began to speak quietly, and with some difficulty. "Your Onkel Adam in Marnheim once borrowed a big medical book from me. It was my own mother's from many years ago, and she gave it to me. Adam should still have the book, and in it you'll find the answers you want. With your uncle away in the army, you'll have to go ask Tante Elise."

I could tell she was finished with the matter and confirmed it by issuing new orders. "Go now and close up the chicken coop for the night. Tomorrow I want you to go around and see if one of the farm families will take them off our hands. With just the two of us at home, I see no need to keep chickens."

I couldn't remember a time when we didn't have chickens, but I was rather ambivalent about the matter. Chickens were alright, except when they got out of the courtyard into the street and I had to chase them down. I liked eating fresh eggs and marveling over new chicks, and it was even downright fun when Papa once brought home a colorful bantam rooster. In quick order, the little fellow had every hen, three times his size, mesmerized and obedient. His duties must have been too much, though. One morning I found him by the garden steps, keeled over dead.

☙

"Why don't you sit down a while and visit," Tante Elise urged as she handed me the book. "That's big and heavy. You should rest some before going home. I have some coffee on the stove."

I'd ridden my bicycle over to Marnheim and was glad I didn't have to carry the huge medical book home walking. It was bigger than our old family Bible. Thankfully, I had thought to bring Mama's cloth shopping bag. "I'll stay for a few minutes, Tante. I am thirsty."

"How is your mother, Märe?" She put a glass of cool, brown liquid in front of me.

"Thank you for asking, Tante. She's not too good lately."

"Has she learned what the problem is?"

"I don't think so. I don't know. Mama just says it hurts down here in the lower part." I touched my abdomen, and remembered how Mama had bent over in pain.

"I must come over for a visit with her. I have so little time with Adam gone and the children…" Her voice just drifted off as she left her chair and moved to gaze silently out the window.

☙

Later in the summer, I talked Mama into letting me go alone to visit Papa in Guntersblum. It wasn't difficult — she was letting me do a lot in my thirteenth year, just as long as people were around. Preparing to leave for the station I asked, "Tell me again, where do I change trains?"

"Ach, Märe. You are something! Now pay attention. On the way you'll change at Alzey. Coming home, you switch in Worms. If you have any problems — "

"I'll remember that they speak German!" We both smiled. It was one of her favorite admonitions.

I had written to Papa if I could visit, and despite some concern about enemy planes shooting at trains, he replied with his blessing. The trip was uneventful, and he was happily waiting at the gate on my arrival. Being a Klein, his hug and kiss came with praise over my longer braids.

I couldn't stay long, only a few hours, so we never left Oppenheim. We had three whole hours to walk around hand in hand, looking at the old town and watching the boats on the Rhein. He took me to sit a while at an outdoor cafe that still offered small bowls of a sherbet.

We mostly talked of happy things, but also Mama's health problems, and how we both missed Erich. I finally got up the nerve to mention wanting to be a teacher, the school in Kaiserslautern, and was relieved when he agreed to go along with it.

"We should have our dreams," he said. "They give us something to work toward. Just don't forget that right now I'm counting on you to help your mother. I'm worried the doctors can't find her problem. Maybe when this mess is over, some of our younger doctors will be able to make her well."

Such serious words made me speechless, and for a moment we both sat at our table silently, watching the pigeons flutter down in search of morsels on the cafe sidewalk.

"Papa, please don't worry. I'll look after Mama and do the best I can to help her. 'Sei brav,' you told me and I will, Papa."

He clapped a hand on the table, got to his feet, and smiled. "I know you will, Annchen! I know you will. Come, let's walk some more. Your train will be here soon."

As we walked slowly toward the train station, I realized for the first time that I was now as tall as Kleine Seppel. And crossing the central square, I also became aware that a number of people nodded and spoke to Papa. I couldn't help remarking about it.

"Ah, that," he laughed. "You know, I come into town quite often. There's no avoiding making a few acquaintances along the way."

That was Papa. A true Seppel in every way, but everyone who had spoken called him "Fritz." I asked him why.

"Seppel is for home folks. Here I use my given name. These folks wouldn't understand our ways around Donnersberg."

How sad, I thought.

As the train carried me homeward, I stared out at the passing jumble of vineyards, villages and woodland, remembering my father's concern over Mama's health. I was baffled. I had accompanied her to at least five doctors in the region, and still she ailed. A couple of weeks before my trip, Mama had broken down and gone to old Dr. Hahn in Kirchheim. She didn't have much respect for him, but he was close, and the trips to other towns had worn her out.

I got home just in time to prepare for one of Fräulein Kiefer's big musical evenings called Elternabend. The 'parent's night' affair took place at the Turnhalle, a large building used for dances, public meetings, and live theater. My music teacher had developed the event for the town's adults, mostly using girls from the various youth groups she worked with. With so many men away fighting in the war, the audience turned out to be nearly all mothers, with a sprinkling of old men, young women and a few small children. Again, Henny and I were entrusted to provide music. Home on a short break from her school in Kaiserslautern, Henny had also been selected by Fräulein Kiefer to play the king in a comedy sketch about a royal family. I didn't get or want any speaking parts, but was content to help backstage changing sets when the curtain was down.

I helped Henny with her king costume and make-up, but never saw the performance. I was busy backstage getting ready for the next act, the musical part of the show. After the curtain came down, Henny hurried back to have her make-up removed and change into her H.J. uniform. That accomplished, we were rushed to center stage, instruments strapped on and ready for the big moment. The house on the other side of the curtain quieted when it was announced that Henny Hemm and Anna Klein would play several selections.

Finally, the curtain slowly rose to reveal standing center stage, a tall girl with a small Handharmonika next to a smaller girl holding a big Handharmonika. Before we could lift a finger to play, the hall erupted in laughter. For what seemed like forever, all Henny and I could do was look at each other and wonder why everybody was laughing. In a moment or two, the hall quieted down again and we went through our performance, receiving at the end a nice round of applause. It wasn't until much later that I realized why the people laughed — a shorter girl with the big box and vice-versa. I was to be sorry no one took a photo of us that night.

Mama didn't attend the event. With Papa away, I had counted on her to come. She refused, and I was more troubled by that than any audience laughing at us. Mama was getting more and more strange, and with each passing day, showed little interest in anything outside the house. When Papa heard that she hadn't gone to the performance, he was angry over her failure to show support of a family member.

Chapter Twenty-Three

It wasn't many weeks after Mama reluctantly turned to Dr. Hahn for help, I had my chance to deal with the elderly doctor. Coming in from school one afternoon, Mama had handed me a small empty prescription bottle. "Take this to the doctor and ask for a refill."

When I got to Dr. Hahn's office, his last patient was coming out. A long wait just to renew a prescription wouldn't have made me happy. "Are you seriously ill?" The sharp tone said clearly he wasn't happy to see another patient in the waiting room.

"Heil Hitler. No, doctor. I'm here for my mother, Frau Klein." I handed him the bottle. "She needs more medicine."

He glanced at the bottle, which apparently served to remind him who Frau Klein was. "Ja, ja. Poor Frau Klein."

My startled expression must have made him realize that I'd heard what he was thinking. Before I could demand to know what he meant by such a cryptic remark, he gruffly ordered me to sit while he refilled the bottle.

In minutes he returned, handed me the bottle with an almost angry thrust. "Here, I renewed your mother's prescription, but you should know she's not sick. It's all in her head. That's where the problem is — it's in her head!"

It seemed like forever that I stood there, struck dumb by his attack on Mama. Each second that passed increased my anger, until finally I grabbed the bottle tight and barged out the door. Taking no more than two steps, I found my voice, and turned to reenter the waiting room. He was still standing there with a scowl on his face. "You are wrong," I shouted, and slammed the door again.

Stomping up the cobblestone toward home I felt hot tears roll down my cheeks, and I knew my eyes were red. Crying is not something I did well. With effort, I worked to halt the tears and bring normal color back to my eyelids before reaching the house. I went up to one of the street-side flowing wells and water troughs. People no longer drank the water, but left the wells in place for passing horses and livestock. I figured if the water was good enough to cool horses, it'd do the job for me.

I didn't tell Mama about the incident, and I never forgave Dr. Hahn his crude, insensitive words.

In early fall, Papa came home for a week to help us prepare for winter. We spaded the garden so it would be ready for planting in the spring, cut down the last of the grapes from the vine on the house, and harvested soup beans that had been allowed to dry on pole vines. As I watched him wrap the water lines against the coming winter freeze, it seemed like another time.

At mid-week, he took Mama somewhere to see another doctor. With school on, I stayed home with Fips, our rascal terrier. As a result, I have no memory of where my parents went — just that they were away two days without explanation.

Finishing my breakfast one morning weeks later, I noticed that Mama hadn't eaten much. She only sat across the table, looking over to me now and then and saying nothing. That didn't bother me, it was just another normal morning. I was about to take my last bite of bread, when I heard the strangest sound — my own name. Only Mama and I were in the kitchen, and she had never called me Annchen. To her I was Märe — forever Märe. I filled my mouth with bread and glanced toward Mama, sure that I was hearing things. She said it again, a tentative smile on her face.

"Annchen — I have something to tell. Something you should know. I will need your help more in the coming months."

"Ja, Mama. Of course, I'll help."

"You don't understand, Märe. Next spring, I will have a baby."

"Mama!" I spit her name out, along with some chewed bread.

"I know you may not like it, having a new baby in the house. Believe me, I understand how you feel. I didn't want another child myself, but the doctor told your father and I that the pregnancy would make me well. I can be well again!"

I thought I was having a bad dream. Any minute I'd reawaken, start my breakfast, and Mama wouldn't call me Annchen — or anything else I'd never heard her say before.

"You do want me well again?"

What could I answer? "Naturally, Mama. I want you like before."

I went off to school and mulled over the news. I certainly couldn't tell my friends just yet. It could be a mistake, I thought, and some of them would probably think it was crazy to have a baby at Mama's age. It occurred to me that Erich didn't know yet. He wrote to us every few weeks, describing his training and letting us know that he would be serving on submarines. He was pleased with the assignment. We were not. There were also photos showing him and some buddies sitting around a big gun pointing out to sea. The best possible news was in his most recent letter, saying, "I'll be home for a whole week at Christmas."

Mama thought that I shouldn't write Erich about the baby — she would tell him in person over Christmas. She was feeling better already, and to me, appeared happier than she's been in a long time. I thought of the medical book that I'd borrowed from Onkel Adam, and wondered if it could help explain Mama's pregnancy?

I had put the book in my bedroom, reading what looked interesting whenever I could. Much of the stuff seemed silly and outdated to me, like a woman shouldn't wash her hair but once a month. I couldn't go a week without washing my hair. Many things written about a woman's health were old-fashioned, and even unreal to anyone who really knows the female body. But then, the authors were all male doctors.

In the section on pregnancy, I was fascinated by one sentence in particular: "Pregnancy renews a woman to wholeness, often curing illness as it brings together all her bodily resources to nourish the baby."

The page had the upper corner turned down.

My mother's pregnancy had naturally made me more curious about the mechanics of getting into the condition. I knew that a husband made a wife pregnant. A thirteen-year-old had to know, or be thought entirely stupid. I wasn't stupid, just poorly informed and naive. As for a woman's sexuality, the 100-year-old medical book had some helpful information. However, it often raised more questions than were answered. Mama simply brushed aside all my efforts at discussion.

I turned to my older friend Henny, now commuting to school in Kaiserslautern, to help in the search for answers. That was a mistake. At thirteen and fifteen, the once small age difference had suddenly become a huge hormone gap. Henny was well along on the bumpy trip into feminine sexuality, while I was still waiting on the sidelines. No wonder she became nervous and blushed when we'd read about the "terrible sin of masturbation," and "Married couples should limit intercourse to two or three times a month."

"What's the matter with you, Henny? We've talked about this stuff before. There's no reason to be embarrassed!"

"I'm not!"

"Ja, you are, and it's making me uncomfortable."

"Annchen, the whole thing is silly anyway. This book was published in 1840. It's all so — so old-fashioned!"

"That's why I wanted you to read it with me. I figured you'd know more about it, being older and all. I told you how it is with Mama."

"It's no different with my mother." Henny paused to leaf through the pages, then snapped the book shut. "Most of this is Quatsch."

Calling the book 'rubbish' was a little strong, I thought, but I didn't argue. Her words provided the needed nudge for my own growing opinion to set aside the old book as ancient history.

Yet, was the book right about pregnancy causing Mama's renewed energy? She had definitely returned to being the cook and housekeeper of old. One thing did become evident to me — the reason why my parents had no new medicines from their two-day trip to 'see a doctor.' They didn't see a doctor. Mama had read the book, and had talked my father into getting her pregnant.

Bad news reached into my neighborhood more often now. The Steinbrecher family just up the street lost two sons, one right after the other. The Steinbrecher girls, Ida and Gertrude, started wearing black, and continued to do so for years. Ida told me of being so devastated she dyed everything black. I felt so bad for the girls losing two brothers, and I had to think about Erich.

In my own family, the death of young Ludwig was bad enough, but it wasn't the end of war's impact on us. Tante Lisbeth's son Willi was missing in Africa. In the same African fighting, the name of Friederich Herbst went on the missing list. He was Onkel Heinrich's son, and also a saddler. In time, we'd learn from the Red Cross that both boys were prisoners of the Americans.

When our trucking business was closed, the telephone had been taken out. Any phone calls made or received now took place at Bossung's Inn next door or Fretz's on the opposite corner. But the fate of family members in the military mostly came by word of mouth. Messages passed from person to person could be amazingly fast. There was always someone in the many surrounding villages coming into Kirchheim daily for business or shopping. If the distance wasn't too far for walking or riding a bicycle, there was no shortage of young ones to carry a message. I did so numerous times for my mother.

By November, the fourth month of her pregnancy, Mama still showed energy and felt good, but stopped leaving the house. Naturally, she had to go across the enclosed courtyard to the outhouse and sometimes into the garden, but both were out of public view. I thought she was oversensitive, and said so.

"I have you to run all my errands," she answered. "I see no need to go out of the house."

I just knew she felt uncomfortable showing herself, embarrassed to be pregnant at her age. It seemed strange to me, because Mama didn't look pregnant. Her cheeks looked healthier and rounder, but her tummy didn't look any bigger than before. I sometimes wondered if she was truly with child.

"Oh, the questions you ask! I never got very big for you or Erich. Some women don't." Her response straightened me out on that mystery, but I still couldn't get her to go out the front door.

Her refusal kept me hopping with more responsibilities added to schoolwork and chores around the house. I did so willingly, if not always with a smile. I had promised Papa, and I wanted Mama to be in good health again. Visits with friends and the mandatory H.J. meetings also remained on my agenda. I surprised myself with how much could be packed into a day.

Following Mama's unspoken lead, I began to discourage friends from coming to the house, and said nothing to them about her condition. As Christmas got closer, I learned that a few family members knew. I didn't tell them, so I can only guess that they heard it from my mother or father. Mama probably wrote to her sisters, hoping that they'd visit, and my father had no doubt informed Oma and Lisbeth in Bolanden. In any case, no one visited, but I was so busy that our increasing isolation on Breitstraße didn't hit me until later.

When I was out of the house most of each day, Fips became Mama's sole companion. He'd pad around after her from room to room as she did the usual pre-Christmas scrub and polish, and be glad to retreat to his warm spot by the cook stove whenever he tired of watching her work.

That year, no lighted Christmas decorations appeared anywhere in town, and not many merchants bothered to decorate their shop windows. There wasn't much on the shelves in the way of necessities anyway, and trinkets and toys were scarcer still. Shopkeepers certainly had no need to advertise, and little motivation to be jolly. There was a slight increase in our allotted ration of sugar, butter, and flour, making it possible for Mama to bake some cookies. The outcome amounted to no more than a few dozen, not enough to share, but we baked more for nostalgia than hunger. Erich would make fast work of devouring most of the cookies.

With Christmas falling on Saturday and Mama not knowing when to expect Erich, she sent me to buy a Christmas tree. I jumped at the chance to pick my first tree for the family, and decided to take my sled along. We'd had several days of snowfall to make it easy hauling my tree choice home by sled, an uphill trip all the way.

I hurried down to the tree lot, pulling the empty sled instead of giving in to an urge to zip along the narrow, winding streets on my stomach. The slower pace gave me time to think about the card from Papa that said he couldn't come home — my first Christmas without him. I bit my lower lip for the tenth time to rid my head of self-pity.

"I must be happy Erich is coming." I said it aloud over and over to myself, trying to push out the ache. Over the weeks, I had managed to buy small gifts for both my parents, and for Erich I had knitted a pair of fine gloves. Thinking about it made me feel better.

&

Mama and I were in the kitchen the following afternoon when we heard heavy footsteps on the stairs. She moved quickly to open the door. There my brother stood, handsome in his navy uniform, a sea sack slung over one shoulder. Mama beamed with joy, hugging her son and pulling him into the room from the cold hall. I hugged him too, not caring about his awkward response. He never had been good receiving my hugs, even though he couldn't hide his pleasure. His shyness in showing affection, as always, was the reason he didn't want us meeting him at the train station.

For most of the evening, he showed us photos of himself and his comrades. We heard in detail about submarines, and were shown drawings of the boat's inner space from end to end.

"Isn't it a bit confined? I don't think you should be in a submarine," Mama said.

"Ja, it's a tight situation, but everything runs like clockwork once you learn how to move about. When we're out at sea, it's best not to think negative things and get on with fighting the enemy. I like it!"

His little speech didn't seem to comfort Mama much, but she said nothing more. Duty on a submarine didn't sound very interesting to me, but I was impressed by his confidence and could only look at him with new respect.

The next afternoon was Christmas Eve, and Erich brought in the tree I'd bought and left in the courtyard snow to stay fresh. We put it in a stand and on top of a small table in the living room. The tree slightly blocked the view of Hitler's picture on the wall. My selection was just a meter and a half high, but by putting it on a table, it nearly touched the ceiling. My family got in the habit of getting small Christmas trees for the limited space in Marnheim and never changed.

"You did a nice job picking a tree." The compliment came as we hung colorful glass balls on its branches.

"I just remembered what Papa always said. 'Full branches, nicely spaced, a straight trunk and a fine crown.'" We both laughed at my poor attempt at impersonating Papa's voice.

&

Christmas Day passed quietly. We had no visitors, but while Mama and I cleaned up after the noon meal, Erich went to see a few of the nearby families whose sons hadn't come home for Christmas. Enne Gass and Franz Wilz were his best friends and he was interested in hearing any news. In the early evening, my brother and I walked alone over to see Tante Lisbeth and Oma in Bolanden. Again, Erich fell into his shy pose as both women patted his cheeks and hugged him. Old Onkel Jacob just shook hands and contented himself sitting on the kitchen wood box, puffing on a pipe that looked to be as old as he. Still mourning Ludwig, Oma was filled with joy at seeing her grandson alive and well in uniform, but a sadness remained in her eyes.

Mama chose the second day after Christmas to have her talk with Erich about the pregnancy. He had had no inkling. No one who knew had said a word. Having left the house to visit some of my friends, I wasn't present for what must have been a painful confrontation.

Returning late in the afternoon, I was surprised to find only Mama standing over the ironing pad, head bowed and earnestly laying the iron to clothes. I asked where Erich was.

She didn't look up. "He left saying he wouldn't be back until very late," she replied softly.

"But, where did he go?"

She still didn't look at me. "I don't know. He didn't say." With that, she picked up the garment and walked past me to the bedroom.

Something told me I should wait up that night for Erich's return. I sat listening to the radio in the kitchen, and pondered how to tell him of my own feelings about having a new brother or sister. Mama went to bed early, still silent about their talk, and I didn't know what to expect. Shortly after eleven I heard the front door, followed by footsteps on the stairs. Nervousness suddenly ran through me, but I put a smile on my face. Finally, the door opened and he stood there, apparently surprised to see me.

"Why do you look so gloomy?" My smile faded rapidly as he gazed at me in anger. "You're not angry because I waited to talk, are you? I thought you'd want to."

He didn't answer or move from the doorway, and I began feeling the cold air from the hallway. "Come in, Erich. Sit down. Can't we talk a while?"

"Go to bed. I don't want to talk. I'm going to bed myself, and tomorrow, just as soon as possible, I'm heading back to my unit!"

"Why are you so grumpy? You have at least three more days, and you promised me a walk in the forest!"

"I won't show my face in this town for another day after what I've heard in this house!"

I knew that this concerned his talk with Mama, but couldn't believe he would react so negatively. I stared at him, not knowing what to say.

"Doesn't it bother you that your mother is going to have a child at her age? It's a disgrace!"

I didn't like it any better than he did, but felt I had to defend her. "You know how sick she's been. The medical book says having a baby will make her well again. It says that. I read it myself!"

"Shit, and double shit!" He was nearly yelling now. "I don't believe that for a minute, and I'll have no part of it. After tomorrow, you'll never see me in this house again!"

I started to cry, but he had turned, slamming the door behind him. The outburst had left me shocked, bewildered, and very hurt. I knew he was being bullheaded about Mama's condition, but I couldn't help but worry that he meant what he'd said. I was sure he really believed a baby would bring shame on us.

I got up and went after him, moving quietly so as not to disturb Mama. Going to his room down the hall I found the door closed and locked. I knocked gently.

"Go away."

It was cold in the hall, and I was more than ready for sleep, but I didn't give up easily. "You must listen," I whispered, hoping he'd hear through the door. "Don't be mad. It'll be fine. Please don't say you're going away forever. Can't you see how much that hurts me?"

There was no answer. I felt terrible for him, though I was also convinced he'd change his mind after thinking about it. Going to bed, I lay for the longest time, unable to erase his angry words. I finally drifted off, hoping Mama would make him understand.

The next morning I found Mama and Erich in the kitchen. They didn't speak, and he was quietly packing his bag. He said little to me until it was time to leave. I offered to walk him to the train station.

"Nay, I'll go alone. I'm going to see Papa first at Guntersblum before going north."

Sudden hope rose up in me. I believed Papa could make him see things right. I decided to stay quiet on the touchy matter in front of Mama, but I prayed it would happen.

I went with him to the street. Saying nothing, he just turned and walked away from me, the bag slung over one shoulder. I started after him, but stopped and shouted, before he could turn the corner. "Auf Wiedersehen, Erich."

Not goodbye, but 'Until we meet again.'

Chapter Twenty-Four

It was the end of January before I could find out about Erich's visit to Papa, and whether he had been able to calm my brother about the pregnancy.

"I don't think he was ready to listen to reason, but he'll come around." Those were my father's confident words in the brief time we could talk during one of his fast visits.

Papa had driven the Luftwaffe truck to Kirchheim in answer to a plea from me. Our terrier Fips had gotten away from the house several days before, and managed to get into another fight with the butcher's dog down the street. The outcome wasn't as lucky for Fips as in the past. He limped home in terrible condition, the worst wound near one eye.

Mama and I did the best we could to clean him up, but without a veterinarian in town, it was all we could do. The eye soon began to fester, and Fips stopped eating. He drank water only if it was brought to his spot by the cook stove. I went to Bossung's and telephoned a message to Papa at Guntersblum. He came the next day.

Taking one look at Fips, he picked the little fellow up and drove him to a nearby sand pit. Using the rifle carried in the truck, he mercifully ended the dog's misery. Papa later told me it was the only time he killed anything in the war.

While enemy bombers continued to use any good weather to menace lives and industry in the big German cities, a new threat struck at those of us living in the countryside. These were the low-level strafing attacks that seemed to suddenly come out of nowhere during daylight hours. Trains, road traffic, and farmers in their fields could at anytime be under attack from low-flying planes with guns blazing. One such incident killed the sister of classmate Helmuth Kelly. The young postal clerk had been sent to Langmeil, one of the stops between Kirchheim and Kaiserslautern, to pick up and bring back mail. Her train had been strafed.

Henny's mother now allowed her to come home from her school in Kaiserslautern only on weekends, and not always then. Because of it, Mama also forbid any further train trips by me to see Papa.

The girl, who had been sent to live with her grandparents across the street from Henny, was having her problems because of the strafing. Margot's home had been in Essen located in the heavily bombed Ruhr industrial area. Her father had sent her to Kirchheim after her mother died in a bombing. The

Hernandez couple she was staying with, were her mother's parents. Margot's grandmother on her father's side also lived in the Pfalz — some sixty kilometers away, and that's where the rub came in. Opa Hernandez didn't have a car, and fearful of strafing attacks, he had refused to let Margot take a train to see the other grandmother in Neustadt.

At first, it was awkward for Mama when Margot began visiting the house in the evenings. She would hide her pregnancy in the bedroom each time the girl came. I finally told Margot about it, then informed my mother hiding was unnecessary. Margot knew and understood. Mama seemed relieved in a way, and no longer left the kitchen when the girl came by.

I had no idea why Margot liked me. I supposed it was because of my friendship with Henny, who she had gotten to know first. With Henny gone much of the time, she looked to me for youthful company. About two years older, the girl was likable enough, but I thought pampered and a bit whiny. I couldn't be too critical, realizing she might still be coping with the death of her mother. That was a subject she didn't talk about much, though she wore a black armband. The biggest thing on her mind, and tongue, was a great desire to see her paternal grandmother in Neustadt.

One evening in early March, Margot sat in our kitchen talking with Mama and me, when the matter arose one more time. "I know how I can go to Neustadt with Opa's approval. He'd let me go with a bicycle."

"But you don't have a bicycle."

"Ja, that's true, but I could borrow yours."

Mama looked up from her sewing, first at Margot and then me. "It's a long way to Neustadt, though I suppose it could be done on a bicycle. Don't you think so, Märe?"

"It could be done, I'm sure. However, I don't have a light on my bicycle. I've waited so long to buy lights, they aren't available anymore. When I ride at night, I take Erich's bike."

"I don't think I could ride a boy's bicycle," protested Margot. "I'll just ride yours there in the daytime."

"Nay, I don't think your grandfather will let you do that."

"Mama's right. The enemy has been strafing everything that moves on the ground in the daylight. You would have to go at night."

"But I don't know how to get to Neustadt," she argued, tears starting. "Going in the dark, I'd get lost!"

"Nay, you wouldn't," I assured her, knowing different. I winked at Mama.

"And you know, they do speak German along the way!"

My attempt at humor missed the mark. Margot was set on directing our talk toward the inevitable question. "So, Opa won't let me go in the daylight, and I can't go at night without a light. He probably wouldn't allow me making the trip alone anyway."

The pause that followed was as pregnant as Mama. Somehow Mama and I knew what was coming.

"You know the way, don't you Annchen? You could lead the way riding your brother's bicycle."

I saw Mama shake her head, but Margot was looking at me and I couldn't lie. "Ja, I know the way. I've gone with Papa several times to Neustadt. I just don't know if you can make it. There are many hills most of the way, and you haven't been riding a bicycle." I could see Mama thought that would change her mind. It didn't.

"I could practice a week or so on your bicycle. I'll have to write to my grandmother anyway, to let her know I'm coming. In the meantime, I can toughen my legs!" Turning to Mama before I could respond, she questioned, "Don't you think we could make it?

"Wait a minute," I said, interrupting. "Mama's due to have the baby in April and I can't be gone when that happens. We haven't had much snow lately, but the nights are still freezing. We could dress for the cold, but should we get heavy snow, there's no way we can go before the birth. Afterwards, I'm not so sure either. The road we'd have to take goes very near dangerous bombing targets. Even Neustadt, the place you want to go has been hit hard."

Margot looked stricken, the effect I had hoped for, when to my surprise, Mama came to her rescue. "It may work out before the baby's due. March is a strange month. It's been known not to have snow at all. Why not plan on going and see what the last week brings."

Margot looked as though she would jump up and hug her. That would have only added to my state of shock over Mama caving in so easily to the girl. The trip she had agreed to wouldn't be without physical demands and perils. I wondered what was on my mother's mind, but I didn't ask.

Trapped by my own admission that it could be done, preparation for the long bicycle ride began. Over the following days, Margot practiced going up and down the hills of Kirchheim on my bicycle. I attended to school and chores, all the while keeping my eyes on the sky for snow clouds. None appeared. In fact, most days were perfect for bombing — cold, but bright and clear.

Approaching the last snow-less weekend of March, it was time to lay out plans for the trip. Mama agreed with most of my ideas — the extra heavy clothing, food, and tire repair kit — but suddenly voiced worry about two girls being seen riding alone. Her worry gave me an idea. I went up to the Hernandez home to tell Margot and her grandparents about it.

"If the weather holds, we'll leave from my house after midnight Saturday. Prepare a sandwich and something to drink. I'll do the same. Most of all, it must be understood that we have to be back in twenty-four hours. I can't be gone from Mama longer than that. Is it agreed?"

Margot nodded agreement, and I continued. "That should be plenty of time to visit your grandmother. I figure it will take around six hours to reach Neustadt. We can rest some, and you'll have the whole afternoon to visit. If we leave there by six, we can be back here around midnight. It still turns dark early, so we should be safe coming home. I want to be far from Neustadt, should the bombers attack it again."

"Sounds like a good plan to me," Herr Hernandez said, nodding at his wife.

"And, I'll be traveling as a boy."

A wide-eyed Margot looked from me to her grandparents, and back. "What? How — "

"Mama gave me the idea, worrying about two girls riding alone in the night. She may be right, and I won't have a problem dressing like a boy. I have Erich's clothes, even his hat and muffler!"

Three nights later and still no snow, but it was cold with frost already beginning to coat the tile roofs. I told Mama not to stay up, we would leave quietly when the church bell struck midnight. (Fortunately, the Nazi officials had left one bell in the Catholic Church tower.) I assured her of my determination to be back by the time the church bell rang out midnight again.

When Margot showed up with knapsack, she found me in shoes with heavy socks, work pants, shirt, sweater and jacket, topped off with my brother's hat and muffler. I had twisted my long braids up on my head, pinning them down under the hat. She readily agreed that, at a distance, I would look like a boy. I silently wondered what Erich and Papa would think.

Leaving the courtyard through the big doors, I looked up to find a nearly full moon. That was both good and bad. We'd see the roadway better, but it also meant bombing attacks where we were heading. I led the way, Margot close behind, since I had the bike light. It would be easier to explain if stopped by a policeman. Down the winding narrow Langstraße into the old town center, out the Vorstadtstraße to the edge of Kirchheim where we left cobblestone for smoother asphalt and the road to Marnheim. It would be asphalt all the way to Neustadt, except for the cobblestone streets of towns and cities on the way. These included Marnheim, Monsheim, Bockenheim, Grünstadt, Bad Dürkheim, and Deidesheim. In between these larger places were many smaller villages and tiny farm settlements.

I spoke for the first time passing through Marnheim. "How are you doing back there? Come up beside me when we get into open country."

"My hands are freezing, gloves and all, but alright otherwise," she said, pulling alongside.

"Mine are cold, too. The wind goes right through the gloves and stings the face. We'll get used to it." I changed the subject. "I was born in the town we just came through. Nothing too special about it."

(The time would come when, as an adult, I changed my mind entirely about my birth village.)

Margot pointed ahead. "What's that? Wait — I see now. It looks like a bridge going across the whole wide valley."

"That's the railroad bridge connecting Kibo with the Marnheim station. Except for the tall stone pillars, the bridge is built entirely of iron. You must have crossed it coming down from Essen. Marnheim is the main transfer point for trains."

"I didn't come by train. My father brought me in his car."

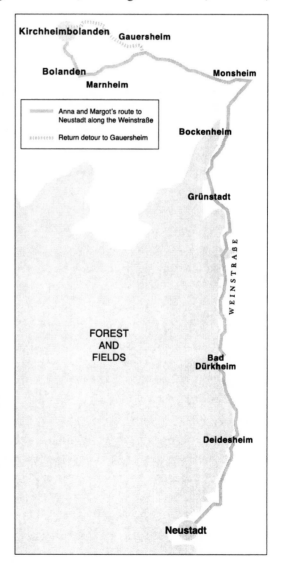

Kirchheimbolanden Gauersheim

Bolanden Monsheim

Marnheim

Anna and Margot's route to
Neustadt along the Weinstraße

Return detour to Gauersheim

Bockenheim

Grünstadt

WEINSTRAßE

FOREST
AND
FIELDS

Bad
Dürkheim

Deidesheim

Neustadt

Yes, I thought to myself, being a big industrial executive, her father would have a car. We fell into silence again for the hilly sixteen-kilometer haul to Monsheim. Pedaling through some farm settlements, the roadway often passed within arm's reach of homes and barns. The aromas and sounds of restless animals were somehow comforting, even warming. Occasionally, a dog roused by our aroma, would bark close by.

Without the many gears available on modern bicycles, pedaling a single speed bike up a hill was punishment. Reaching the top of one hill, I stopped a moment to let Margot catch up.

"I'm fine," she smiled, breathing hard.

"Good. I just wanted you to know that we'll soon hit a very high hill outside Monsheim. Don't try to pedal it. We'll walk our bicycles. At the bottom of the hill we'll turn onto another road toward Grünstadt and the Rhein valley."

Just outside Grünstadt, we finally stopped to rest on a rural bus stop bench.

"Let's stay here a few minutes, and have a sandwich and tea. I'm sure we're near halfway to Neustadt."

Margot plopped down next to me and started rummaging in her knapsack for food. "I'm glad to stop. My legs feel like lead. What kind of sandwich did you bring?"

I had just opened my mouth for a first bite. "It's just bread with some butter and slices of cheese. What's yours?"

"About the same as you, only Oma put in cold cuts. Would you like to split with me?"

We ate in silence, and drank cold mint tea. It tasted good, but I started cooling down and I thought we'd better move on. Before either of us could move, sirens in Grünstadt blasted the night quiet. A trembling Margot grabbed my arm, as we stood frozen in place. Soon a low rumble from the west reached our ears — bombers!

We waited and saw streams of lights to the east begin searching the black night. The loud roar of big propeller engines overhead kept us rooted to the spot. There was no place for us to run and hide anyway. After the initial shock of the siren's sound, Margot had calmed and loosened her grip on me. She said the sound of planes wasn't as bad as the bomb explosions that followed. She should know.

I knew that due east from our location was Worms, and that's where the group of planes passing over us were heading. Just as the flak started up around that city, we saw more lights come on to the south toward Ludwigshafen and Mannheim targets. It wasn't long before the flak and flares from anti-aircraft guns filled the night sky over the Rhein valley. The thunder and ground vibrations of bombs exploding short kilometers away now joined the tumult before our eyes. The spots of fire's glow began to pop up and spread along the eastern horizon — adding to the illusion of one of those blazing sunsets, but on the wrong side of the world.

It was over in minutes. The German anti-aircraft gun crews were still trying, even while the first returning bombers passed over us. They were more widespread in the sky and not making such a terrible rumble. We decided to leave our lonely bus stop.

"How many kilometers did you say it was from Kirchheim to Neustadt?"

I'd been expecting the question for the last ten kilometers, so I was ready to tell the truth. It wouldn't have stopped her from making the trip, but I didn't see any need to scare her.

"I told your grandparents it was about fifty kilometers. I then realized this easier bike route was more like sixty or sixty-five. I didn't think you could pedal the shorter, but harder way."

"I couldn't make it if we had many more hills like those."

"The land starts to level out now. The last half should be easier. Let's get going."

It was strange that only one vehicle had passed us since leaving Kirchheim. I expected that the coming dawn would bring a change. The lack of traffic brought Margot up next to me so we could talk easier.

"This is better," she said. "No big hills."

"We're now on what is called the 'Wine street,' and when it gets lighter you'll see why — only vineyards in every direction for as far as the eye can see.

At Bad Dürkheim, home of the big "Wurstmarkt" and wine barrel restaurant, we started running into more cars and trucks on the street. Many of the vehicles were mopeds, a small-motorized scooter used by workers. Margot slid in behind me as more and more of these zipped past us, obviously people going to jobs in town and elsewhere. There were a few cars and an occasional military truck going in both directions. We had to be careful until reaching open country again, and on to Deidesheim.

Deidesheim was our last big town before Neustadt and upon arriving, I caught sight of a clock on a church tower. A quarter past seven. We were running late, though not bad considering the extra kilometers. Tired as we were at this point, our spirits perked up laughing over an incident. Passing a bus stop on the edge of Deidesheim, a bunch of boys all started doing that common female-appreciation-whistling thing. They couldn't have been aiming their whistling at me dressed as a boy, and as if I could care. That set of hormones in me hadn't started throbbing yet. I looked at Margot who wasn't especially pretty, just sort of normal and neat appearing. She looked at me, and we burst out laughing so hard our legs could hardly pedal.

It looked to be another sunny day dawning, as the skyline of Neustadt came into view. No smoke was rising, and I was glad it hadn't been on the target list of the latest raid. It soon became evident however, that the city hadn't escaped. On the outskirts, houses and barns, and even the famous vineyards, showed scars from explosions. In town, great sections of buildings along our way had been leveled.

"You do remember where your Oma lives?"

"Not exactly," Margot shouted. "Let's get off and walk a little." After dismounting, she thought a minute. "Oma wrote in her letter that Rotkreuzstraße is a main street. It shouldn't be hard to find."

Easier said than done, and the reason became shockingly apparent the farther we walked. Whole blocks of buildings had been turned to rubble by the bombings, and along with missing houses were street signs. Yet most of the buildings remained intact and inhabited, and we saw people out getting a new day started. After several minutes, I stopped a woman who looked to be a cleaning lady and asked directions. She kindly walked with us to a nearby intersection and pointed the way. Mounting our bicycles, I heard her wonder aloud if the address we wanted was still standing.

We were relieved to find the grandmother's apartment building unharmed, though a building on one side was leveled. Margot said she lived on the second floor, so we left the bicycles in the ground floor hall and climbed the stairs.

A small and handsome old woman answered our knock, hugging us both into a spacious apartment. "Oh, I can't believe it. All that far, and on bicycles! I'm so glad you're safe. Come, come. I have some coffee and bread. Would you like a hard-boiled egg? They're cold, but the coffee is hot."

I was so tired, if she had spoken any faster, I wouldn't have understood a word. The food sounded good and we ate with appetite. Afterward, I asked to lie down. Margot joined me in sleeping until noon, when Oma offered us soup and bread from her meager rations. I decided to rest some more and let the two of them visit. Amazingly for me, I fell asleep again instantly and woke up about four o'clock.

Coming out of the bedroom, I saw Oma and Margot deep in conversation. The old woman looked up. "Surely, you can stay over for two or three days. You need to rest for the long ride back."

Margot had a look of complete agreement, which made me angry. She knew my situation and my promise to Mama. "I'm sorry. I can't do that. I promised my mother to return tonight." I was disgusted with the Essen girl for putting me in the position of seeming ungrateful, but I tried to keep my composure. "Thank you, for being concerned, but I must leave within the hour. I expect Margot to come with me, otherwise I don't know how she will find her way home safe. I also promised her family in Kirchheim that I'd bring her back."

It was now Margot's turn to become angry. "No, I'm staying here. Don't worry about me finding the way. I'll go back when I'm good and ready!"

I glared at her a full minute. The kindly old person next to her really seemed in need of company, but that didn't change the fact the girl had broken her word. It also meant I'd have to ride the sixty kilometers back alone, mostly in the dark.

"Alright," I said. "I'll leave now instead of six. That'll give me some daylight to get out of the area. Just remember the bicycle you have doesn't have a light or the tire repair kit."

"I'll work something out," said Oma brightly. "Maybe she can go back on a train. We'll see."

I turned away to retrieve Erich's coat and hat, letting my braids hang out. Thanking the grandmother for the food and bed, I left the apartment without looking at Margot again. All the way down the stairs, my mind was working overtime.

"Put her on a train!" I muttered to myself angrily. The whole reason I made this trip was to keep her off the trains! How am I going to explain this to Herr Hernandez?

Finding it warmer than expected, I removed my sweater and stuffed it into the cloth sack hanging from the handlebars. Part of a sandwich and half a bottle of tea were still in the sack. Without Margot to be concerned about, I hurried along and made good time out of Neustadt.

It was still bright daylight passing through Deidesheim, and on into vineyard countryside again. A few kilometers short of Bad Dürkheim, I heard the sound of planes and quickly stopped. Two small dots low in the sky were coming fast in my direction, looming larger in size with every heartbeat. Two older people on bicycles up ahead on the tree-lined road had also halted, and were already running toward the embankment. Mesmerized by the approach of the planes, I finally realized they were the enemy looking for vehicles and people to strafe. Dropping my bicycle, I made my legs run to the grassy slope by a tree. The noise turned deafening just as I threw myself down and hugged the earth. Roaring side by side the planes flew over, but didn't fire their guns. From my vantage point, and in my state of mind, the planes seemed to touch the tops of trees before flying straight up and away. I thought I'd stay put, in case they decided to return. After another minute or so I heard a voice speak.

"It's alright young man. The planes are gone. You can come up."

I slowly rose, not sure it was me being talked to. I'd never been called a 'young man' before. As I stood, my braids, which had fallen beneath me, came in view to the woman standing above.

"You're not a boy at all, just a young girl!"

"Ja," I answered, climbing up the slope. "I'm a girl." I picked up my bicycle. "As you can see I have a boy's bike. It's easier to pedal with trousers on." I rode away before the couple could ask about the rest of my male attire.

After the airplane incident, I wished for night's darkness. It finally came soon after rolling through Grünstadt. Fewer cars and trucks passed me by, and I made good time on to Bockenheim, and the big hill near Monsheim.

Before sailing down the steep grade, a cold drizzle began and I stopped to put on the heavy sweater under my coat. Only then did I remember the half sandwich and tea, making me hungry for the first time. But a heavier rainfall told me not to stop, and instead head for home by way of a short cut through Gauersheim. There I could stop at Tante Sannchen. The slight detour was over a hilly gravel road, but driven by the cold rain, I made record time.

Sannchen remained close after Onkel Heinrich's death, though less than a year later, she remarried and moved into her new husband's home. I didn't know where that house was, but I knew the village of Gauersheim and would find it.

"You give Seppel my regards when you see him." An innkeeper was nice enough to point a finger toward my aunt's house. He also knew my father.

I looked like some drowned ghost when Tante Sannchen opened the door. She gasped and jerked me into the hall, all the while marveling. "Gott im Himmel, Märe, what are you doing here, and all soaked! Come quickly into the warm kitchen and take off those wet clothes. Ach, sit here child and let me hang that coat by the stove. Have you eaten? I'll fix something."

I always found it a wonderful trait in Sannchen to think of food any time a relative or good friend stopped by, no matter what time was on the clock. When I looked at the one on her wall, it was after ten. She was the only one up. Her two young girls were in bed, as was her husband, who I called Herr Schreiter, not Onkel.

While she hurried around frying potatoes and slicing off some sausage, I explained my day. She punctuated my tale with "Ach, you poor girl" throughout. A half-hour later after eating, I suddenly felt very weary, which prompted my aunt to urge me to stay the night.

"Nay, Tante, but many thanks. I must go on, Mama will be worried. I should be there before midnight. The rain isn't too bad and who knows, tomorrow it may snow."

The coat wasn't dry, just mighty warm and that felt good as I readied my bicycle again. My aunt stood in the doorway watching and asking me repeatedly to stay, but I just thanked and hugged her "auf Wiedersehen."

Back on the road, and the final few kilometers. I thought about Tante Sannchen and realized my leaving in the rain reminded her of Heinrich. He caught his death riding a bicycle in bad weather. I still missed my favorite uncle, but smiled thinking about the man who was so much a part of my early years. He wouldn't have been surprised by my latest adventure — more likely he'd be proud.

I hoped Tante Sannchen wouldn't worry too much, and pedaled faster toward home and Mama. I knew that after the ride I had just taken, I would survive.

Chapter Twenty-Five

Long before the Neustadt trip, I'd tried forcing the matter of clothing for the baby, but Mama proved to be of little help. Since Christmas, her daily mood swings were going way up and down, just as they had before the pregnancy. At best, she got dressed and did some light cleaning and cooking, but I often came home from school to find her still in bed. Her willingness to make decisions had disappeared, except on rare days. The low days brought only silent stares for answers. I tried to attribute these swings to the pregnancy. I couldn't think of any other reason. She made no move to help me understand any other cause.

If there had been any baby clothes left from Erich or I, Mama had given them away years before. Another baby had no place in my parents' plans after I was born. Now everything had changed, and it was left to me to find some way to get clothes and diapers. The latter didn't worry me — I could use old bed sheets to produce diapers. It was little gowns and such that I hadn't yet tackled on the sewing machine. Baby things in a store were rationed, like everything else, and a special permission slip from City Hall was required.

Most of my close friends at school had now been told about Mama, and from one of them I learned that the slips were available. I rushed home to ask Mama what she thought. I discovered her in bed, a bad sign, but her response struck me as stranger than usual. For long minutes, she stared at me blankly and said not a word.

"Mama, I know we have the money. Please say something. We need to get clothes for the baby!"

I waited for an answer, though her vacant look almost changed my mind. Her eyes suddenly focused on me, and she smirked. It wasn't an expression I liked on her, but it was better than none at all.

"You can try," she finally said, moving to leave the bed. "There's money in my purse, all you'll need."

I got it and hurried out, hoping I'd broken the bad spell that had made Mama depressed.

Entering the door of the rationing office, I was pleased to see there was no line. The last person served was turning to leave, and I marched right up to a balding man with a pencil thin mustache seated at the desk.

"Heil Hitler. I'm here for permission slips to buy baby clothes."

"You look a little young and not at all pregnant. Why should you need such a slip."

"It's not for me. My mother is pregnant." I had thought it would be an easy matter. How I wished that Papa could be there to handle the man.

"So, it's for your mother. And do you have a document from a physician affirming her condition?"

I wasn't prepared for that. Mama hadn't been to a doctor since before the pregnancy. "Nay, I haven't such a paper."

"Then I can't help you. If your mother is really pregnant, I need proof." He got up and walked away. On his desk was a small bust of Hitler, and I wanted to throw it at him. Instead, I turned and left for my house, disgusted and frustrated.

Telling Mama about it, she didn't appear surprised, and I knew not to suggest that she visit a doctor. There was only Doctor Hahn, and I think she sensed he might deny her condition. I could tell something had already happened in her relationship with Hahn.

Two other possibilities for baby clothes occurred to me. Both Frau Andres next door and Tante Gusta in Bolanden had had babies in the last two years. I could ask them, but in the meantime it wouldn't hurt to check the trunk in the attic. I really didn't expect to find baby clothes, distinctly remembering that Mama had given them to my namesake aunts. Still, I might find something useful.

The steamer-type trunk sat under the window at one end of the attic, and I wiped off the top and heaved it open. Just below the lid, a removable deep tray extended across the length covering the main compartment. Only lightweight things such as gloves and lace hankies lay in it, and to my delight — a large wide brim black straw hat. I lifted it out and placed it on my head in fun. It was then all I could do to extend my hands far enough apart to stick my fingers into holes at the ends of the tray to bring it out.

The things stored below were covered by an old pillow slip. I lifted it off carefully, perhaps fearful that ghosts might rise up. None did, though something far better rose up, helped by my hands. I had reached for a neatly folded, irresistible dress — so beautiful that I couldn't believe I'd forgotten about it.

How many years had it been since Mama showed me not just this dress, but several more of similar style that lay with it? They were from the turn of the century, from her youth. All were very frilly and elegant. The material was a kind of gauzy voile in all shades of white, except for one black dress. It too was fancy, with lace trim everywhere and puffy sleeves. Another dress had intricate beading on the bodice that added a subtle sparkle. Mama had said they were mostly for summer. I had last seen the dresses as a child, and I remember being fascinated but quickly disinterested. They had been, after all, much too big for me. In the years between, I acted more like a boy than a girl — according to Erich — and fancy dresses had no appeal for me. All the harder to explain then why I suddenly had to urge to put on one of the dresses, right then and there. However, not in the cold attic!

Deciding on the first dress and a long pair of fingerless summer gloves, I went down to the comfortably warm kitchen, the straw hat was still on my head. As was Mama's new routine, she had remained in the bedroom.

Quickly I removed my school clothes and prayerfully slipped the new to me fancy white frock over my head and buttoned the back. It fit perfectly over my waist and hips. Of course, I didn't fill out the lacy bodice like Mama, but the shoulders fit. I tugged the sleeves until they looked perfectly puffy — maybe too puffy for my square shoulders. I didn't have high heel shoes to wear, so the wide skirt hung nearly to the floor. I had to walk on my toes to raise it a little. Looking in the small mirror over the sink was useless for an overall inspection. I tried the hat in various positions. Finally, I found slightly tipping it to one side pleased me the most. I put my braids in front, threw one back, then both back, but nothing looked right. In order to see myself in a full-length mirror, I'd have to risk Mama's reaction to my foolishness in the bedroom.

I didn't want to startle her, and called out before entering the room. She turned from looking out the window just as I moved through the door. I knew she might get angry and it was only childish excitement that made me chance it. To my relief, and real

Kristina VanOss captures the moment beautifully when a very pregnant Mama found pleasure in seeing me in one of her stunning turn of the century dresses. She soon unbraided my hair, brushed it down my back, and then topped it off by placing a black, wide-brim fancy straw hat on my head.

surprise, Mama smiled and chuckled.

"Ach, you have my dress on!" She walked toward me, saying I should turn around. "It fits you nicely. I'm amazed."

I looked in the mirror, and she looked with me. I pulled at one of the braids. "Ja, I like it, too," I said. "But somehow these braids don't look right."

"Come, I'll show you how your hair will look best with this dress." Sitting on the bed, she loosened my braids. She then brushed my hair until it shined, laying the result down my back and put the hat back on my head.

"Now, look at yourself in the mirror."

I couldn't believe what I saw. My hair flowed down from under the hat to drape my shoulders, then fell to well below my waist in waves. Brushing my hair out had changed my whole image. As I rarely looked in the full-length mirror I had not really noticed how long my hair was unbraided.

"This was one of my good summer dresses when I was around eighteen or nineteen."

Mama lifted and touched the flared skirt. Her hand smoothed the material over my back and shoulders with an almost loving touch. She seemed to be reliving a happy moment in her life, and her hands were in contact with the past, not with me. I didn't fully realize it then in those terms — I just liked her caressing touch.

"Mama, did you go dancing in this dress?" I began swishing back and forth in front of the mirror, watching the skirt flare out. As I did I became aware that Mama was sitting on the bed, humming one of many songs she used to sing.

Finally, "Ach, Märe, you know I've said we had little time for such things!"

I was disappointed in the answer, but even more in her brusque tone and the lost touch of her hand. I went on dancing and turning, refusing to lose the magic, even though I didn't know how to dance. I simply twirled about like I had seen in a movie, humming a waltz melody. On one turn, I caught Mama smiling at me, and I came to a stop in front of her. "Why are you smiling? Do I look strange? I know I can't dance."

"Nay, nay. You look and dance just fine. Someday you'll dance the night away. It's just that you reminded me of, well, something I hadn't thought about in a long time. My sisters and I used to twirl around and sing in our fancy dresses at home after church on Sundays. But only when we were alone. Your grandfather would have thought it sinful to dance on the Lord's day, and our brothers would have laughed at our silliness."

As Mama talked, she moved to sit on the side of her bed. I joined her, placing myself carefully so as not to harm the dress. She took my hand and held it on her lap while she reminisced. At one point, she was nearly apologetic. "I don't want to leave the idea in your head that I never had happy times. I went to dances only with your Papa, and even then, not very often."

Daylight had faded outside the bedroom window, and we both knew without saying it that the present needed attention. I stood up, made one more twirling motion away from her, and took a last look in the mirror.

"Isn't it sad?" I said. "I'll soon outgrow this beautiful dress. I haven't stopped growing. Papa says I may end up a head taller than both of you!"

"What's so sad about that?"

"Because I'll never have a photo of myself as I look right now."

❧

As there was no light in the attic, I waited until the next day to return Mama's dress to the trunk. In doing so, I discovered another treasure folded on the bottom. It was my Opa Jean's uniform from the Franco-Prussian War in the late 1800's. I had no idea what rank or position my grandfather held in the Kaiser's service. In the midst of another war, I had little interest in old conflicts. But I was impressed with the dark green uniform, made of fine wool and trimmed with red flaps on the shoulders. Red striping trimmed the collar and jacket front, along with two rows of fancy brass buttons, and the red striping also decorated the outer seams of the pants.

Opa Jean Herbst

I have a picture of Opa Herbst in the uniform, young and dashing with a head of wavy black hair, and wearing a full beard with mustache. How the uniform came into Mama's possession, I was never certain. I assumed she took over its care when her mother died. I carefully put the uniform back in the trunk below the dresses and closed the lid.

❧

Only weeks remained in the seventh grade with Lehrer Lawaldt, and I found it hard to accept. Going to school everyday to my favorite teacher was the only pleasure I'd had since taking on nearly all the housework. Mama found it increasingly hard to bend and lift, and limited her efforts to cooking. I really didn't mind the extra workload, except for the time it took. All of the chores — washing and polishing floors, and doing the laundry — were all done by hand. Working class families weren't likely to have washing machines and vacuum sweepers. These appliances were certainly known and available, at least they were until the war. Papa would have convinced his wife to buy and use such labor-saving devices early on — had there been no war.

In the beginning of April, I got more nervous. My mother hadn't said exactly when the birth would take place. I'd done some backtracking on the calendar and figured it had to be in April.

Still, there were other things to do besides worry about the arrival of a baby. Some of my girlfriends in class wanted to give Lawaldt a farewell gift. I suggested giving a photo of all the girls, and it was agreed upon.

As it turned out, three of the twenty-four girls bowed out, probably for lack of money. Somehow, I regretted that the twenty boys in class didn't participate, if only for remembrance sake. The idea was brought up to invite the boys, but it was voted down. "Let the boys do their own gift," someone said. Soon thereafter, twenty-one girls secretly gathered at Photo Haus Ims to pose.

I sat on pins and needles waiting for the resulting photo. Being wartime, there was a shortage of materials, and we heard only one click of the shutter. We were told it would be a week or more before twenty-two copies of one frozen moment could be picked up — like them or not.

It was Wednesday morning, April fifth. Leaving for school, I stuck my head into Mama's bedroom to say goodbye.

"Don't go to school, Märe. Find the midwife."

I realized it wasn't going to happen the way I'd planned. There was none of the control I expected. "Which midwife? There are two!"

"Get Frau Walter, of course," she quietly answered. I marveled over her calmness, grabbed my heavy sweater, and raced out of the house to run down to the Walters' home on Gasstraße. I'd already rounded the corner, when I had to run back to tell Rosalinde across from our house to inform Lehrer Lawaldt. From there, I started running again down the Langstraße, through the town center to the Gasstraße. I'd never been to the midwife's house and had to take a moment to find the right door. After knocking, I didn't bother to wait, and pushed through the door to find myself in a kitchen with a startled young woman at the sink.

"Please, I need Frau Walter!"

The woman wiped her hands dry. "I'm sorry, Frau Walter isn't here, but I expect her soon. Where do you need her?"

I managed to answer in a rational fashion. Explaining the situation at Breitstraße One, I asked that she have the midwife come quickly.

"Yes, I'll tell her. Now go back and try to calm down. Things don't go that fast!" That was a comfort. I had no idea how fast babies were born.

Back at the house, I found Mama up and around, just as steady as could be. I put more wood on the kitchen-stove fire. Because of the midwife's delay, I was told to go and get Frau Rösel. "I think there should be another woman in the house until Frau Walter gets here."

Frau Rösel had already learned about the pending birth from daughter Rosalinde, and was waiting to see if her help was needed. When she entered our door, I ran down to Bossung's corner to anxiously await the midwife. My eyes searched the Langstraße for as far as I could see to the first curve, hoping to see her familiar figure pedaling a bicycle. My welcoming committee of one wasn't really necessary. Frau Walter knew every centimeter of Kirchheim, but I waited and worried just the same. Looking up to the clock on the Catholic church tower, the hour hand was nearing nine o'clock. Where was Frau Walter?

Neighbor women started going by in ones and twos, on their way to see what could be found in the shops. "Guten Morgen" — "Guten Tag," was spoken several times as they walked past, no doubt wondering what had me standing on the corner. If I hadn't greeted them, my name would have been forever blackened. In my town you speak to passersby, especially people from the neighborhood.

I finally spotted the midwife coming up the hill. In another minute, she was telling me of having just delivered another baby, then asked a few questions about Mama. I answered as best I could. At the house, she propped her bicycle against the wall, took a black bag from the back and stepped through the door with a sigh.

Showing her upstairs and to the bedroom, I saw the small figure suddenly go ramrod straight as she went through the doorway. She ordered me to stay in the kitchen and keep the fire hot and the water kettle going. I was obviously being excluded from the birthing process, except to provide the hot water. From the bedroom, Frau Rösel heard the midwife, and came out in the kitchen a few minutes later.

"Don't worry, Annchen," she said. "Your mother will be fine. Frau Walter talks like that because she thinks young girls shouldn't witness a birth."

"Why not? I'm nearly fourteen. I should be in there holding Mama's hand

— or something!"

Frau Rösel, whose singing and laughter I always liked, chuckled and patted my hand. "That may be, but she believes you will be scared off from wanting to have children of your own if you see a birth."

"That's crazy!"

"Hush now. I'm going back in. Everything will be just fine."

Making myself busy, I puttered about, sweeping the floor and wiping the table a dozen times. I listened and waited, finally deciding that the walls were too thick for a baby's cry to be heard through. Frau Rösel came in the kitchen a few times to carry back more hot water. I was glad she was there, but I began to think they were all taking a bath, so much water was leaving. Shaking the thought from my head, I kept heating water and watching the clock.

At precisely eleven o'clock in the morning, I heard the first cry, and became nervous with suspense. I had something, a brother or a sister, but which? I heard footsteps, and the midwife came in, her sleeves still rolled up and an apron pinned to her bosom. "You have a brother, a healthy little guy. That's for sure." The little woman continued drying her hands, as though she didn't know what I wanted. "You can go in and see them, soon as we clean up a little more."

Frau Rösel then appeared, exclaiming the news all over again. "Ach, what a beautiful little boy."

This only added to my fear. I didn't remember ever liking babies. How was I going to react to him? Would I hate him?

The midwife reappeared with a bundle of soiled linen and laid the pile on the floor. "Leave it here until I return later. I have to look them over yet." She put on her coat, picked up the black bag, and started for the door.

"Many thanks, Frau Walter," I said, quickly. "Thank you for coming so quickly."

She just smiled and turned to go. "Let your mother sleep soon."

There were no further instructions, and I had no idea what to do for a newborn baby. Frau Rösel came back from the bedroom, ready to return to her own home. "I'll be back later with some chicken soup for your mother." Stepping into the hallway, she turned and smiled. "I think it's safe to go in now." She said, nodding toward the bedroom.

I stood there alone for several minutes. Though not a praying sort of person, I made pleas for strength and patience many times during my wait. That day in the kitchen, I prayed hard that I would love my new brother.

Slowly, I entered the quiet bedroom, tiptoeing to where Mama lay. Our eyes met, and she was smiling, first at me, then at the bundle in the crook of her arm. She moved a corner of the blanket so I could see, and there, a round little red face greeted me, topped by a helmet of black hair. Mama watched my reaction and smiled more broadly. I couldn't stop staring at his sweet face, so peaceful in sleep.

"Do you like him, Märe?"

"Oh, Mama, he's so beautiful. He looks just like Erich with that round face and those little fists he makes." I couldn't resist the urge to touch him for the first time. I slowly put a finger on one of his round cheeks, amazed at its softness. "Peterchen," I murmured.

Mama and Papa had promised earlier that I could name the baby. I can't think now what I proposed for a girl, but there was never any doubt about a boy's name — Peter Herman. The second name was a compromise with my father. He said we should follow the old German tradition of naming at least one son after a famous leader. Of course, Herman as in Herman Göring, was Papa's big boss in the Luftwaffe. I didn't care. No one was going to call him Herman — not if I had anything to do with it.

I wanted the name to be Peter for my Opa Klein — not the original Seppel — but the one who really brought renown and good fortune to my Klein family in our Donnersberg region. It took an entire world economic recession to finally bring 'Kleine Seppel' down. And I knew Oma in Bolanden would be so proud we had honored her late husband. I thought having a new Peter in the family would bring happiness. In many ways, he did just that.

I left Mama to sleep, and went to Bossung's to telephone Papa with the news. He was delighted, and promised to come home soon. On my way back to the house I ran into Frau Andres, who gave me one of her baby bottles. The news of Peter's entry into the world was traveling fast on the street.

Frau Walter returned as promised to check the sheets, and advised me to give my mother lots of liquid and keep her in bed for a week. Noticing the worry on my face. "You've got to be all of seventeen, there shouldn't be anything you can't handle I'll tell the Health Department to send a nurse to check on those two in there."

"I'll be fine, Frau Walter. My father's coming home for a few days. But I'm not seventeen. I'll be fourteen in July."

She left, shaking her head. The next morning I fixed some fennel tea, just as the midwife said I should. Mama couldn't start nursing for hours yet. The tea was for Peter, who had begun to whimper for food. I was so thrilled when

Mama allowed me to sit on the bed and hold him while giving him the tea from Frau Andres' bottle. I wasn't allowed to do anything else for the moment. The midwife had said that only she would bathe and change Peter for the first few days.

The birth had taken place on the Wednesday before Good Friday. By the time Papa got home on Saturday, I had matters fairly well in hand. The Health Department had sent a woman to help with the laundry and clean the house, apparently a one-time service when someone had a baby. One look and my father agreed Peter reminded him of Erich. "I just hope he grows into another Seppel like Erich." Papa and I were in the wash kitchen working. "How would you like permanent help here until this war is over and I can be home?"

Before I could answer, he explained. "Frau Hofmann, the woman who does the laundry for me in Guntersblum, could live with you here in this big house and help with all the chores. That way she'd be away from all the bombing and be useful. You'd like her, she's a widowed lady. She could sew for you, too. How does that sound to you?"

"Papa, it sounds fine to me, but I don't think Mama will agree. Have you asked her?"

"Nay, I wanted to talk to you first. We'll see."

He was to leave Monday after Easter, and if he asked my mother, her answer must have been no — Frau Hofmann never came. The reason was probably because of an incident Easter evening.

On Sunday afternoon, my father had said he would walk to Bolanden to visit his mother. I remained home to bake traditional yeast cakes, but the day was uneventful until late evening.

Mama and Peter were sleeping, and by eleven I was in my bedroom, ready to do the same. It had been a long day and I was tired, both from work and from waiting for Papa's return. As I turned back the bed covers, I heard a stumbling noise from the stairway. Mama's bedroom was closer to the hall, and I feared she'd be awakened. I knew it had to be Papa, and I hurried out to hush him.

There he was, starting to enter her room and tripping over the two steps up. When I got to him, he'd decided to sit on the top step in the dark, mumbling and laughing about something only he understood. Not wanting to turn on the bedroom light and really disturb Mama, I went and switched on the living room light. It partially illuminated the bedroom door and steps. Right away, Papa saw one of Peter's little sweaters on the chair by the door. He picked it up and studied it in a cock-eyed fashion.

"Look at my jacket. It shrunk." By the sound of his voice, I knew he was 'happy drunk' — not 'incoherent drunk.'

I was angry and disappointed, but had to bite my lip to keep from laughing. Papa looked so comical holding the tiny sweater on to himself. I couldn't see Mama, and she said nothing, but I knew she lay there disgusted. I went to help my father up and over to the extra bed.

I whispered loudly in his ear, "Papa, what have you done? You promised. Why didn't you stop?"

He chuckled, but offered no resistance to my help. In seconds, he was quiet and sound asleep. I looked over to Mama and Peter, across the room in the shadows. The baby hadn't awakened, and still only silence from my mother. Tears stung my eyes. *Damn you, Papa. Why can't you behave, at least for Mama's sake!* The words echoed loudly in my head, and for a moment I was sure I had actually spoken them.

The next morning, he remembered nothing, not even how he had made it home. I reminded him of that 'magic button' on his neck that stopped the flow of wine.

"Well," he sighed. "I can only say it didn't pop last night. Ach, it's always different in Bolanden, where I know so many people. I only stopped by Kroneberger's Inn to say hello. It would have insulted the owner had I refused his offer of a glass."

"And the offer of everyone else in the place, I'm sure."

"Well, I didn't spend a pfennig all evening, that's certain. I checked this morning. But you're right. I should have quit early and come home. I wouldn't be in hot water today."

"Oh, Papa, can't you "sei brav' for me, like I do for you?"

He smiled, reached across the table to pat my cheek, and asked for more jam for his bread.

❧

During the few days that remained in seventh grade at Easter, is when the girls gave Herr Lawaldt our gift, framed and wrapped in pretty paper. We watched with anxious eyes as he carefully opened the package. We needn't have worried. The oversized photo of us seemed to please him. He was speechless for the first time in three years. Finding his voice, he looked at the group in the picture, then to the girls seated before him. That was easy to do, since all the girls were seated together on one side of the room.

"I'll keep this picture of you in a place where it will remind me often of our three years together. Many thanks, girls." He stopped to take in the entire room. "I'll miss all of you, and I wish you well in eighth grade. Good luck!"

Herr Lawaldt had liked the picture, but for all of us in it, you can be sure there were twenty-one critical opinions.

Over spring break, I discovered lice in my hair. I was horror struck. Someone had passed lice on to me, and in my mind, it was the worst possible calamity. Immediately, I had visions of girls I'd seen who gotten lice. Shaved heads, covered with cotton caps, told the world of their affliction.

I had to save my hair and avoid the public shame of lice, but for the time being — I had to wait for a solution.

Chapter Twenty-Six

By May of 1944, the daily barrage of victory news on German radio had ceased. After events in North Africa and the Allied landings in Italy, Germany went from an offensive to defensive posture overnight. Our news reports were undoubtedly censored, but over time a vivid picture still developed that didn't bode well for Germany. Nazi commentators couldn't totally gloss over the bad news from the east and west. Every setback on the battlefronts resulted in more deprivation at home. The real truth was all around us, and it gave more and more people the courage to risk turning to another source of information — the BBC German language broadcasts.

It may seem ridiculous that we feared being caught listening to foreign radio. Naturally, it was impossible to police every radio in every German kitchen and living room, but in a totalitarian state, constant surveillance in each village and town wasn't necessary to establish fear. You worried about the neighbors and their possible ambitions in and loyalty to the regime. The Gestapo didn't need an agent in every block, only people willing to report the sins of their neighbors.

The shortages in food and materials for the civilian population worsened, compounded in 1943 and 1944 by the poor potato harvests. The scarcity of this main staple in our diet did as much as anything to dampen German spirits. In the past, any shortages were supplemented by shipping the product in from another place, but bombing and strafing attacks on transportation made this nearly impossible.

As the month wore on, German concern rose sharply over a possible enemy crossing of the English Channel to France. There was troop movement throughout the Rheinland, and all available men and machines were ordered west to reinforce the coastline. By June, it had proved to be a useless effort. All of the bunkers and barbed wire had made no difference when the Americans, British and French came crashing ashore. They called it "D-Day." We called it by the French word "Invasion."

For us, the event hit with a force as great as the collapse at Stalingrad. Silence fell on Kirchheim — a silence only slightly interrupted by the occasional strident voice of someone who believed in Hitler's V-2 rocket bombs. Again, we were showered by pamphlets from the sky encouraging Germans to stop fighting. As before, the young were sent out to gather the pieces of paper to turn in to school officials and police. Many of us doing the collecting were confused, even while remaining firm to our H.J. pledge to the Führer. Hitler's V-2 would save the nation. We just had to believe it.

❧

As yet, I didn't have to worry much about feeding Peter. Mama continued to breastfeed, though she took little interest in other matters in or out of the house. All the housework, except washing diapers, now fell on me. The energy shown by Mama in pregnancy had dissipated. She remained in bed with Peter next to her for longer and longer periods of time. Mostly, she read the Bible, and I tried to keep her informed. She approved of the Kirchheim authorities drafting all old men and young boys over sixteen to erect barricades at all entrances to the city. However, I agreed with many of my friends who said such meager efforts were useless — we'd all seen the Wochenschau newsreels showing tanks crashing through stone walls.

"Please, Mama. Go out in the garden and sit in the sun." Every nice summer day I urged her, remembering what she had once said to me about the 'healing sun.' She would never go, and even worse, she refused me in silence. Not answering was becoming a habit, and I wondered if part of it was over worry about my brother.

After Erich had left us in a huff, we heard nothing for months. I wrote to him regularly, describing Peter's progress and sweet nature, and hoped the lack of mail from him was caused by sea duty, not anger. Finally, in early July, a letter came. He explained in a somewhat cryptic fashion, that he'd just been able to catch up with his mail. While he was never allowed to state specific information about assignments and missions, we were able to figure out that he'd spent some time in Denmark. He covered quite a lot in the letter, but didn't acknowledge his new brother.

❧

On July twentieth, the radio brought shocking news of an attempt to kill the Führer. We were reassured that Hitler was only slightly hurt, and he took to the air himself a short time later, promising to punish the perpetrators and fight on against all enemies inside and outside our country. This time, not many people found inspiration in his words or voice. After a few days, the incident amounted to no more than another hammer blow to numb the senses. We all had problems closer to home to worry over.

When I first discovered I had lice, the urge to find the culprit who'd passed them on to me was strong. I came to believe that the girl who sat in front of me in class was the culprit. My friends didn't have lice. It had to be the girl who

259

was always dirty and smelled of urine. Only people like that, I figured, had lice. Her hair was such a mess that I couldn't tell, but that didn't stop me from lashing out at her during a recess.

"You always smell bad. Don't you wash?"

My friend Else pulled me away before I could proceed with the attack. "Don't say mean things to her. Don't you know she comes from a very poor family? She has to sleep with a younger sister who wets the bed. Leave her alone."

It made me feel sorry for the girl, but I didn't apologize. She could still wash, was my thinking. I also didn't reveal my own problem, which was getting worse despite my efforts. I begged Mama to help me. Her response was curt. "You're big enough to take care of it."

I was positive my friends couldn't help, even if I had the courage to tell them about it. I was certain that they would shun me. No mother would allow her daughter to associate with a person who had lice.

I took pains to make sure that no one stood behind me for long. Lice are not plainly visible, but their eggs are. Being in the back row helped, but one day our new teacher Frau Christman called on me, and asked me to the blackboard for a math problem. I went to the board and wrote out the calculation under her direction. She stepped behind me, saying I should solve it. The very idea of her eyes on the back of my head made me uneasy and I froze. The figures on the board suddenly meant nothing. All I could feel were eyes inspecting my head. I just knew she was going to order me from the room.

"I have to sit down. I can't finish it." The words exploded from me as I turned without permission to rush back to my desk embarrassed and near tears.

At the end of the day, Frau Christman asked me to stay for a minute. "Annchen, what happened at the board? You could've done the problem. I wouldn't have asked you otherwise."

I wanted to spill my insides out to the woman in front of me, to tell her everything and ask her help. The fear of a shaved head and shame kept me from it. I could only manage a weak excuse. "I'm sorry, Frau Christman. I don't know what came over me."

My rapport with her hadn't been the same as with Herr Lawaldt — nothing terrible, but after this incident, it never really improved.

To the uninitiated, having head lice may sound like a simple hygiene problem, easily cured with a special shampoo or medicine. In 1944, that was definitely not the case. We had a few quack remedies, but other than shaving the hair, kerosene was the only method, and only if done right. Even then, the treatment might have to be repeated. I bought some kerosene at old Bender's shop down on the Langstraße. I must not have applied it right. I found no relief, but worse still, Mama and Peter got the lice from me.

I managed to rid Peter of them, but had no success with Mama. Her scalp had been scratched open, making the use of kerosene too painful. She had stopped washing and brushing her hair. What had once been long, beautiful braids became a tangled, matted mess constantly scratched at, and a scalp with open sores and dried blood that emitted a bad smell. I was getting more frantic by the day, pleading with her to get up, to wash herself, to wash and brush her hair. It was not as if Mama never got out of bed. She did, usually when I was in school. I could tell that she had been up, though not to dress and clean up. I would have helped to wash and brush her hair, but she wouldn't let me.

By late summer, the pressure of school and our lice problem had reached the breaking point. Papa hadn't been home for some time, and our contact was limited to the mail. I had previously hesitated to bother him with a situation easily remedied by Mama. I finally realized that it wouldn't happen, and wrote to Papa. He came through the door two days later. I stood before him in the kitchen, just feet away, my body trembling and tears flowing from grief and shame, relief and joy. I wanted to hug him, but feared he'd shove me away because of the lice.

"Where's your mother?"

I pointed to the bedroom. He left me standing there, but returned shortly, very angry.

"Why have you kept this from me? Mein Gott! What has become of this family? Come here. I want to look at your head."

I'd never seen my father in such a rage, and I began to shake harder. All joy and relief that he had come were gone. He inspected my well-brushed hair and scalp with a brutal touch. When he was through, I felt a terrible guilt in having let him down.

"It's too late, much too late. I have to cut the hair off both of you!"

"Nay!" I'd jumped to my feet, screaming and bawling. "You can't do that to me. Please! Please, Papa, say you won't cut my hair! The shame, Papa. Don't make it so I can't go to school again! Please, I'll do anything to get rid of them, but don't cut off my hair. Papa, please don't." I collapsed back into the chair and buried my face in my hands. For a moment my father said nothing, then left to go back into the bedroom. I cried and continued to plead aloud despite his absence, and after a while, he returned and walked over to me. Again he inspected my bowed head, more gently than before.

"Ach, my Annchen, what have we come to." His voice was gentle as he softly massaged my shoulders and back, helping me regain control of myself. "Your mother's hair is a lost cause. There's no way to even wash and brush it. Nay, it can't be saved. I'll have to cut it off."

I shivered at the thought, which probably made Papa think I was going to start up again.

"Nay, Märe, don't worry. Your head is in much better shape. We'll try a treatment first. You said in your letter about trying kerosene. That should have worked. You must have done it wrong. Is there any left to use?"

"I emptied the bottle, and Herr Bender probably won't give us more. He wasn't happy to part with the liter I got."

"So, Bender has kerosene. Isn't it amazing what he has stashed in that old musty shop. Get me an empty wine bottle. I haven't talked to bachelor Bender in far too long a time.

I was sure Papa hadn't spoken more than a few words with the shopkeeper in years, still they must have had a good visit. My father came back with the bottle filled all the way to the cork with kerosene.

I knew that what Papa was about to do saddened and angered him. He always loved Mama's hair — her beautiful, beautiful hair. To cut it off hurt him deeply. He couldn't understand how his wife, once so proud and meticulous, had let herself go down so completely.

He brought Mama into the kitchen and placed her on a chair. I checked on Peter and returned to watch. My mother gave no argument — she said nothing at all. I couldn't stop the tears that came and ran down my cheeks, dropping to the floor as silently as the hair piling up at Papa's feet. He had decided not to cut her hair at the scalp, and he explained. "I'm just going to get it to where a comb will go through. Then you and I will wash and dry it before I put some kerosene on and wrap her head."

"Papa! You'll hurt her with kerosene. Don't you see all the open sores?"

"It's either that, or all the hair has to come off. Don't worry. We must at least try."

When it came time for the kerosene, I knew it must have hurt. She bit her lip, but made no sound. He wrapped her head with brown paper, also soaked with the smelly liquid, then put on more paper to seal it. I swept up the hair on the floor and threw the whole pile into the stove to burn. Mama was told to sit still while he took care of me.

Everything was done with the window wide open. Kerosene isn't as explosive as gasoline, but it would have been foolhardy to take chances. Papa didn't want me to take apart my braids, saying that long loose hair would turn into a hopeless mass of tangles. He started by saturating my scalp, then pinning each braid on top of my head. He put extra kerosene at the base of each braid before soaking the rest on top.

"That should do it," he said, starting to wrap and seal his handiwork. "It would have been better to put each braid right in the bottle, but they're too thick."

Mama didn't move from the table. She'd fixed her gaze on a spot near the stove and stared at it for more than two hours. Papa had fixed some tea and sandwiches for us, but she'd only sip at the tea. I stayed close to fresh air by the window, and away from the stove. Peter began to fuss, and Papa brought him to the kitchen and spooned creamed wheat cereal into his mouth. He didn't like the kerosene aroma or the two strange creatures with the wrapped heads. The little guy was also not accustomed to Papa, who must have seemed a stranger. He didn't cry, but looked mighty uncomfortable.

My father had given up trying to make conversation with Mama — she wouldn't answer. He and I talked, mostly about Peter and how I should find a carriage to take him for walks in the fresh air. "He needs to see other people and learn there's something besides walls of a bedroom." I agreed, but silently wondered how I'd find the time.

Nearly three hours had passed when Papa and I took Mama to the wash kitchen to shampoo her head. He rinsed and lathered her hair a second time. Now cut short, it was quickly towel dried and combed. I didn't know what to say as I looked at her. There was no doubt that Papa had to trim and make her hair more presentable, which he did the next day before a third wash. I could only think that the transformation of my mother was complete. In both her behavior and appearance, she had become a person I didn't know.

While I waited for my own hair to dry, Papa stripped all the linens from the beds, and he and I boiled everything in the big wash kettles late into the night. Mama and Peter were then settled in a clean bed.

It was late when we finally turned in, but the next morning, promptly after breakfast, another hair wash was ordered, and a new close inspection of our heads.

"I can't find any evidence of lice," he said to me. "But you will have to work at scraping the dead eggs from your long hair. They stick like glue."

I worked like mad to do just that over the next several days and it worked. Neither Mama nor I had further evidence of lice. I thanked God and Papa.

ॐ

Mama remained listless and withdrawn, and seemed resentful that her husband had come to help in our emergency.

Standing beside her bed, he pleaded with her. "Tell me what's wrong. I'll take you to another doctor. Tell me the problem. No one can help when you don't talk."

There was no response.

"Can't you get up and take care of a few things? It's too much for Annchen alone. You were such a proud woman. What's happened to you?"

Again, it was like speaking to a stone.

On the third day, Papa left us again. "I'll try to come home soon. I can't tell you just when. This war is heading toward the end, and things are more hectic. It doesn't seem you'll be getting any help," he said, nodding toward the bedroom. "Just do the best you can. Don't let things pile up. It's harder to catch up. And try to keep on top of your schoolwork. I'll write to a couple of your aunts. Maybe they can come by and help you."

He left, and the aunts never came. Everybody had problems of their own. I didn't do too badly on my own, and it helped that eighth grade offered nutrition and cooking classes.

But I found it harder to participate in my classes. So much had changed for me that instead of having freedom to think about lesson problem solving, my mind was now muddled by worries at home. Girlfriends were no longer invited to the house. When there was time to visit, it was at their homes. I kept all of them in the dark about the conditions at home, and I certainly couldn't tell Frau Christman.

As autumn set in, we were told in religion class that we needed to sign up for extra catechism studies. It was required for confirmation in the spring and at the end of eighth grade. A person could graduate without confirmation, but it wasn't done often. All of my friends wanted acceptance in the church, and so did I. The problem was having the energy and time for catechism study on top of everything else.

I asked around the neighborhood, and learned that Frau Baum had a baby carriage I could borrow. It was the high-type with big wheels and good heavy springs, easy to maneuver over rough cobblestone. I'd bundle Peter into it for an outing, whenever I had a spare moment. The first trip was to Bolanden on a

Sunday before the bad weather set in. Oma and Tante Lisbeth had not yet seen the boy, who by then was seven months old. Oma now never left the house, and my aunt was apparently too occupied to visit Kirchheim. I missed her visits, and needed her help, but I couldn't be upset. Lives had been turned upside down by the war.

The gentle rocking of the carriage kept Peter dozing on the way, a good thing, too, since it took me nearly an hour to reach Bolanden. It usually took me half that time.

Tante Lisbeth was tickled to see both me and our new addition to the Klein family. She helped me carry the carriage into the house. My tiny Oma sat in the kitchen, and I kissed her thin face and placed the boy in her lap. Her bony hands caressed his face and head while her dark brown eyes sparkled with tears of joy. Over and over she spoke his name softly. This was the reason for my visit. She needed to see and touch the boy named for her husband.

It was during this visit that I learned of a near riot by a few Bolanden farmers. The story came from Onkel Jakob. He rushed in after our arrival from working at his one-man sand quarry. He had just run into one of his farmer friends. Jacob was much older than Lisbeth, and hardly talked much. I always figured it was because my aunt never let him get a word in. This time, anyone could see the old man was agitated and had something to get out.

"What's the matter, Jacob? Something go wrong at the pit?"

I expected him to say yes, because working alone he sometimes did get into trouble with shifting sand. One time, he got buried in a sand slide and almost suffocated. When he struggled, more sand came down to bury him until only a hand and part of his face was left to see. It was Papa who had come along for a load of sand, heard him moaning, and pulled him out. That wasn't the problem this time.

He sat on the wood box by the stove, and started removing his boots and talking at the same time. "Something terrible has happened! Burgey's Heiner just stopped me on the road and told me. You want to know?"

"Naturally, old man, get on with it." Tante Lisbeth was getting impatient, as usual, whenever Jakob decided to talk. He had a way of identifying persons by family name, then given name. If he wanted to report what a person said, he'd stop and ask if the listener was interested. It always exasperated my aunt.

"Well, Heiner just came from being with a bunch of farmers that went into the forest where one of those enemy planes came down. They found the two pilots alive and started beating on them, and were going to hang them on the spot, had the police not come along." Jacob paused to look around, as though checking to make sure we were listening.

"The pilots were taken away to Kirchheim for treatment," he continued. "It's an awful thing, but folks are upset about planes shooting at them in the fields. They don't think that's right either."

I sat silently for the whole story, partly in amazement at hearing him say so much at one time. All during her husband's tale, Tante Lisbeth clapped her hands together, saying repeatedly, "Gott im Himmel!" By the end, she was thoroughly disgusted. "This awful war, why can't it be over right now!"

I understood her anguish. She'd already lost her young brother Ludwig, and still hadn't learned the fate of two missing sons, Walter and Willie.

Evening dark was coming, so my aunt and I packed Peter back into the carriage for the trek home. The weather had turned colder, and I hated leaving my aunt's warm kitchen.

I had to think of Mama waiting at home alone. She had once kept a warm and welcome kitchen. Now, I couldn't be sure I would find the fire still going in the kitchen stove.

Kirchheimbolanden Photo Section

Breitstraße One in winter. Our house abuts Bossung's Inn. Mama is at the Shell gas pump. Tante Lina looks out an upper window. Cousin Helmi and myself are in the doorway. Over the large door behind Mama hangs the beautiful wrought iron blacksmith symbol with a horse and anvil. Note that it now hangs in the Kirchheim museum.

Daughter Kristina's image of my first day at Breitstraße One. It is a bit fanciful with me standing at a window, watching passersby. It was in November and quite cold. I can image what Mama would say about me standing in an open window! Still I do like the sketch over the old photo above.

The school I attended from 3rd–8th grade, ending with church confirmation. The building with the windows was K–8. The wall to the right belonged to a separate school for higher grades. The courtyard is actually much larger than it appears.

In the garden of my new home at Breitstraße One. We didn't own a camera, so this rare photo of me was no doubt taken by a visiting relative, checking out Kleine Seppel's decision to move to Kirchheim.

Kirchheimbolanden Jewish Synagogue. Just as the Klein family was moving from Marnheim to a new home in Kibo this local landmark fell victim to the infamous 'Crystal Night' destruction sweeping across Germany. An irony is that the next building to the left is St. Paul's protestant church. The synagogue was never rebuilt.

Kriegsmarine (Navy) enlistee. Erich did not want any thing to do with serving in the Wehrmacht (Army). But submarine duty worried Mama.

Erich at 16 and in the Labor Service (Arbeits Dienst), the step before military service.

The war is over and it was time for Erich to start courting the butcher's daughter. I thought Ida was one of the town's prettiest girls.

Erich with a few comrades from the crew on break from submarine duty. This was taken at the port of Cuxhaven on the north German coast. We saw him just one time during his entire service.

Another Nazi outing for older teen girls. On some occasions like this Henny and I were the "entertainment."

Some girls of Hitler Youth from villages around the area. I knew the three Kirchheim girls seated in the front. Since all were four to five years older than I, nodding acquaintances was all we were until later years.

From right to left: Tante Dina, sister of Mama who married a French soldier after the so-called "Great War," Jean, the only son, and Raul, husband and father. I never knew Dina and Mama never saw her again after she left to live in France. Mama and Dina died within a month of each other.

Papa and friend at another airbase. This was his last assignment — a phony airbase near Guntersblum. It was not far from Kirchheim, making it possible for him to make quick visits when I needed him.

From right to left: Myself with the Hand-harmonika, cousins Elsbeth and Helmi. We are at the Ziegelwoog, a small lake.

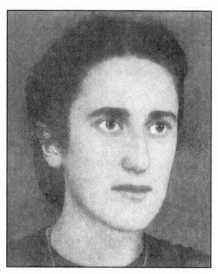

My beautiful cousin Elsbeth, some four years later than in the picture on the left. She had to leave nurse's training before completion to returned home to fight a losing battle with Multiple Sclerosis.

Someone snapped our picture after a long train ride to see Papa at Gießen airbase north of Frankfurt. Mama had a problem only Papa could fix.

The Oelbergstraße goes up a steep grade from the old shopping area inside the old walls to St. Peter's church where I was confirmed. Here you must turn onto Langstraße and continue upward to my Breitstraße.

Myself (back row) with some of the girls at the end of the 7th grade. It was a gift to our teacher of three years — Herr Lawaldt. There were more girls in the class, but as with any volunteer idea, not everyone wanted to join in.

This photo was taken about the same time — at age 13.

Long before Mama's death in 1946 I had become Peter's mother as well as his sister. This photo taken with an old box camera shows Peter not long after recuperating from severe injuries in a traffic accident.

Forefront: Herr Steitz in one of the several shoe production workrooms of his Marnheim company. This is where Seppel got my confirmation shoes.

Transferring from the one Weierhof switchboard to the 30-position board in Kaiserslautern was really exciting for me. The above happens to be the four position Sunday crew. I am at the far end. The all-male technical fellows were always taking pictures when the boss had "left the building."

Most of the operators also worked an occasional shift on the three positions for information. New operators were not assigned until after several weeks on the job, and then only for one day a week.

Headquarters building of the 138th Artillery at Weierhof Kasern. The telephone switchboard was also located here. The military frequently hosted events for the public as above.

Weierhof — Soldiers on parade. Seen in the background is a building used for housing many services, including an infirmary for minor medical help. Note the truck with the Red Cross.

Elfriede, a life-long friend on her wedding day. It was not uncommon for brides to wear black in those days. Her new husband, Manfred Denzer, would become renowned in the art of woodcarving. His work can be found in many places; private and public.

Seems odd to see only the bride coming out of the church following the marriage vows. My new husband said he wanted to take a photo of me in my wedding dress leaving the church. The event was not very long after Elfriede and Manfred tied the knot.

Papa's last photo.

On our honeymoon in June 1956 we stopped over in Verona for a foxtrot. We sang and danced in front of the Opera House at midnight in Vienna. Then on to Salzburg for a visit with Mozart, Switzerland, Holland, Belgium and France — all in 30 days.

275

Chapter Twenty-Seven

Not long after Papa had come home to help me conquer the lice, his job with the Luftwaffe changed again. The movement of German reinforcements into France following the Normandy invasion brought a renewed demand for supplies. He once more drove a supply truck and an immediate benefit to me was quick visits to Kirchheim. Some lasted as little as fifteen minutes, when he was pushing his luck. There were times when he came and went and I didn't know it until returning home from school. When that happened, he'd leave a note for me, usually with advice and always with encouragement.

I was grateful that during his earlier three days at home, he and I together chopped enough firewood for the winter. The last of the garden was also harvested — mostly a supply of dried soup beans. I was glad about it because Mama had stopped helping with the work entirely. Breast feeding Peter was her only contribution, and about all that allowed me some breathing space to tackle schoolwork. Earlier, she had been doing some cooking, and the boiling and washing of daily diapers on top of the cook stove. That ended abruptly one day when I returned to find the pot still filled with dirty diapers on a nearly cold stove.

She and Peter were in bed, keeping warm under the comforter when I entered her room. I was tired and angry, a full load of other chores and school-work lay ahead of me. "Why are there dirty diapers still in the pot? Mama, you know we need clean ones for tomorrow!" And while I was at it, "Why can't you at least keep wood on the fire?"

"I can't wash anymore. The water — it electrocutes my hands. You'll have to do it."

That she'd answered me right away was surprise enough, but what she said stunned me. I was angry, and let her know it. "Water doesn't have electricity in it!" But her response remained the same. "I can't touch water." She said it over and over.

An awful feeling hit me and I had to shake off the shudder that raced through me. A sick feeling replaced it. Had there been any doubt before, it was gone. My mother was sick in her head, and it frightened me. I wasn't afraid for my physical safety or for Peter's. Somehow I knew Mama couldn't harm her children, but I feared that I alone couldn't defend and protect the family reputation, or keep us alive until Papa was home for good.

The cooking and general house cleaning I could handle. Our meals were simple, and Peter required only a creamed hot cereal to supplement breast milk. Dishes, dusting and cleaning floors had been mine to do for a long time anyway. It was the weekly pile of laundry that demoralized me, especially in winter. I'd let it get ahead of me, something Papa had warned about. Before I knew it, there was two weeks of laundry facing me.

Winter made doing laundry hard, because nothing could be hung outside to dry. I tried it, and ended up with frozen bed sheets that had to be brought up to the kitchen for thawing. Our kitchen could accommodate only a few large frozen articles at one time. Some items could be hung in the still warm wash kitchen, but even that only partially helped in drying so much laundry.

I began to develop an appreciation for what my mother had done as a housewife and mother over the years. In the future, I would never agree that housekeeping and child-rearing done well, isn't a full-time job. At fourteen, I wasn't prepared to do the job well, and without help and advice, I sometimes failed. My consolation was knowing that even Mama never kept house while going to school six days a week.

The time came when I thought Peter should sleep in the youth bed that had once been mine in Marnheim. It was already set up across from Mama, and I hoped that it would force her to get up more often to tend to him. It worked for a while. Sometimes I caught her making happy small talk to the boy, but shut it off the instant she saw me.

She began to answer any question I asked with the same response. "Go ask your father!"

At first, stunned by her reply, I'd just leave the room. After several more times, I'd had enough and would shout at her. "Stop it, Mama! Stop saying that to me. You know Papa's not here. How can I ask him anything? He's gone, Mama. I have only you to ask!"

I hated myself for being angry with her, but I didn't know how to deal with her madness any other way. Sometimes I wondered if I was going mad too, but I refused to let her silences or crazy words keep me from talking. I started forcing news and gossip about school, friends, the war, Erich and Papa onto her without let up. And I would push her to make decisions or help me do so, but usually to no avail.

Bad news came from all sides. My friend Hannelore's father was killed on the eastern front. Only weeks before, her brother Hans had been drafted by the SS. Tall and blonde, he was a true example of the Aryan race and a perfect recruit for Hitler's special service.

Within days, there was more sadness for my family. Tante Gusta's husband Ernst was reported killed in action, also on the eastern front. He was a Swiss national, a cheesemaker, who had come to the area as a young man and married my father's sister. As a Swiss, Ernst might not have been drafted into the army. He was shamed into volunteering by Tante Lina, who said he had a duty to his adopted country. Gusta and four children never saw him again.

❧

Herr Kasper, the shoemaker stopped by, not only to reopen his shop downstairs, but also to ask about three small vacant rooms upstairs. He'd married a girl from a nearby village and they already had a baby boy, months older than Peter. His army service was ended by injuries he never discussed. Papa made one of his short visits a few days later and quickly agreed that the Kaspers should move in. He thought it would be good to have them in the house.

My prayers for normal adult company and wisdom were answered. Frau Kasper, shorter than I, had naturally curly, short black hair. Her face was ordinary and made almost stern by wire rimmed glasses. I wondered if she and I would get along, and soon found her pleasant and helpful, a seamstress and knitter. That sealed our friendship, though out of respect I couldn't call her Maria. That wasn't done unless invited.

Frau Kasper gave me several items of clothing for Peter from her son Rudi. She also guided me, over many evenings, in sewing other things for my little brother. I often felt like I was intruding, but with Herr Kasper spending a lot of late nights in the shop, she seemed to like my company. Of the three rooms they had turned one into a kitchen, just like the refugees from the Saar in earlier days.

Herr Kasper worked long evenings in his shop because Christmas was approaching. He now made more new shoes than make repairs to old. I was curious as to how he got new leather with a war raging. The answer was that farmers brought him the leather, having him use the nicer quality sections to make them shoes and boots, and letting him keep the lesser materials in payment. Like a magician, he turned the leftovers into shoes for people who paid cash. And while nothing was ever said about it, I could tell the Kaspers didn't have to rely solely on their ration cards to put food on the table. Shoemaking could be a valuable trade in hard times.

❧

I began to think about Christmas. It was clear that Erich wouldn't come home, and Papa was questionable. Because it was Peter's first Christmas, I was determined to make the occasion as normal as possible, in spite of the rationing and lack of toys in the shops. I remembered an old carpenter in Marnheim who made a few wooden toys each year for pleasure and extra money. I knew just where Herr Werner lived and worked.

While it was early December, little snow had fallen and I decided to bicycle to Marnheim. I found his shop near my first school and went in. I expected him to recognize me, and of course, he didn't right away.

"Guten Tag, Herr Werner. Perhaps you remember me? My family moved away a few years ago. My name is — "

Peering intently over his glasses at me, his face suddenly brightened. "Ach, ja," he interrupted. "Naturally I know you. Mariechen's little girl. Ah, but you're not so little anymore, are you? Ja, ja, I remember. People called your father Seppel, but that wasn't his name, right?"

"Ja, Herr Werner, his name is Fritz Klein, and I'm Anna."

"But of course. How is your mother?"

He would remember my mother better, she being a Marnheimer. I didn't think I should mention her problems, so I replied she was fine and jumped right into the purpose of my mission. Explaining briefly about my baby brother and my desire to give him a wooden toy, I asked if any of the little trains on the shelf behind him were for sale.

I had no sooner stated my case, he turned and lifted down a locomotive and three passengers cars and placed them in my hands. The workmanship was beautiful, and I screwed up my courage. "How much, please?"

His face wrinkled in a broad smile. "You have the train. A gift from me. After all, we are old acquaintances!"

I couldn't believe my luck, and must have said 'Danke' a dozen times. Herr Werner seemed almost embarrassed by my gratitude. "It's nothing," he said. "Just give my regards to your mother."

Mama wasn't aware of my visit to Herr Werner until my return and placed the train before her, describing my visit. She surprised me with a fleeting smile, touching each piece with a finger. "Herr Werner was a friend of my father," she said. "Ja, little Peter will like it." I put the train away.

The day after my outing to Marnheim I felt chilled, and knew I must've caught a cold. My whole body began aching, and I put myself to bed. By midnight, my fever raged. I went from not enough cover to throwing everything off. There was no aspirin, and no mother who cared. I started hallucinating, yelling out in the dark. Mama had always helped me through those awful feelings of fear, confusion, and panic that came with the high fevers. Now, she lay in the next room uncaring. Oddly, I was aware of that, and I desperately worked to find an opening to reality.

I jerked myself into a sitting position, panting and struggling to free myself of wet bed linens and the heavy comforter. When my eyes adjusted to the darkness, I saw Mama standing in the doorway. It must have been my yelling that brought her that far. Light from the kitchen outlined her shadowy figure, and reflected dimly across her face. The cold expression I found there sent a shock to my brain. She doesn't care whether I live or die. Not at all.

The fever was still with me, but my mother's vacant eyes told me I must find strength to fight it alone. How long she stood there I can't say, but long enough for me to regain control over mind and body. Fixing my covers and finding the pillow's dry side, I heard myself tell her to go back to bed. My head hit the pillow and I promptly fell into deep, undisturbed sleep. In the morning, I awoke refreshed — no fever or lingering signs of illness. The quick recovery amazed me, but as I thought of it, I understood. I had to stay well. I had no choice.

৯

Christmas of 1944 was the first in my life that no cookies were baked in the Klein house. Ever diminishing food stocks in the shops made ration coupons almost useless. Coupons did no good when flour, eggs, butter and sugar couldn't be found. I had hoarded enough to make a small cake, nothing more. We made a few cookies in cooking class, a few to share on the last day before school break. Frau Christman led her all-female class in songs, but with little enthusiasm from me. A lot of us were missing Herr Lawaldt's storytelling from a Peter Rosegger book. As I sang, I kept thinking of the Peter waiting for me at home, my only sunshine on a dreary winter day.

Walking home in the afternoon, the absence of snow reminded me how miserable winter could be. The unusual weather seemed to fit the gloomy mood of Kirchheim's people. This year there weren't even Christmas trees for sale in the town's marketplace. Reaching my front door, I had made up my mind to do as Papa had done in years past — go and cut a tree down in the forest after dark.

As I passed Kasper's shop door, it opened and the shoemaker stopped me. "Annchen! You've been worrying about a tree, and I want one too. Today a customer told me they're cutting trees just the other side of Haide. Want to go with me? We could ride our bicycles."

There was one benefit of no snow. It was a kilometer to the village of Haide and trudging uphill in a foot of snow, wouldn't have appealed to me. As it was, we could use our bicycles. I checked on Mama and Peter, gobbled down a slice of bread, put on extra clothing against the cold, and left with Herr Kasper for the forest by Haide.

People were carrying trees of every size. A couple of old men working for the forestry service stood about directing newcomers to locations where it was permitted to cut. Our turn came, and in no time found what we wanted — two trees a little over a meter high. Kasper had a saw and nipped off both in short order.

We paid and left for home. Finding a tree without a sneaky trip in the night excited me so much, I ignored the stinging bitter cold pedaling home. We left the trees in the courtyard until the next day.

In the meantime, I attempted to clean for Christmas, as Mama would have done. It had to satisfy to have the floors clean without the usual waxing. Missing were the wonderful mixed aromas of baking and freshly polished floors. Only the fragrance of a new-cut pine tree would grace the house this time.

The sun came out to brighten Christmas Eve day, so I took Peter for a carriage ride. He looked cute under a load of blankets with only his face peeking out into the cold. After putting him down for a nap and with Mama still in her bed, I busied myself putting up the tree on the table near Hitler's picture on the wall. Carefully, I took out the boxes of colorful glass ornaments and proceeded to decorate the tree alone and in silence, a first for me. The final touches included the pointed blown glass piece for the top and the placing of a special ornament, different from all the rest. Instead of a ball, it was blown-glass formed into a tiny, roofed manger. Looking inside the silver interior, the figures of Mary, Joseph, and the Christ child appeared in a background of glitter. The candleholder clips were left in the box. No candles were to be had. It didn't bother me. Sunlight poured through the windows, making the ornaments sparkle and shine. The little train went under the tree.

Waiting as long as I could, I gently woke Peter for his first look at a Christmas tree. He seemed to know something wonderful was in store, and he wrapped an arm around my neck, his face all smiles as we quietly left the bedroom. Mama didn't stir. I'd prepared for the moment by building a fire in the small heating stove to warm the living room. It was a luxury, but to me, the occasion called for warmth.

"Look, Peterchen, your first Christmas tree. Isn't it beautiful? Someday Papa and Erich will be home and we'll all celebrate and have fun with presents. Oh, what do we have here? Look, it's a train!"

The wooden train had no chance of winning Peter's attention from the silver balls that glowed in the sunlight. We both laughed and giggled as I began playing a tantalizing game of stepping near and jumping back before fingers could grab a shining prize. Later, Peter played with his train. For the moment, all of our joy came from being together in front of the glimmering Christmas tree.

Then, while he quietly played with one of my braids, I held him close and found myself softly singing a childrens' carol.

"Kling, Glöckchen,	*'Ring, little bell,*
kling-a-ling-a-ling	*ring-a-ling-a-ling*
Kling, Glöckchen, kling."	*Ring, little bell, ring.'*

I suddenly became aware that Mama stood in the doorway behind us. There was no pleasure on her face, and she said nothing. When I looked again, she was gone.

Chapter Twenty-Eight

Christmas and New Year passed in a strange kind of loneliness for me. Peter and Mama were in the house, but there was only so much one could say to a baby, and my mother responded about as well to my efforts at conversation. She had just turned forty-three in December.

The Kaspers had gone to her family's home in Ruppertsecken for the week, so quick visits with Hannelore or Elfriede had to be it for meaningful conversation. One thing we talked about was confirmation, only three months away. It seemed like there was plenty of time to prepare, but I had none of the required black clothing and shoes. Neither of them had extra dresses or shoes they could lend me, though they both pushed me to come to catechism studies so I could participate.

That no one visited us over Christmas brought to mind one of Mama's truisms: "Those who don't come, don't have to leave." Such sayings are embedded in our culture, and that one never failed to have an impact on me. It perfectly describes my mixed feelings of disappointment and indifference.

Though she wouldn't offer any advice on my clothing problems, I felt my mother would want me to go through with confirmation. Her family had always been strict adherents to Martin Luther and the church. In what I thought was an effort to please her and my friends, I broke my own rule to keep problems at home. I went to see Henny's mother. Henny had confirmed two years earlier, and I needed advice.

"Ach, Annchen. I had no idea you had no one in the family who could lend you a black dress. Of course you can use Henny's. I have it stored away. Come, let's try it on you right now."

It fit wonderfully, and I could have hugged and kissed Frau Hemm. I promised to take good care of it.

"I know you will. In fact, keep it to wear for the Lord's Supper service on Easter. They like to have you wear black for that, too. I'm sorry there aren't shoes to go along. Henny took them with her to Kaiserslautern."

"That's alright, Frau Hemm. I'll ask Hannelore's mother if she has an extra pair."

I thanked her again and left, almost skipping with happiness the short distance to my house. But my mission to Frau Rihlmann's failed. All of the shoes were too small for me, but she did offer me a pair of black stockings. I thanked her as well. Confirmation was beginning to look like a sure thing. It had come down to finding a pair of black shoes. I began working on it by going to city hall to get a Bezugschein, a permission slip to buy a pair in a store.

The second month of 1945 was about to give way to the third when Ertell's store announced a new supply of shoes. I got there and waited in a line that continued to grow behind me. The store allowed three persons in at a time. No one ever came out the same door, so we all figured they must have been let out the back door, not a normal practice.

There were only about twenty people ahead of me when I arrived shortly after two o'clock. As time passed — one hour, then two hours — we who still waited, began to suspect that other people were entering through the back.

"This is taking forever," I heard someone say. "How long can it take for three people to pick out shoes?" The windows in front were covered, so we couldn't see in. The grumbling became intense as I reached the front and it became my turn. I looked up at the clock on the main tower — I'd been in line for nearly three hours. I hoped they had my size in any kind of a black shoe. I wasn't going to be picky.

The door started to open, then stopped at a point just wide enough for a head to come through. "Sorry, we're out of shoes."

"What!" A woman's voice behind me screamed, and I was shoved into the door. The shopkeeper no doubt expected such a reaction, because his feet were planted firmly against the door to prevent entry. He needn't have worried. I didn't like being shoved and I shoved her back. The door slammed shut.

"Why did you push me away?" The woman was now shouting at me. "We could have gotten in there to see if he was lying!"

I thought she was going to hit me when I already felt bad enough. My hopes for a pair of black shoes had been dashed. At that moment, Herr Lawaldt stepped between us, took my arm, and guided me away from the woman. I couldn't imagine where my former teacher had come from. I'd looked down the line of people many times and had never spotted him. Now hurriedly walking through the main tower entrance toward Langstraße, he released my arm.

"Annchen, you have to start being more careful while waiting in lines. People are getting more angry every day. It could get nasty for a young person unaccustomed to the rage of adults."

I didn't know how to respond to his act of kindness. My emotions had to be brought under better control. We walked on to where Langstraße and Schloßstraße, the street he lived on, came together. I was glad for the extra moment, because I wanted to congratulate him in a calm voice. He had been promoted to an administrative position and we no longer saw him in school.

"I'll leave you here. I know you go up Langstraße, and I turn here."

"I miss you, Herr Lawaldt." It wasn't exactly what I'd intended to say, but I did miss him. He smiled.

"I miss all of you, too. Believe me, being an administrator isn't half as interesting as our three years together. Now remember what I said. If this war isn't over soon, our people may forget their manners entirely. Auf Wiedersehen, Annchen!"

I almost said, 'Heil Hitler,' but caught myself in time. I knew in my heart that my old teacher would not like to hear that from me. "Auf Wiedersehen, Herr Lawaldt. Thanks for everything."

Before turning to go home, I looked back toward the shoe store. The crowd had dispersed, except for one man who still banged on the door. Walking on, I thought of Papa. In his last letter he'd promised to come home soon. I picked up my pace, knowing he needed to hear from me. Maybe he could help me find shoes. If anyone had the answer, I knew it had to be 'Kleine Seppel.'

It became a habit now to do schoolwork late in the evenings at the small table near the kitchen window. That way, after supper I could finish the chores and make sure Mama and Peter were settled for the night. Only then could I give full thought to school lessons, and be up and ready to answer an air raid siren.

The bombing raids still came nightly, except in very bad weather, and lately they were much earlier. I often didn't bother going to bed. When tired, I just folded my arms on the table and laid my head down, counting on the siren to wake me. It could happen that I sometimes woke up in the morning, in the same position. The weather had kept the enemy away, there had been no siren to rouse me.

That was not to be Friday night, March second. It was about nine-thirty, and my homework completed. I'd just put more wood in the kitchen stove to keep it alive during the night. No sooner had I sat and put my head down on folded arms that the shrill warning came. For a moment, there was a strong temptation to ignore it and sleep. Mama never went, and the wardens never asked about her. Why not stay home? My promise to Papa to always take Peter to the shelter proved stronger, and I moved quickly to get the boy and be on our way.

The shelter was half a block away, and the entrance in the courtyard of the apartment building owned by Fräulein von Hirsch. Hannelore and her family lived in the same building, though I never saw them or the royal lady. Apparently they preferred going elsewhere. Herr Dietz, an air raid official from the neighborhood stood at the door holding a small lantern to help us find the way in. He, along with block warden Herr Lander, made sure that everyone had arrived. Earlier in the war, the rule had been strictly enforced, but that had long since turned lax. Many people now only went in daytime raids.

By dim lantern light we again searched our way down the long stone stairs into the musty air some twenty-five feet below ground level. With no handrail, I had to be careful carrying the boy. We weren't the first to arrive, or the last. Within minutes, most of the scattered benches were filled by women, children, and a handful of old men. The heavy door above was closed with a loud clank, and there was a momentary silence. The murmur of voices began again, but now more subdued. As my eyes became accustomed to the shadowy light, I saw no strange faces. It gave me a feeling of comfort, but at the same time, I felt a kind of fear as I imagined being buried alive with people I knew so well.

Despite all the commotion that brought us almost daily to this shelter, I couldn't help being fascinated with the sanctuary. The underground room, with its high arched ceiling, was really an enlarged area in what had been an ancient tunnel. It was said that the tunnel ran all the way from the old Prince's palace nearby up to the forest by Schillerhain. The story went that in the olden days, persons living above would gather in the deep assembly space in times of danger and find safety by following the tunnel to the forest. Once again, it was being used to escape possible death. Only now, there was no way out except up the stairs.

I hardly ever spoke to the people around me, but I would speak softly to Peter, awake or asleep. Waiting for the all-clear siren, most of the small children took up sleeping positions. Now and then one would cry or ask to go to the toilet. There was none, just a bucket at the far edge of the lantern's glow by a damp wall. "Soon we'll be back in our beds again," I whispered to Peter.

The first time Mama and I had gone down into a bomb shelter, I remember her repeating, "God help us if we're trapped in this place." We had heard of people buried alive in Kaiserslautern. She often asked what good a shelter would be against a direct hit.

I now heard the old bachelor, Herr Lander, telling someone nearby how he had information that the planes were heading for Ludwigshafen and Mannheim. As he said it, we could hear planes overhead flying toward those very targets. Now it was a matter of waiting for the return flight. The sound would be completely different. Coming in from the west, the bomber engines sent out a heavy laboring throb. Returning, emptied of their deadly loads, the sound was more like the easy roar of race cars.

Most nights, as we left the shelter, our group couldn't resist looking to the east where the horizon glowed from the fires burning in the target areas. As the land dropped away low and flat to the Rhein from our hilly area, it wasn't difficult to see, and even hear, the distant havoc.

Our wait was longer than usual, and Herr Lander was agitated. He wanted to go and check the outside situation. Herr Dietz reminded him that the all-clear had not sounded, a fact he didn't seem to care about.

Frau Andres cried softly and clutched her two little girls closer. Just weeks before, her two-year-old Helga had died of leukemia. I liked my next door neighbor and her little girls very much, and felt sorry for her. Herr Andres was Papa's card playing friend, and was also away serving on a far battlefront.

In a near corner was Frau Rösel, surrounded by her four children. It was sad how much work she had with Kätchen, her youngest. Rumors had it that Kätchen wasn't quite right in the head. Such gossip seemed to be a natural part of neighborhood life, and it made me wonder at times what was being passed around about my family.

Of course, I knew or had heard something about most of the people gathered in the underground room. With little to do but talk to Peter and look around, I couldn't help but study some of the people hiding with us. Fräulein Schmidt was a person I was very curious about. She also sat by herself, and spoke to no one. I only knew that she'd never married but had a son, now serving in the army somewhere. Seated just a few steps away from her, also alone, was Frau Usner, a friendly, talkative woman. She was the only Jewish person left in town. Married to a Christian man, she had a son, Walter, who went to school with Erich. Herr Usner had died. Walter was old enough to be in uniform, but he remained at home, though never came to the shelter.

Waiting, I thought of my own mother in her unprotected bed at home. Was she staring at the dark ceiling or studying her Bible by a dim light? The Bible was kept under her pillow — maybe she was praying. She always seemed to be having a conversation with God.

My body was getting stiff from sitting so long and holding Peter. I stood up, and was about to break the rules by walking around when a loud shout came from the top of the stairway. Apparently Herr Lander, tired of waiting, had opened the door. The roar of the bombers returning entered the cellar with a frightening loudness before the steel door could be slammed shut again. This was followed by a new sound, muffled but terrifying. It reverberated like a huge empty barrel falling down a flight of stairs.

A terrible thunderclap and violent shaking hit our sanctuary, knocking those of us standing onto the dirt floor. A cloud of dust descended from stone joints in the ceiling, making it hard to breathe or see, but the shaking didn't bring down any stones. Amidst the crying of young children came the realization of a new and horrible prospect. There was relief that the shelter remained intact, but had the apartment building collapsed on top of us? Were we trapped?

In my arms, Peter was still whimpering after the shock of the explosion and our fall to the floor. I covered his face so he wouldn't have to breathe the dirty air. I could see Frau Usner walking around, holding part of her shawl over her mouth, asking if anyone had been hurt. No one had been. One or two voices worried aloud that more bombs might be dropped. Herr Dietz started up the long stairway, telling all who could hear that he was concerned, but not enough to keep him from making sure we could escape. He had finally put into words what we all feared, and the room became oddly quiet as he neared the top, and twisted the big handle on the door.

With a hard push, the door opened wide, allowing in both the low roar of fire and a blinding brightness. Almost at the same moment, there came the unreal sound of the all-clear siren. Herr Dietz rushed halfway down the steps and urged us to come up and go back to our homes. The bomb, he said, had fallen on Seyler's leather tannery works a few hundred meters away. Many of us were still frightened as we made our way slowly toward the bright glow above. Firefighters with their equipment were already arriving as Peter and I came out into the open courtyard, adding to the frantic scene before us.

Like moths to fire, several in our group in the cellar joined others from the neighborhood to move closer to the heat and flames. We soon were ordered back.

"Go home! Go to your homes!"

Stunned by this singular attack on Kirchheim, the survivors dispersed quickly. We were still Germans obeying authority.

Peter was asleep in my arms when we got home. I don't remember if I slept again that night. At school the next day, I saw Elfriede, who told me of the damage done to her house from the bomb blast. Her parents' farmhouse is near the tannery, but fortunately she and her family were in a shelter, and unhurt when much of the roof on their house was blown away.

In the light of day, we discovered that the one bomb, dropped so recklessly by the enemy, had not destroyed the tannery or its tall smokestack. Instead, it had flattened the tannery's office building across the street, killing one man. Bookkeeper Ernst Butz had been working late alone. He too had ignored the siren, thinking it was safe in Kirchheim. The city records would record that only Herr Butz died as the result of a bomb blast on March 2, 1945 at 10:20 p.m.

In a few days, the town had settled back to normal. As for me, I still hadn't solved my problem of finding shoes for confirmation. The day following the bombing, I wrote to Papa telling him about it, and about my lack of black shoes. I doubt the shoes had anything to do with his decision, but a bomb had fallen near his house and he finagled a three-day furlough to come home to see for himself.

"I'm here now, so you can stop worrying. We'll find shoes for you. First, I want to see the damage at Seyler's."

After a bite to eat, I prepared Peter for cold weather. Papa wanted him to have some fresh air while we walked down and over a short block to Haiderstraße where the bomb hit.

A deep crater, bigger around than the building once sitting there, was now fenced off. My father stared at it in disbelief. "Mein Gott! That must have been a huge bomb to make such a hole."

"It was awful, Papa. The explosion knocked me and others in the shelter to the floor." I pointed back to the von Hirsch property where Peter and I were when the bomb came down.

He let out a whistle of surprise and relief. "That's close. Just a matter of meters and it could've been more tragic." My father was silent for a moment as he looked down into the gaping crater. He knew that Peter and I, and everyone, couldn't have survived such a blast.

"Thank God," he said. "Do you understand now why I ask you to always take Peter to the shelter? Poor Butz could be alive today if he'd taken heed of the siren!"

"I understand," I said. It was a weak reply, remembering the times we didn't go. "But I don't know what to do during the daytime raids and I'm in school. I can't run home and get him!"

"I know. But bombing attacks on small towns and villages haven't occurred as much during day raids. We'll just have to hope it doesn't change. Are you afraid?"

"Nay. Not anymore. Not for myself. I do worry about Peter and what will happen to him in this awful war. With you gone, he's my only joy."

We stared silently at the damage for a few more minutes. Papa held Peter in one arm, the boy cautiously responded by putting one arm around his neck.

He had no interest in what a bomb had done. His attention was on a man he didn't quite feel sure about. As long as I was in sight, Peter stayed quiet, but I'd learned to read him very well. With Papa not around that much, I made a point to show the boy how happy I felt when he did come home.

Some people came to stand and look with us. If it had been another place and time, Papa would have jumped right into small talk with them. Now he only nodded or agreed with a word or two about their complaints or worries. After the last person walked on, he indicated that we, too, should go home.

"War is an awful thing," he said after a few steps. "Innocent people on both sides die, whole towns are destroyed — and for what good purpose? Well, Adolf started this mess, and we went along, so we asked for it." We were about to turn the corner onto Breitstraße when he stopped and put a hand on my shoulder. "Believe me, Annchen, this war will be over soon. Very, very soon."

I had never seen my father's face so melancholy, yet he also seemed relieved to have spoken his feelings aloud to me. We went on home, spending the rest of the day working around the house. Nothing was said at any time before turning in about shoes. Trusting Papa to keep his word and not wanting to nag, I kept quiet. But as I pulled the bed covers over me, I wondered what he had in mind.

꙰

School was out at two o'clock the next day, and when I got home I found Papa taking the bull by the horns as usual. Two weeks worth of laundry had been boiled, washed and rinsed. I should have felt guilt, but I decided to be grateful instead.

"Hang it out on the lines quickly," he said, not letting me off the hook entirely. "When you're finished, we'll take the bicycles and go over to Steitz in Marnheim."

"Steitz? The shoe factory? But, Papa — "

"I know what you're going say, and it's true. They make only work shoes, but a new shoe is a new shoe. So hurry it up. We need to go!"

I didn't argue. I just hoped for black ones. Leaving the house later, I made sure to take the permission slip from city hall just in case. It was no news that Papa had known the Steitz family for years. As a small child in Marnheim, I was aware of the small shoe factory near the cemetery. No more than twenty people worked there. On the way over, Papa said the factory always refused to sell shoes retail — that only wholesalers could buy. His remark was accompanied by a wink.

When we arrived, the workers were beginning to leave for the day, but the offices were open. Papa led me directly into and down the hall to the owner's door. He was not the least bit shy, opening the door and walking in after a brief knock.

"Guten Tag, Herr Steitz. I'm glad to see you again, and looking so well, too!" My father didn't greet him with the expected 'Heil Hitler,' though it seemed to me that since Steitz supplied boots and shoes to the Wehrmacht, he could have been a big Nazi supporter. But my fears were unfounded. Herr Steitz returned Papa's greeting with a hearty handshake and broad smile.

It never ceased to amaze and please me that so many people knew and liked Papa. Herr Steitz shook my hand, saying something about how Seppel's daughter was taller than Seppel himself. It was true, and Papa grinned. "Ja, Herr Steitz, and I don't think she has stopped growing. She'll still have to show respect, though, and not spit on the top of my head."

I know my face progressed through ten shades of red as the two of them went into a fit of uproarious laughter. I couldn't help but join them, after recovering from my momentary shock. I don't know why the Seppel humor, and Papa's quickness, always took me aback. I should have been used to it.

In any case, that appeared to be the right moment to bring up the purpose behind our unexpected visit. Papa, suddenly began acting as if we were taking up too much of the man's time, and made quick work of explaining my situation, asking if he could help.

"Seppel, you came by at the right moment. Let's go out on the floor. We're just wrapping up an order of new work boots, and, I think, some low work shoes. Sadly for your daughter, we're now in the brown season. We do black in the fall."

My heart sank, but I could see by my father's face that I shouldn't show disappointment.

"That's too bad. But I'm sure Annchen will be pleased with brown. Right, Annchen?"

"Ja, Papa."

We continued through the work area with its cutting tables, heavy sewing machines, and individual workbenches. Herr Steitz opened another door and entered the shipping room. There in front of us was row after row of work shoes and boots, all brown. Papa later called it "a soldier's fantasy come true, especially right now." He added how short supplies were for the troops.

"These will be paired and boxed tomorrow for shipment," Herr Steitz said. "Go along that row over there. You're likely to find a fitting size in that section."

He and Papa stayed put and chatted while I immersed myself in the smell of new leather, checking sizes on the row designated. Size was the only question, since there wasn't a shade of difference in color or style. I eventually found a pair of low work shoes and returned to the two men, who were talking about the war in quiet tones. I thought they sounded more resigned than angry about what was happening.

"Ah, you found a pair. That's good." Papa reached in his pocket to bring out money and I handed Herr Steitz my slip.

"Nay, nay, Märe! What would I do with a permission document from the government? I don't sell retail!"

I would have been embarrassed had he not given my father a nudge and a wink. "Keep that," he added. "Maybe you'll have luck next time at a store —of course, if the war doesn't end first."

With many thanks, and our best wishes to Herr Steitz, we departed for home with the shoes wrapped in paper.

Riding side by side, Papa looked at me. "Seppel got you new shoes. So, they're not black. Is that so bad?"

"Papa, please! Don't think I'm not grateful. The color doesn't matter anymore. I have a black dress and stockings, and I'm sure there will be others wearing brown shoes. Believe me, Papa. I know what Seppel has done for me, and I know the shoes will wear better than any I could have bought."

"Are you sure you really want confirmation? You know it doesn't make any difference to me. I'll still think you're good as gold!"

"I know, Papa, but I want to. And, I'll be carrying Erich's hymn book he had for confirmation?" He smiled and I continued. "It's family tradition to be in the church. Don't you agree?"

"Ja, ja. I'm just sorry it'll be impossible for me to be there. I doubt if any family will come or give you the usual party."

"I'll be fine. Maybe one of my friends will have a party. If not, that's alright, too."

While I prepared supper later, Papa again tried to visit with Mama in the bedroom. He didn't share any of their words with me, but I could tell his deep unhappiness on his return to the kitchen.

In the morning, as we hugged farewell, I could see he was pleased with me, and with Peter's health and progress. The little fellow was already able at eleven months to walk around, with the help of furniture to hold on to.

"Remember that I'm always thinking about you," he said. "Try not to let your mother get you down. We have to believe help for her can be found."

࿎

My mother's long hours in bed during the day began to disturb my nights. Often I awoke to unexplainable sounds, and would find her sitting in the dark whimpering, moaning, or talking. It was sometimes hard to describe just what she was doing, and she never responded to my questions.

There were other sounds keeping me awake as well. Off in the distance came the exploding sounds of the enemy's artillery barrages. It seemed only days before that the enemy had come crashing into Germany. For us in the Rheinland, any last minute miracles to turn back the invaders were needed now. Each day, the shock wave blasts from the big guns came closer.

I had spoken to Pastor Schott a week before Palm Sunday, and convinced him I would be ready to participate, even without having attended catechism studies. I strongly suspected that any other year he would have refused me outright. I think he was getting nervous about going through with the confirmation. Reports of enemy progress toward us from the west and south were not encouraging. So my lack of study became the least of his concerns. He approved, and put me in the seating arrangement for the church service. Schott insisted that I be in the final rehearsal, and I agreed. As it turned out, rehearsal had just started when the air raid sirens sent us to the shelter.

The air raid was a relief to me. I had feared making a fool of myself by not knowing any of the answers. Sitting in the shelter, I knew I wouldn't be unhappy if the sirens went off again on Palm Sunday. I couldn't count on any disruption though, so I put my mind to remembering every detail of Henny's ceremony two years before, and Erich's before that.

The trick to passing the test, Erich had boasted, was to be first one with your hand up at the beginning. The pastor, wanting to impress the congregation, starts off with easier questions. Then, with the harder questions, he targets the students who haven't raised their hands at all.

Anyone who has given correct responses two or more times would not be called on again, and are free to relax.

I recall him nearly jumping out of his chair to get the pastor's attention. He gave answers to two questions, then sat back and only raised his hand occasionally. Of course, the Pastor ignored him to give others their turn. I decided

293

to chance the same tactic.

On Palm Sunday morning, I dressed in the black things I had and put on the brown shoes. As I left the house, the word was passing along the street that Bad Krueznach, thirty-five kilometers away, had fallen to the Americans.

Peterskirche was my destination, and it was packed with people. As Papa predicted, no one of my blood had come. I took my assigned seat with the class and waited with Erich's beautiful hymn book clasped in my hands for luck. The wait was short, as the pastor didn't want to be interrupted by any air raids. There was an organ anthem, singing, and the usual prayers. Pastor Schott introduced the class to the congregation, and began the testing that would give us acceptance into the church and adult responsibility. I could feel the tension increase with each word. He posed the first question and I listened very carefully, my hand ready to fly up.

"Martin Luther!" I said. Hands had gone up all around me, but it was my name he called on for the correct answer.

He went on, and it surprised me how many answers I knew. The religion classes in school over the years and my prayer meetings with Mama had done me more good than I realized. I kept putting my hand up, but it wasn't until the sixth question that he recognized me again to recite the twenty-third Psalm. Halfway through my recitation he interrupted, "Gute! Danke. Next —"

I don't think I heard all of the next question. I was so relieved to have gotten that far with the Psalm. Afterward, I made my way through the crowd outside the church, speaking a few words to classmate friends, before walking home. I told Mama that I was going to visit Henny. Because of illness, my friend had come home to spend a few days away from her school in Kaiserslautern. She would have come to my confirmation as I had gone to hers, had she been feeling better. She knew I wore her dress, and I wanted to tell her all about the service.

When I walked into the Hemm house, Henny's mother greeted me with a cake to celebrate my confirmation. I was dumbstruck. Tears flowed from joy, and I couldn't thank her enough. I felt terrible that I had once believed she didn't like me. Henny had tried to tell me different, but I didn't really believe it until that moment. I had been feeling so alone and worthless after leaving the church.

Henny got a kick out of my shock, and explained to me later how she had told her mother about the situation at home.

I could hardly wait to write Papa about my big day and how I did in the question period, but I really wanted him to know about Frau Hemm and my surprise cake. I already knew what his reaction would be. I could hear him say it: "Why are you surprised? Good friends care. They help each other, in good times and bad."

It was true.

Chapter Twenty-Nine

Monday morning, March 19.
I went to school only to have Frau Christman dismiss the class early. "Tomorrow was the final day of school for you anyway," she said. "The way matters are going, the administrator thinks you should all be in your homes."

No time for sentimentality, we all left and scattered to our respective houses. As I neared the Freier Platz across from Bossung's Inn, I saw and heard clearly Frau Gass standing in front of her farmhouse. She was highly agitated and shouting loudly to a neighbor.

"Frau Gass. Have you heard bad news?" I'd walked over, half fearing she'd gotten a black-edged envelope about her sons Helmuth or Enne, both in the army and good friends of Erich. "Is it one of the boys?"

"Oh, nay, child. Praise God that it isn't the boys," she said, looking skyward. "It's Frau Usner. The Gestapo came in the night and hauled the poor woman away!"

I was stunned. The old Jewish lady had shared a small apartment in Frau Gass' house with her son. "But that's crazy!" I said, finding my voice. "Couldn't her son stop them? He's not Jewish — at least, not all Jewish."

Frau Gass looked at me silently for a moment. "I'm surprised you don't know. He left here secretly weeks ago. Frau Usner wouldn't say where her son was heading." Looking at her neighbor friend and back at me. "The whole situation is insane. Everything is collapsing all around, and the Gestapo is still arresting Jews!"

At that moment, we all heard the commotion making us look up to see German soldiers coming down the Breitstraße. I cried at the sight. They came in ones and twos, in uniforms and boots so ragged as to be hardly recognizable. All appeared completely dispirited.

I ran up the street to my house to get away, to shut my eyes, but I couldn't. I found myself drawn to my bedroom window and I opened it, hoping the cool air would clear the tears from my eyes. More stragglers passed below, and I heard Herr Lander hollering at one.

"Where are you coming from?"

"From the west, old man," came the answer. "We ran out of gas and had to leave our equipment — tanks and trucks, all left behind."

"Where are you going now?"

The soldier stopped and stared at him, then walked on, hollering, "Home, if I can get there!"

Cleaning up after the noon meal later, I heard boots pounding up the stairway. For some reason it didn't frighten me, though I expected no one. The door jerked open and there stood my Papa, out of breath and excited. "Come quickly, we need to take care of some things fast. Don't stand there. This is important!"

For a moment, the urgency of his voice had me frozen in place, but I soon moved to obey.

"I had to come. I took the Luftwaffe truck and drove all the back roads I could remember to get here. I'm sure my commander considers me AWOL and will have me shot if I don't get right back!"

"Oh, no Papa!"

"Don't worry about that. Come. I'll get by. We've got to do some things."

I went with him, first to the living room. "Let's get this picture of Hitler off the wall. Take the picture out of the frame and burn it. Also, get the flag and burn it, too." He then almost ran into the bedroom to talk to Mama, leaving me to do the job.

I burned the picture, but couldn't bring myself to put the flag in the stove. I hid it for later use. Walking back to the bedroom, I got there in time to hear Mama screaming. "You're crazy, we're going to win. I know we are. I know it!" Her voice broke into sobs.

"Woman, you know nothing! I can't believe you haven't heard the artillery at night. They are almost here and they're going to go house to house searching for our soldiers. Look out your window and see how our boys are in flight! If you talk in favor of Hitler, they'll line you up on the wall. Do you hear me? Now help Annchen, and keep all the windows closed and doors locked!"

As we left and passed through the living room again, he stopped. "Get that bomb off the cabinet. I'll get the two rifles and meet you in the garden."

The 'bomb' in question was nothing more than a souvenir. About the size of a two-pound loaf of bread, it was defused and sitting on its tail fins. In the garden, he rapidly dug a hole and buried the rifles and bomb together. I stood and watched, worried about him. To me, he was wrong to rip through the house looking for any slight evidence of Nazism. Besides Hitler's picture and the flag, we really didn't have anything to implicate us in that way.

"Listen to me now," Papa said, taking me by the arm toward the courtyard doors. "I must go back to my unit before they really do send someone to shoot

297

me. Don't be too brave. Keep the doors locked. There won't be any more air raids. The Amis are too close, they won't bomb their own troops. Stay inside until it's over. It may be tomorrow or the next day, but it's ending. I'll try to come home soon."

'Amis' was our slang for Americans. I fought my emotions as he grabbed me and held me hard to him for a long time. Climbing into his truck, he drove away. I ran after him, and stood watching as the truck turned at Bossung's and disappeared. Slowly, I walked back into the house. I locked the door and sat down on the stairs. I wanted to cry, but knew there was no time for tears.

All day, the stream of German soldiers running away from the Amis continued through Kirchheim. I could feel their emptiness and confusion, but I didn't share the fear on some of their faces. For some reason I wasn't scared. I could find nothing on the radio about the retreat, and the radio signals out of Baden Baden and Berlin were filled not with despair, but with ringing calls to arms. "Victory is still in sight!" Such words continued through April, but for us in the Pfalz, defeat was at hand.

Tuesday, March 20.

Again, the true war news came by word of mouth along the street. The latest was that the Amis had taken control of the rail lines in Kaiserslautern, Grünstadt, and nearby Marnheim. All remaining and intact units of our Seventh Army in Kirchheim got out, but not before blowing up the beautiful iron railroad bridge connecting us to Marnheim and the world. Everyone was disgusted about it, calling the destruction crazy — with a few other choice words for the SS idiots responsible. Out in the countryside near Marnheim, huge stone structures at each end of the iron bridge still remain as monuments to stupidity.

The ladies of our town went en masse to city hall for a visit with Bürgermeister Knieriemen. I saw them while on my way to check the food shops downtown. Later Henny's grandmother said they had gone to tell the mayor to tear down the barricades at the road entrances into town. The women demanded no resistance to the Amis, and Knieriemen obeyed.

Wednesday, March 21, 1 a.m.

I hadn't been asleep long when the sound of trucks and a low flying airplane startled me awake. There was shooting, and the plane flew away. A vehicle screeched to a halt in front of our house, quickly followed by frantic calls of "Water," in English. I ran to the window, and against Papa's orders, opened it to look down on the street.

A fire was burning up one of the truck's tires, and I could see three men running about hollering and trying to smother the blaze. There was a public well up the street, but of course they wouldn't know about that. I only knew a few words in English, and 'water' was one of them. I ran in to Mama to tell her some Amis needed water.

"Nay," she answered. "Don't open the door!" By the time I got back to my window to look out, I could see that someone had brought them water in a bucket. It was Frau Andres from next door. The fire was soon out, and I thanked God for it. Papa once told me fire near the gas tank could make it blow up and our house was but a meter away from the truck.

I continued to watch as the soldiers unloaded the truck and carry everything into Andres' little house. As I lay in bed, I worried what they would do to the little mother of two.

Suddenly, my bed shook as an awful rumble began out on the street. I had fallen asleep again. I ran once more to the window to be greeted by dawn and tank after tank coming down the hill, part of the endless parade of Americans rolling into Kirchheim. Every now and then the floor under my feet stopped shaking when the convoy halted. After the initial tank incursion, it was mostly all trucks loaded with young men sitting in the back. Sometimes, when the trucks stopped for a few minutes, I could look at them closely. These Americans, the ones Papa said would search every house, had a most unusual habit of chewing without eating. The puzzle was solved within hours when the soldiers began sharing something new to Germans — chewing gum.

As the new day's sky lightened, trucks loaded with soldiers continued their stop-and-go passage by the house, and on down Breitstraße to Neumayerstraße, around the Schloßgarten, and into the heart of town. An entire group of trucks carried Negro soldiers, but whether white or black, all looked in need of food and rest. In want of food myself, I went over to check on Mama and the boy. She was awake, and had been up and around, though only as far as the kitchen. She'd have to go into the living room to see the invasion along Breitstraße, and she would not.

I dressed and fixed hot wheat cereal for us, and afterward, decided to risk venturing down to the street. Cautiously unlocking the front door, I stepped out and saw that many children of the neighborhood had already stationed themselves at the sides of the street. They all seemed to be waiting for something. The trucks had halted momentarily, and small packages came raining down from the soldiers high up in the open trucks. Children of every age clambered around, grabbing at anything hitting the cobblestones. Someone near me ripped open an oddly marked flat bar and yelled "Schokolade!" One of the bars fell at my feet. A little boy I recognized looked at the bar, then me. He knew there wasn't a chance against a girl twice his size, so he waited and watched.

I glanced up at the faces on the back of the truck. They were really just boys up close, laughing and throwing away something none of us had seen or tasted in a very long time. One of them, smiling broadly, motioned for me to pick up the bar at my feet. I wanted to — the urge was strong. My mouth watered with the memory of chocolate. Erich wouldn't have hesitated a second. I reached down for the slim package, and handed it to the small boy. The line of trucks jerked forward again, and I turned to reenter the house. I couldn't keep the chocolate. The conquerors must not be allowed to think of me as another hungry German child.

⇛

I noticed that we no longer had electricity. Apparently, the Americans had cut it off to prevent people from listening to German radio broadcasts. Other than that, it was no inconvenience to me. Light at night and listening to the radio were all the use we made of it. Since we didn't have candles or oil for the old lamp, the day had to be planned accordingly.

Outside, the traffic had slowed and the three soldiers at Frau Andres worked to repair the tire shot out by an airplane in the night. Since Luftwaffe planes hadn't been seen in our skies for months, the attacker must have been American or British. The damaged truck left soon after.

Day was ending when a new, small group of trucks pulled over and stopped in front of the house with some commotion. Curious, I stepped out, as did the Andres' children and others. One of the soldiers jumped off a truck and walked over to us.

"Guten Abend." The young man spoke in perfect German with a heavy Pfälzisch accent. "Wohnt die Frau Steinmetz noch hier an dieser Straße?" (Does Frau Steinmetz still live on this street?)

The familiar sound coming out of this person in an American uniform left us wide-eyed and speechless for a minute. Then, almost in unison, we answered. "Ja, da oben links in dem blauen Haus!" We all pointed the direction, the blue house next to Henny's.

He left to walk up to the house in question, and several smaller children followed. I stayed put, and it was just as well, for I learned one or two facts from the soldiers on the closest truck. One of them pointed toward the disappearing soldier. "Alfons Steinmetz. Son. Frau Steinmetz' son." I understood, and it hit me with surprise and shock.

I had always known the widow Steinmetz as just a nice old neighbor woman living next to Henny. A quiet person, and also hard of hearing, she had grown children, but they were all gone when I came to the Breitstraße. Alfons had obviously ended up in America, only to return wearing the enemy's uniform.

For most Germans, there were enemies, and then there were real enemies. The Russians and the French we considered bad enemies, but Americans were thought of more like kindred folk — a nicer sort of foe. We hated defeat by anyone, but had always liked and been fascinated by Americans.

It was getting dark, and without electricity, I didn't wait around for the son's return. Getting ready for bed was more important. One wonderful aspect of the war's end for us — a good night's sleep. There would be no more air raids, no threat of bombs, and no dashes to the shelter. Lying in bed, I heard the trucks pull away and wondered what happened when Frau Steinmetz opened her door.

Thursday, March 22.

News of the amazing visit by Alfons Steinmetz to his mother was on a special fast track in the morning. No doubt embellished by the time it got to my house, the story of reunion was heart warming just the same. Everyone I talked to expressed happiness for the son's return, even if he was with the wrong army.

By noon, word had circulated through the town that occupation by the Americans was complete. All city and district officials appointed by the Nazis were under arrest and being sent to prison elsewhere. Kirchheim would officially capitulate on Good Friday, the next day.

A proclamation by General Dwight D. Eisenhower, written in German, was hung outside City Hall and posted in other locations. It began: "An das deutsche Volk! (To the german people!)" The small 'd' in the spelling of 'deutsche' was insulting. (The standard language rule is that the name of a nation and its people is always capitalized.) It wasn't considered an oversight. The small 'd' appeared throughout the proclamation, and this act of further humiliating the German people wasn't lost on us.

Good Friday, March 23.

With official capitulation came a curfew. The townspeople had two hours in the morning and another two in the afternoon to be out and about. All other times, everyone had to be inside, children included. All radios and weapons were to be turned in promptly. I did neither. The rifles were already buried in the garden, and I wouldn't give up the radio, one of the few valuable things we owned. I hid it in the attic until the order was rescinded. We couldn't listen to it anyway without electricity.

Saturday, March 24.

Electricity was restored, but not the right to have a radio. I was sorry for little Peter, who couldn't go for a long outing. I wondered too, how our families were doing in Bolanden and Marnheim. I could be sure Oma and Tante Lisbeth were glad it was over.

In the afternoon, Pastor Schott got the word out that he'd been given permission to hold rehearsal that evening for the Lord's Supper (communion) for my class. It had to be over, and students returned to their homes, before dark.

March 25 — Easter Sunday

Once again, I donned the black dress and stockings, put on the brown shoes, and with the black hymnal in my hand I walked to Peterskirche. Along the street, I encountered American soldiers everywhere. One of them stopped me, pointed to my dress, and in English asked: "Why?" It was another word I understood, but I couldn't explain the reason for wearing black. So I lifted my hand toward the church tower and walked on. Once inside our ancient sanctuary honoring Saint Peter, a kind of peace washed over me, and I realized this was the one place still protected from the turmoil outside. And for the first time, I had the wine and bread of the Lord's Supper.

The Americans erected a large tent on the nearby Freier Platz, across from the Catholic church. That intersection had suddenly become important to the Americans. The tent primarily sheltered soldiers guarding the crossroads, and others patrolling the adjacent streets. Other checkpoints had been set up throughout the city, but our road intersection was a strategic spot. To the north and west were the towns of Alzey, Bad Kreuznach, and two major cities on the Rhein — Mainz and Bingen. To the east was Worms, also on the Rhein river. Southwest were Kaiserslautern and France, and due west, Trier and Luxembourg. It was little wonder that a major checkpoint was established on Freier Platz, also the location of a memorial statue from a long forgotten war.

And there was some irony in that an early Nazi event occurred at the foot of the statue. In May of 1933, long before my family had moved to Kirchheim, local Nazis held a book burning there. Seeing a photograph of it, I was surprised by how small the pile of books on fire, compared to the very large crowd of onlookers.

American authorities made their headquarters in the district court building a block farther down Neumayerstraße. To house officers, and some top non-commissioned officers, villas of some of the affluent families on Glaserstraße were confiscated. Owners were given just hours to pack up belongings and find living arrangements elsewhere.

The curfew put in place the first week of occupation remained in effect the entire time the Americans stayed, though the hours a person was restricted did change once or twice. Only farmers were given freedom to work in their fields anytime. By the second week, all persons over the age of ten were required to carry an identification pass. I went a short distance to get one at the courthouse on Neumayerstraße, the downhill continuation of Breitstraße.

Immediately upon entering the building I stepped into a wide hallway, lined on one side with office doors every few meters. On the other side was a wall, with no doors. I'd been in the building before, and quickly saw a difference. On this day, the entire length of the wall without doors was covered with a photo display. Just one other person, a woman, was in the hallway, and she walked slowly and silently, looking at the photos.

I stopped to glance at the black-and-white pictures. In my head, a voice screamed, "These can't be photos. They have to be drawings!" But they were real photographs of real people. Emaciated people in striped clothing with shaven heads, in groups and alone, staring vacantly at the camera lens. I was repelled and fascinated all at once by the pictures. Some had names over big iron gates. I'd never heard before of Buchenwald, Gurs, Auschwitz and Theresienstadt. Every picture had a description underneath written in German. I read all I could in disbelief. The Gestapo, SS, and Nazi party were accused over and over with committing the atrocities shown. But the charges didn't stop there.

"Germans! You did it! You killed millions of these innocent men, women and children! Nobody else. You!" If someone came in or passed as I walked along, I was unaware of it. What little I had in my stomach churned, but I couldn't turn away. The reason for my being there was forgotten until the woman, the one I had seen earlier, came out of a door with a paper in her hand. She looked at me, or maybe right through me to all of the terrible photos lining the hall, it was hard to say. Then, she hurried out, saying, "That's the office."

Remembering my purpose, I walked in not knowing what to expect. I found two Americans, just standing at one side of the big office watching German women sitting at desks. A few of the women were helping people. One desk had a sign that read 'Registration,' and a man was just leaving. I went over, repeatedly telling myself not to say 'Heil Hitler' to the woman. She told me to sit, shoved a card in the typewriter, and matter-of-factly asked, "Name, age, address." Her fingers flew over the keys, jerked the card out, and stamped it. "Carry it at all times!"

I wanted to ask her, a stranger, if it was true, if it really happened — what the photos in the hall showed. I couldn't. The two officers seemed to be looking at me. "Is there something else?"

I jumped up. "Nay, danke." I rushed out and down the hall, looking neither left nor right until reaching fresh air. The bright, sunny spring morning that greeted me should have cheered me, but it didn't. Everything had suddenly turned ugly. I had to talk with someone who could explain.

Mama was in the kitchen feeding Peter when I got home. She did that when she was in the mood or had no choice when I had to be out looking for food. Sitting down across from her at the table, I tried describing the photo display and what the Americans had said about us. All the time she never looked at me, keeping her attention on the boy and smiling at him with each spoonful of warm cereal. Only subtle changes of expression on her face told me she heard my words.

I begged her to help me know the truth. "Do you think the Germans could really do all those terrible things?" There was no response. "Mama, look at me! I need to know!"

Finally, she turned her face my way, and with a blank expression, slowly shook her head from side to side. I couldn't tell what it meant. I was a fool to talk to her. She cared nothing about what was happening in the outside world.

With the arrival of the Americans ending the war for us in the Pfalz, Mama had only gotten worse. It wasn't so much a physical as a mental slide. I couldn't tell how much pain she had — she wouldn't have complained to me directly. She did start pacing the floor from room to room for much of each night, often calling out Erich's name and generally worrying aloud about his fate. She never spoke of Papa and his fate. Since my bedroom was next to hers, these roamings always kept me in turmoil and tired me out. There were times when I shouted her back into bed.

"I'm so worried about Erich," she'd say.

"Mama, I'm worried about both Erich and Papa, but we'll hear something soon. We'll get word they're both safe. Now go to bed!"

I wasn't at all sure when we would hear of my father and brother's whereabouts. I didn't know if they were safe at all, but I could not allow myself to think the worst. Over the weeks and months to come, even as other men returned one by one, I had to believe that no news was good news.

In the meantime, there was plenty to keep me busy. Mama had decided to add one more burden. No more would she go to the courtyard outhouse, but instead used the bed pot day and night. The pot had always been an emergency substitute for the outhouse at night, and was almost never used for bowel movements. This changed, forcing me to replace the pot with a bucket half filled with water, and a lid for the top to cut down on the smell. Naturally, I emptied and cleaned the bucket. It would have been understandable had she not been able to make the short trip outside.

The other decision had one positive outcome — no more washing diapers. I convinced Mama to put Peter on the pot when he showed signs. Thankfully, the boy grasped the concept in no time. But if I couldn't be there to supervise, I'd have stool to clean up on the floor, beds, and wherever he managed to leave his mark. It was another troubling sign of my mother's mental state.

Soon after my futile attempt to reach Mama about the courthouse experience, I waited for a chance to visit Hannelore. It was the first time I had to show my new pass to the sentry at the corner. Nearing the intersection, I saw the soldier, again just a lanky young man, standing in the middle of the road, his rifle slung over one shoulder. I went over and handed him my pass.

As he took the pass I said, "Don't shoot." I'd wanted to say that to some American ever since the soldiers arrived. (That phrase was one I practiced with Henny many months earlier.)

He laughed. "You speak English?"

"Nay," I stammered. "Only words." He ignored the answer and went on talking to me. I was sorry I'd spoken to him, but I had wanted to use a phrase I'd seen in the little German-English booklet issued to my father by the Luftwaffe. It contained only phrases such as "Hands up," not enough to make conversation.

"So, your name is Ainchin. You're not German — no blonde hair and no blue eyes."

I understood him, and how badly he said my name. "Not 'Ainchin,'" I corrected. "Annchen. Germans nicht — not all blonde."

He gave me my pass back. "That's not what uncle Adolf said."

I smiled back at him and walked on, though it was several steps before I realized the 'Uncle Adolf' he referred to was our Führer. It made me laugh, and I had the urge to tell him how I felt about it. But I didn't know how.

Reaching Hannelore's door, I looked to my right across to the Freier Platz, where the big tent stood. Soldiers were sitting outside playing cards and listening to music coming from a big speaker. Some young boys from the neighborhood hung close, watching them. It all seemed unreal. I never could've dreamt such a scene.

Frau Rihlmann, Hannelore's mother, was in the living room sitting by the window when I came in. "Ach, Annchen. How nice you came by. Come sit by me."

She was alone, mending clothes and watching the activity outside and below the second floor window. All of Freier Platz and the crossroads were in view. I'd just pulled a chair over to join her when Hannelore and her older sister Anneliese came in. It was a surprise to learn that Anneliese had just come from the tent. Her four years of English at the Gymnasium was being put to use by the Americans. I liked Anneliese very much, probably even better than Hannelore at the time, though I was jealous of her ability to fluently speak and understand English. Of course, she was closer to my brother in age and had had the chance to get more education.

Anneliese was stable and sensible compared to the flighty, but lovable Hannelore. The only real fault I found in the oldest was that she allowed Hannelore to draw her into constant verbal battles. I think all those kinds of things struck me because there were no sisters in my life.

Our visit had only started when the royal landlady, Fräulein von Hirsch, stopped in for a visit. The elegant old lady had a way of dominating conversation, so she talked and we listened. At the right moment, Hannelore nudged me. "Come, let's go out so we can talk."

Usually, I liked listening to the Fräulein tell tales of how it used to be, but this time I was glad to leave. I'd come over to talk about the terrible pictures at the courthouse. We went into the kitchen and I gave her no time to start up with foolish gossip.

"Hannelore, have you gotten your pass?"

"Ja, of course. Isn't it wild having these Americans here? You should see all the handsome ones over at the tent. With their helmets off they're downright — "

"Hannelore!" I interrupted, angrier with myself than her. I should have known not to ask her a serious question. "I'm not interested in handsome guys. I want to know if you looked at the photo display."

Before she could answer, Anneliese joined us, hearing my question as she came through the door. "I looked at all of them," she offered. "I nearly got sick. Mama went with me and was shocked also. She said she'd never heard of those camps, and has no idea where they are. Even Fräulein von Hirsch saw the display, and you know she always has an opinion."

"What did she think?"

"She thinks it's not true. Germans couldn't do that, she said."

Hannelore continued to be quiet, so I pressed on with Anneliese. "And what do you think?"

Her answer came only after a long pause. "I can't believe photos like that can be faked. It must be true. I just don't know what to do about it."

Mama had fixed a simple supper for herself and Peter while I was out, and had gone back to bed. The dirty dishes were left on the table. I ate what she had left for me, and cleaned up the kitchen. I liked playing with the boy after supper, but had missed out because of my visit to Hannelore's. I peeked into the bedroom and saw him fast asleep.

Peter had become my biggest joy. It was as though God had looked into my future and had given me what I needed. I knew some children could be lively to the point of distraction, and that's not what I needed. When I could play with him, I was always pleased how he'd pay attention and catch on to things quickly. At just over a year old, he grasped ideas immediately. For his age, I thought his quiet and meticulous efforts amazing. As long as I didn't go too far from his sight, I could go about my work unhindered by any need to constantly entertain or discipline him. I called him my "Goldklümpchen" (gold nugget).

❧

New regulations governing citizen behavior were made known by way of our Litfassäule, Germany's famous round advertising columns, most often found standing in front of public buildings and along major streets. Of course, not everyone ran down to one of the columns everyday to see what was new. It only took one person from a block to check, and everyone soon knew the word. For the first few days, all inns and taverns were closed. On reopening, American soldiers couldn't go in, with the exception of military police. It was their job to make sure only a certain number of German patrons congregated at a table, an effort to prevent conspiratorial meetings.

On the whole, people were surprised and pleased by the Americans. Most of the young men seemed well behaved, and fairly friendly. I always felt a kind of comfort when I encountered a foot patrol or a jeep passed while making my rounds in town. I noticed right away how quiet their steps were when marching or just out on foot patrols. The reason was their boots. Unlike the leather and steel bottoms of German boots, the Americans had rubber. The marching of our soldiers on cobblestones could be heard blocks away.

I liked the Americans because they didn't bring destruction to my pretty town. They made few demands on me, and didn't chase my family and me from our home. But more than this, they brought an element completely new to us. I can only describe it as a casual spirit unencumbered by the strict formalities of European culture. This is not to imply that as soldiers these Americans didn't have strict military rules to obey. But their behavior and attitudes, I later came to realize, sprang from a special American-style freedom. In Germany, one didn't go much beyond "Guten Tag" to a total stranger, or question anyone in authority. And one certainly didn't mingle uninvited with persons of another class. I would later learn that in America there were very definite class distinctions and separation, but we didn't see it in the first Americans arriving in Kirchheim.

Naturally, being occupied by Americans had its negative side. Ending up on the losing side was no reason to celebrate, even if you'd opposed the war. For young people like me, it was harder. Years of indoctrination in the Hitler Jugend created a strong idealism that turned to bitterness in defeat. Most of the older Germans had sensed the real possibility of losing their war long years earlier, but the youth woke up to that reality only when the conquerors rolled in.

The young people had counted on a miracle. Wiser heads knew that there were no miracles left. The very young children and the very old were the luckiest German survivors. The first couldn't comprehend the blow to our pride, and the second had lived it all before and knew about survival.

To lose a war by overwhelming forces was hard enough to accept, but to stand personally accused in the slaughter of millions of innocents in concentration camps and elsewhere was devastating. The methods used by the Americans, British and French to lay the genocide entirely on us were intended to crush forever our pride and spirit. It was never said to us that it was known the guilt belonged entirely to the Nazi leaders and their criminal followers. Instead, it was easier to lay guilt on Germans like me. That didn't make it so, but it did exact cruel results.

The first time I knew with absolute certainty that the death camps had existed was on June nineteenth. On that day, Frau Usner returned to Kirchheim from the camp at Theresienstadt, her head shaved. Understandably, she would never forgive the people of Kirchheim for allowing it to happen.

As a Kirchheimer and a German, I was saddened and ashamed, but accepting blame is another matter.

Chapter Thirty

The arrests of nearly all of the top local Nazi officials got underway immediately, and most were imprisoned. Henny and I were completely shocked to hear that one of that group was Karola Kiefer, our former music teacher. We couldn't believe that it was true, but if it was, we felt a terrible mistake had been made. Later, word came that she had been tried and sentenced to the prison in Landau.

When Fräulein Karola Kiefer told us she could no longer be our instructor in late 1943, we were crushed. We had admired and appreciated her immensely. She had given two very young girls a special gift of her time and knowledge of music, art and books. We were young girls easily molded by a strong personality. She took that responsibility most seriously, but never tried to indoctrinate us politically. She instead sparked in us a life-long desire to learn more about the wonders of our world.

As a Bund Deutscher Mädchen leader, Fräulein Kiefer was responsible for the older teenage girls' activities, and though we played our instruments for many of that group's programs, Henny and I were too young to be members. But, as her students, we observed her methods. In all that time, I never heard her espouse Nazism. She could have, BDM was, after all, a party organization. Why she didn't, I couldn't say. Perhaps in coming from a cultured family, and being the daughter of a poet, she believed a young girl's guidance didn't need politics. Remembering her love of the arts and young people, it's the only guess I could make. Of course, I knew nothing of her activities as the war wound down. I simply couldn't believe she'd betray the decency I knew.

The day she parted from us as a teacher, Henny and I were given a choice from gifts she had purchased. Henny got a necklace and I took a small hand-carved and painted wood trinket box. Lucky for me Henny took the necklace. I had my eye on the round box decorated with colorful flowers, mostly Edelweiss. As was her style, Fräulein Kiefer didn't explain in detail why the lessons must stop, only that her BDM responsibilities had grown. It would be years before the truth surrounding her arrest and imprisonment became known.

In any case, after losing her as teacher and by 1944, life began closing in on me. The happy times with Fräulein Kiefer and my Handharmonika had to be set aside.

The identities of the real hard-line Nazi leaders in Kirchheim really didn't matter that much to the American army authorities in the beginning. There were the obvious Nazi scoundrels to be rounded up, and then there were those fingered by revengeful neighbors as 'Nazi leaders,' but were in fact innocent. It would take a very long time for the allied authorities to sort out the phony charges from the real. In some cases, like Karola Kiefer, many were never given the chance to clear their names of the charges.

∼

After the first weeks of April had passed, and with no American soldiers coming into the house to inspect, I decided to bring the radio down from its hiding in the attic. Though raised to obey authorities, there were some things I was willing to risk punishment. The radio was one of our treasured possessions.

Turning the radio on for the first time in weeks I learned one thing right away. The station we listened to the most, Südwestfunk (Southwest Radio) in Baden Baden, was in the hands of the Americans. They and the British were moving fast. It seemed to be the same wherever I tuned to a German station, with the exception of the powerful Radio Berlin. I felt more guilty and nervous about tuning in this last voice of Nazism than I had when Erich and I listened to BBC broadcasts. Both were forbidden, yet the strident voices from Radio Berlin held me in a mesmerized state of sadness and tears. The most ardent believer had to now know that the words from Berlin matched nothing in reality.

The very last broadcast I heard from Berlin announced Hitler's suicide. Not much was said on the broadcast about Hitler's death, and I remember not caring anymore. It was all over. Berlin capitulated on May second, and Stunde Null or Zero Hour, came on May ninth. I heard it all on our radio, the final lying down of arms by the Germans. Americans called it V-E Day. Later, I saw masses of people cheering in London and New York in movie newsreels. I cried on that day, but not for Hitler or Nazism. I knew something had gone terribly wrong. My tears were for all the dead, and for my missing father and brother, for Germany, and for myself. The fates of Peter and Mama were in my lap. I had sole responsibility for our survival until Papa and Erich came home, and I wasn't sure they would.

∼

The tent on the Freier Platz stayed up just a short time. In appreciation for all her translating work, Anneliese was given the record player and several records by the soldiers before moving on. In the spare moments I could spend with her and Hannelore, we'd listen to American songs over and over again. "You Are My Sunshine" and "Boo-Hoo, You've Got Me Crying For You," were two of the tunes we soon learned to sing. Frau Rösel whose second floor apartment was directly across from us, had picked up the lyrics of "You Are My Sunshine" earlier when the soldiers repeatedly played the song.

People usually kept their windows open in nice weather, and one afternoon an American patrolling Breitstraße, started passing under Frau Rösel's window. Standing behind her curtains, so as not to be seen, she began singing the song in her lilting soprano. I watched the scene from my window, and I smiled as the soldier stopped and looked around in complete puzzlement. He caught sight of me sitting on the windowsill and pointed a finger. I quickly shook my head, and indicated Frau Rösel's window. I understood his confusion. Her voice carried well out into the street and bounced off my house. He listened for another minute, chuckled and walked on.

But not everything was so pleasant in those first days of occupation. Rumors and accusations flew through Kirchheim and neighboring villages on the matter of who were the real local Nazi leaders and supporters. Fingers pointed right and left. Many people were arrested, both guilty and innocent. Eventually, most of the harmless party members without influence and those found free of party connection were released. It also happened that some real Nazi leaders and workers remained free, or were released after questioning. It was a hectic time and regarding imprisonment of people without strong Nazi ties, the Americans seemed to need scapegoats. As for those who had really lined their pockets under Hitler, it was rumored that the Americans needed people who knew how to run the bureaucracy. Hence, the people who had been running it before stayed in place.

After May ninth, the Americans named a new Bürgermeister for Kirchheim, my fourth grade teacher, Ferdinand Schardt. The reaction of the people was mixed. Some were indignant. "What does a school teacher know about being Mayor?" But more people defended Herr Schardt. "At least he's clean!" they said. Being barely more than a kid myself, my opinion didn't count for much, but I do recall wondering how he would do in the position. He'd not only been my teacher, Schardt was also a neighbor, living just a half block away.

Along with his appointment came the rapid return of postal service, a daily newspaper, banking service, and out-of-town bus service. Kirchheim folks also had train service for a short time, but only to the north toward Alzey and Mainz. All other points had been blocked by the senseless destruction of the rail bridge toward Marnheim. Eventually, rail officials canceled northbound service too, finding it impractical. New bus service to Marnheim station enabled Kirchheimers to again travel anywhere by train.

The impact of permitting Germans to travel was instant and overwhelming. Hungry people from every devastated big city in the Rheinland swarmed into the countryside by any means possible — overcrowded trains, cars and trucks, motorcycle, moped, bicycle, and even hired taxi. Lots of city people had money, but quickly discovered that farmers weren't very interested in money. They preferred good quality silver-plated knives, forks and spoons, Rosenthal dinnerware, fine jewelry, good men's suits and pretty dresses, and even fancy underwear, if clean and not mended. Any of these material things the farmers took in trade for a little bit of food.

I saw a man pedaling up our hill, a heavy suitcase hanging from each handlebar. The struggle was too great and he finally got off and started pushing the bicycle up the grade. First, he removed what once must have been a handsome fedora hat to wipe his brow. His suit appeared worn, but was obviously tailored for him. Store-bought suits were easily identified by their bagginess. It was just as obvious he wasn't from our part of the Pfalz, and didn't know the territory. The northerly direction he was going had mostly forested hills, and few farm villages for long kilometers. My ride to Neustadt had been a picnic compared to what he had in store.

I had nothing to trade, just ration coupons and money to use whenever food shops offered anything. Again I stood in lines, only to hear too often that what I needed was sold out. I began following the lead of several neighbors who made nocturnal visits to farmers' fields and orchards to steal anything edible. For me, it was always fruit, and I never took it from the trees, only what had fallen to the ground. I already felt guilty for stealing, and if someone came along, there was nowhere to go when caught up in a tree. At least on the ground, I could run like the wind.

Scrounging on the ground in the dark could mean a disappointing harvest upon inspection at home. Apples and plums were often wormy and badly bruised under the kitchen light. Better than nothing I'd tell myself, as I cut away the bad parts to make sauce. Some people were caught by farmers, resulting in warnings by authorities of stiff penalties, but it didn't stop me. The best time was two or three in the morning, after the farmers got too tired to stay alert. Not once did I encounter a soul, whether it be a farmer or another thief. It would have been a mistake to carry a burlap bag on the street, and it wasn't necessary. Any Kirchheim kid knew all the garden paths that criss-crossed the neighborhood. Everyone used them to get around.

May was garden planting time, and without seeds, I worried what to do. I'd just been talking to Frau Andres and Herr Kasper about it. Our lodger Kasper wanted half the garden for his little family. I didn't care — half of nothing is nothing. Hardly a day later, we all heard the word that the Merz hothouse and garden center near the Schloßgarten had seedlings for sale. As with everything else, these were rationed according to family size. I hurried down and stood in a line, and for a change, got my share. I remember carefully carrying the tiny plants home to put in my half of the garden. The seedlings included lettuce, cabbage, and brussel sprouts. Merz was reluctant to part with any seeds, but I managed to come home with carrot seeds as well. Planting my half of the garden, the promise I'd given my father came back to speak to me, "Ja, Papa, I'll take care of things."

But, occasional greens and salvaged fruit didn't make a complete diet. I was able to still draw from the dwindling supply of old potatoes in our dirt floor basement. We'd always bought a year's supply of potatoes in the fall. By early summer, almost a year later, any remainders were shriveled and sprouting eyes. I longed for bread. Including Mama, Peter and myself, rationing permitted only enough bread per week to provide slightly more than a slice a day for each of us. For a growing teenager, that was not enough, especially considering the lack of other hardy foods. I finally got hungry enough to try and do something about it.

Riding my bicycle over to Bolanden, I had in mind to visit a few minutes with Oma and Tante Lisbeth, but with the real purpose of speaking to Tante Gusta. The latter had started up her route again delivering dairy products to the doors of well-off clients in Kirchheim and elsewhere. Having lost her husband in Russia, she had a war widow's pension, but it wasn't enough. Until recent weeks, she'd stop by Breitstraße infrequently to check on us and maybe drop off some extra butter. The visits stopped altogether when she became disgusted at always finding Mama in bed. Tante Gusta, a mere sister-in-law, didn't believe in my mother's illness any more than Mama's own blood sisters did. I couldn't do much about that, but there was something I needed to ask her, and it wasn't going to be easy. She didn't believe much in me either.

"What brings you to Bolanden, don't you have enough to do at home?"

"Tante, I want your opinion about something, since you know the baker next door."

"Naturally I do. Been buying his goods for years. What are you getting at?"

I believe she already had some idea, but I answered anyway. "I'm going to go over there and ask him to sell me a loaf of bread. I don't have a ration coupon, only money. Do you think he'll do it?"

A look of surprise spread across her face, as though she had expected I was going to ask her to do it. "I can't say I know. All I'll tell you is this — tell them loud and clear that you're Seppel's daughter. That will wake up some memories. Fritz is known far and wide, especially in his home village. Go now and hurry on home. I'm sure that little boy is needing you!"

Walking into the small bakery next door, my courage almost left me when I saw two housewives still doing business. I didn't know the woman waiting on them, but from what the other ladies were saying, I took it that she was the baker's wife, and not a happy one at that. My hope was fading fast. I stayed back until one housewife left, and then the other. The door closed, and the baker stepped out, apparently thinking the last customer of the day had departed. He spotted me. "One more customer, Mutter, then we can lock up."

I think it was because he called his wife 'Mother' in such a kind way that I could speak at all. I closed my eyes in a quick silent plea to my father: 'Please understand, Papa, I'm not begging. I have the money.'

"Ja, Guten Tag," I began. "I'm Kleine Seppel's daughter. I was wondering if you could sell me a loaf of bread. I have the money, but no coupons."

Both froze like statues, the wife uncomfortably staring at her flour-dusted husband. I prayed no one else would intrude. Suddenly, a twinkle of recognition came to the little man's eyes and spread until his whole face smiled. "So, you're Fritz's daughter! It's been a while since Seppel — ach, but how is your father?" Both of them had relaxed somewhat.

"I don't know. We haven't heard anything since the end. Not about my brother Erich either. It's just my mother and I, and a little baby brother."

The smile left the baker's face, and he turned to his wife. "Ja, Mutter, we know Seppel. Let's help out and sell her a loaf."

She brought down a three-pound loaf from a shelf and wrapped it, taking my money. "Please say nothing about it."

I promised, thanking them profusely as I went out the door to fly home. I must have flown, for I don't remember pedaling the bike at all. From that day on, working from a list of village bakeries in the area, I made a point to visit every one where Papa had delivered flour in the 'old days.' Knowing it was important not to wear out my welcome, I made sure not to go back to the same bakery too soon. I didn't always get a three-pounder — in fact, most times it was just a one or two-pound share. That was alright. At least Seppel's daughter was never turned down completely, not by bakers anyway. It may seem like a small advantage, but not to have to worry about bread was a godsend. Others could have their inside tracks with butchers and farmers, I was more than satisfied that the bakers remembered Seppel.

I didn't bother Mama with my methods in getting the extra bread. While she ate some of it, knowing what was happening in the world was of no interest to her. No longer did I speak about those things with her, only of mundane matters of the household and concerns about Peter.

In June, good news came about Walter and Willi, sons of Tante Lisbeth. Walter came home after twenty-two months in a Russian prison camp, and word arrived that Willi was safe and sound in a prison camp in Texas. Everyone talked about how Willi was captured in Africa and transported all the way to America. He, too, would come home soon. Almost every week now, Kirchheim welcomed home its men. They came in ones and twos. Some had lost fingers, hands, arms, feet, or legs. Like soldiers of all nations in any war, there were also those whose scars were not so visible. Still, no word came about Papa and Erich.

It would take almost ten years for Kirchheim officials to make a final accounting of our losses. By the middle 1950's the list included 237 confirmed dead and ninety-seven continued as "still missing." This total is out of a 1939 population of 3,838 people or about ten percent. Other communities suffered worse, but 334 lost was bad enough. Kirchheim was grateful for every man who did return. In 1946, the population had jumped to 4,483, attributed solely to the influx of refugees from East Germany and elsewhere.

The cheer felt in seeing our men as they returned was sharply offset by other news during the first part of July. Germany was being divided into four military zones — the British in the north, Americans in the south, Russians in the east, and the French would have the Rheinland in the west. For us in the Pfalz, it amounted to déjà vu. The French had occupied us after the First World War, and it left a bitter taste. Pfälzers had memories of how they took our food, timber, and pride only twenty-five years earlier. Of course, the animosity between the Germans and the French went back centuries. Now, in 1945, it would again be the French, not the Amis or the Brits, who would sit on us.

A large number of townspeople were already hired and working for the Americans in various jobs, including domestic work. The French would also need workers, but it was said that neither the money nor the relationship would be as good. It proved true. We had nothing to say about it.

❧

The week of July fifth, a new set of soldiers planted themselves in

Kirchheim and throughout most of the Rheinland. And, for the Pfälzer who remembered the last time, there came some shock with the new occupation. This time the French command settled in whole companies of troops from their African colonies of Algeria and Tunisia. They were dark-skinned Arabs, not Negroes, but that made little difference to many Germans. For my part, I'd developed an interest in foreign countries, and an acceptance of other races. I had never accepted the Nazi doctrine of the "Master Race," especially the blonde and blue-eye version. At any rate, the presence of Arab-French troops in Kirchheim continued to be a contentious matter to the end.

The regular French troops and officers segregated themselves from their Arab counterparts. Arab officers also lived separately from the ordinary Arab soldiers. The latter, as a group, took over the Traube Inn on a main street downtown. German women learned not to pass the place alone and never at night. The soldiers hung out from all the windows yelling in their guttural Arabic to any woman passing near.

Officers and non-commissioned officers, both white-French and Arab-French took up quarters in villas and in ordinary homes. In all cases, Germans had no say. On our street, probably ten households had to give a room to one of the new occupiers. We didn't, but across the street, Frau Rösel had to take in one of the Arab officers.

Her new boarder looked to me to be in his mid-twenties. He was tall and handsome, capable of setting any woman's heart aflutter. My own feelings weren't helped by his black wavy hair, tan complexion, and eyes so dark they may as well been black. All of these physical features left no doubt he was Arab, yet unlike the others, he wore a regular French uniform, including the usual hat, not a turban. I wasn't informed about French military ranks, and I couldn't tell what position he held, but other soldiers saluted him on approach.

His room faced out on the street, and since Frau Rösel's second floor was slightly higher than ours, I soon learned he could look directly into our living room and my bedroom when the windows were open. It was a shock one afternoon, as I cleaned, to glance out and see him standing in his open window, his black eyes staring at me. Quickly turning my head, I went back to my dusting, hoping that his inspection of my activity was momentary. It wasn't. Each time I peeked out of the corner of my eye, he was still there, watching my every movement. I left the room.

On July fourteenth, the French made their presence known in a big way by putting on a parade in celebration of their Bastille Day, a national holiday.

The Arab contingent provided the most interesting display for the German onlookers. The baggy pants, colorful cutaway jackets, cummerbunds, swords and turbans pleased the young and scared the old. Right up front, marching between two tall Arabs coming down Breitstraße, was a big-horned ram mascot. All of it, as the parade continued through Kirchheim, was accompanied by a kind of music we'd never heard. I don't know what my neighbors thought, but I found the sights and sounds strangely fascinating. It was like glimpsing into a different world.

The French festivities were followed the next day by the first non-celebration of my birthday, not that I'd ever been accustomed to big parties on the occasion. In my family, birthdays weren't treated that way — just a small gift and maybe a special food dish to eat. Still, it was a family event, and I missed Papa's hug and birthday peck on the cheek, and Erich's usual teasing. Mama no longer cared to know the day or month, and wouldn't have responded had I mentioned it.

I decided after our noon meal to take Peter for an outing. Not many days before, I'd returned the carriage to Frau Baum and she, in turn, had let me borrow a primitive stroller. Unlike the carriage with its big wheels, the stroller was equipped with very small wheels, not the best for pushing over cobblestones. Peter found the whole experience funny, and laughed all the way down Langstraße. It brightened my day. I was also glad Frau Kasper saw me leaving the house and asked me to buy her some stationery at Gau's office supply shop. It was a treat just to go into a business where you didn't have to stand in line. I liked looking around in Gau's, but it was more comfortable when I had something to buy.

Upon my arrival, I immediately saw that the stroller and Peter would have to be maneuvered up the steps to get in the front door. I decided to park the boy next to the steps and have a talk. "Peterchen, I have to go in here for just a minute. You can wait in the stroller, can't you?" I had bent down to his eye level as I spoke. "You'll be fine, right?" Naturally, he couldn't answer in words, but I knew his look of agreement, or so I thought, and entered the shop.

The boy had a quiet way of crying, that I considered a blessing, until that day. Having finished my business, I stepped out to find Peter, with tears flowing, and a young man kneeling down attempting to comfort him. Had he only cried louder, I would've heard and rushed out sooner.

The man glanced up at me. "Ah, here's your mama, little girl."

Before I could say thank you, he was gone. I wanted to shout after him, "You're wrong! I'm not his Mama, I'm his sister!" I didn't — it would have made the situation more embarrassing. The boy's dark brown hair, falling in natural waves, was shoulder length. Despite knowing both my father and brother would be unhappy about the Dutch-boy look, I couldn't bring myself to cut it. Obviously, the rather handsome stranger couldn't be blamed for mistaking the boy's sex, but I resented being called his 'Mama.' Somehow I felt it didn't bode well for my future if, having just turned fifteen on that very day, some good looking guy thought I was already a mother.

Peter's crying stopped the instant he saw me, and he returned to his happy self before I could get the stroller moving again. Walking along mostly empty shop windows, I caught sight of a woman's reflection in the glass. About ready to turn around to see who it was, I suddenly realized the person was me. When had I started looking that old? The young man's reaction now made sense.

My clothes were far from youthful. My dress was an old, drab brown affair of my mother's, altered to fit. I wore socks and the brown shoes Papa had bought. I'd been experimenting with my hair, and for my birthday, instead of two braids hanging down, I'd made one braid and coiled it into a mound on the back of my head — just like a lot of older women in town.

The very thought of it struck me funny and I began to laugh. "Now, that's a joke, isn't it, Peterchen? All I have to do is look like this everyday, and no boy will ever bother me. Except for you, of course. You don't care if I look like somebody's mother. Right? Well, who cares about boys anyway."

I'm sure my words held little meaning, but my laughter had him giggling along. Reward enough for my birthday, I thought.

The uphill push on the stroller gave me time to think about my clothing problems. I had to come up with more clever ways to lengthen my old dresses so they wouldn't look odd. My girlfriends were having troubles too. We'd all grown so much since dresses could be bought, or even the materials to make them. It was about all we talked of during our infrequent get-togethers. Sometimes the subject of boys came up, usually instigated by Hannelore, who seemed to think of little else. Our visits were soon to be rare indeed. Hannelore was being sent to Stetten, a nearby small village, where she'd live and work with a farm family. Her mother, now a war widow, came up with the idea, no doubt seeing a solution to the food shortage situation. I think she also saw a need to keep her daughter occupied.

Henny told me she'd be leaving to return to Kaiserslautern, where a job had been arranged in the labor office. Of course, the teacher's school there was shut. Neither of us would fulfill our dreams by that route. Margot, my companion to Neustadt, had already left Kirchheim, and was back with her father in

Essen. My close friend Elfriede, like me, felt she had little choice but to stay at home — she to help on the family farm, and I for reasons out of my control.

When Peter and I reached the house, Frau Kasper didn't answer my knock. I decided to deliver her stationery later in the evening, and went about preparing the supper meal. Always optimistic, I hoped Mama would start eating more. Sometimes it was a chore just to get her to the table.

It was nearly dark outside when I remembered the stationery and crossed the hall to knock on the Kaspers' door. She opened it and invited me in. Sitting at the kitchen table was Herr Kasper, trying to make himself understood by the Arab officer from across the street. Both glanced at me briefly and went right back to the matter in question. I felt my heart thumping wildly. If Frau Kasper hadn't pulled me to a day couch, insisting on inspecting the stationery in my presence, I would have raced back out the door. I tried listening to her comments, but couldn't help looking over at the two men. It became apparent that all of the gesturing was about some necessary repairs to a leather gun holster.

Time was ticking away as I sat on edge, and all the while Frau Kasper wanted to talk about things I suddenly had no interest in. Finally, I made excuses to leave and started for the door.

"Annchen, could you wait just a minute?" Herr Kasper's voice held me back. "I think Armand and I have finished our business. Could you show him down to the door, then lock up for the night? We'll leave our door open a crack until you come back."

I was surprised he'd asked me — after all, Armand wasn't my company. It was still my house, but the halls and stairway had no lights, and I felt it would be better if Herr Kasper escorted his guest, the man who'd watched me from his window, down the dark stairs.

"Ja, of course, Herr Kasper. I'll show him out." I'm sure my expression was not happy, but I indicated to the tall soldier that he should follow me.

Approaching the spiral staircase, and knowing how tricky the first narrow steps could be, I warned him loudly over my shoulder. "Be careful." I don't know why I didn't open our kitchen door across from the stairs. It would've provided some light.

All went well down the stairs, and as I led him along the hall to the front door. I had to feel my way along with a hand on the wall. Fumbling at the big lock key, I started to open the door, turning to move out of his way. Instead, he pulled me to him, his arms firmly encircling my waist in a close embrace. I had little time to breath, let alone yell out, as he lifted me and kissed my mouth. Though he hadn't grabbed me roughly, it was strong enough that my feet barely touched the floor. His lips were so surprisingly soft and warm that my entire being seemed to float away. No previous girlish daydreams could have come up with such a feeling. My arms hung limply at my sides and didn't return his embrace, though something inside me wanted to. He kissed my lips for one long moment, but made no further demands.

It would be a while before I learned how to return my own desire in a kiss. I have since thanked God many times that Armand, if that was really his name, didn't take advantage of my vulnerability. Perhaps he realized, when I didn't respond, I was too young and innocent. He gently released me to slump back against the wall and, without a word, he left.

I locked the door and leaned against it for a long time. Several minutes were required to calm my shaking before attempting the stairs. Grateful now for the blackness that enveloped me, I quietly went up, passing Kasper's closed door.

I stayed in darkness, sitting on my bed — my mind and emotions swinging wildly, reliving the wonderful sensation of my first kiss and talking to myself.

So that's how it is to be kissed! I can't allow it to happen again — not for years — I'm too young. Does he think Peter is mine, too? I've got to tell him it isn't so. No! I'll never let myself be alone with him. He can think what he wants! I wonder if he liked my lips? No, I can't think about that! I've got plenty of time to find someone else to kiss. I've got to keep my mind on Peter and Mama, and getting food, and sewing clothes.

Getting under the covers, I wondered if kissing always makes your heart pound — and what would Henny say about me being kissed on my fifteenth birthday?

It was quite some while before sleep came.

Chapter Thirty-One

Any fears I had of further encounters with Armand ended when, three weeks after my birthday, he departed Breitstraße and Kirchheim. There had been only one other uncomfortable time in his company, when Frau Andres had asked me to walk with her down to the cemetery. My neighbor wanted to place flowers on daughter Helga's grave. The little girl had died of cancer earlier in the year.

I agreed to go with her, a welcome break from my house duties on a nice early evening, and a chance to talk to someone who answered back. When I met her on the street a few minutes later, I was surprised that her other two girls weren't along.

"Where are the girls?" I said. "Surely not in bed already?"

"Nay," she replied. "They're visiting their grandmother in Oberwiesen for a few days."

Walking down to where the Neumayerstraße began, we exchanged notes on the fates of Papa, Erich, and her husband Heiner. He was still missing in Russia. There wasn't much to tell, since neither of us had received any news. Reaching the corner at Amtsstraße, across from the court building occupied by the French, Armand suddenly appeared. He had stepped out the building's front door, and Frau Andres shocked me when she stopped and waved at him, indicating he should join us.

What's the matter with her? I wanted to turn around there and then.

"Bonsoir!" Smiling, he had walked over to us.

I said nothing, but Frau Andres began rattling on in German, with an occasional French word thrown in. She invited him to join us. I really wanted to turn around and go home, but seemed to be unable to make excuses.

I couldn't help but look at him as he listened to Frau Andres. Seeing him for the first time close up in broad daylight, I got that thumping feeling again. This stranger from another land was indeed, quite handsome. But that didn't mean I wanted him to come along. I prayed he'd say, "No." Instead, he stepped to my side and started walking along.

All the rest of the way to the cemetery, I avoided looking at him, and directed all conversation to Frau Andres. At our destination, I quickly took the water can from her and walked away to a nearby faucet. As it filled, I looked back at them standing before the grave. I could tell she was trying to explain who was buried there. Returning with the water, I heard him say, "Je comprendre," his face filled with sympathy. When we left, I made sure Frau Andres was in the middle. No one should think there was a connection between us. I reasoned that walking next to my neighbor wouldn't create talk, since she was older. And besides, her being married with children, I believed, protected her from loose talk.

At my house, I excused myself in a hurry and went in. A week later, Armand was gone, though not forgotten.

❧

Sweeping out the driveway a few days later, a strange yet somehow familiar young man stepped off the street and through the open passage door. A shock wave hit me when I looked up. He was wearing a navy uniform and was carrying a sea bag. Expecting terrible news, I couldn't make my mouth work.

"Is this the Klein residence?" He said.

"Ja," I finally answered. "I'm the daughter." I leaned on the broom handle for support.

"I saw your brother Erich two weeks ago. He's alive and well, and wanted me to tell his family that he would soon be home. He's in northern Germany working for a farmer."

My emotions went from despair to elation so fast, it was all I could do to keep from running up to embrace him. "Please," I said, "tell me more. We've waited so long to hear. When do you think he'll come?"

"I really don't know," he replied. "It was a coincidence I ran into him. He looked familiar when I saw him, and I asked where he was from. It was a shock to learn we came from the same town, even the same neighborhood."

"I remember you now," I interrupted. "You went into the navy long before Erich. I saw you once on the street when you were home visiting. My friend Henny Hemm was with me, and she said you're from the Wingertstraße."

"Ja, I went into the navy in 1941, and now I'm home for good," He laughed. "Well, not quite. I came here first to give you the news. Now, I must be on my way up the hill."

"Ja, please. Thank you so much for stopping to tell me."

I had many more questions that I didn't have the heart to ask. The man looked so weary, and in need of family and rest. Erich would soon be home. That was all I really needed to know. I flew upstairs to tell Mama, sure that the news would bring her out of the dark place to which she'd retreated.

She did seem to perk up a little as I excitedly related the news. "Now you can stop your worrying. Erich's coming home. He's alright!" I could've

322

jumped out of my skin with happiness. Instead, I grabbed Peter and swung him around and around. "Soon your big brother will be here," I gleefully shouted. "And won't he be surprised and proud over what a fine boy you are!"

Everything was working out. The Kaspers had told me they were expecting another child and would be moving to Ruppertsecken, shoe workshop and all. I was sad to see them go, but it would give Erich his bedroom again. The news of my brother also got my hopes up about Papa. I had so much to do to get ready for their homecoming — Erich's for sure.

"Mama, please won't you get up and help me clean? If you can just do some things in the house, I could get in the garden to weed."

Her rise in spirits had lasted all of a few minutes. No help was forthcoming, and I was frustrated. Through Onkel Adolf, who continued to work in Kirchheim, I got word about Erich to Oma and the folks in Bolanden. In turn, he gave me the good news that three other Klein family members were just released from prison camps. My uncles Otto and Rudi were home in Bolanden, and my cousin Fritz in Monsheim. Now, if we only heard from Papa. We all needed "Seppel."

❧

As local farm crops ripened and harvesting began, the French took a share for themselves to ship back to France, a repeat of past behavior after 1918. The angry atmosphere simmered. Our young men were warned to avoid encounters, especially with the Arabs, who were rumored to be carrying knives in their boots. Most German men had more important matters to worry over, and stayed away from them. Personal and family survival took top priority.

With the French skimming off food supplies, a thriving black market became a big source of food for the local populace. For all practical purposes, money took a back seat to bartering.

❧

A postcard arrived from Erich. He didn't say where he was, only to expect him soon. I put it on the glass cupboard door to remind us, though it proved unnecessary. My brother walked through the kitchen door late in the evening on August twenty-first. I'd just come from checking on Mama and Peter and would have, in a few minutes, gone down to lock the front door. The Kaspers had moved out, leaving the house lonely, especially at night.

Erich must have taken the stairs two at a time because he was in the hall before I realized someone else was in the house. He startled me, opening the door so quickly. Then, for what felt like the longest time, he just stared at me. I wanted to run and hug him, but something about his expression held me back.

Suddenly, he smiled — the Seppel smile I loved so much, and opened his arms. I was there in a flash and hugged him tight.

He laughed. "You changed so much. I thought I'd entered the wrong house."

"I've grown taller, haven't I?"

He held me out at arm's length. "Ach, I expected you to be taller. It's just, well, I didn't think you'd be wearing your hair like an old lady. You look a lot older and — "

"I don't feel like a little girl anymore. Let's just say I'm an old fifteen."

"So, now I have an old sister, huh?" Still studying me with a smile, he took off his jacket and sat wearily on a chair. "Tell me then, old sister, is Papa home?"

The look on his face seemed to expect good news, something I couldn't give him. I shook my head sadly.

"Nay?" The Seppel smile vanished. "Haven't you at least heard from him?"

"Nothing at all," I said, knowing that the news ruined his day.

With elbows on the table, he ran the fingers of both hands through his hair repeatedly in an all too familiar gesture of anger and frustration. "Where's Mama?"

I was ready to say something about her condition when the door opened and Mama stepped in. A spark flared briefly in her eyes.

"Erich, thank God you're home safe." She must have sensed his presence while lying in bed.

Erich jumped up and hugged his mother, though the look on his face was the same as when he first saw me. He then brought her over to the table and pulled out a chair. "Come, sit down Mama. Tell me how you are."

"Ach, there's little to say. I haven't been well and can only stay a few minutes. I must go back soon — to my bed."

The last had come with a sad sigh. It'd been the most said in days. Erich wouldn't know that, but he'd learn. "Erich," I said. "You must be hungry. Could you eat some bread? There's also some sliced sausage. It isn't much... and I'll heat water for tea."

He just nodded and kept looking at Mama. I could read his mind: What has happened here? Why is her hair cut off? Why is she so disheveled and unclean? What have I come home to?

I gave him the bread and sausage, and put water on the stove to break the awkward moment. He looked up at me. "Did Karl Heinz stop by to tell you I was coming?" I nodded and he continued. "I was working for a farmer up north. It was alright. The old man kind of took a liking to me. Had me in mind for one of his daughters, I think. That's when I decided to try to get some release papers from a prison camp, you know, so I could travel freely. That's when I ran into Karl Heinz. It's a long story. The rest I'll tell later. Right now, I'm glad to be eating some good Pfälzer bread!"

Erich had not yet asked about Peter, and I waited patiently for him to do so as he continued.

"So, how's the food supply? It's probably a good thing I came home — a man in the house again. Otherwise, you'd probably starve to death. Tomorrow I'll go look for a job so we'll have the money to buy things."

"Wait a minute!" I was mad and wishing for another heavy ball bearing to conk him on the head. Mama took that moment to shuffle back to her bed. "We don't have a problem here with money. Our government support started up again right after the Amis came. We have money! You just can't buy much with the meager rationing."

"I didn't mean — "

"You just listen," I interrupted again. "We don't have a big supply of food, but we aren't starving. There are still some vegetables in the garden. I even made raspberry jam. And I've been getting more than our share of bread. According to the ration coupons, you have just eaten your week's allowance. But, don't fret — I'll get more for you tomorrow." I paused to let it sink in. "More than money, you need to help us find different kinds of food, and things for the house!"

"What about meat?"

After my blast, I was surprised he could only ask about meat. Sorry to have gotten so angry, I answered more calmly. "I usually get all I can with the coupons, which isn't much. The meat shops often have more sausage than fresh meat. Now and then the city offers meat at the Freibank. I hate it, but I always go."

"What do you mean by 'Freibank'? Surely the city doesn't give away meat!"

I also thought the name was misleading, because there was nothing free about it. "No, you have to pay so much a pound, and while you sometimes get more, the meat is awful. Except when they offer wild boar, which isn't often. It's usually horse meat or that of a hundred-year-old cow. It's so tough I have to cook it for hours just to make it chewable. I wouldn't bother to go at all, if we could live without it."

He listened in silence to my explanation, mulling over the real facts of our situation. "So this is what Germany has come down to — Freibanks and horse meat." He was silent again, and I sat down across from him at the table.

"Erich, why haven't you asked about your brother?"

"My brother!"

"Ja, your little brother Peter. He's such a sweet boy. Haven't you thought about him at all?"

"What about him? We don't know each other and there's nothing to ask until we get acquainted tomorrow. Right now, I'm more interested in what's wrong with Mama. She looks and behaves not like my mother at all. Why is her hair so short?"

It wasn't easy, but I explained all that had happened during the twenty months since Erich had stomped out of the house. How he'd been right that her pregnancy wouldn't improve her health, about the lice, her black moods and the awful silences. I tried to make him see that, though he'd guessed right, that her pregnancy wouldn't cure her, but Peter was not to blame.

"And, besides," I lowered my voice almost to a whisper. "Doctor Hahn once told me he thinks her illness is all in her head. It made me angry at the time, but what if he's right? What if she did get depressed about you and Papa being gone, and about the war. Maybe now that it's over and you're home — well, maybe she'll get better."

"God in heaven! Why isn't Papa here? I wish now I'd never come home."

Anger flared in me again. Had he not seen I was doing my best? With all of my strength, I held my tongue. The subject was changed to heating up some bath water on the stove, which we did. While waiting for it to get hot, I helped him set up the bed in his old room across the hall. Then, as he readied his bath in the kitchen, I bid him good night, adding something that had been simmering in my head. "I also wish more than anything to have Papa home. Until he comes, and I believe he will, we can still hold it together, just the two of us." I closed the door before he could reply, and went to bed.

The next morning, Peter and I were already in the kitchen eating when Erich got up and came in. The little fellow immediately came off his chair to stand next to me. The big brother laughed. "Come here, Peter, let me take a look at you."

Peter just moved closer to climb on my lap. "Well, I can see he doesn't like me," Erich offered, his smile fading. "And what's with the long hair? You trying to make a girl out of him?"

"Erich, stop it!" I pulled the boy onto my lap and stood up. "He's never seen you before. What did you expect? Now just stay there and I'll bring him to you so he'll know it's alright."

Peter had started to cry quietly, but I turned on the charm to let him see how I liked this stranger in his life. "This is our big brother Erich. And he's come home to stay with us now. Isn't that nice? You don't have to be afraid of big brother!"

"He's probably afraid 'cause you never take him out to see people."

"And what do you know about how often I take him out? I wish you had stumbled over the stroller in the hall last night. Then you wouldn't lip off so quick!" I laughed so he wouldn't think I was serious, and went back to my chair. "All children this age take time to warm up to new people. Just be friendly and he'll like you."

Erich muttered as he stepped over to the sink to wash up, "If you say so." He turned and took another look at Peter. "It'll be a lot easier if he doesn't look like a girl! I'm not going to be seen with him on the street like that."

"I'll get his hair cut soon. Until now there's been little time for haircuts." It was a white lie, but only a tiny one. "With you here, it'll be easier to get it taken care of."

That seemed to satisfy him, and he went to work charming Peter until we all were laughing like silly fools. After breakfast, our conversation took a more serious turn again. He wanted to know of friends who had already come home.

"None of our closest friends are home, except Helmut, who was badly wounded. He lost parts of both hands. Isn't it awful? Then there's Werner Diehl, who was in your class. He's staying with his aunt on the Wingertstraße." Erich hadn't considered Werner a close friend, but knew him well. It was hard to tell the rest. "Werner came home months ago with both of his lower arms missing. I feel so bad for him."

Erich just nodded glumly and sat quietly in thought. After a few minutes, we went down to the wash kitchen where he dumped out his sack of dirty clothes.

"Would you wash these clothes for me? I'm going to take my bicycle and go see Werner and Helmut, then probably ride over to Bolanden to see the relations."

That was the big difference between Papa and Erich. My father would have offered to help me wash the pile now at my feet. I said nothing, letting him go without argument.

News now raging on the Breitstraße claimed my neighbor Frau Andres was known to be pregnant. With her soldier husband away for almost two years, the speculation was rampant as to the man's identity. I knew, but said nothing.

∾

My brother told me in the next days about his sojourn up north following the collapse of Germany. I found it a fascinating tale, and had him write it down for me later. When he did, it certainly gave me another view of what occurred at the end where Erich served. This is what he wrote:

"I served on U-boat 1205 in the German navy, based at the port of Kiel on the Baltic Sea. My rank was like that of corporal in the army of the Amis.

"Our base and wharves at Kiel were heavily damaged by bombing toward the war's end. In the final weeks, little was done to repair the destruction. But our duties went on, moving around and through the mess to take on supplies. It happened that my U-boat was in port on May second, and with the British enemy closing in from every direction, the orders suddenly came to scuttle the boat right there in the harbor. I felt no particular sadness going about helping to sink her, though I liked being in the U-boat service.

"Once we put 1205 on the bottom, the crew was ordered to proceed over land to make a last stand at Flensburg to the north, near the Denmark border. Seven of my comrades and I, all from southern parts of Germany, thought the order was crazy. It would not only take us farther from our homes, but the word reaching everyone made it clear that the British forces were fast tightening the noose around Kiel. The eight of us made a pact to leave the others and try to break out to the south.

"We hung onto the diving gear from the boat scuttling job, packed our sea bags to make them water-proof, and looked for food. Someone said they heard about food supplies delivered the day before to the commissary. We went there to find the building heavily damaged and no guards. Each of us filled our bags with as much smoked sausages and canned food as we could carry. My bag was too heavy to carry far. Another comrade got the idea to load the bags on a large hand wagon.

"Loading the wagon, we began our journey just after dark. By dirt lanes and side roads, over the next eighteen hours, we managed to get about seventy-five kilometers inland to the southwest. Every moment we worried about surprise encounters with British patrols. Worse still was the SS. Any German soldiers caught in flight were automatically executed by the SS. We knew that, and maintained a sharp lookout until reaching a wooded area near the Elbe river in the late afternoon of the second day. From this sheltered vantage point, we saw the first British patrol on a road some distance away. At dusk, we moved the last few kilometers to the Elbe and hid in a reed bed.

"In the early gray of the next morning, we put on our diving gear. It was our plan to swim the river under water, pulling the bags along the surface. Each of us then tied ourselves to the man in front with a long rope. It was agreed that everyone carry a knife in the hand to cut the rope in an emergency. When everything was ready, the first man entered the water, then the second, followed by the third. I was sixth in line.

"The man in front of me had just stepped off the bank when a shout came from behind. 'Halt! Hands up!' The fifth man cut the rope and disappeared, his bag making rapid progress across the wide Elbe. I and two unlucky comrades slowly turned, hands raised high, to watch three Tommies approach, their rifles leveled at us. Our only weapons were the knives, and we'd already tossed them to the ground.

"When they found we only had clothes and food and were simply trying to get home, the tension eased considerably. We were allowed to strip off the diving gear and get back into our uniforms. It came as a surprise, when ordered to march toward a nearby road, that we were permitted to take our heavy bags. I, for one, was happy when finally arriving at Elmshorn, where we climbed aboard open bed trucks with other prisoners. After a while, as each truck filled, we moved off toward the south. No one knew the destination. Somebody thought it might be Pinneberg. He was right. At about noon, the trucks pulled through a barbed wire enclosure surrounding the Pinneberg airport.

"The prison camp was more than crowded. It was hard to move around without stepping on someone just lying on the ground. There were only two makeshift barracks, already full. One housed only females, all uniformed women of the German navy and air force. The other was filled with members of the SS. The rest of us remained outdoors to sleep and eat. I didn't mind. The weather wasn't bad and I preferred fresh air to being cooped up in a building with either women or the SS.

"We quickly discovered the kitchen facility set-up too small to handle the proper feeding of everyone, which made the three of us twice as glad to still have our bags. Food from the kitchen became less important.

"Not many days later, the loudspeakers blared out in German about the final capitulation and the war's end. We had already known of Hitler's suicide.

That news came as we were about to scuttle the U-boat.

"On my eighth day in camp, as I stood near a gate, another announcement came on the loudspeakers. The British wanted mechanics and truck drivers immediately. Moving fast, I made my way to the designated location and found myself, along with fifty others, selected for a job outside the barbed wire. Picking a German officer to lead us, the British told us to go set up a camp to the north near Itzehoe, then round up every abandoned military truck and car within a fifty kilometer radius. We did just that.

"On an open field outside the northern city of Itzehoe, we brought together in little more than a week over a thousand vehicles. Most were heavy hauling trucks, and since the British provided us with little food, we took some of the better trucks and traded them to farmers for food.

"After another four weeks, I quietly prepared a sedan I'd brought in earlier for another escape attempt. By that time, it was felt that guards were unnecessary. At four in the morning, I drove out of camp, going directly across fields, down farm lanes and on side roads to avoid patrols. The camp was north of Itzehoe, and I wanted to again head south. By full daylight, I came to a farm in a very small place called Mordorf, and decided to lay low for a while. It was good timing with the growing season. The farmer needed help and he agreed to take me on. There were a couple of daughters in the house, something I didn't feel too comfortable about. I wasn't aiming to put down roots, only to stay long enough to figure a way to get home.

"By the end of eight weeks, pressure from the old man to stay and marry one of his daughters was all the push I needed to plan a new escape. Using the excuse of needing a haircut, I left the farm after the noon meal to go into Itzehoe, the nearest big city. What I didn't let them know was that I'd packed my sea bag and put it in some bushes by the road. After retrieving the bag, I caught a ride on a farm truck heading in that direction. Reaching Itzehoe, I right away ran into another British patrol. One of the two soldiers spoke German. In questioning me and, my lack of proper papers, I was told release papers were now being given out rapidly to ordinary prisoners with no connection to the SS. They took me along to their headquarters, and before evening, I was free to travel openly.

"With the papers in my pocket, I could've grabbed the first ride south. I wanted to, but I didn't. Standing by the road, the same farmer who'd picked me up earlier saw me and stopped. Opening the passenger door, he asked if I needed a lift back home.

"I smiled, though I couldn't tell him the reason. I wanted to tell him to drive me all the way to Kirchheim, but instead agreed to let him take me back to the farm. It had to be my conscience tugging at me. I couldn't leave the farmer without giving my thanks for taking me in.

"As I feared, my farm host wasn't happy I wanted to leave, though I think it had more to do with the harvest work just starting, than marrying off one of the girls. However, he allowed me to stay the night, and I got a fresh start toward home in the morning.

"It took me over three days to come south, mostly on trucks carrying everything from beer to vegetables. Sometimes I sat up front in the cab, but more often as company to whatever was being hauled on the truck bed.

"Nearing home, I caught a ride just outside Mainz as it was turning dark. The driver said he and his two boys were heading in the direction of Worms, and if I wanted to go, I could hop on the load of freshly harvested carrots. I did, and promptly fell asleep.

"The pocket I'd made in the pile of carrots to lie in must have been comfortable, because in my exhaustion, I slept right through Worms where I'd planned to jump off. I was jerked awake riding over some railroad tracks entering Karlsruhe. The driver hadn't said anything about Karlsruhe, and I found myself having to backtrack fifty kilometers just to get to Worms. There, I knew it would be easy to find a ride to Kirchheim. If not, I'd walk the twenty-seven kilometers.

"I got lucky, catching a lift all the way back to Worms on one truck. It was the last leg from Worms that took most of the day. One ride was on a farm wagon pulled by a dilapidated tractor. Walking the few kilometers would have been faster than the ride I got on that old beast. Two more short rides by truck brought me to Marnheim. I walked the rest, getting to the house late in the evening. I remember entering our kitchen and not recognizing my own sister for a minute. It was the first time I had ever seen her with a large knot of hair at the nape of her neck. I could see she made it with a thick rope of braided hair. Shocking — she'd grown up!"

ʘ

Ja, I had grown up, and now it was up to the two of us to keep the family whole until Papa's return.

Meanwhile, the rest of the neighborhood was waiting expectantly for Heiner Andres to come back from the prisoner-of-war camp to his pregnant wife.

Chapter Thirty-Two

Erich found a job within days of returning home. Being the new chauffeur for the commander of the Gendarmerie suited him perfectly. The French police station was just over a block away from the house at the corner of Neumayerstraße and Amtsstraße. His easy humor and mechanical talents won him quick approval by his boss.

People seemed to instantly trust my brother, as they did with Papa, but it still surprised me the night Erich showed up at the house pushing a disabled motorcycle into the courtyard. The machine had been sitting around the police compound in disrepair and was ready for the junk heap. The "Chef," as Erich called him, didn't believe it could be fixed, so he was allowed to haul it home. A few days later, the commander and his staff stood in amazement when my brother showed up for work driving it. Not long after, he traded the machine to a shepherd for a sheep to slaughter. Meat, and mutton in particular, wasn't my favorite food, but I was hungry, and grateful for his wizardry in mechanics.

Food was ever on the mind, Erich's most of all. With his good looks and instant charm, he soon had the German female cooks and kitchen help at the police garrison supplementing his food intake. Sometimes he got enough to bring home and share, but not much and not often. In truth, our French masters had little more than we did in their diet. Paris expected the Germans to provide what was needed to support the army's occupation, which led to hard feelings. At least the Americans hadn't taken what little food we had.

Mama's mood swing that went up with Erich's homecoming fizzled within an hour, and she fell back into silence and isolation. He tried to cheer and motivate her, but without success. Disgust and frustration quickly followed and he started spending more of his free time away from the house, often at the home of Ida Steinbrecher. Just up a short distance from us on the Breitstraße, Ida was the girl who had accompanied our family to church and shared confirmation with Erich. I had long forgotten any possible attraction between the two. After all, they had both been fifteen and I was ten, and there was no time to be thinking about love in bloom.

Over the years I rarely spoke to Ida. Later, I learned she had been aware of my friendship with Henny, who lived across the street from her, and had been resentful of our friendship. In her mind, my friend had too much free time, and that meant Erich's sister had a similar problem.

Ida's life was very different than Henny's or mine. Her father was both a farmer and a busy house butcher, and his services were in great demand by other farmers when they were ready to slaughter. With an older sister and four brothers, it seemed reasonable to assume the house and farm chores got spread around. Not so, I learned. Ida was forced to do all the hard field and barn work. Her sister had convinced the parents she was too frail for outside work. Two brothers still at home were too young for more than light work and the two older brothers had been killed in the war. Everyone on our street felt terrible when the brothers were killed in Russia. It was a blow to the family, and though I didn't know her well, my heart went out to Ida. She began wearing only black, and didn't stop until long after the war.

Her situation was the reason I saw little of Ida until she broke away and got a job as a telephone operator, and even then I only caught a glimpse of her as she passed by going to and from work.

From what little contact I had with Ida, I did think of her as nice. Also I admired her small, trim body and lovely oval face framed by natural dark curls. She was easily one of the prettiest girls in town. Still, I didn't make any romantic connection between her and Erich, not even when he began spending time at the Steinbrechers. His reasons to me were entirely practical. Herr Steinbrecher was ill, and he was there strictly to help with the work. In return, he said, there was sure to be extra food for us.

It became routine for Erich to come home from his daytime chauffeur job, grab a bite, and head up the street. He did bring home potatoes and such for his labors, but something else was going on besides "helping out." I eventually figured that out. Ida's father died in early winter, further strengthening the connection. Frau Steinbrecher started counting on Erich to give direction to young Richard and Dieter.

I didn't go to the funeral of Herr Steinbrecher. The day was bitter cold, and I thought it best to stay at home with Peter. Erich told me later about the wake at the house following the burial. Already a somber affair, the raw nerves and emotions of those in the house weren't helped by the actions of young Richard. It had been so cold at the cemetery that he'd nearly frozen his hands. On arriving back home, and with everyone else gathered in the living room, Richard plunged his hands into a pan of hot water on the kitchen stove. A bloodcurdling scream brought everyone running to the kitchen to find him writhing in agony. He had never been told that frostbitten hands went in cold water, not hot.

❧

Meanwhile, the happiness felt upon Erich's return from the north soon withered between us. His criticism of me, especially of my cooking skills, sprang from the general dismay he felt over Mama's condition and Papa's absence. Not knowing our fate kept us both on edge.

There were times when a strong parent was needed to stop the childish encounters we still had. A good example was when Erich brought home a wild rabbit, skinned and cleaned, and expected me to prepare a gourmet meal. The poor animal was his reward for guiding his French boss on a hunting excursion in nearby fields.

"Take this," he said. "Brown it good, so you can make a nice gravy. Then throw in some potatoes and carrots and roast everything together."

"Wait a minute!" Having been handed the skinny victim, I could see immediately that unlike an old laying hen, the creature before my eyes had not a gram of fat showing anywhere. "How am I supposed to brown this thing? We have no lard, no butter. There's no fat of any kind for browning! If you want to eat this unfortunate animal, I'll have to boil it."

"You dummy!" A stick of dynamite would have been less explosive than his reaction. "You can brown meat without fat. Mama did it all the time!"

"She never did," I shouted back. "It's impossible."

"She did. And you can too," he yelled. "I've got to get back to work. Cook that rabbit right and have it ready for me tonight!"

Carrying the rabbit with some disdain before me, I went in the bedroom to ask Mama how to brown it without fat. No answer. Back in the kitchen, I boiled the poor creature.

Such bickering encounters didn't happen everyday, but often enough to add unnecessary misery to the struggle we couldn't avoid. We tried most of the time to keep our flare-ups from harming the survival of the family. Erich willingly helped me in the garden, kept us in firewood, and tried to keep the house in good repair. My cooking improved with time — and when good foods were available. Housekeeping, and laundry in particular, always required too much of my day, and one of my biggest challenges was keeping us all in clothes.

Erich's work clothes always needed mending, but the old pedal sewing machine gave me the most pleasure in creating new garments from old ones. It was impossible to buy new materials in a store, but I had lots of clothes that Mama had stored away. Many things dated back to the turn of the century, including her father's uniform. I turned it into a charming pair of pants for little Peter, among other things. I knew nothing of following patterns. I simply took a garment apart carefully and studied how it had been put together — adjusting the size for the new wearer. Since Opa Herbst's heavy wool uniform was green with bright red piping and stripes, it was perfect for designing Peter a mock

Bavarian Lederhosen, bib and all.

Becoming more daring, I refashioned some of Mama's old fancy dresses, and they became passable blouses and skirts. Now much taller, and more filled out than Mama, I could no longer wear the dresses. Besides, they would have been too frilly and impractical. What started from necessity — the creation of clothes to wear in a desperate time, turned into a real pleasure for me. I found myself dreaming of becoming a clothes designer, but any dreams in my head had to wait for Papa.

I remembered the large Nazi flag Papa wanted me to burn, and brought it out of hiding for one of my bright ideas — a useful red kitchen apron trimmed in black and white. So much for National Socialism.

After much pestering by Erich, I took Peter to a barber to have his beautiful curls cut off. A former schoolmate, Theo, was the apprentice, and had the task of providing the boy's first haircut. The little fellow made no fuss sitting on his special platform, but the tears flowed as Theo got started. "Annchen, halt mich," he whimpered. Peter's entreaties to 'hold me' turned into a running joke that went on for years. Whenever Theo saw me on the dance floor or in the street, without fail he'd open his arms with a most passionate plea, "Annchen, halt mich." He wasn't my type, but I couldn't help laughing. Naturally, I'd have to quickly explain the story to anyone with me, especially to a dance partner!

Peter no longer looked like a girl, and Erich was so proud he insisted that I dress the boy up to show off at his work. I was glad when he did, as it gave me a break for personal time.

I kept constant check on Mama, but I was truly alone as she never spoke and rarely left the bedroom. I had given up on my mother. No one came to see her, except a Deaconess nurse now and then. For whatever reason, none of her sisters and brothers came, and Papa's side stayed away, too. It was clear that Erich and I gave her no comfort or hope. All she accepted from us was food and my efforts to keep her clean. A staring silence was our only reward. My single thread of hope was the possibility of my father's homecoming, and that she constantly read her Bible. It was always within reach.

᷒

It was early November. Erich and I spent all of a Saturday afternoon splitting and stacking firewood for a cold winter that was already nipping at our heels. Peter was in the courtyard with us, amusing himself with sticks from the kindling pile. We'd left the big passage doors open to the street, and while the boy knew better than to wander out into traffic, when I saw him eyeing the opening, I decided it would be best to close off the temptation. Stepping over to the passage, I was nearly run over by a young man on a bicycle coming into the courtyard. He dismounted, laughing and apologizing for the scare. For a moment, I was at a loss as to who it was. Erich had no such problem, throwing down the ax to come over and shake the visitor's hand heartily.

"Ach, Friederich, so you're home already!"

"Ja, ja. Guten Tag, Erich — Annchen." Spotting Peter, he added, "And who is this young fellow? Erich, you're not married already!"

"Nay. Certainly not!"

"This," I added quickly, "is our brother Peter. His coming is a long story you can hear later." Peter was pressing himself to my leg as I spoke, shyly eyeing the newcomer as my hand caressed the top of his head.

"Well, hello, young Peter. I'll shake your hand, too!"

Peter already knew about shaking hands, but waited to get my blessing. "It's alright, Peter. This is Friederich. He's been gone a long time and didn't know about you." Peter didn't understand, but knew it was fine with me to shake the man's hand, and did.

Settling the boy onto my lap, I sat on a chunk of wood to listen as Erich and Friederich caught up on each other's lives. Onkel Heinrich's only son had been captured by the Americans in Egypt and kept a prisoner there until his release. His father had died during this time, and he'd come home to a new situation. Tante Sannchen had remarried, and he now had a stepfather and a different house. His younger sisters, Hilde and Johanna, were also well into womanhood. It seemed to me that he was going about visiting relatives hoping to find familiar ground. It was impossible. Almost everyone and every household had changed.

"I passed through Gauersheim a few days ago and saw your mother," Erich explained. "She told me of the Red Cross letter saying you were fine and coming home. I don't think she expected you so soon though."

"She didn't, and things got a little hectic around the house when I showed up. I'd heard about my father dying, but it was a surprise to find mother married again." A kind of awkward pause followed his comment, and I could see he was thinking about his father. Onkel Heinrich had trained him as a saddler, wanting his son to take over the shop in Marnheim. Turning to me, he spoke again. "So, you've grown up, too. No more little girl with the big eyes. What are you now, seventeen?"

Though I often felt much older than seventeen, I shook my head. "Nay, far from it. I turned fifteen in July."

Erich seemed to want to get off the matter of his sister's age, so he quickly brought attention back to his own capture by the British and recent return home.

Friederich had a little different tale. "I have no complaint about how the 'Amis' treated us in the camp in Egypt. I think most of us knew it'd make no sense to try to escape. Where could we get to in North Africa? So we settled down to wait out the duration of the war. I even picked up quite a bit of English. But the best part for me was the music. They played it on loudspeakers all the time. American music I like, especially Bing Crosby. He's the greatest singer they have!"

German radio stations were already playing American music, including songs by Bing Crosby who we called 'Der Bingel.' However I silently disagreed with my cousin that he was 'the greatest.' Besides, Erich changed the subject again.

"What are you going to do, start up your father's business again?"

"I don't think so," Friederich replied. "Times have changed. There wouldn't be enough work to feed a village saddler these days. I'll find something, but it won't be making harnesses or doing upholstery work." He was right. That way of life was dying.

It was our visitor's next comment that made Erich and I nervous, and I had to do some fast thinking. Friederich asked to see his Tante Marie. My brother suddenly became uncomfortable and silent, leaving it to me to discourage a visit with Mama.

"I don't know what you've heard about Mama's illness, but she stays in bed and really doesn't want visitors. I'm sorry."

He seemed surprised to hear how seriously ill his aunt was, but accepted my excuse without question. "I'm very sorry about Tante Marie. Perhaps some other time, please give her my regards."

I felt both relieved and guilty over the matter. Mama had never said she wouldn't see visitors. My words were based solely on the fact that she'd made no effort in two years to see people, even when she'd had better health. And if she wouldn't talk to her own children, would she talk to a brother's son? Neither Erich nor I wanted to face the embarrassment, for us or for Friederich, if she were to just lie there staring at him.

"I should be going, I see you have more wood to split." He turned to mount his bicycle. "Thought I'd stop in Marnheim at Onkel Adam's on the way home. I'm sure he'll be relieved to know there won't be another Herbst in competition with him. Who knows, he may even buy some of the equipment and materials Papa had."

After he left, Erich decided he'd finish the firewood the next day. He was aching to go up to Steinbrechers to see Ida. He told me of the many people from cities like Worms and Kaiserslautern who were constantly knocking on their door wanting to trade for food. Naturally, I counted myself lucky to have a brother who traded his labor for butter, eggs and potatoes.

Erich often took Peter along, something he liked doing. He said everyone liked the boy, especially Ida's sister Gertrude. It wasn't very long before I joined the parade to the Frau Steinbrecher household. One or two times a week was all I could spare, and then it was usually to help churn butter. That she would let me take some home made me happy.

Another unhappy offshoot of the French occupation were the unsavory women who wandered into our midst from the big cities to ply their trade in bars and bordellos that had suddenly sprung into existence. The town where I once felt safe on any street, became an obstacle course for women with innocent intentions. Next, we started hearing about local girls who were getting into the 'oldest profession.' At first, I felt shame for them. To me, they painted all German women with the same brush. In time my opinion would soften, but for the moment, nothing could be done about prostitution. It was legal. The public was told that our government controlled any problems of sexual diseases by requiring regular medical examinations of the women involved. Nothing was said about the men who frequented them.

December of 1945 and the coming Christmas season looked to be a bleak time for us. I busied myself sewing up a rag doll for Peter then decided to make a teddy bear as well. An old brown dress of my mother's worked out perfect as it had a plush side to it. A walk over to Marnheim was rewarded by a supply of toy building blocks from the old man who had given me the train. I felt good about those things, but the fact that we still had heard nothing of Papa made everyone cross. Erich and I had to watch our tongues, our tempers being so short.

"What good is a tree if we don't have candles for it!" It was Erich's reasoning for not wanting to cut down a Christmas tree.

"I don't care," was my firm reply. "I didn't have candles last year, and we liked it just as much!"

He cut a tree.

❧

I was hating the cold winter, a feeling I'd never experienced before. The weather made drying the laundry impossible. More than once, I wanted to burn the dirty clothes rather than do the wash. Too young to know or think how Mama had handled the drying problem, it was only much later that I remembered that in winter she washed more often and therefore had less to dry at one time. I was waiting until there was nothing left to wear. But Mama didn't talk to me anymore, and I was bound to learn the hard way. For Christmas, I tried to have everything clean. Most of all, I made sure we had a few simple cookies. Some tradition had to be observed.

Soon it was New Year's Eve and I heard no bells ringing. Erich was up at Ida's, and I went to bed early. As I drifted off, I realized there were things to be thankful about. My big brother had made it home safe, and though I'd worried at first, he'd grown as crazy about Peter as I was. We were both amazed by the boy's sweet nature, and he gave both of us more reason to work in harmony, at least while he was in our company.

Early in January, a postcard arrived from the Red Cross. I remember shaking so much I could barely hold it in front of my eyes. The words swam around as I read them over twice — three times — to make sure there was no mistake. Papa was safe and coming home.

Peter must have thought I'd gone crazy running and shouting my way back up to the kitchen where he sat on his little stool. I grabbed him up to swing around and around, all the while laughing and yelling. "Papa's coming home!" I cried from joy, and repeated over again the blessed news. "Papa's coming home at last."

I wanted to rush right down to Erich at the Gendarmerie, then thought better of it. I knew my joy would be hard to contain, and would make Erich uncomfortable in front of his French bosses. He was never one to demonstrate emotion to outsiders. So I waited, but in such a numbed state, no thought was given to preparing supper. Of course, I told Mama. She lay in bed and only turned her head away.

"Mama, can't you be happy. Papa's coming home to make everything right!"

Her response this time was to hold out a clinched fist. "Here!" The word came out in anger as she slowly opened the hand to reveal a new anguish.

It was her wedding ring, the gold band had split in two. I took the two narrow bands, both quite fragile, from her hand. I'd never seen anything like it, but a shutter ran through me as the words of a folk song filled my head. Mama often sang it while working around the house.

"Er hat mir treu Versprochen, gab mir ein Ring dabei. Er hat die treu gebrochen, mein Ringlein sprang entzwei."

(He promised to be true, gave me a ring as love's token. He betrayed me, and now my ring is broken.)

She stared up at my face knowing I was remembering. At one time I loved hearing her sing the words.

"Hör ich das Mühlrad gehen, ich weiß nicht was ich will. Ich mocht am liebsten sterben, da wärs auf einmal still."

(When I hear the mill wheel grinding, I don't know what's best. To die is my greatest desire, for only then I'll find rest.)

"Ach, Mama. It means nothing that the ring broke. That old song was just about silly superstition. I'll take the ring to a jeweler. It can be fixed like new. Papa would want me to."

"Throw it away! Nothing — nothing can be fixed." She turned away and closed her eyes.

When Erich got home, I first gave him the good news, which brought what I can only describe as a sigh of relief. Then I showed him the ring and what Mama said. He remembered the song too, but insisted the ring would be repaired. He put the thin round pieces in a teacup in the cabinet.

Now that I knew Papa was alive and would soon be home, I wanted to bundle up Peter and walk over to Bolanden. Oma and Tante Lisbeth needed to know the news. Sadly, I had to hope Onkel Adolf would pass my message. He was still plowing snow for the city and going home to Bolanden every night. I couldn't go because the weather was bitter cold and I had no warm coat. The weather also kept me from riding my bicycle to neighboring village bakeries to buy extra bread.

❧

More and more, I heard about people from the bigger cities moving to Kirchheim and the surrounding villages. With the French troops occupying so many properties, living quarters were scarce. I kept thinking about Papa and what he would say about everything.

The kitchen was a mess, all strung with lines so I could dry laundry overnight. Erich made his usual comment about it when he came home late from Ida's. I had just suggested strongly he go to his room and sleep when a loud knock sounded downstairs.

"I'll go see who it is," he said, and went down the hall to the window overlooking the front door below. "Who is it?" I heard him holler. There was a momentary silence, then his footsteps raced back down the hall to the staircase. "It's Papa," he shouted, pounding down the steps.

"Thank God," I screamed joyfully, and raced after him.

A blast of cold air hit me at the bottom of the steps. I could make out two figures at the other end of the shadowy hall shaking hands. I ran for Papa and held on tight, laughing and crying all at once. It had been nearly a year since he'd driven away to an unknown fate. He'd come home again, just as he promised. It was Thursday evening, January 24, 1946.

"Come, come, Märe! I didn't get here to be choked to death." His voice squeaked just like it did when he challenged me as a child to squeeze harder. I backed off, feeling not a little embarrassed to be acting like a kid again. He rubbed his neck and laughed, putting an arm around my waist. "Come, let's go up. I need to be where it's warm!"

We all climbed the stairs, letting Papa go first. Erich hauled up a big sack Papa had handed him. I was glad I hadn't begun to hang the wet clothes. That would have been a rude greeting for his homecoming. In the kitchen light, it was clear my father was tired and cold, but he looked slightly heavier. He sat down wearily on a chair by the stove to warm himself, staring at the lines overhead.

"I was getting ready to dry laundry," I explained. "I see," he replied.

I'd also been ready to make some mint tea for myself, and had hot water on the stove. It would now be three cups of tea with no sugar, all I could offer to drink. No one seemed to mind. After a few minutes, Papa asked the question I dreaded.

"How is your mother and little Peter?"

Erich jumped right in, and in a way I was glad. The news of Mama's terrible decline came best from someone else.

My brother's revelations on our mother's condition were filled with more frustration than mine would have, but it hit close to the mark. Papa listened intently as Erich described the useless efforts to get Mama to see a doctor, and our failed attempts just to get her talking. When he finished, Papa got up and walked quietly to the bedroom. I perked my ears intently, but heard no voices in the nearby room. I figured that Papa was just standing in there, studying the sleeping figures of his wife and son. In only a few minutes, he returned to the kitchen and sank slowly into his chair. A hand brushed imaginary crumbs from the tabletop, and he appeared to stare at nothing.

"I tried to speak to her gently, to tell her I'm home and everything would be alright. I know she heard me — " His voice trailed away into silence as Erich and I waited and watched his expression.

In only a moment, his eyes began to focus on us again, a smile gently coming to light on his face. "On my way home," he said, "all I encountered were dispirited people. There's no room for that in this house. We're all together again. That's what matters!" He paused, starting to stand. "I'm tired now, but tomorrow is a new day, and the three of us are going to start making things right." He slapped the table, his eyes still on us. The smile was still there, but the look was sharp.

It was an expression we'd witnessed many times since childhood. It told us that it was time to start again, and above all, not give up. As if to reinforce the point, he added, "Come. Let's get this laundry up on the lines and go to bed."

Seppel was home.

Chapter Thirty-Three

On his first day at home, Papa took Erich's bicycle for the short trip to Bolanden to visit with his mother and sisters. I wanted to go along to witness the joyous reunion, but there was much to do at home and I was still without a winter coat.

His visit was uncharacteristically short. Just three hours later, I heard his footsteps and familiar happy whistling in the stairway. In quick order, I learned that he'd not only seen the Bolanden family, but had also gotten a job on the way home.

"I hired on as a mechanic for old Hirschbiel down at his shop. It'll do until I get my feet on the ground and take in the lay of the land."

Somehow, none of it surprised me. Papa hadn't said a thing about job hunting when he left, yet I knew his restless mind. Sitting around the house wasn't for him. Even when forced to stay at home, he would be constantly tinkering, repairing, or planning next year's garden.

"Don't worry," he added. "I won't start for a couple of days. We need to get ahead of the housework so you can get some work clothes mended for me."

So it went. Without further comment, he jumped right in, helping me catch up with the laundry, the cleaning of floors — in short, a general straightening and sweeping out of places long neglected. Since we were alone at the task, I think he wondered about all the time Erich spent with the Steinbrechers, but said nothing.

Little Peter was a constant companion as we worked, usually staying close by me. He was still sizing up this man called "Papa." It was during one of our breaks from boiling laundry that I heard for the first time where Papa had been for almost a year. We were resting at the kitchen table with cups of tea.

"After leaving you, I managed to catch up with my unit just as the men were preparing to move with other units to the east side of the Rhein. Soon as we got across, some idiots blew up the bridge, as if that was going to help."

"Some SS blew up our railroad bridge," I interrupted. "Not long after you drove off."

"What foolishness. She was a beautiful old bridge," he replied. "Anyway, after the SS blew up the bridge we used to cross the Rhein, we found ourselves trapped just the same. There were a few hotheads who wanted to shoot it out. Fight to the death, they said. Several of my friends and I quietly walked away,

343

got rid of any guns, and kept walking with hands raised until reaching the Americans."

"Weren't you afraid they would shoot, even with your hands up?"

"Nay, Märe — well, maybe at first, but I was more scared of being shot in the back by the SS. We were lucky though. In no time we reached the American patrols without further problem. To our relief, we weren't treated harshly. We were able to sit on the ground for a while, then we were loaded on trucks heading south into Bavaria."

"Bavaria! All this time I thought you were a prisoner somewhere in France." I could see he was startled by my conclusion, so I quickly explained. "You see I got the idea when you said your commander would probably have you shot for being AWOL. I thought maybe you decided not to go back and tried to escape going the other way.

He laughed. "Nay. Not me. Much as I know where I might hide out in the Pfalz, I couldn't run out on my unit."

"Of course not. I'm sorry Papa."

"Ach, don't worry about it. I can see where you could have been misled. Instead, I ended up in good hands on a truck ride to a small village near Stuttgart. There we had the tables turned on us. We went into a prisoner-of-war camp previously used to house British and American prisoners. What do you think of that?"

I didn't know what to make of it. His story was so different from what my mind had conjured up over the months of his absence. "At least, you fared better than prisoners of the French."

"It wasn't bad. The Americans were better to us than we were to their people, I'm afraid. Except for not letting us write to our families. The Red Cross said you would be notified in time, but it never occurred to me that you would think I was dead.

"In my mind you were alive, but only because I heard nothing."

"Not only alive," he laughed. "But with the best job in the camp. Right away I volunteered as a helper in the kitchen!"

"That explains why you looked heavier to me."

"That's the problem with eating without working." He patted his stomach, and chuckled, "Don't worry. I'll be your skinny Papa again in no time.

The old pedal sewing machine now got a workout, patching old clothes into wearable condition for the two men. It was impossible to buy materials or threads, so seams often had colored thread mismatched to the shade of the garment. Papa never complained about it, and his presence kept Erich's tongue in place and my own as well. That was Papa's effect on the house. He insisted on a home of hardworking tranquility. If he thought one or the other of us was going too far, our names, spoken in a certain tone along with a look, was all it took to restore harmony. That may sound all too easy, but we had been raised to respect our parents.

My workload as surrogate mother and housekeeper was not reduced by my father's return, but it was lightened considerably. No matter how long his day at Hirschbiel's, he never hesitated to wash supper dishes or do a dozen other chores when I had my hands full with Peter and Mama.

One benefit from the busy pace of survival was how the days and weeks flew by. A warmer spring arrived, and I hardly knew where winter had gone. Spring brought with it a bit of shock for Breitstraße — our next door neighbor Frau Andres had a baby. This usually happy news spread quickly on the street because, as everyone knew, Herr Andres was still a prisoner of war and hadn't been home for nearly two years. People wondered who the father could be. I knew, but said nothing. After all, I'd been kissed by the man.

The baby girl was beautiful from the start, and very different from her older sisters with her black curls and dusky skin. It was an anxious wait for Herr Andres' return. He was a walking tinderbox — the loss of even a pfennig at cards sent him into fits.

The neighborhood wait wasn't long. Herr Andres returned from prison camp on May eighteenth, and every ear in the neighborhood listened for the explosion. It didn't come. He told Papa later that when he'd walked into the house and saw the baby, his first thought was that Frau Andres was babysitting. And before she could even break the news, he had picked the child up, instantly falling in love. Besides, he said, how could he leave his own girls! He stayed and raised the girl without recrimination or regret.

Herr Andres returned to his job in the stone quarry, and to playing cards with Papa in his usual competitive fashion.

During the months following war's end, finding enough food was difficult but not impossible. By my efforts, and later with Erich's help, some variety of things to eat was somehow managed. Papa's return proved to be our salvation, however, because 1946 was the beginning of the real test of our will to survive.

By late spring, many factors including poor harvests, and war reparations to France among them, combined to create near-starvation for most Germans.

Happily, Papa proved to be ingenious in providing for his family, especially in bringing home the food we needed. Through barter, and promises of future favors, he made sure we always had something to eat, even if it was the same dish for every meal.

One evening he hauled home a fifty kilo sack of wheat grain. In the blacksmith shop he then rigged up an electric grinding stone, making it possible to turn the grain into flour for baking. A little coarser grind was perfect for making a hot creamy wheat cereal, and a final sifting gave us a coarse whole grain mash. In better times, the latter would have been fed to livestock. Boiled and served with a little sweet syrup, it made for a filling and nutritious supper.

The city continued to have the open air 'Freibank' market behind city hall. These were less frequent and the meat offered was now only horse. Chunks of the tough flesh laid on a rough wood plank, and whatever the family size, that's how the cleaver fell. I'd stand in line dreaming that someone had shot a wild boar, but when it was my turn, I usually found what was left of a horse's rear end. I tried to make it palatable for the others, but one or two bites was about all I could stomach.

∾

The warmer weather made it possible to get out again and occasionally visit Oma and my aunts in Bolanden. During these times, I made friends with Tante Gusta's daughters, particularly with Gretel, who was my age. With her blonde hair and big blue eyes, she looked just like one of the old-fashioned dolls I had once craved. She was fun to be with, and I was glad to have found a female cousin my age with whom I could relate.

But it was not to last. Papa came home one day from a visit to Bolanden with the awful news that Tante Gusta had kicked Gretel out of the house. At only fifteen, the girl had been made pregnant by one of the French soldiers who boarded in her mother's house. No one in the family would speak of Gretel's fate. I believe my father knew where the girl went, but because he didn't spread gossip in or out of the family, he remained silent. Perhaps the episode made him concerned about preserving his own daughter's virginity, the less said the better.

∾

It was in May that Mama took a turn for the worse. She began to refuse to eat, and accused us of trying to poison her. No amount of persuasion worked, and in desperation, Papa called in the help of the Deaconess nurses. A Sister Caroline answered the call. She looked to be about sixty years old, and I never saw her smile. Nor did she ever offer any encouragement or comfort to us who stood by worrying.

She came for about a half hour every second day, sometimes bringing with her some soup. We were not allowed to be in the bedroom during her visits, and I never learned of what they talked about. I remembered seeing her around town prior to our contact, often walking at a fast clip. She wore the traditional navy blue cape over a fully gathered skirt of the same color, and a crisp white-dotted Swiss cap. She turned out to be as crisp and dark as the uniform. Departures from our house were always accompanied by the order: "Just keep her comfortable."

While Sister Caroline didn't speak to Erich or I about Mama's condition, she did talk to Papa, though never at length. Even when Mama showed a rapid weight loss, the nurse never expressed deep concern, gave any remedies, or spoke of any need to put her in a hospital. I'm sure Mama told her, as she had us, that she wouldn't see Doctor Hahn, the man who called her crazy.

Mama's complaints of being poisoned grew worse. In midsummer, a circulation problem added to the steady weight loss. She told the nurse of being cold, especially her feet. Sister Caroline said we should add a hot water bottle to our daily 'comfort' duties. Mama's limbs were cold to the touch, but the bottle did seem to ease her.

Through the summer and into the fall, Mama could still get up and walk with help. Two days a week, the nurse had me heat water and prepare a bath in the kitchen. The sight of my mother being guided into the kitchen, stripped of her gown, and lowered into the portable tub remains with me. With every passing week, her body shrank to a horrible resemblance to those people I saw in the pictures at the courthouse.

Peter was often present during these baths, and I remember on one occasion, he came over to where I was seated, awaiting further orders from the nurse. "Ma-hee," he said, pointing a little finger. "Ma-hee."

"Nay, Peterchen. Not Ma-hee," I said, as quietly as I could. "That's our Mama. Please say Mama."

Tears stung my eyes as he answered, "Ma-hee." The little fellow just couldn't understand.

He had heard his older brother and sister say "Mama" to her, but somehow the name 'Marie' that Papa used, stayed in his head and couldn't be changed. Before the sadness of it could really overwhelm me I picked him up and went into the bedroom to change the bed linens. Working furiously to control my emotions, anger rose up, anger at myself for being too stupid to know what to do to make Mama whole again.

The downward slide in her condition advanced rapidly by late fall. She was too weak to feed herself. Papa and I took turns feeding her, if she ate at all. Sometimes, just a turned face told us the answer. Passing a bowel movement into the bucket also ended she could no longer sit up.

The nurse brought us oversized cloth diapers, but I still had to change the bed linens frequently each day. We had no waterproof liners to protect the sheets. Her cleanliness became my biggest daily chore. Those days the nurse didn't come, I took on the task of bathing Mama from head to foot. Sometimes Papa helped when he was home. For his sake, I had to control my emotions enough to bathe her emaciated body. It suddenly became important to me to show her as well.

The first time I removed her gown, my stomach cramped and I wanted to escape the room. I could feel her eyes watching my reaction as I started to apply the wash cloth to little more than skin on bones. Something inside me clicked. I'd found what I called my 'numb switch.' The cold reality that Mama was dying could no longer be denied. I had to allow her the dignity of being kept clean.

In November, the rectal bleeding began. It seemed to puzzle Sister Caroline, but again she said nothing about taking her to the hospital. One day, while the nurse was in the bedroom, my father followed, saying, "I must take her to the hospital!"

"Nay!" Mama's loud protest could been heard in the street had the window been open.

Papa walked out dejected. Moving in silence to the kitchen window, he stared out for long minutes at the cold, leaden sky. Finally, with a deep sigh, he turned, touched my arm without a word, and left for work.

During the daytime, Mama made no audible outward signs of suffering. It was in the long nights that my father and I knew how she suffered. We both heard her moaning and whimpering. When Papa came home from prison, he'd set up a bed in the living room, which connected to her bedroom, as did my room. All efforts we attempted to comfort were rejected. My father said it as only a guess, but he believed the nurse may have given Mama morphine, when suddenly her nights became more peaceful as winter set in. How the sister came to have morphine, and under what authority it was used, are questions I didn't care to ask. I never saw her give injections of any kind, but I would have favored any effort to release Mama from her pain and despair. Papa may have been told the truth about any drugs, but was pledged to secrecy.

❧

Death took Mama December 19, 1946, eight days before her twenty-fourth wedding anniversary and sixteen days after her birthday. She was 45 years old.

On that day, Sister Caroline arrived in an unusual rush, telling me the job of washing Mama would be mine. As she couldn't stay long. Neither Papa nor I questioned the Sister's unusual change of routine. I went ahead, preparing food for us and soup for Mama. In only minutes, the nurse came back through the kitchen ready to leave. Something was said about returning in two days. Seeing the bowl of soup cooling on the table, she added, "You can take that in to her now."

Usually, I didn't go into Mama's bedroom right after the nurse had been there. That day I did, leaving Papa and Peter at the table eating. Entering the room I was immediately aware of a strange aroma. I walked over to the bed, looking around to try to find the source, and even looked to see if Mama was lying in a mess. She wasn't. I figured it was my imagination, and knelt down on the floor by the head of the bed, placing the bowl on a chair pulled up next to me. I'd found it easier to feed her by resting an arm under the pillow, lifting her head and chest up to help her swallow. When she wouldn't eat, she simply turned away. This time, there was no sign of refusal. When I lifted and brought the spoon to her mouth Mama turned to me, fluttering eyes staring blankly at mine. I'd become accustomed to that expression over the weeks, but a squeeze or nudge always got her to accept the food.

I touched the spoon to her lips. "Mama, please eat. The soup is good. The nurse brought it." The last was a white lie, but I would try anything to make her cooperate.

At my words, her eyes opened and fluttered at me each time I urged, but her mouth stayed closed. Finally, I put the spoon down and eased the pillow back to the mattress. I left the soup by the bed and went to the kitchen, hoping to get Papa to try. He got right up, leaving the food on his plate. I remained for a moment with Peter to keep him eating, then followed to see if Papa was having any luck.

At the door, I could see he wasn't trying. He'd laid her back on the pillow, his one hand smoothing Mama's hair, the other hand closing her eyes.

"She's gone." It was all he said. My father hadn't looked in my direction, but must have sensed my presence.

"Gott sei dank!" I shocked myself by thanking God out loud, but I knew no other emotion. Mama was dead — and I thanked God.

That my father felt the same relief about Mama's release from misery I have no doubt. But his understanding and lack of rebuke at my words didn't ease my guilt. As if sensing my feeling, he wasted no time putting into motion things that had to be done.

"It's over," he said softly, removing a hand from her eyes. The act of standing up seemed to break the spell of melancholy within him. "Go look after the boy. I'll go and order a coffin and send the Leichenfrau up here. Your mother has to be washed and dressed before rigor mortis sets in."

My brain was spinning, but finally managed to speak as he started down the stairs. "What about Erich?"

"I'll stop by the Gendarmerie and leave a message."

Stepping back into the kitchen, I saw Peter going toward the bedroom. "Nay, Peter, come here." I swept him off the floor and held on tight. He made no struggle to be put down. I'd held him that way so many times, maybe he understood I needed his comfort. There were no tears. It was an awful feeling wanting to cry, but could not. Every fiber in my body demanded tears, yet none came. After a time, I sat Peter down with a pile of blocks to play with, while I cleaned the kitchen. And, there was water to heat for the Leichenfrau, the person called upon to wash, dress and lay out the dead.

When Papa returned with Frau Meyer, He'd made another decision.

"We'll have to carry her down to the wash kitchen to be laid out. There is no way we can carry a coffin down those winding, narrow steps."

He was right of course, but Frau Meyer and I regretted the need. How awful to have family and friends visit the departed in a wash kitchen, however neat and clean. I could see that Papa felt bad, too. However, he'd never let that get in the way of doing what was necessary.

"You stay here with Peter," Papa said. "Frau Meyer and I will carry your mother through the living room and into the hall so he won't see anything. As for Erich, he drove his boss to Worms and won't know about this until he returns tonight."

In a few minutes, Frau Meyer returned for a wash bowl and warm water. In those brief moments, it came to me that I wanted Mama to wear her one pretty nightgown. I got it and asked her to tell Papa. She didn't question my choice, nor did my father.

By mid-afternoon, having put Peter down for a nap, I went to the wash kitchen to offer my help. Frau Meyer had left, and none was needed. Papa had removed the two large tubs on one wall, and Mama was laid temporarily on a stretcher resting on stands at the head and foot. The pine coffin, all that could be ordered, was not expected until the next day from the carpenter. I saw that Papa had tied a kerchief around Mama's head, holding her jaw closed.

"We can take it off by the time the coffin arrives," he said. "Come, we were finished here. I need to have something to drink."

I knew that what he really wanted was time to think on the events of the day and how it would affect the future.

When Erich arrived home that night, Papa explained about Mama's last moments and what had been done since. "Let's go down to the wash kitchen," he concluded. "You'll want to see her."

"Nay! I don't want to see her like that. I'll remember what she looked like alive!"

I looked at Papa and found him as shocked as I was with Erich's behavior. "But, you must Erich," I said, trying not to shout.

"I will not."

"Then you stay here with Peter," Papa ordered. "Annchen and I have things to do."

The wash kitchen was cold. Papa wanted to check on Mama's condition and, I think, just be with her a few moments alone with me. Inspecting the kerchief holding her jaw closed, he again smoothed and caressed Mama's head. Frau Meyer had brushed her hair to lay behind her head, as if to hide it's shortness. Under the dim glow of the single light bulb hanging overhead, her terribly thin face appeared even more pitiful. Earlier, we left her there covered only by a nightgown. Now Papa asked me for a clean bed sheet to cover her. He didn't cover the face, but tucked the sheet just below her chin.

There was nothing more to do, yet neither of us wanted to leave Mama alone. Papa rearranged things, then put them back where they were. I wiped already clean surfaces. When we caught ourselves searching the whitewashed walls and ceiling for non-existent cobwebs, we knew it was time to return upstairs to the living.

❧

A local cabinetmaker delivered the coffin early the next day. Frau Meyer showed up soon after to help Papa place my mother in it. There was no satin lining. The inside matched the outside — pine wood stained a dark brown. The

351

coffin lid, with its simple elevated design, was set off to the side. Going down to the room later, I saw that the white sheet now covered her body from the waist down. Above the waist, pillows were used to raise Mama slightly, with the area around her head filled with fresh evergreen sprigs. The first of several evergreen wreaths, decorated with ribbons and dried flowers, must have arrived earlier. Papa had placed it on top of the open coffin at the foot. All the wreaths came from neighbors. In winter, evergreens were customary as fresh flowers couldn't take the cold, and that Friday was more than cold — it was bitter cold.

Papa thought Erich should report to his job as usual. He seemed useless around the house. After all was finished, and the Leichenfrau gone, my father spent much of the day in and out, making arrangements for the burial the next day. I was left to escort any visitors to where Mama lay and accept more wreaths sent by neighbors. For both of us, there was much to do and little time. Papa found a burial plot, the hearse, and a minister. He notified relatives near and far, and, I learned later, visited city hall to record the death of his wife. During one of his brief stops at home, I rushed some of our own flour, eggs and butter up the street to Frau Leber, who ran a small bakery. She agreed to make some plain cake for the wake.

The death certificate, dated December twentieth, stated that on the word of the deceased's husband, the death of Maria Klein, born Herbst, had occurred the previous day. The cause was an unknown five-year illness and "psychose." That was all the information Papa had to give, and it was accepted without question.

By late Friday afternoon, people from the neighborhood began stopping by to see Mama and express their condolences. A few dropped off black-bordered sympathy cards at the door without coming in. Frau Rösel from across the street did go into the room, and was deeply shocked. She hadn't seen my mother in over two years, since the birth of Peter. Mama had secluded herself well. Frau Rösel was one of the few who allowed tears to fall at the sight of what two years had wrought. I was against showing her body, but Papa wanted people to know that she had really been sick.

All the relatives had received word, though no one came on Friday. It was to be expected, as none lived in Kirchheim and the weather was so terribly cold. It left me wondering who, if anyone, would come out for the burial service held in the cemetery. Saturday would reveal the strength of family ties.

Papa had purchased black armbands. None of us had black clothing, and the armbands had to substitute.

᷉

Erich kept his word, and didn't cross the threshold of the wash kitchen until the hearse arrived Saturday after noon, and the coffin lid sealed shut by men who accompanied the horse-drawn hearse. Only then did he agree to join Papa and I in following the black carriage. Frau Andres came over from next door to watch Peter while we were at the cemetery. Leaving the house with us were Papa's sisters, Lina, Lisbeth and Gusta. Tante Lina came the farthest, driving from Monsheim with her son Fritz. Other relatives from Marnheim and Bolanden were there, but I was in no mood to record all their names in memory. Those who had looked upon Mama's emaciated body were already speculating that it had to have been cancer that killed her. It was the first I'd heard of that possibility.

The new day had brought no moderation in temperature. The breath coming from the nostrils of the two horses in front of the hearse shot out like steam from a train locomotive. I was ill-prepared for the cold, having only Mama's blue spring coat with a sweater on underneath. All my scarves were colorful, and I refused to wear one around my throat or on my head. The others must have thought me crazy, and they were probably right. I didn't even have my long hair to help keep my head warm. Weeks before, I had convinced Papa to let me cut my hair short.

The horses were started at 2:30 p.m. My father, brother and I were the first walking behind the plain roofed hearse with open sides. Papa was in the middle. Right behind us came the relatives, then Ida Steinbrecher. As the procession began, I heard house doors open and people stepping out to join us. I caught sight of Frau Rösel leaving her house bundled up. Thinking it would be disrespectful to look around each time a house door opened, I kept my eyes straight ahead all the way down Breitstraße, Neumayerstraße, around the Schloßgarten, and on to the cemetery.

Though the cold stung my face and ears, I was grateful for the lack of snow. There was only a dusting of white along the street and in the cemetery as we approached the burial plot.

Pastor LaFrenz, a new minister in town, waited for us by the open grave. Two boards were laid across the hole and the men with the hearse quickly lifted the coffin and placed it on the boards. The pastor, who knew only what Papa had told him about Mama, motioned for the three of us to step closer. The others closed in a semi-circle behind us. The sermon was short. There was so little Pastor LaFrenz could say of the woman being buried, and it was cold.

But, even in the short time he recited the service, I had to think about

Marnheim — Mama's village. For many years, it was tradition there for burials to have the sounds of Lehrer Bauer's violin and the voices of village school children singing hymns. Mama went to many graveside services in Marnheim through the years and, she who never cried, came the closest to tears when the violin played and the children sang an old hymn by Johann F. Raeder.

Harre meine Seele	*Rest my soul,*
harre des Herren	*rest in the Lord*
Alles ihm befehle,	*He understands everything,*
hilft er doch so gern	*Trust him to help*
Wenn alles bricht	*When all is broken,*
Gott verläßt uns nicht	*God won't abandon us*
Größer als der helfer	*The need is never greater*
ist die Not ja nicht	*than the helper*
Ewige Treue, Retter in Not	*Eternal Truth, rescue is needed*
rett auch unsere Seele	*Rescue our souls*
du treuer Gott	*O faithful God*

I felt great sadness that no hymns would be heard at her graveside. Wanting to cry for her. I just simply couldn't, even as the final prayer ended and the coffin was lowered. The numbness in me still refused to give way to tears.

Pastor LaFrenz picked up a small shovel and scooped three loads of dirt down onto Mama's coffin. "In the name of the Father, the Son, and the Holy Ghost. Amen." The shovel was handed to Papa, then to Erich. I was next, punching the shovel into the hard pile of dirt to add my share. One by one, most of my relations took their turn with the shovel. Looking behind me for the first time I could see that perhaps fifteen friends and neighbors had joined our procession down the hill, and most were now moving off rapidly to the warmth of homes. Erich had gone over to Ida and I stood with Papa, who was thanking the pastor.

Our Oma Klein was missing from our midst, unable to come. Old and frail, the ordeal would have been too much. Suddenly Papa moved to rejoin the family for the walk home in silence. It was much too cold to talk. I was sure Oma was at home remembering — remembering how hundreds of people had come to help her husband off to his eternal rest in much better weather.

Everyone who came to the cemetery were invited for coffee and cake, but the cold had taken its toll, and only a few relatives joined us. Just as well, since the living room, the usual place for a wake, still had Papa's bed in it. There had been no time to move it out, therefore our guests had to crowd into the kitchen. I kept busy serving the cake and wheat coffee, but I was struck by how little was said about Mama. I thought it had to be another result of the war — she was just one more victim, and any fond remembrances were too painful to express.

Extra food had been brought in for anyone staying for supper, but it proved unnecessary. People left early. They all lived in other towns, and could not be blamed for wanting to get home before dark. Long before suppertime Papa and I were alone again with Peter. Erich had left to visit Ida.

That first evening with Mama truly gone from us passed quietly, but the day would come when Papa and I would have to talk about the guilt I felt.

Chapter Thirty-Four

The Christmas that followed four days after Mama's burial was a very quiet affair. A tree was cut and decorated in the usual spot, but no one felt like exchanging gifts. There wasn't much available in the stores anyway. The left-over sweet bread from the wake had to suffice as Christmas cake.

"Where's Ma-hee?" Peter asked, pointing to the empty bed across from his.

"Mama," I corrected again. "Mama is no longer here, Peterchen. She was taken to heaven."

He couldn't possibly have understood 'heaven,' yet my answer must have satisfied. He never asked again about 'Ma-hee.'

Mama's death would have been sad at anytime, but especially so at Christmas. Except for the last years when her health and mind had failed, I know it was a favorite time for her. It was not about gifts. Giving gifts played a minor role, whether the money was there or not. Christmas for Mama meant family traditions, like baking cookies and cakes, and visiting relatives. Most important was attending church to hear again the carols played on Mozart's mighty organ. Papa and Erich had no problem joining in on the pleasures of holiday food and fellowship, but were less enthusiastic about the religious aspects. Only I shared Mama's devotion to church. Now, with all that had happened — I began to waver.

As the last of the church bells rang in 1947, I went to work cleaning and disinfecting Mama's bedroom. It didn't seem right for Papa to sleep in the living room when the bedroom was available. He had arranged for a painter friend to come in and redecorate as part of the clean-up. Painting was something we could have done ourselves, considering the hard times, but only he had the stencils for various design overlays on the new paint. In any case, I'm sure my father didn't pay all cash for the work. There were always favors that could be done for his friend.

Peter's bed was moved into the living room for a short time required by the painter. My father tossed out the three-piece mattress on Mama's bed, and the bedstead stored away. He was about to throw out her pillows and the big comforter.

"Don't do that," I pleaded. "Feather pillows and comforters aren't easy to get. Let me clean them."

A strange smile came to Papa's face: "You know the ticking has to be boiled after removing the feathers. Can you do that without feathers everywhere?"

"I can just see it," Erich hollered out sarcastically. He had been sitting and gobbling down his breakfast as usual to be at work on time. "When I come home tonight, it'll be filled with blowing feathers. Don't let her do it, Papa."

"Hold your tongue, son. Shouldn't you be on your way?"

"Ja, Ja, I'm going, but I still think she'll make a mess."

As soon as the door closed behind my brother, I made another try. "I won't make a mess. I know just how to take out the feathers. Everything will be done in the wash kitchen."

My father was never one to turn down a challenge. I could see on his face he was going to let me try, though not without humor and a warning. "I can see you have some Herbst blood mixed with the Klein," he laughed. "But I won't be happy if Erich has something to throw in our faces!"

I worked hard to not give my brother the satisfaction of gloating, because I had bitten off almost more than I could chew. It took most of the day to empty out the feathers and boiled the tickings, and I had to use every tub and container in sight to keep the feathers safe. It took another three days before the heavy tickings were dry enough to be refilled. At the end I vowed silently to never tackle such a job again.

The New Year wasn't many weeks old when Ida burst in on us one evening in tears. Her mother had kicked her out of the house in a dispute over marrying Erich. To our surprise, Frau Steinbrecher didn't want my brother for a son-in-law. With both my father and Erich helping to keep the widow's farm going, the news was a shock. For months, everyone who knew Erich and Ida expected them to someday marry.

It was bewildering to me. Whenever I visited Steinbrecher's they acted as though we were good people. Papa quickly offered Ida one of our empty rooms, but she declined, saying that it wouldn't look proper until after marriage. After she and Erich went to his room to talk over the problem, Papa and I cleaned up the supper dishes.

"If that doesn't beat all," he mumbled. "Must be something going on there. It wouldn't surprise me if the old lady refuses to let Ida have her own belongings." Papa's words proved true.

It was decided that Erich would go with Ida to her Tante Felleis. The sister of her late father lived at the edge of Kirchheim, not far from the old railroad station. It was a long walk, but Ida thought her aunt would take her in.

Tante Felleis was a childless widow, and quite fond of Ida. After settling in, Ida soon found a job working as a maid for a local dentist. We decided to announce the engagement at Easter and hold the wedding in the summer.

During the waiting period, my future sister-in-law became a frequent part of evening life in our kitchen. With each visit, I grew to like her very much. We were all angry when we learned she was allowed to take only her clothes from home. The dishes, silver and linens she had gathered for the marriage were locked up. Papa said she should take the matter to the police, but understood when Ida refused. To her it wasn't worth the ugly public mess created.

Letting Ida know us better, we made several visits to Bolanden and Marnheim to meet the extended families. Everyone said Erich had made quite a catch. But all too soon Ida was also caught up in family sorrows. On March thirtieth, my dear Oma died.

Charlotte Klein, at seventy-nine years of age, had lived a full fifteen years beyond her husband — long enough to witness the rise and fall of Adolf Hitler and suffer the loss of a son and a son-in-law in the war. By the time my father returned home from prison camp in early 1946, it was clear Oma was failing. Previously, she had fiercely maintained an independent life in her own quarters in Tante Lisbeth's house. As the end grew near, Lisbeth had taken over the cooking and cleaning — chores too much for Oma to handle. Still, my tiny, white-haired grandmother went right on greeting visitors with smiles and kisses to the last. Over these final days, I went to her often — sometimes with Papa or Ida, but mostly with Peter. Bedridden near the end, I'd sit by her side with the boy on my lap as she related more memories to me about her husband — my Opa Peter.

I'd heard all my life that the area had never seen as big a funeral as the one for my grandfather. Finally broken by the world-wide depression, he was still remembered as the richest man in the district. The procession to the hilltop cemetery at the edge of Bolanden had been as long as the eye could see, or so the story went. Having been a small child at the time, I'm sure all I thought about was hanging on tight to Papa.

Sad as I was about Oma's passing, my grief was made greater by the news that Tante Lina insisted her mother be cremated. The thought of it sickened me. Papa didn't agree with his sister, saying his mother deserved a proper funeral, but he didn't want to start a family argument.

Crying so easily over Oma's death only complicated my feelings of guilt about Mama. The months following her funeral had brought no easing of the burden. The only person I could talk to about it was Papa, but how could I admit to having no love for my mother? How could I explain being unable to express sorrow for her?

During waking hours, thoughts of Mama were shoved aside without effort. My time was never empty of things to do. When every job is done by hand, every meal started from scratch, the mind has little room for prolonged remembrance. Even sitting and knitting, a pure pleasure for me, required some planning and attention to the click of the needles.

The nights were another story. The frequent restless efforts to fall asleep drove me crazy. I was unable to forget her accusations of being poisoned by me, or the long silent stares in answer to my pleas. During those nights when exhaustion allowed immediate sleep, I often woke with a start at three or four in the morning. A reoccurring dream of seeing Mama's uncaring eyes staring into mine from the doorway, always brought me upright — struggling to find reality. The nightmares were nothing more than a memory from the past. No one stood in my bedroom doorway.

Not long after Oma died, an opportunity came up to speak about Mama privately with Papa. Supper was over and the kitchen cleaned up, and for once, Ida hadn't joined us for the evening. Erich had gone to see her instead. After putting Peter to bed, I returned to the kitchen, where my father sat at the table reading the newspaper and listening to music from the radio.

I sat down across and started in on socks that needed mending. It was not unlike many of our evenings, with he and I listening to the radio and catching up on hand-work until bedtime. My father rarely left the house after dark, and if he did, it was only to go across the courtyard to tinker in the workshop.

"Papa, can we talk?" I don't know what possessed me to start the subject.

"Of course. What is it?" He folded and set the newspaper aside.

"It's about Mama," I answered, getting right to the point before losing my nerve. It also gave him a chance to back out of the conversation.

"I've been waiting for you to talk about your mother. I know you've been troubled." Seeing the surprise on my face, he hurried on. "You've never been able to hide your feelings, even as a little girl. So, tell me."

"Ja, Papa. Well, how can I say it? All I know is I can't cry about Mama. I feel terrible about it, but I can't grieve over her death. Not the way she was, so cold and uncaring. Mama killed all my love for her a long time ago."

Speaking out that way about my mother was new for me. Having begun, there was so much I had to unload.

359

"Märe, I saw for myself the bad state of your mother during the months after I came home. It must have been difficult for you dealing with her alone."

"I've never blamed you for not being here," I said. "The war took you away. But the worst part was not having anyone to talk to as she turned cold toward me. The hardest was when I finally realized she didn't love me. I thought her craziness would pull me in too. Peter was all that kept me sane." I stopped, but Papa nodded for me to go on.

"My prayer for Mama was your return. I believed it was God's answer, only I was wrong — wrong to have such faith. I now know believing in God and prayer is stupid. The Bible was all Mama trusted at the end. What good did it do her?"

There were many painful memories I still had bottled up, but attacking Mama all at once would have only made the sadness on Papa's face worse. I lowered my eyes to the mending again and waited. The music from the radio seemed to match the somber moment.

He waited, and said nothing.

"Papa, I'm sorry. It's just that those years alone with her robbed me of understanding. I truly want to feel sorry she had to be sick and die so young, but why did she have to hate me? Why wouldn't she believe I wanted her well again?"

"I don't know the answer," my father finally said. "Something was turning bad in her mind, even before I was taken back in the Luftwaffe. It was hard for me to see it as anything more than the war getting her down at the time. I should have known better after that business with the lice. I was shocked at her condition, and how bad things were at home. I should have gotten you more help."

"You tried, Papa. Remember? The war was ending and all the relatives had their own problems."

"Ja, ja. The war — the damned war that Hitler brought on our heads. Her beloved Führer and his war made it impossible to get the doctors she needed. Maybe that's what made her sick in the head as well. Hitler was not the savior she thought. She'd never admit it though, not even when our trucks were taken away. Her dreams of prosperity and being a businesswoman were smashed. Yet, none of it made her blame Hitler. Nay, it was me she lost faith in, and in you, too. For that, I'm sorry."

"Why? We did nothing wrong!"

"Don't you worry about it. Your only fault was loving your father. She couldn't stand even that, as her doubts about me got bigger."

My mouth opened to protest, but he hushed me. "Listen. Your mother married me, but never really came to understand the Seppel ways. She believed that success came only from hard work. My father taught me a different lesson. He lived by hard work, but not without good humor and fun, and friendship toward everyone. Do you remember what your Oma always said about your Opa?"

I had to think about my many visits to Bolanden. Oma liked talking about Kleine Seppel, and his many beliefs. "Do you mean how Opa believed it was important to make good friends along the way, because only they will help you up when the world knocks you down."

"Right, and I hope you never forget it. He also believed it never hurt to extend friendliness to the women folks. They have the biggest influence on their men, he would say. Your mother found that the hardest to understand. Long before the war, before you were born, she'd accuse me of being unfaithful if she saw me tipping my hat to a neighbor lady. At the time, I just laughed about it. I thought she would change, be more optimistic and see the advantage of the friendly approach. And, she never understood why my mother meant so much to me."

It was hurting Papa to speak ill of Mama, and I pleaded with him. "You don't have to say anything more. I just wanted you to know why it's been so hard for me to mourn for Mama."

"But that's my point Annchen. You have to believe the problem was always inside your mother. A collapsing world and being sick weakened her mind and will to live. Don't think about how she was toward the end. That wouldn't be fair." Papa paused, then sighed. "Ja, your Mama wasn't the most affectionate woman, not at all like your Tante Lisbeth or your Oma. For her, keeping a clean house and looking after our well-being were the only ways she could show love. We shouldn't forget she made a good job of it — until the burdens of life overwhelmed her. Maybe our tears will come when all we remember are the songs she loved to sing."

Papa switched jobs. There was an opportunity to drive a truck again, something he wanted. A young war veteran, Kurt Butz, lived on the other side of town, and was determined to have his own trucking business. He had the truck, but he'd lost both legs above the knees in the war. My father would drive, but only until a way could be worked out allowing Kurt to operate the truck entirely with hand levers. In the meantime, Papa had the chance to be back on the road with an eye out for a suitable used truck, and for making contacts to get back into business himself. Kurt knew my father's plan and didn't care. He was happy just to have the temporary help.

Almost at the same time, Erich had the bright idea of towing home an abandoned tank that had been still sitting in a field outside town. Without warning, I was suddenly confronted with one of our small German tanks sitting in our courtyard. Apparently, it had run out of gas during the German retreat through our area. The French authorities didn't seem to mind if Erich and others claimed such abandoned equipment for salvage. That was his plan, to use the tank parts for something. He just hadn't decided the what the 'something' would be.

"It's an R.S.O.," he announced proudly, as though I was supposed to know what that meant. "Sister, don't you know anything about German military tanks? R.S.O. stands for Raupenschlepper-Ost"

It didn't help me at all to know what I saw from the kitchen window was a 'Caterpillar Tractor-East.' "How nice," I said sarcastically. "And what am I supposed to tell the neighbors about our new war machine — oh, sorry — the R.S.O. standing in our courtyard?"

"You leave that to me. I'll put it to good use. You'll see!"

The idea he came up with wasn't all that bad. When he and Papa discovered the engine still worked, Erich approached the city fathers with his novel notion. He wanted to repaint the small tank, drive it into the forest, and hired it out to the forestry service to haul harvested logs. He was ahead of his time. Under our system of government, Kirchheim controlled the forest around it, and the officials refused. They believed the tank tracks would tear up the paved roads leading into the forest. Disheartened, Erich sold off parts from the tank until nothing was left sitting in the courtyard.

At least the neighborhood boys had their fun climbing all over the 'Caterpillar Tractor-East' as long as it lasted. I got into the cramped two-man machine just once, and it made me twice as glad not to see anymore souvenirs of war out my kitchen window.

❧

There was little chance during my duties of keeping house to visit friends. We might meet and chat a few minutes on the street while shopping, but there were never any real sit-down visits. The radio became my daytime companion in the house, along with Peter. I couldn't converse much with a baby brother, and not at all with the radio, though I did sing along to some of the old melodies played. Peter got a kick out of his sister's voice. My childhood voice had long since turned into something far short of Mama's lovely soprano.

After a lifetime of listening to mostly Nazi-oriented programs, I was fascinated by the new offerings on German radio. Of special interest to me were talks about people and events in America, such as Abraham Lincoln and the Civil War. I also found a program on the newest clothing styles for women, both interesting and ironic. It was a subject dear to my heart, yet most Germans couldn't buy any of the clothes talked about, or the materials to make them. There was also a program that devoted a whole hour to the qualities of a good wife in Germany. By the end, I couldn't believe how I'd wasted time listening to someone explain how to make life easier for a husband.

With little else to do, evenings I had the usual knitting project or mending, and hanging on to every word of a mystery program. Mysteries and series about historical events always captured my interest. Many Germans, myself included, tired fast of news of the Nuremberg trials while they lasted. I was listening when the bulletin came over about Herman Goring's suicide. And, it was the radio again that told me the fates of other Nazi leaders. When all the news seemed to be bad, I'd search the dial for any station playing music. The daily struggle often went better with the sounds of music. Otherwise, it was too easy to fall into the gloom of wondering — what is going to become of me?

Because of Oma's death, the engagement party for Ida and Erich was postponed for a couple of weeks. In a way I was glad, as it allowed time to get extra ingredients for baking enough cakes. Ida helped me bake, though it wasn't one of her talents. Not surprising, she had always been the outside-worker at home. Her mother and sister had always taken care of cooking and baking. With marriage just weeks away, Ida looked to me for a crash course in the kitchen. The whole situation seemed odd — she should have been teaching me.

The party couldn't have been nicer, the first happy occasion in our house in far too long. Ida's aunt was more than generous, providing a delicious meal for us and a few friends and relatives prior to cake and coffee. Peter must have wondered about all the laughing, happy people around him. It was a new experience for him.

The weeks leading up to the July wedding seemed to whiz by. Again, Papa and I managed to gather extra food for the occasion. Dictated by the times, the wedding was a simple affair. Erich and Ida stood alone with two witnesses before the city registrar to satisfy the legal requirements, then, with family and friends rushing behind, a quick walk to the church to make it alright in the eyes of God. The walk back to our house was at a slower pace, with bride and groom leading the way. Erich looked so handsome in his dark gray suit, which had been purchased through the black market, along with the wedding rings. Ida was the loveliest bride in a black satin dress that reached her ankles. A lacy white veil covered her head, and dark curls surrounded a sweet face made all the prettier by happiness. It wasn't unusual for brides to wear black when I was young.

My friend Hannelore came over to help me with the wedding dinner, served around our extended table in the living room. Ida wanted to lend a hand in the kitchen, but we shooed her back to the merrymakers waiting to eat. Papa had filled all the available wine glasses for a toast. Where he got the wine I could only imagine. Our Pfälzer wine still wasn't all that available. The wedding had been a late morning event, and a whole day of feasting lay ahead.

I appreciated Hannelore's help, but sent her home soon after the dinner clean-up. Alone again, I sat in the kitchen for a moment enjoying the peace. The faint sound of happy voices from the living room added to my contentment as I opened the window to allow the afternoon breeze in. It made me smile to see the swallows all in a row on the electric line. The fork-tailed singers were the one thing that never changed year to year.

Turning to sit down again, I was startled by one of the birds almost hitting my head as it flew into the kitchen. Circling the room, it settled on top of the cupboard and began singing as so many had done before. Listening to the repeated refrain, the words to the swallow's song rose from somewhere in my memory.

"Als wir fort zogen — " It was Mama's version of what the swallows sing, and I began to hum the tune.

Little Peter rushed through the door, frightening the bird into a quick exit through the window, and breaking the memory of Mama's song. Somehow I was sorry for the interruption.

"Papa said you should come."

"Ja, Peter. Tell him I'll be in when the coffee is brewed."

&

The long happy day wound down to final best wishes and goodbyes from the guests late in the evening. Ida's few belongings had been brought up from her aunt's house, so it was a simple matter for the newlyweds to retire to Erich's room. They would use the adjoining room as private space to have friends. Family cooking and eating would be as before. A honeymoon was never discussed. Such things were for better times.

With Peter finally down for the night, I rejoined Papa in the kitchen. He was already finishing up the dishes. Seeing how tired I looked, he urged me to bed also, saying he had the job well in hand. I didn't argue.

I was very weary, but content as I laid my head down. My mind whirled with thoughts of the day. There was so much excitement, and not a single sour note or problem. There was real happiness in our family again. How good it felt to have people in the house gaily talking and laughing, and swallows flying in and out of the kitchen singing their songs.

The ceiling began swimming around. I was crying, but didn't know why. The harder I tried to stop, turning from one side to the other, the stronger the terrible sobs filling my throat. I buried my face in my pillow to silence them. Papa was only a door away and I didn't want him to know how much I hurt.

But I knew he was by my bed before his hand touched my shoulder.

"Dear Märe, why do you cry? Surely you can't be so unhappy about Erich and Ida."

"Oh, Papa," I cried, my face still buried in the pillow. "It's not that."

"Then tell me. Why do you cry on this of all nights?"

Sitting on the side of my bed, his strong hands and arms turned me as he spoke. I found myself sitting up, my head on his shoulder. I had so little control over my sobbing; it was difficult to finally get the words out about my feelings of guilt and shame. How could I explain the endless days of silence Mama made me endure, no longer recognizing the daughter who loved and wanted her well again? How could she think I would poison her?

When I finally spoke it had to be the truth. I could never lie to Papa and I knew that only he would understand my torment since Mama's funeral.

"I don't know, Papa. It's crazy. I can only now tell you how I miss Mama. In the kitchen today — a swallow flew in to sing Mama's song.

"Oh, Papa, I miss her so. I miss all the songs she once sang."

His arms wrapped me in a gentle embrace, and without saying a word, he absorbed all the tears finally unlocked by the song of the swallow.

Chapter Thirty-Five

My brother and his new wife had agreed that she would stop working after the marriage. The extra money from her job would have come in handy, but few women of the day worked a regular job once they were married. It was tradition in our family for the wife to stay home. In other families, the war and its aftermath had already turned tradition upside-down. I was more than happy to have Ida at home. Finally, there was someone to help share the household work, and I was sure she'd become a good friend in the process.

It was a while before Ida, who lacked cooking experience, tackled much at the stove. But she was a willing student, and rivaled my own abilities in no time. I was by no means an expert chef, but did come armed with Mama's handwritten recipe book, and my own slim book of collected recipes I'd begun as a child. It wasn't long before we began to cautiously experiment. Girls my age were expected to have built their own cookbooks.

In cleaning, laundry, and gardening, Ida was a true help and soul sister from the start. Best of all, we could talk. It was nice to have the drudgery of doing laundry cut in half by good female conversation. We often stood side by side without complaint, rubbing our knuckles raw as we scrubbed clothes on wash boards. We saved our grumbling for the men.

Ida could also knit, a helpful talent considering the constant need for sweaters, stockings, scarves and warm headgear. A source for yarn was the problem, except for what we might recover from old garments. Any yarn salvaged from an old sweater was often too weak to reuse entirely. Yarn from two or more sources would have to be used, resulting in some interesting color combinations.

The Seppel bartering talents and mechanical abilities came to the rescue once more. Papa had received a quantity of sheep wool in trade, and Erich acquired a pattern for making wood parts to change the treadle sewing machine into a wool-spinner. He took the plans to a friend who used his wood-turning tools to create the parts. After assembling the unit, it replaced the sewing machine on top the cabinet and connected to the drive belt.

After a few false starts, Ida and I got the knack for spinning. Our reward for several evenings of labor was enough yarn to make new sweaters for everyone. Since the yarn was all the color of the natural wool, we used a combination of new spun yarn and old dyed yarn to add variety. The spinning and knitting went on as long as wool was available.

Machine sewing was something else Ida wouldn't do for several years. That was alright since we had but one machine and sewing was my favorite occupation at the time. Recycling clothes was a necessity, and for me, a challenging art. Almost every stitch Peter wore, including his underwear, came from old adult clothes. Papa and Erich were always in need of having shirt collars turned, or created anew from cut-off shirt tails. Fortunately, German men's shirts had extra long tails. The only article I didn't feel qualified to re-model was a new winter coat for myself. Papa sacrificed his old, long air force coat, which I took to a seamstress downtown to style into something more suitable to my figure. Unhappy news from Bolanden reached us in early fall. My cousin Elsbeth had been sent home from Speyer, her career as a pediatric nurse cut short by a mysterious illness. Tante Lisbeth's only daughter had been losing strength over several months, and all efforts to find the cause had the Deaconess nurses' group and numerous German doctors baffled.

Ida and I immediately walked to Bolanden to visit Elsbeth. Except for some trouble in walking and speaking clearly, she looked and acted as normal and sweet as ever. We also learned that Tante Lisbeth was bound to take her 'angel' to any doctor in the land to find an answer.

In late summer of 1947 Kirchheim officials announced the arrival of dried lima beans from America. The beans were free, and doled out according to family size. I went down for our share. While not a strange food to us, the flat beans were not a staple in our normal diet.

Reaching home, I dumped enough for a meal into a pot of water to soak overnight. Ida was the first to lift the lid in the morning, and called me in from the garden. She wasn't happy. "Look. This is what the Americans sent!"

The top of the water was covered with black bugs. The beans were infested. "Annchen, we can't serve these. Let's dump them."

"No, no — wait," I said. "I remember my mother soaking beans in salt water when she suspected bugs. Why don't we try that."

The beans the men ate that night came with our silent prayers.

Our reaction to the bug-infested beans may appear overwrought and ungrateful, but it wasn't. Even though Germans were a defeated people under occupation, we still had pride. At the time, the contaminated food seemed another effort to degrade us.

Meanwhile, up the Breitstraße at the Wilz family farm house, some surprises were cooking. Franz, the son, was a friend of Erich. Daughter Elizabeth was the one who'd carried on a secret romance with Josef, a Polish prisoner of war. He had been assigned during his captivity to work on the Wilz farm. Elizabeth and Josef married in 1946, around the time the father died. There was another daughter, Sophie, who was younger than Elizabeth and crippled by childhood polio.

She had to walk with a cane, bent forward with a severe limp. Still she was known as a hard worker with a kind disposition. Witnessing that optimistic outlook on life, it was hard to feel sorry for her. Finding a young man to marry, though, seemed out of the question.

Ida and I got to know the whole family better in the years following the war when Josef asked for our help in the field harvest. Anyone could see Elizabeth was pregnant just months after her marriage. And each passing week brought with it more speculation all around that it was sure to be a multiple birth. Elizabeth was huge.

One morning, as I finished sweeping in front of the house, I could almost feel the buzz in the air. An unusual number of women up the street gossiping with each other had caught my attention. Normally, the ladies were too busy at that time of day to be hanging out of their windows. I noticed a boy coming my way. It was Wolfgang, a cousin of the Wilz family. Older than I, his approach seemed curious. He hardly ever made a point to speak to me.

Without so much as a 'Guten Tag,' the boy started right in with a disgusted tone. "Have you heard what happened up the street?"

Ida and I had been waiting for word of the birth of Elizabeth's babies, never doubting there'd be more than one. I told him so.

"Not Elizabeth," he replied. "Sophie. It was Sophie! She had a baby last night."

"You mean Elizabeth. Sophie's not pregnant."

"Yes, she was! There's a baby girl to prove it."

"But how? Who?" Stunned, I could only stammer.

"I know who the father is," Wolfgang said in a knowing tone.

He went on to identify the father as a returning prisoner of the British, who'd passed through Kirchheim some months earlier. The man had stayed a few weeks helping Josef before moving on. It was only a strong guess on Wolfgang's part and never proven, but then, no evidence was ever given to the contrary.

Elizabeth soon delivered her twin boys, making it three babies for Frau

Wilz to be a grandmother to. The uproar over Sophie eventually quieted down to simple amazement that she had hidden her pregnancy from both family and neighbors so well. It was no mystery to Ida.

❧

As was his style, Papa stayed on the move from dawn until dark with never a complaint. Driving for Butz, he also kept a sharp lookout for a good used truck. The quicker he felt his own wheels rolling underneath him meant a big leap for the green twig. I knew of his search, and like my mother before me, took a less hopeful view for success. New trucks weren't widely available yet, and most people with a decent running vehicle were not apt to sell. Again, I underestimated Papa. He found both the truck and the bank financing to buy it. We were back in business. Someday, I told myself, I'll truly learn to trust what he called the "Seppel way."

With the truck, Papa could wheel and deal in earnest. In fall, he showed up in the courtyard with a small load of sugar beets. Sugar was one of the most severely rationed food items, and he'd set out to alleviate our shortage — not by making sugar, but rather sugar syrup.

Cleaning and preparing sugar beets for syrup-making on a cold fall evening was something neither Ida nor I had ever done. Tossing all other work aside, we followed Papa's lead in scrubbing each beet in tubs of cold water set up by the truck. Stiff brushes had to be used to clean away all traces of dirt. Then, cutting off the tops and bottoms, we passed the beets on to Papa and Erich, who took turns shredding them. Papa had borrowed a shredding board similar to those used to shred cabbage for sauerkraut. None of the work was easy, but seeing how the men struggled with the shredding, the women could hardly grumble.

Once shredded, the beets were rushed into the wash kitchen to be boiled in the same copper kettles used to boil laundry. The cooking process, we learned under Papa's guidance, softened the pulp and draws the juice. Working in assembly line fashion, Ida and I watched the kettles and kept the fires going. Now and then, the men would put a batch into a wine press, also borrowed, then squeezed out the liquid. The latter went back into another kettle to boil down further. The final boiling took hours, until Papa was satisfied with ruby-brown color and consistency of the syrup. It was four in the morning when the last of it was funneled into sterilized wine bottles and corked.

We had beet sugar syrup through the winter, spring and into summer. The greatest pleasure, though, was later that morning, after a few hours sleep. We all dug into steaming bowls of creamy wheat cereal, liberally dosed with fresh

369

syrup. Teasingly, I told Ida it may be well to keep the syrup locked up, considering her husband's sweet tooth.

At the time, my personal hunger was not for sugar, but for bread. There were moments when I felt I could eat a whole three-pound loaf of fresh baked bread without help. When a person's diet isn't well rounded, it's easy to feel that kind of hunger.

The one commodity Papa and Erich wouldn't barter for or buy on the expensive black market were cigarettes. Both smoked moderately when cigarettes were available, but lately that was almost never.

It was not uncommon to see someone along the street quickly bend over, pick up a cigarette butt, and put it in a pocket. It was all accomplished, of course, with the hope that no one saw such behavior. Unfortunately, it was witnessed too often, and a joke was made about: "How low the Germans stoop to get the discarded cigarette butts of the French."

My father found his answer to the problem by buying young tobacco plants in the spring to grow in the garden. The greenhouse allowed him only ten plants, but he was determined to grow and harvest a winter's supply. Enlisted into the project when he began cutting off the larger outer leaves in fall, I was shown how to cut them into fine strips. Papa then sprinkled my output with sugar water, and spread the lot on cookie sheets to dry slowly in the oven. The tobacco had to be turned frequently and kept from drying completely.

I won't forget the first cigarette Papa rolled from his homegrown efforts. Erich, Ida, Peter and I stood in the kitchen, waiting in watchful silence as Papa carefully packed the paper and began to roll. He licked it lengthwise, his fingers gliding along the seam to seal it. He then struck a match. The moment was somewhat akin to watching one of our local wine tasters sniff and 'chew' a new vintage for quality.

Putting one end of the cigarette between his lips, he lit the other end with a flourish. That first puff, I think, had us all involuntarily sucking the thing along with him. His was the only cough though, followed by another drag and a smile of approval.

❧

"I think you should start dancing lessons."

My father's announcement startled me. I knew that both Elfriede and Hannelore were taking lessons.

"I'd like to, Papa. It's just — well, Mama hasn't been dead a year, and we're still in mourning. It wouldn't look right!"

"We've mourned long enough. Your mother wouldn't want you missing out on learning to dance with your friends. Go down tomorrow and see if you can get in."

I had started lessons the previous year with Hannelore. Elfriede's parents wouldn't allow her, saying she was too young and could wait a year. For many reasons, I'd decided to quit at the end of the first lesson. In my mind, I would wait until Elfriede could come along. The year-long mourning period for Mama changed with Papa's decision.

Hannelore insisted on signing up with us. She didn't like Elfriede and I doing something without her. She'd already learned the waltz, polka and slow-fox the previous year. One benefit of having her around was the young men she brought along. She'd met them at village dances in the area, so they came experienced. There were never enough boys in the classes to pair up with all the girls. For once, Elfriede and I had to admit Hannelore had the right idea. There's no doubt I caught on to dancing much quicker in the arms of experience.

The lessons were at the Turnhalle, the town's community center or public hall, and the same place where Henny and I had made such a comic hit playing our Handharmonikas years before. Things had changed for everyone since then.

Another Christmas and New Year slipped by with only a glimmering of brighter days ahead. On the radio in December, we heard of some new economic program approved by the American government that would affect Germany. During the early weeks of 1948 the Marshall Plan, as it became known, had little practical effect on daily life. We had no idea what to expect. The British and American occupation zones were combined early in the year, but that had no impact on those of us still in the French zone. Rumors had it that bigger things were coming, but no one knew exactly what.

The Marshall Plan did have one immediate result — the start of the Cold War and the complete separation of Germany into two states, east and west. By June twenty-fourth, the Soviet Union stopped all land traffic in and out of East Germany. For the Americans, French, and British, that also meant road and rail access to Berlin. Apparently this was the Russian reaction to the Allies announcing earlier their intention to create a federal republic in the western zones. Answering the blockade of Berlin was a massive airlift of supplies to the city that lasted for almost a year. All of this kept the Germans around me nervous. One couldn't afford to miss any news bulletins as long as the crisis lasted.

To divert our attention from the tumult to the east was an event that changed our lives for the better overnight. For us in Kirchheim, it came on June twenty-first. The Nazi Reichmark was dead, replaced by the Deutschmark, and every person in our town was issued sixty of these new Deutschmarks, whatever their financial condition. The new money was considered more stable and brought with it an abundance of consumer products literally within hours.

On June twentieth, passers-by found little or nothing in shop windows or on shelves, a condition that we'd lived with for years. By the next morning, all were filled to overflowing. There were abundant household items, clothing, and other factory goods in every store. Food continued to be rationed and in short supply, but in just twelve hours shops went from scarce to bulging with wearing apparel, books, toys and cookware. There were dolls too, all with perfect legs, unlike the war-time doll Mama ordered for me.

The money change had been publicized, but few people were ready for sights like I found the morning of the big day. Passing a shop window on Langstraße, I froze in my footsteps, my eyes staring in disbelief at a huge display of new cookware not seen since my early childhood. I wondered where had it all come from. While mesmerized by the sight of all the shiny aluminum pots and pans, my mind kept asking the question over and over. Then the truth dawned on me, and I felt my face heat up in anger. The shop owners had been holding out on the townspeople. They had the merchandise all the while, stored away, waiting for the new money.

Papa was angry about the deception, too. He said we would drive to Ludwigshafen to spend our money. We weren't alone in our disgust with local merchants. It took awhile for them to win back customer loyalty. Soon after the money change, Papa and I did go to the Rhein river city and spent every pfennig on clothes. I talked him into getting new shirts he sorely needed. As for me, I would never again have to put on underwear that had been worn by someone else first.

ॐ

The money change reinforced my father's earlier decision about getting back into the trucking business. Orders for his services got to a point where Erich could quit the French gendarmerie job and join Papa in the truck cab. Ida didn't seem too happy with the decision. She thought the job with the French offered security. This bone of contention between a regular paycheck and risky self-employment remained on the back burner for a long time. In the meantime, summer and fall business was so good that we could actually hope for the best Christmas in years. But life wasn't without terrible scares from another direction.

My new sister-in-law shared every chore but one — the raising of Peter was left entirely to me. There was a day in midsummer when I had reason to wonder how well I did the job. At four and a half years old, the loving and obedient boy hadn't yet given me a moment's worry.

He'd taken to watching neighborhood activities from the second floor living room window. In nice weather, I'd open the window so he could see better, and sometimes I joined him in watching children on the block play, and greet neighbors as they past. It was my habit through the day to have him within sight as I worked, but now he wanted to 'watch the other kids' by himself more than ever.

"Annchen, can I sit on the doorstep?"

Erich and my father had taken advantage of the longer summer daylight, and had left right after supper to make a short haul. Ida and I decided to cook up some jam from the gooseberries and currants picked in our garden that morning. We headed down to the wash kitchen, with Peter tagging along as usual. When his question came, I thought it understandable that he had no interest in watching the tedious job of boiling fruit down, so I gave in to his wish. Besides, I had sat on the front door step many times as a child.

"Ja, you can go and sit there, but don't you leave the step. I want to see you when I look down the hall. Understood?"

He gave me his serious nod and ran down the hall, seating himself well in view. I turned to help Ida rinse the fruit. "He'll be fine," I said, making a mental note to check on him every few minutes.

The berries never got into the boiling kettle. An awful commotion reached our ears from the street before we got that far. For a long time afterward, I relived the moment, the sound of a motorcycle engine roaring up the Breitstraße. "It's that damned Günther again," I said, heading for the hallway.

Racing for the front door with Ida right behind me, I was shocked not to see Peter on the step. In seconds, I was through the door and onto the street, but a bloody and limp Peter was already being carried toward us in the arms of Richard Fink, an old classmate of mine who lived up on the Wingertstraße. He must have been passing by when the accident occurred.

Another young man of the neighborhood stood across the street next to his motorcycle, his head bowed. Günther, who lived farther up the street, was always racing his motorcycle up the steep street.

"What happened?" My words, but I knew instantly that Günther had struck Peter. I still cried out the words, maybe hoping that it was all a nightmare, and I would wake up. A crowd was already milling about.

"He's hurt bad, Annchen," Richard said calmly, which had the odd effect of helping me keep any further outburst in check.

"Let me have him, Richard," I begged. Peter was moaning, and I wanted desperately to comfort him.

"Nay! I probably shouldn't have picked him up myself, but I don't think we can wait for the ambulance. He has to get to the hospital now. Come along and hold his head up as we walk."

I knew he was right. Peter could die waiting. There was a terrible bleeding wound on his forehead, and blood ran from both the left arm and right leg. The leg was twisted. Richard held him straight out, like cradling a log, causing the boy's head to flop back and jerk with every step. With one hand, I held his head up as the three of us rushed along over the cobblestones.

The only sound coming from Peter was a soft whimpering. His eyes were open and alert, and I dare not let him see me cry. Richard said I should keep talking to him, something I found difficult in my emotional state. It couldn't be easy on my school friend either, holding Peter out in front of him all the way and trying his best to soften his jarring footsteps. Richard's strength and determination were all that kept me sane racing down winding streets to the hospital, more than a kilometer from the accident. The journey must have taken only ten or twelve minutes, though it seemed like an hour.

By the time we walked through the hospital door, my arm and hand ached with fatigue. I could imagine how Richard felt. Nurses rushed forward to relieve his burden.

Miracles do happen. The one worry we all said aloud approaching the hospital was whether a doctor would be there. He was, but just barely — Dr. Eugen Sießl was walking toward the door to leave for the day. He had Peter in the operating room in only minutes. It was our further luck that Dr. Sießl was a highly regarded surgeon.

We waited and I prayed. Papa had always said that praying was the same as hoping. I had plenty of reason to hope. Richard wanted to wait with us, but I saw no reason and urged him to go home. My thanks, then and later, could never be sufficient for what he did. It was strange how this young man from my school days came back into my life and took command at such a critical time. Since school, we'd barely spoken more than a simple 'hello,' even though he'd been one of the few boys in class I liked. Unfortunately, he was shy, and never showed the least interest in my direction. But after carrying Peter with such strength and care that day, he has had my gratitude for well over fifty years.

While Ida and I waited for news of Peter's condition, Papa and Erich rushed in. They got the news from neighbors upon returning home. What they said to my father must have made him frantic and he had every right to be angry with me. I was, after all, responsible for Peter's safety. The dam holding back my emotions broke soon after Richard left us, and when Papa saw my state, he had not a word of recrimination. Erich held his tongue as well, seeing how stricken Ida was. While I was entirely to blame, she somehow felt responsible too.

The nurse came to tell us that Peter had a bad concussion to the head, his left arm was broken below the elbow, and his right leg broken in two places. He'd lost a lot of blood, and had many bruises and abrasions. That he was alive seemed a miracle. The broken arm had an open wound which had to heal before a cast could be applied. The healing would take two to three weeks, then the arm would be re-broken to be set properly.

As soon as we'd been informed that Peter was out of danger, Papa asked to see Dr. Sießl. He later told us his talk with the doctor covered the boy's injuries and outlook for recovery, and the matter of payment. Having just started up his business, we had no health insurance. A deal was worked out on the spot for a future job hauling some medical equipment for the doctor, and the hospital bill was paid in cash. (It was only later that Germany instituted socialized medicine.)

After a while, the four of us were allowed into the ward to be there when Peter woke up. There were eight beds, all except one occupied by adult men. My father knew a couple of them, and he and Erich visited while Ida and I sat by Peter. Only willpower stopped me from crying out at the sight of the bandages that covered much of the little fellow's head and arms. His right leg was bound in a cast and held up in the air by pulleys and wires.

The waiting was the worst. Terrible thoughts of what I'd done filled my mind. We had been told by the nurse that the boy's head injuries may have caused brain damage. I thought it had to be God's retribution, because I hadn't wanted Peter at first. I tried to keep my sobbing under control, and gritted my teeth, but the tears flowed unabated, wetting my cheeks and the apron I still wore.

"Annchen, don't cry."

It was Peter's little voice, and it seemed to come from my own fierce wish that he'd speak, that he wouldn't be brain damaged. Papa and Erich stepped over, and Ida stood up. My eyes fixed on the bandaged face, not really expecting what was there. Only one eye showed, and it was looking straight at me. His little tongue kept darting out, moistening his parted lips.

"Annchen — — "

"Ja, Peter, I'm here. And here's Papa and Erich, and Ida, too."

"Annchen, don't cry."

I couldn't believe my ears. He was in such pain, and he didn't want me to cry! I forced a smile for him. "I'm alright, Peterchen." The words tumbled out as I fumbled to wipe my cheeks. "Do you hurt bad? We can get the nurse to give you something."

"My arm — it hurts." His eye moved from the arm to the elevated leg, but he made no further comment.

He looked in awful shape. I wanted to touch him, but dared not, fearing I'd cause more pain. The other three around the bed didn't say much of anything to Peter, maybe because he wouldn't stop looking at me. I did see Papa's smile of encouragement and love, but he, too, was afraid to touch him. His hand just patted the bed near the uninjured leg. Soon he stepped out to speak to a nurse, who followed him back in with medication. She didn't say what, but it was the tiniest pill I'd ever seen.

"That will help him sleep," she said, checking the head bandage and the broken arm that couldn't yet be in a cast. She suddenly looked at the four of us, badly shaken and looking it, and a smile brightened her face. "Don't worry. He'll be well taken care of here." She motioned to the room with her hand. "These fellows will let the nurses know quickly if Peter needs us."

I followed the movement of her arm, looking for the first time at each man there. It was comforting to note that most of them didn't look that bad off and would, indeed, be aware of my beloved brother.

❧

Peter couldn't have been in better hands. The nursing staff, and the patients who came and went over his seven-weeks stay, adopted the boy with total heart. My family would learn many reasons to be thankful for all their kindnesses. We could see the result of constant attention during daily visits over the weeks that followed. In time, we all began to wonder if the abundant loving care wasn't spoiling him. He never cried when our visits ended. It may have been my imagination, but sometimes he looked too happy when I left.

❧

The boy was in the hospital just a couple weeks when I was invited to do sewing for pay. Tante Lisbeth in Bolanden and Tante Sannchen in Gauersheim asked that I come weekly to their homes to mend clothing on their own machines. I never learned if Papa was behind it, but I'd been moping around the house about Peter. He said it would be good for me to get away from the house twice a week, and earn my first pocket money in the bargain. I liked sewing, not to mention the pleasant company of my aunts. Mending work pants and such, however, wasn't the most challenging work. After a time, it became boring. My answer was to come up with a grand fantasy with every push of the pedal. It wasn't very realistic, but it was nice for a little while to dream of becoming the 'great clothes designer Anna Klein.' It helped pass the time until Lisbeth or Sannchen brought me tea and conversation.

I'd been giving a lot of thought to my future. Clothing design really appealed to me, though I hadn't the slightest idea how to go about doing it. Earlier attempts to have a seamstress take me on as an apprentice had failed. Times were bad, and there wasn't enough work. If Elfriede and Hannelore were unhappy with their lives, they never said. I didn't speak to them of my discontent either. The reality was that my father needed me for a few years, or until he remarried. He'd recently mentioned some casual interest in a widowed lady. If he did marry, all I could see was a blank page for me.

Ida was saying I should start dating — in short, find a husband. That wasn't for me. Marriage meant diapers, and I wanted no part of more diapers. Not for many years.

Peter's recovery was amazing. His last two weeks in the hospital were mainly spent in therapy, and he performed so well that they let him home early. Except for some scars, he was entirely well again, both in body and spirit. As December approached, Papa thought the boy should get a visit from Pelznickel, as I had at about his age.

The old man who played the part for me had died years before. I volunteered, much to Erich's disbelief. With a little help from my friends, a long black hooded cloak was found. Someone came up with a scraggly white beard and mustache, and I went to work to make it all fit me. Easiest to find were a tall staff and long chain. As December sixth drew near, a few cookies were set aside from those we'd begun to bake. In Peter's absence, I practiced my gruff old man's voice on Ida. When he was around, we talked about 'old Pelznickel,' and wondered aloud if he'd show up again.

On the evening of the appointed day, everyone worked hard at making all seem normal, but I worried about Erich. The supper dishes were cleaned up. Papa buried his nose in the newspaper, and Erich got Peter interested in tuning in radio programs.

"I hope no one minds," I said finally. "But I did promise Elfriede a short visit tonight."

"Sure, sure. You go ahead," Papa said.

Erich gave me a wicked smile, and stuck out his tongue.

"You run along," Ida urged. "We'll put Peter to bed later."

I left, but not for Elfriede's. Going out the courtyard door, I moved quietly over to the workshop building. Since a light could be seen from the kitchen window, I had to ease along in the dark to where the costume was hidden. My foot caught on what turned out to be a long steel pipe. Luckily, I grabbed it before disaster happened — namely a clanking, crashing noise to ruin my deception. The pipe hadn't been there before, which aroused my suspicions.

Once in disguise, the return to the kitchen went undetected, right up until my loud knock on the door. All in all, it wasn't a bad performance. Peter was completely fooled. All his reactions were like my own on that long ago evening in Marnheim. Shock was followed by acceptance. I faltered just once, but he didn't seem to notice.

When I asked if he'd been good, he nodded. Then, in my best stern voice, I asked, "And the family, have they been good?"

"Our sister Annchen hasn't been good," came a taunt from Erich, who was sitting safely out of my reach.

Before I could say something out of character, Peter had already turned, raising a hand as if to strike his older brother.

"She is good," he shouted. "Annchen is a good girl." He turned back to me. "Don't believe him!"

I could have hugged and kissed him, but satisfied myself with handing over the sack of cookies and making a quick exit. Closing the door, I heard Ida and Papa laughing and applauding my performance.

For everyone, having Peter whole and well again was the best Christmas gift of all.

As for that long steel pipe so carelessly left in the work shop for me to trip, I never did discover whether Erich was the culprit.

Chapter Thirty-Six

Harry S. Truman started a second term as President of the United States in 1949. Most Germans around me didn't pay all that much attention to American politics, except to that which might affect our situation. From what I could tell, Truman's re-election was considered good for us. The positive mood about him probably came from his support of making the western zones stronger economically and creating a German democratic government. Certainly the western allies had more practical reasons behind their new attitude, aside from comfort and prosperity for West Germans. One bad outcome of this development for us was the increase in cold war tensions with the Soviet Union. The Russians still held many hundreds of German prisoners. At the time, I cared not at all about the politics of it. My family and friends desired only peace, and a chance to walk tall again.

Inside my own four walls, another kind of cold war had started — one which I had about as much power over as the turmoil outside between the east and west. The widowed woman Papa showed some interest in didn't work out, in spite of once bringing her to the house to become acquainted. I got the feeling that, nice as she appeared to us, she pushed my father too hard toward marriage. Instead, he turned an eye toward a woman on the Langstraße who I also knew slightly. Frau Rolf had a small housewares shop, an offshoot of her late husband's plumbing business. He had died in the war. My mother and I both knew the woman and thought well of her.

The problem came from Ida. She was outspoken about Papa spending so much time with Frau Rolf and not helping Erich enough in the business. It was true that Papa let my brother take care of more hauling jobs, though it didn't seem too much to me. Erich seemed to enjoy being more responsible. Ida felt otherwise, and kept up her attacks on Papa with extreme words. Through it all, I sat on the fence. I'd grown to like Ida very much, and tried to understand her viewpoint while trying to do the same for Papa.

I knew how he hated disharmony in the family, so it shouldn't have surprised me when the decision came. One evening, following another blast from his daughter-in-law, he stood up from the supper table and looked each of us over. Since Erich and I made no effort to defend him against her criticism, his disappointment was complete. If she'd attacked my father personally, I'd have been the first on my feet shouting her down. What she attacked was his ongoing romance, something I, too, was unsure about. She said it put an undue burden on her husband. Again I didn't defend Papa, choosing instead to say nothing. It must have hurt him deeply.

"If this is how all of you feel," he said slowly, "I'll arrange to move out tomorrow. Frau Rolf will be glad to have me. You can stay in my house, but I'll take Peter with me!"

Just the idea of my father leaving his own house stabbed my heart. That it meant losing Peter also twisted the knife. I don't know why I didn't speak out. It was crazy for him to go. If Ida and Erich were that unhappy, I thought, they should leave. But Papa had given it more thought than we knew. Obviously, his son had no means of support and no place to go. He knew Frau Rolf would take him in, along with anyone he wanted to bring along.

"Annchen," he said, almost pleadingly. "You can come along with me too. It's up to you."

"But there is hardly any room down there. Where would I sleep?"

My initial reaction was to go with my father, then I thought of Frau Rolf's house. Aside from the small shop fronting on the street, the living quarters didn't amount to much. I had recently socialized with the young girl Frau Rolf had hired as a live-in maid. Her tiny room, I was shocked to learn, was under the stairs leading to the attic. I tried to picture myself in such a tight space not much bigger than a closet.

"I'm sure a room won't be a problem," he said reassuringly. "For a while, you may have to share a bedroom with Peter. You won't mind that, will you?"

Before I could reply, Ida jumped in with something I had not thought about. "Don't go! You will just be Frau Rolf's new maid, and it won't be easy to leave like all the others have?"

"It's not true," Papa shot back. "Naturally, you'll have to help with the chores, but that's no different than you do now."

My head was spinning, and I was speechless. After a minute, I sat down and looked from one to the other. Peter, who had been listening to all of it in silent wonder, scooted off his chair to come stand by me.

"Papa, I have to think. Why does any of this have to happen? Everything was going so well. Maybe tomorrow I'll know what to do."

"You mull it over," he answered, walking toward the door. "I'll be back for my things tomorrow, and you can tell me then."

It wasn't until after Papa left, apparently to stay the night at Frau Rolf's, that Ida spoke again. "Why don't you get Peter in bed, then come back. Erich and I want to talk to you."

Helping Peter prepare for bed I felt numb again, and wondered whether Mama had been right that happiness always turns into despair. I stayed with Peter for awhile, holding him tight. I knew he alone would be going with Papa, and it was sure to make him cry, so I said nothing. I couldn't handle tears on his last night in the only house he had known. He fell asleep, and I returned to the kitchen.

Papa had also made it clear, when he announced the move to Frau Rolf's, that there wouldn't be an immediate marriage. She was afraid of losing her widow's war pension. He would keep the truck and pay Erich for his share. Ida didn't scream about that, and I knew why. She had often talked of getting her husband into a nice payroll job in a factory. The small 'share' amount expected from Papa would force the issue.

Meanwhile, the two of them thought I had to be worked on to stay at Breitstraße One. Returning to the kitchen, I let the words fly at me, but I already knew my course. Going with my father meant leaving the house I loved so much, and Ida's argument that the arrangement with Frau Rolf was immoral also had an impact.

"What will the neighbors think?" That question still guided my life in 1949. The moral codes had not yet changed in towns like Kirchheim. Living as man and wife without church sanction, while not illegal, was considered immoral. At nineteen years of age, if I went to live under the same roof, I would be labeled immoral. All the love for my father couldn't overcome an impossible situation.

When Papa returned the next day to collect his and Peter's clothes, I told him my decision with real heartbreak. I felt even worse for my little brother — he was so confused about it all when I walked with him down the Langstraße to his new home. Our father was already there unloading things from the truck. At the door, and with Frau Rolf looking on, I told Peter of how he was now going to live here — in the simplest of terms.

"It's going to be fine. I'll stop by often to see you. And, remember it's not very far to Breitstraße. Sometimes you can come to see us."

He didn't cry, though for a moment I thought he would. We hugged, and I made a fast retreat up the hill.

The next day, I went out to find a job. I was too old to apprentice in any German business, which wouldn't have paid much anyway. Erich directed me to a French army office, where I was approved to work as a maid. This led to a half day job with a French family, an army adjutant and his wife and child in a local apartment. He had the very un-French name of Schönenberger, and could speak excellent German. I discovered that he came from the Alsace-Lorraine region of France, which bordered Germany. His wife welcomed my house-cleaning help, but I soon found that she hated Germans.

She called us 'Boche,' a derogatory name meaning swine. Little Jean-Pierre, called me that whenever I tried to interact with him. The four year old was already well taught in his mother's hatred. I didn't try to fight it, at least not in any obvious way.

Madame Schönenberger loved to knit. I heard the click of needles upon arrival, and right through washing a pile of dishes, scrubbing laundry in the bathtub, and other chores awaiting me each day.

I left around noon, and often to the same sound. I wondered at times whether Madame clicked her way through bath, lovemaking and sleep. Perhaps I was a bit jealous, not being able to knit all day myself, and because what she produced, I had to admit, was beautifully done. Having to wash many of the garments, close inspection of her designs and patterns left no doubt that I was far behind in my knitting ability. After a few months, I did find courage to ask her to show me how to do a particular pattern I liked. Her quick agreement surprised me, as she wasn't the most gracious or generous of ladies.

Being a maid to the Schönenbergers was never a pleasant task. I couldn't understand how they could get through an entire weekend without washing a pot or pan — not to forget the sink full of dishes I faced every Monday. The Madame had also filled the bathtub with all kinds of clothes to soak — from work pants to fine underwear and blouses — with no attention to separation of colors.

Perhaps an older, more experienced maid would have forced a change in the habits of her bosses. I worked for Schönenbergers from July of 1949 to July of 1950 without complaint, at least to them. But Ida and my girlfriends got a regular earful. I did try to think of the positive side. It was only a half-day task, and as my first job, I worked toward getting a good recommendation for my next job.

To help fill out a day, I hired myself out to work afternoons for local farmers. Often, Ida went with me. The pay wasn't much — 32 pfennigs an hour — but I found the work more satisfying than doing the Schönenberger laundry. Farmers such as Josef up the street always needed extra hands in spring, summer and fall.

I considered both jobs menial, and a far cry from Papa's rosy predictions. One way I fought off the gloom of this reality was to give myself over completely to weekend dancing. A local revival of the American big band sound coincided with my predicament, and every band in the area took up the music with fervor. The long drought in displays of public gaiety had ended in 1948, and weekend dances in Kirchheim and the surrounding villages suddenly became a draw for young people. Having finished with dancing lessons, and no longer responsible for Peter, I was more than ready.

Initially, I did more listening than dancing to the music. Shyness was part of it, but mostly I loved to just hear what we called 'swing' music. Local bands playing the area learned fast that few young people liked to polka and waltz. We wanted the Woodchopper's Ball and the One O'clock Jump, and certainly nothing slower than Moonlight Serenade. Some groups played American big band better than others. Villages like Orbis, a short walk through the forest from Kirchheim, got to be a hot spot for dancing because the band there sounded great. They had six or seven musicians, while most groups had only four or five on the bandstand. Naturally, none of them could match the real Benny Goodman or Glenn Miller, but we didn't care. Just as long as they came close to the original, we happily danced the night away.

The best dance band of all was right in Kirchheim at the Turnhalle. My first music teacher, Fritz Keitel, had formed a twelve-member band that played nearly every week, loading the hall with so many dancers that my friends and I rarely found room at a table. But once I started dancing, sitting down didn't appeal anyway. I wanted to be on the dance floor often, and with as many different partners as I could entice to ask me. For a long time I never went to a dance with a man, though many tried to be my exclusive partner. My only company to and from the dance halls were Elfriede, Hannelore, and other girls from my school days or the neighborhood. We'd all show up as a group, buy tickets, and stand inside the entrance hall waiting to be asked by single fellows, who were usually standing around gathering courage to ask.

Older people, including many married couples, came to the dances. They were the ones who took up the table space. Some danced to the slower tunes, but mostly they came to hear the music, drink, and sing along. Occasionally, married men, fortified with wine, would come up to the girls asking for a dance. My group had a favorite way of handling them. We'd laugh very loud and shout over the music, "Go back and ask your wife!" That did the trick.

For more than a year, no matter how bad the week went, nothing got in the way of Saturday nights and my craze for dancing. Most often my friends and I stayed in Kirchheim, but every so often we'd make walking visits to other village dance halls for a change of pace. Kirchheim was surrounded by many villages of all sizes. Oberwiesen, Gauersheim, Marnheim, Bischheim, Bolanden, and Orbis are only a few of these. Orbis was quite a hike, so I usually tried to convince Erich to drive us over. Soon after the family break-up, and refusing to listen to Ida's wishes to get a payroll job, my brother had found an old truck to begin chasing his own dream.

Since Erich was a non-dancer, he'd just drop us off. We'd then get home however we could. Sometimes a nicely infatuated farm boy was more than willing to pull us home on a wagon behind a tractor. Otherwise we walked, getting home at about four in the morning. Once I convinced Erich to drive a big group of us, girls and boys, all the way to Bad Dürkheim, some forty kilometers away. We had heard of a special dance that was part of the annual Wurstmarkt carnival, and of course, we had to go. On that jaunt, my brother had to stay and bring us home, so Ida came along. Neither liked to dance that much, but there were lots of other attractions to occupy them. A number of young men from around the vicinity jumped at the chance to go, no doubt encouraged by Hannelore. It was a bumpy ride on the bed of the truck, but we made it a gay affair singing all the way. Coming home, the bumping and swaying of the truck had a bad affect on the few who'd overindulged all evening. Mixing dancing and drink was something I didn't do. Erich didn't enjoy cleaning the mess that came from those who'd relieved their agony over the sides of the truck bed. The Wurstmarkt trip was the last time my brother chauffeured to a dance for anyone other than the always sober Elfriede and me.

It didn't take long to discover that shyness and dancing are sorry companions. Conquering the first to enjoy the second required some fast education on the art of being fun, but not too friendly toward partners looking for more than a dance. Hannelore liked to tease the boys, always looking for romance. Elfriede and I made it known up front that we'd come only to dance. If we decided to do some kissing along the way, we made sure roaming hands stayed put. Shocked the first time a hand landed in forbidden territory, I lashed out at the poor fellow with a chopping blow much harder than needed. He still nursed a bruised arm the next Saturday.

The incident had a happy ending. At the next dance the victim of my outrage cautiously approached to ask for a turn. He looked so apologetic, I couldn't refuse. After all, he was one of the better dancers.

"How is your arm?" I managed the question as we began a fast swing step.

"It still hurts," he hollered, twirling me around.

"That'll teach you to beware of girls with older brothers," I shouted, laughing. "We learn early about self-defense!"

"I should say so," he shot back. "I had to tell my mother that I accidentally shut the barn door on my arm!"

That's all it took. We both started laughing so hard, it was useless to go on with the dance. There would be other dances, but no romance. Maybe he shouldn't have introduced me to Kurt from a nice family in Oberwiesen. Kurt was clearly interested in me, but after the first blush of being flattered, I immediately backed off. He was the first of several kind and thoughtful young men whose desire for something permanent scared me away. When laughter and music turned to tender looks and serious talk, the dreaded sound of wedding bells pounded my ears.

Following Kurt's attentions, I set my eyes on his cousin Karl, another regular at the dance halls. A local shepherd who was also a good dancer and fun person, Karl was lusted after by most of the females. He, in turn, was in love with my friend Elfriede. She didn't feel the same, and brushed him off, which I found hard to understand. But her loss was my gain, and I went after him.

I threw myself into the weekly dances looking for a happy respite following another week of demeaning work for the Schönenbergers. Fun-loving Karl made it easy for anyone to forget their miseries for an evening. The son of an Oberwiesen farmer, he was my age, tall and good looking in a happy sort of way. Karl seemed to be smiling or laughing most of the time. His congenial ways were just beginning to make him widely known and welcome at any community social function. If the other fellows were jealous of his popularity with the girls on the dance floor, they were hard put to show it, since they liked him too. Besides, until Elfriede, and later me, everyone understood he came for the fun of dancing, not to steal someone's girlfriend. It was a lucky girl who got to dance with him twice.

I think he took a longer look at my friend because she was a farm girl. In those days, it was expected for farm boys to marry farm girls. Sadly for Karl, he learned that Elfriede had enough of farm labor. There would not be shearing of sheep for her. I had even less interest in being a farmer's wife, but I found myself attracted to the happy shepherd. Perhaps, his humor reminded me of Papa.

That such a fantastic dancer had decided on raising sheep also sparked my curiosity. His flock, then numbering a hundred animals, had started with just a half dozen when he was fourteen. He said that while he had no experience with sheep, he knew by the eighth grade that shepherding was for him.

All the reasons feeding my interest in Karl were the same ones for pulling away when the relationship took on serious overtones. My views on being a shepherd's wife hadn't changed at all, but more important was one more discovery — he couldn't stop flirting with other girls. The break up didn't bother him at all, and we remained friendly enough to enjoy an occasional dance.

Ș

When going to a dance in Oberwiesen, we usually walked the five kilometers from Kirchheim, taking forest paths instead of the longer road route. Returning along the same path at two in the morning provided thrills of an eerie sort, but when the three of us linked arms, all fears dissolved. The darkest path couldn't shake our sense of immortality. This all changed the Saturday night Hannelore deserted our partnership.

We should have seen it coming. Hannelore had been acting crazier than usual about a particular young man from the village, and he and his parents convinced her to stay overnight with them following the dance. Our pleas to come home with us fell on deaf ears, and we sadly prepared to set off without her. A group of fellows gathered around Elfriede and I, alerted by our fuss with Hannelore. At first, some of them offered to escort the two of us on the forest journey. We refused the offers, being more afraid of them in a lonely forest than other possible dangers. Walking us to the edge of the village, the betting began, most of it in good-natured fun.

Ernst, the shortest among them, started it. "I'll bet half-a-Mark some wild boar is going to make a five-minute meal of them!" (At the time, a Mark was worth about twenty-five cents.)

"That's five minutes longer than it would take to swallow you," I heard Karl gleefully answer. Then he added his own taunt, "I'll bet a Mark they come running back before reaching the first tree."

Elfriede whipped around to confront the tall shepherd. Waving her finger under his nose, and with an edge in her voice, she mocked him. "If we're only worth one Mark to you, we'll take that bet and raise it to twenty!" She turned to me. "Won't we?"

With a roar of laughter rising all around him, Karl shouted, "That's too much. All bets are off!"

As the laughing died behind us, we made our way across a small valley meadow and stopped to gather courage before entering the forest. Looking back, the moon was bright enough for us to see the fellows, still standing where we'd left them. They saw us as well, for the hollering began again. "Come back. You're doomed!" The words echoed across the grassy slope, al-

386

ready wet with dew. We turned away and plunged into a pathway not quite as familiar as hoped.

We'd gone only a few meters when Elfriede, her arm already linked tightly in mine, moved closer. The path was plenty wide enough for walking three-abreast.

"You're not afraid, are you?" I said in a whisper.

"Nay, not really," she said, squeezing my arm harder and picking up the pace. "It won't hurt to walk a little faster though, just in case Ernst is right about wild boar!"

I saw no reason to practically run and perhaps stumble in the shadowy gloom. "We don't have to go this fast," I said, slowing my step and loosening her hold. "Erich says wild boar only attack if they're cornered. I think we should —"

Just off the trail a few meters from us, a loud grunt that only a hog could make, stopped my tongue in mid-sentence. It took but another second for two very scared females to jump toward what appeared to be a large tree. In hindsight our actions would not have kept an angry boar from mauling us, if that was the goal. A boar's sense of smell makes sight unnecessary in finding an intruder in darkness.

Getting as close as physically possible to the tree and each other, we held our breath and waited in silence. It provided a chance, the first since entering the wooded domain, to really hear the sounds of the forest at night. There was a thumping in the distance, perhaps a small deer pawing the earth. Above our heads a sudden flutter of wings was followed by a scampering of small feet over leaves and debris on the forest floor. One could imagine a mouse or other small creature rushing to avoid the claws of a hungry owl. Insects and birds called to each other, and the boar's grunts could still be heard, though growing fainter.

Cautiously stepping back on the trail, I said, "I wanted to suggest earlier that we should sing. It'll give the animals advance notice that we are here." Elfriede laughed, took my arm in an easier hold, and began singing at the top of her voice. I joined in, and by the time we broke into another meadow near the village of Orbis, our terrible noise must have scared off every living creature within earshot. It was four in the morning.

Not long after our memorable jaunt we both got invitations to a wedding. Hannelore's decision to marry came as no surprise.

છે

Papa had paid Erich a thousand Deutschmarks for his share in the business when they broke up. It amounted to about 250 dollars at that time, certainly not enough to buy a truck of his own. Approaching a local bank for a loan, he was refused. The bank demanded collateral, and he had none. Papa had already taken a big loan to buy his truck, using the house as collateral. An angry tension took over Breitstraße One. Besides not wanting her husband to stay in trucking, Ida let everyone know her opinion about Papa.

She begged and nagged Erich to get a job with BASF, a huge chemical conglomerate in Ludwigshafen. Many Kirchheim men worked there, commuting by train, but my brother was more than adamant about remaining independent. It was a family tradition with both the Kleins and Herbsts. Very few family men had worked on a payroll over the generations, and Erich was determined to keep it that way.

He finally traveled to Worms, where he walked into the biggest automobile and truck dealership in the city. The owner found himself confronted by a determined and very persuasive young man. After some minutes of give and take, he finally agreed to finance Erich's purchase of a used truck. Considering that there were few trucks still on the road driven by wood gas, one might wonder who got the better deal. The vehicle was truly a relic from the early days of mechanized transport. No doubt the people at the garage expected to see it back on the lot again soon, ready for another dreamer without cash. If so, they wrongly judged the true mechanic stoking wood as he drove back to Kirchheim.

The truck looked like most five-ton trucks, but had a few marked differences. Just behind the cab, on the driver's side, was a boiler tank containing a large chamber for wood, and a smaller fire chamber below. No water was used. The start up process required ten minutes. When the wood in the upper chamber reached the right temperature, gas was created and sent to the engine.

Other local truckers, owners of gas or diesel models, heard about Erich's 'antique,' and would stop by the house to see it. Many were disappointed, because Erich would be gone, working the truck and making money. In time, he paid it off and bought a used diesel, keeping the woodburner for parts. People had snickered about the wood gas relic, but my brother told me there were only two problems with it. It stunk to high heaven and had no power on hills. Otherwise, he loved the beast.

Around mid-1949, with Erich struggling to survive on his own and Ida continuing to bad mouth Papa, the occasional visits by Peter came to an abrupt stop. Word was sent up from the Langstraße that he wouldn't be allowed to see us. Frau Rolf had heard of Ida's negative comments. I didn't like all of the bad things my sister-in-law said about Papa's living arrangements, but at the time, her strong personality overwhelmed me. Except when it came to the question of working for himself, Erich also lacked the strength to go up against his wife.

Frau Rolf's reaction quieted Ida for a while, but that didn't help the hurt when Peter ran away from me one day. Walking into the town center, I caught sight of the boy and called out. I was so happy to see him, and just wanted to talk. Instead of coming to me, he ran back in the direction of the Rolf house. It tore my heart so, I had to find a place to cry.

The situation drove me harder to find more work and more fun. Mornings I worked at Schönenbergers, and when farmers no longer needed me after the summer harvest, I found another cleaning job to fill the afternoons. This time my employer was only a few steps from the house, and a German. Frau Klag owned a butcher shop on the Freier Platz. Her husband had been the butcher, but when he failed to return from the war, she hired a man to do the work while she ran the shop. My job was to clean the upstairs living quarters. It was no more than another maid's position, but at least Frau Klag's demands were in line with my own knowledge of a German household.

As much as a child pays attention to such things growing up, the Klags and their meat market were familiar to me. Both Mama and I had bought there through the years. Being a part-time maid for the widow had never entered my mind. When she asked, I grabbed at the chance to earn more money while keeping my mind off family problems. The pay wasn't any better than at the Schönenberger's, but Frau Klag was a pleasant woman whose criticisms and compliments came in equal measure. One memory that stays with me about my time with her involved another former classmate of mine.

The back of the apartment overlooked the courtyard much like our layout at home, except the back of the butcher shop closed off one side. The house, another building with animal stalls, and a wall completed the enclosure. The concrete floor was easily washed down and swept after an animal had been taken out from a stall and slaughtered. I avoided being anywhere near a window to observe the scene whenever that happened.

Alfons was an apprentice of the butcher, and usually the one who did all the dirty work, like washing down the courtyard after a slaughter. One day, to my surprise, I watched him bring out from a stall an old cow. Curious about the small, wiry young man's behavior, I stopped my cleaning to watch. Alfons had not to my knowledge ever killed an animal — not by himself anyway, and he was alone. Leaving the docile animal standing by the back door of the butcher shop he stepped from my view, then after a moment he returned and placed something on the cow's forehead. Shocked because I knew what that object was in his hand, I couldn't avert my eyes in time to avoid seeing what happened. I wanted to scream out, "Since when are you allowed to do that?" It would have been too late and drowned out by the shot.

Normally the gun-like tool, properly used, will instantly fell an animal. This time all hell erupted. Alfons hadn't reckoned on a last-second jerk of the cow's head, and severely wounded the poor beast instead of killing it. It was all the young apprentice could do to jump away from the charging, very angry animal as it crashed into walls, knocked over benches loaded with pots and pans, and cause a ruckus that must have been heard far and wide. I even backed away from the window, fearing the animal might somehow crash into my second floor refuge.

The next sound brought me back to look out on a worsening scene. Alfons had climbed a heavy drain pipe coming down from the roof gutter, while an enraged butcher who'd rushed from the shop, dodged and chased the still rampaging cow. He kept trying to reload the killing tool, screaming swear words at a shaking Alfons, who still clung to the pipe. Finally, he got the animal into position for a fatal shot. That should have ended the racket, but the butcher wasn't through yet with his young assistant. Marching over to the downspout, he ordered the boy down and quickly grabbed him by the shirt with one big blood-stained hand. His other hand chopped through air all around the poor lad's head, while raging on about his stupidity. Alfons saw the same thing I did, and probably had the same fear. His eyes never left the waving fist that still held the killing tool.

છે

In late fall, we got the awful news. Papa had run over and killed a young girl with his truck. The tragedy occurred after he'd completed a delivery in Bolanden and he was backing up to leave. He'd seen a group of children playing nearby, but was unaware when a couple of them ran over to jump up and hang on to the tailgate. The girl fell. The screams of witnesses were all that told him that something had gone terribly wrong.

The court later found him innocent in the girl's death, but already his life had changed forever. He couldn't rid his mind of having killed her. Not even war had made him take a life. He blamed himself for not having someone make sure that the children stayed clear. Perhaps his despair could have been eased if the village people, his lifelong friends, had rallied to him. Only our family members remained loyal. Papa was depressed, and decided to stop driving and take on a hired man. When Erich heard of it, he predicted that history would repeat itself. During the war, when my father had taken on a hired driver to work in his absence, our trucking business rapidly failed. Wages and increased equipment failures, ate up all the profits.

About this time, a happy announcement came from Breitstraße One. I thought it was wonderful, though in the beginning, Ida vehemently disagreed. She was pregnant. The idea undoubtedly scared her, as it does for some women the first time around. The situation was such that she also believed they weren't financially ready. The man responsible pooh-poohed her fears, saying he was ready to have a son. A more than even chance the child could be a girl had never entered his mind.

On April 9, 1950, a girl, Brunhilde, joined the family.

In July, Adjutant Schönenberger informed me of his immediate transfer back to his home area of Straßbourg. He asked me if I would come along and be his family's maid on a live in, full-time basis. In spite of my huge desire to see something new, I wasn't at all fond of his wife. There was a new little girl at home to do things for, and many fun nights of dancing ahead.

I didn't mention those as reasons for refusing, and though he was disappointed, he wrote a nice letter of recommendation and arranged a job interview. This time I was directed to a French battalion headquarters located in the villa of the Schloßgarten. Adjutant Montuir spoke to me in broken German for a few minutes, then sent me alone to discuss the position with his wife. They lived in a spacious apartment overlooking our ancient cemetery where I'd once performed exercises in the Nazi youth group. It had long been turned into a play area, which became handy as my new family included three children. Madame Montuir, to my great relief, was a gracious, lovely woman. Her kind manner quickly put me at ease as we conversed in a stumbling mix of languages. In less than ten minutes, she asked me to come not half days, but all day. Something told me to say yes, and she immediately brought out the children for proper introduction, followed by a tour of the apartment and an explanation of my duties.

The children were polite and attentive. I thought it would be a headache dealing with them only in French. I was wrong. They soon became charming teachers of the language, improving my skills. Nine-year-old Roger was an older brother to four-year-old twins, Jean-Jacques and Regine. As for the apartment and my duties, I didn't trust my ears when Madame said she would help in all the work and that I would eat my meals at the table with them. I learned she was a woman of her word the following Monday when I became a daytime part of the Montuir family. Unlike my previous French employer who'd used me strictly for cleaning, Madame Montuir not only assisted in the work, she brought me into the caring of the children and food preparation. Her name was Helen, and her husband's name was Roger. I addressed them only as 'Madame' and 'Adjutant.' She called me 'Anni,' a name I had to get used to.

Madame was very specific about every aspect of her life — the children, house, food, and clothes. My day began at 8 a.m., after breakfast at home. It usually ended following the evening meal clean-up around six o'clock. If they had a military or social function to attend, I'd stay on with young Roger and the twins until their return.

Every morning around ten, without fail, Madame presented everyone with two squares of chocolate to eat. I remember how this ritual continued to surprise me for weeks. It didn't matter if I was hanging out a window washing it or under a bed dusting, there would come a tap on whatever part of my body she could reach, followed by a smile, and an extended hand holding the chocolate morsels.

Noon and evening meals were prepared from scratch, the French way, and she insisted I learn about the foods and methods of cooking. Naturally, some things I loved, and others I could only tolerate. French cheeses were all wonderful. Strange to me were the seafoods that proved to be a struggle from plate to mouth. Snails tasted like tender pieces of veal, but it didn't help — I saw the little creatures before cooking. Still, I would try anything for Madame at least once. I could do no less for someone who generously taught and respected me as a person. As our relationship developed, she refused to call me a maid. "You are not my maid," she'd say, in her lovely French-accented German. "You are Anni, and we work together!"

She treated me more like a daughter, and I was soon comfortable eating at the family table. It took a little longer to feel at ease at the Madame's frequent afternoon coffees. She enjoyed friendship with a few select women, wives of other soldiers in the French command. One or two were often invited to come for coffee, perhaps twice a week. On my first such occasion, I expected to have on a little white apron and do the serving, but when the guests arrived, I was formally introduced, sans apron, as simply 'Anni.'

After we both served refreshments, she invited me to sit with them. Until I got a better grip on the language, the conversation made my head swim.

Whenever Madame was invited to a friend's apartment for coffee, I didn't attend. I stayed with the children — usually just the twins — as Roger went to a French school established in town. At age ten, he was sent to a boarding school in Mainz, and came home on the weekends. I missed the lad, but the twins were a joy and the daily outings a special pleasure. The little boy and girl weren't identical in appearance or personality. Jean-Jacques was slightly taller, while Regine was quicker in mind and body. In behavior and sweet nature, however, they were adorably the same.

There was one small, constant tug-of-war between the lady of the house and me. She wanted to learn German, and I wanted to speak French. She usually won out, insisting on knowing how to say this or that in German the whole day. Over the months, it dawned on me that I was picking up a lot of French in the process. Maybe it wasn't an unfair exchange at all. Madame also asked about my life, and expressed interest in visiting Breitstraße One. I'd only been working perhaps a month or two when the matter came up. Talking to Ida, I found her delighted by the idea of meeting this 'different French woman' that I talked about nightly. So it was arranged. One fine fall afternoon, I escorted Madame and the twins to coffee with Ida and baby Brunhilde. The two women hit it off so well that the visits to Breitstraße became a regular occurrence.

In the meantime, and in spite of my good luck in finding the Montuir family, the idea of spending my life as a maid or paid housekeeper depressed me. Though I felt happy anticipation going to work each morning, I just had to be careful not to become too settled in.

Chapter Thirty-Seven

I'd been home from Montuirs just minutes when more upsetting news about Papa rushed through the kitchen door. Ida was attending to Brunhilde's evening bath while Erich sat at the table studying the well-worn manual for his truck. My usual talk with Ida about the day's events had just begun when running footsteps on the stairs made me stop. Ingrid, the teenage daughter of Frau Rolf, practically burst through the door. Out of breath from running up the hill, her eyes darted to each of us as the words came out like a series of small explosions. "Your Papa is in the hospital. He's had a stroke!"

How could it be? Papa was not even fifty years old. Looking at my brother and then at Ida, I could see they were thinking the same thing. Adding to our shock was just seeing the young girl standing in our kitchen. I knew Ingrid, and had nothing against her personally, but the break between our families was complete. We no longer spoke when meeting in public. Her message had shattered that silence. Surely it had to be a true emergency to bring her into our house.

When we got to his hospital room, Papa tried to smile for our benefit. The familiar grin I'd known all my life was now oddly lopsided, and sad to see. The nurse told us before we went in that he was paralyzed on the left side and that he wouldn't be able to talk. Apparently, my father wasn't about to let that stop an effort to greet us. All that came forth was a babble of sound.

He finally stopped, chuckling at his own futile struggle. With his good hand, he gestured for me to come to his right side. I couldn't say anything, but buried my face in his half-embrace.

When Madame Montuir heard about Papa, she generously urged me to make short visits to the hospital during work. It was less than a block from the apartment, so it was possible to do without too much disruption. Visitation wasn't quite the same as when Peter was hospitalized. While I looked in on Papa two and three times a day, Erich and Ida went less often. Understandable, I thought. Ida had Brunhilde to care for, and my brother seemed to work day and night. I crossed paths with Frau Rolf and Ingrid on occasion, and our conversations were short, stiff and polite. "Fritz is looking better today, don't you agree, Annchen?" It always made me feel strange when someone I wasn't supposed to like used my name endearingly.

Papa improved gradually. He obeyed the doctor and nurses in his daily therapy sessions, and always attempted to make fun of his condition. It tore my heart to watch him try so hard to talk those first weeks, but the therapy and his own battle to regain speech did begin to pay off. When Frau Rolf took him home, he could walk and speak, and with time he got better. Like his father before, plans to restore the Kleine Seppel name filled Papa's head. Could he succeed where my grandfather had failed?

One of Mama's superstitions had been that things happen to people in bunches. It wasn't hard to believe, especially since Papa's stroke so closely followed the accident killing the young girl. Then, with Hannelore's marriage still fresh, Henny announced that she too would be getting married. Henny, my kindred spirit and longtime music partner, broke the news on a weekend visit. She lived and worked in Kaiserslautern, and had been dating a handsome young man who worked for the railroad. Henny Hemm would become Henny Zirkel, which seemed to put more pressure on Anna Klein to do something about her last name.

The Kirchheim wedding was a tiny affair, as Henny came from a small family. Of her circle of friends, only myself and a female co-worker from her office made up the wedding party.

࿘

Cousin Elsbeth's worsening condition in Bolanden began to concern people far outside her family and the village. Her mother's relentless search for help in curing the illness had hit a wall with every German doctor she could interest in the case. They couldn't identify what it was or offer much in the way of treatment. By 1950, the story of the young Bolanden girl's condition had spread over the Donnersberg region. Newspaper articles appeared, and cards, letters and flowers came to my aunt's house for Elsbeth almost every day. This constant flow of kind sentiments, from friends and strangers alike, both embarrassed and encouraged her.

She was the same age as Erich, and I had idolized her nearly all my life. At the time of her return from Speyer, my visits to Bolanden were more regular and I found her always cheerful — still able to perform some physical tasks. It was a long-standing joke in the extended Klein family that my aunt had four rascal sons and one beautiful angel for them to adore.

I was away when the American army doctors took an active interest in Elsbeth's case, and I can't say how they became involved. Tante Lisbeth said that she didn't know what brought the Americans to her doorstep. We had just one small contingent of them in the area when Elsbeth was taken to the American hospital in Heidelberg. Not long after being put through a battery of tests, the diagnosis finally came. The Americans called it Multiple Sclerosis,

395

and that it was an incurable disease. The news was devastating, but the doctors offered some hope that ongoing medical research might solve the mystery of the illness soon.

The Americans went beyond mere diagnosis, by providing tests and experimental drugs in an effort to find answers. None came. As for Elsbeth, she thought it a blessing to finally have a name for the enemy within. Knowing that it had a name seemed to make her more serene. Over the three years before she died in May of 1954, no person who spent any time in her company could fail to notice that serenity. Elsbeth's calm endurance through painful test procedures and sickening side effects amazed everyone. She had just one request of the doctors — her mother was to always be at her side.

"Elsbeth didn't allow me to cry in her presence," Tante Lisbeth said to me a few days after the beautiful spring day Elsbeth was buried in the Bolanden cemetery. "All that love from her shining eyes always blocked my tears," she added.

It took all the strength of sons Rudi, Walter, Willie and Günther to keep my aunt from joining Elsbeth in the grave. The girl's loss was so greatly felt that nearly a hundred people followed the casket, but not a single one of them wanted to participate in the usual wake that followed a burial, and none was held.

By the end of 1950, most German soldiers from Kirchheim, still in prison camps, were freed to come home. These last had been unluckily caught by the Russians and held in Siberia. None wanted to talk about it. Looking for fun, like the rest of us, some of them started showing up at the dances. During the annual late-summer Kirchheim carnival, "Residenzfest," one particular former prisoner paid too much attention to me. The festival celebrates the town's former status as residence of a royal family, and had always been the year's major event.

Call it fate that a man would come into my life in the midst of turmoil. No sooner had friend Henny married when my last companion and best friend, Elfriede, also got that look in her eyes. The object of interest, I learned, was Manfred Denzer, the son of a cabinetmaker in Bischheim, a tiny village just a kilometer away. I was starting to feel deserted, though she still walked with me to the dance halls.

When things got really serious between the two, she insisted that I 'chaperone' them on outings. The evening Manfred took her to meet his parents, I was there, feeling totally out of place, but I'd do anything for Elfriede. She was a lovely and shy girl from a strict family, and tended to look on romance cautiously.

To me, Elfriede was the mirror image of the American movie star of the day, Joan Fontaine. I could understand Manfred's interest of course, but wished he'd hold off his courting for another ten years at least. Sadly for me, he was already a qualified, talented part of his father's trade, and could support a bride.

And now, in an already trying time, Leopold enters to confuse and complicate my life further. At our first meeting, he said to call him Leo, to which I indicated no interest one way or the other. He laughed, but his persistence at the Residenzfest dance was a warning I failed to heed.

The first time I saw Leo, he was sitting at a table with a group of Erich's friends, and they shouted and waved as I danced by. Otherwise, I wouldn't have noticed the newcomer at all. Blond men didn't attract me, and certainly not anyone who appeared to be no taller than myself. Still, I was curious about any new face in the crowd, boy or girl.

"Willi?" I said to my partner. "Who is that blond fellow sitting with the rest? He can't be from around here."

He peered at the table over my shoulder. "That guy? He's from Kirchheim. His name's Leo Ratch. You don't remember him because he's over thirty. Just got returned from five years in Siberia. You don't want to meet him!"

"Of course not," I laughed, taking a twirl under his arm. "I've no interest in old prisoners of war!"

The dance ended, and after thanking Willi, I started making my way over to Elfriede and Manfred, who were just sitting down at our table. The way was suddenly blocked by Leo Ratch, just as the band started up a slow waltz — not my favorite dance.

"Would you permit me this dance?" He said politely.

As I had guessed, he was only my height, but clean and trim, with sharp blue eyes and a pleasant smile. I figured that having just returned from prison camp, someone should dance with him.

"Ja, if you like. May I know who's asking?" I didn't want him thinking I'd already inquired.

"I like to be called Leo. Leopold is a rather stuffy name, don't you think?"

We began to dance. "And your family?"

"Ja, ja. It's Leo Ratch, and I live with my widowed mother not far from the old Liebfrauenkirche. But you wouldn't know that. I've been away many years."

"I can't say I remember you. My name — "

"I know who you are," he interrupted. "Your friends told me."

"They are really my brother's friends. Please! — don't hold me so close! I don't like it!"

From the moment we had begun dancing, his hold had grown tighter around my waist, closing the gap between us. With my warning, I pushed him back.

"I'm sorry," he laughed. "But it's the way I was taught."

"Not where I learned. I don't dance close with anyone!"

I kept my distance until the waltz ended, thanked him, and turned for another try at reaching Elfriede when the band started up again. It was a slow fox, my second least favorite way to go around the floor. Leo stepped quickly around to face me again, his arm encircling my waist, and began moving.

"You wouldn't deprive an old soldier a second slow dance. That stuff they call 'swing' is too fast for me."

"Ja," I replied. "You're probably too old for the swing step." The put-down was deserved. He was acting as though I was there for his pleasure alone.

My effort to set him straight turned his already ruddy complexion a deeper red. Anger flashed across his face, replaced quickly by an unconvincing laugh. "You got me there, and a good one, too!" His arm tightened around me. "Let's say I've still got what it takes."

I put some space between us again. "Just keep your 'taking' at a distance, please."

"You're very quick. I like that!" His words came with a genuine laugh, and I relaxed a bit to the band's Moonlight Serenade, a tune I liked very much. "You work here in town?"

What a chatterbox! I thought it, but answered anyway. "I work for a French family on the Schillerstraße."

"You mean in the big house by the old wall?"

"That's it. Why?"

"I live just a stone's throw away!"

Before I could reply, he pulled me into a tight embrace right in front of the bandstand, and I brought my foot down hard on his ankle. He instantly released me and jumped back, nearly bumping into a couple dancing by.

"I warned you, Herr Ratch. Now go back to your friends!"

For the rest of the evening, I asked partners to keep our dancing away from the end of the hall where Leo Ratch sat.

"Well you can't blame a guy for trying."

That was Manfred's response when I complained about the encounter to him and Elfriede. She wasn't surprised by my anger, and admonished her intended husband for not being sympathetic.

I stopped her. "Please don't say any more, Elfriede. I don't want you two arguing on my account. Manfred's right. It shouldn't be a problem. My sister-in-law says men try all the time. We both know that's true. What makes me mad is when they don't take no for an answer!"

I thought I heard Elfriede say something like 'Amen.' It was hard to tell in the din of the dance hall.

The episode was entirely out of my head a few days later as I walked home from work. It was still daylight, and I was enjoying the early fall evening when the door of a house I was passing flew open. Out stepped Leo. His sudden appearance stopped me in my tracks.

"Hello. It's Anna Klein, I believe. I've been looking out to see if you'd walk by on your way home."

"So this is where you live." Unhappy with the unwelcome intrusion, it was all I could think of to say.

"Ja, ja, this is it. I can see you're still mad. Please don't be. And please don't kick me again!"

His answer came with a playful laugh, and a quick step back. He held out a hand with something white and square. "See? I've written a letter of apology. Please take it."

I found myself accepting the small envelope, and not knowing what to say.

"Don't speak yet. Read it, and if you find forgiveness in your heart, maybe you'll agree to a movie this weekend. You can tell me when you pass by tomorrow."

That's how it all started with Leo. I did go home and read his note, a beautifully worded apology that included a bit of poetry about innocent intentions and simple friendship. I swallowed it from the first to last word. What can I lose? My last girlfriend would soon march down the aisle. All the men my age acted young and stupid. Certainly none would think to write a girl poetry.

Saying yes to the movie invitation swept me down a path I would forever regret. All was fine at the start. Leo was the perfect gentleman, impressing Ida so much that she encouraged his coming to the house nearly every evening.

Erich wasn't happy about finding Leo in his kitchen all the time, and he didn't particularly like the idea of his sister dating a man older than himself. But he said little. Arguing with his wife over her belief that I should marry didn't appeal to him, and I know he didn't want me dating French soldiers, as many girls were doing.

On more than one occasion, he'd take me aside. "There are lots of guys around here your own age." That just stiffened my resolve to stay on course. The fellows he went on to name wouldn't stuff my mailbox with poems like Leo did. Besides, I had no real complaints about the relationship, outside the few I kept brushing off as unimportant.

As fall had turned to winter, my days became a routine of caring for the Montuir family during weekdays and having Leo's company on evenings and weekends. For a while he still took me to the Saturday dances, but all had suddenly changed. None of the other fellows asked me to dance. Surprised and disappointed, it dawned on me that I'd cut myself off. Who of my former young partners would dare intrude in a war veteran's territory. Sadness welled up in me that I promptly dismissed as foolishness. After all, I hadn't decided the friendship was permanent.

It became clear with each passing week that Leo didn't enjoy going to the dances. He wasn't a good dancer, and took to the floor only for slower numbers. When a fast tune started, and with no other guy willing to risk asking, on occasion I'd dance with a girlfriend. Even that created tension. A gloomy mood would set in, and he'd want to leave. His real worry, of course, was a fear that my friends in the younger crowd would win me back. He needn't have worried. I hadn't yet developed an adequate defense against the flattering interest of an older man. As it was, the Saturday dances were soon replaced by movies. It didn't matter. The fun had gone out of dancing.

Whenever Leo spent an evening in our kitchen, and that was almost nightly, he talked non-stop, with only an occasional break for any reaction from Ida and I. It hadn't taken long for Erich to formulate his escape — the truck always needed repairs. Early on, Leo didn't seem all that strange or boring to Ida and me. We were curious to learn about his life and interests. To my amazement, he had an opinion on everything — usually life in Siberia, politics, and soccer. Soccer was my least favorite sport, but since I mostly spent these times knitting, it was easy to focus my thoughts elsewhere when the subject came up.

I wasn't accustomed to going out, except on weekends, but I did wonder why Leo was content to spend all of his evenings in our kitchen. Gradually, I began to see his game. He had, without my consent, decided to act like we were married. Considering that he went home to bed alone every night, it was a strange behavior. More important, I remained a virgin.

Leo's possessiveness created more doubts, and I could no longer easily shove them aside. The romantic poems of undying love and urgent desires grew in proportion to my wish to end it. However, my efforts to squelch his ideas of marriage failed. The reason was simple — I couldn't bring myself to make a clean break.

I had even met his mother, a nice, quiet wisp of a woman. Not long after, on a surprise visit to her house, I discovered him shouting and shoving his mother around. He quickly turned jovial and polite on seeing me standing there in shock. "Just a little family squabble," he explained. "Nothing to be concerned about." I'd never seen Leo angry, so the incident was forgotten until weeks later when Frau Ratch brought it up privately.

"Perhaps you shouldn't think of marrying my son. He has a violent temper."

It was a warning from someone who knew. Yet, I didn't know what to think. A few days before, I'd heard through the grapevine what she'd told a neighbor. "Annchen is a nice girl, but doesn't have a thing to bring into a marriage." Her conflicting behavior confused me all the more. I wondered if she was trying to step between us out of fear for me, or because I had no property or wealth to offer. I would have demanded an explanation from anyone my age, but with Frau Ratch, I silently resolved to be stubborn. I didn't want to marry her son, of that I was fairly certain. Still, it wouldn't hurt to worry her a while longer just for the insult.

The down side of my decision, was that Leo stepped up the pressure to marry, and at the same time, have pre-marital sex. On the first, I continued to claim no immediate interest, and on the matter of sex, my response never altered from "not before marriage." He never failed to laugh at my resistance.

"You're too old fashioned about sex. No one waits until they're married these days! Where do you get those outdated ideas? When you love someone, you show it. That's the way it's always been."

"I'm not so sure I love you. What about that?"

My meager attempts to make him mad enough to stop bothering me didn't work. A momentary flush of redness came to his cheeks, but he quickly covered it with laughter.

"Ha! You're too inexperienced to understand what love is. After sex, you'll know. Believe me!"

And so the sexual arguments went on, right through spring and into summer, and right past my twenty-first birthday in July. He was determined to win, if not the battle for my hand, then my acceptance that sexual intercourse revealed true love. I finally gave in, and found my own answer. If there was a man who could make a woman awaken to love through sex, Leo was not him. Shame and disgust, not love, were all that came from abandoning my principles.

Papa believed every bad experience had a good side, but trying to find any good from my terrible moment of weakness was near impossible for me. I could only think of running, and that chance came sooner than expected. Adjutant Montuir had received transfer orders, and Madame asked me to come along and stay with the family. I agreed without so much as a second thought.

Subtle changes were happening with our French occupying force. Slowly, individual soldiers and whole companies started leaving Kirchheim. The French still maintained a headquarters operation in the Schloßgarten, but something big was definitely in the wind. Madame had no knowledge of it, but like a good wife of a career soldier, she didn't ask questions. She just packed up to follow her man to his next post. He was already there waiting, north of us in a much larger city called Wetzlar.

On a bright, sunny morning in late July, I joined the family climbing aboard a military bus to begin a new adventure. Saying goodbye to my family was sad, but the day before was harder. It was the first time that I revealed my plans to Leo. I made sure Ida was present to help defuse what I knew would be a difficult and angry situation. But seeing his pain, I backed off my intention to end our relationship then and there. What came out was a cowardly excuse.

"I need to get away. You should forget about me and find someone else."

Chapter Thirty-Eight

The bus took us to Mainz, where we switched to a train. I found it ironic that our destination of Wetzlar was so close to Gießen, north of Frankfurt. It was to Gießen that Mama and I had traveled to visit Papa at the Luftwaffe base. Eleven years later, I'm aboard another train rolling through the same landscape, maid to a French family. Watching the scenery flash by my window, images from the past filled my head. That ten-year-old girl, happily greeting her father at Gießen, had been truly blessed by ignorance of life's future twists and turns.

The bus ride was free, but Madame paid for my train fare. The Montuirs, in fact, paid my monthly wage of seventy Marks themselves. (In 1951 terms, that was about $17.50.) It was an important difference between the French and American occupying forces. Americans paid all their German employees, including maids. American policy at the time was to back up West Germany's economic recovery. Easy for rich America, the French said. France's economic position, however, wasn't much better than our own following the war, and its army couldn't afford to pay for maids. When I began work for the Montuirs, I had wondered if one or the other had family money that enabled the hiring of a maid. The answer, was that both came from moderate circumstances, and employing me was possible only through Madame's resourceful use of her husband's army income.

Our first home was in a confiscated German villa at the edge of Wetzlar. As we drove away from the train station, I was struck by the remarkable absence of war devastation. I could see nothing disturbed around the station. The city center also appeared untouched. I'd expected worse — the bomb damage at nearby Gießen was well-known. No doubt Wetzlar's industrial sectors were heavily bombed, but the still intact old city center buildings and stunning cathedrals excited me. All thoughts of missing my family faded with the new exciting possibilities of exploring my new home.

Madame Montuir was clearly as surprised when we pulled into the villa grounds. It wasn't grand in the sense of showy wealth, but the house was large and situated in the middle of gardens. The real grandeur was the gardens, all lush with flowers and orderly rows of vegetables. We discovered that the owner retained rights to the gardens, and the view provided beautiful evidence of his love for growing things. Later I'd have a chance to see him working diligently among the rows. I somehow felt guilty being in his house.

My room was in the attic. The large airy space was intended for servant's quarters, and had been nicely furnished for the purpose. All of the furnishings in the house belonged to the owner, and Madame insisted throughout the weeks of our stay that all of it be treated with respect.

Any drawbacks I'd worried about in becoming a live-in maid didn't occur. There were subtle changes to be sure, but most had to do with adjusting to the full-time relationship. If anything, Madame drew me closer into the family, and became even more like an older, wiser sister. She was only twelve years older, so she couldn't boss me like a mother, though at times she tried. As before, evening meal clean-up ended my day. I was free to go to my room, go to a movie, or stay downstairs until bedtime. And, as in Kirchheim, I was still 'Anni,' not the maid.

Madame took serious her role as protector, which was fine with me. She had earned my respect, and I wasn't above needing and accepting her advice. Her protective attitude didn't take long to show after we settled in. Another French couple and their German maid, stayed with us a week while awaiting assignment of quarters. The girl, Marianna, enticed me to go with her a couple of evenings to a nearby inn. Leaving the villa the first evening, the makeup piled on her normally clean face had me wondering.

On reaching the inn, I quickly realized Marianna was no stranger to the place. And while the establishment had all the appearance of respectability, the presence of so many French and American soldiers made me nervous.

"Ach, Anni," she said, laughing. "This Gasthaus is alright. All the boys who come here are really nice!"

As we passed some booths, a few of the soldiers invited us to join them. I assumed the invitations were just for drinks and talk, but really understood only some words spoken by the Americans. Looking at me, Marianna turned everyone down. We found our own table and ordered drinks, mineral water for me, a beer for her. About to question her familiarity with the inn, my eyes caught sight of two big uniformed men coming through the front door. They were the same men I'd seen earlier passing the villa several times in their open military police jeep.

Sweeping their eyes over every inch of the suddenly quiet room, their search finally stopped on us. I suddenly felt guilty, though I'd done nothing wrong. It was an odd sensation. The face on the bigger of the two broke into a big grin as he nudged his partner and pointed in our direction. Marianna was facing away from the door, but seeing my expression she turned and laughed, waving at the newcomers. She'd said nothing about meeting anyone, especially military police. My discomfort level was growing by the second.

"Hiya, Marianna," said the older of the two. His name turned out to be Smitty. "How're things going, sweetheart?" Looking at me, he added, "Who's the girl?"

"She's a maid for a French family where I'm staying temporarily. Anni's new to the area. She can't say much in English, so I guess you fellows are going to have to devote all your time to me!"

I hadn't known Marianna could speak English, and with such apparent ease. I got the gist of her answer, and felt stupid for tagging along. Still, my curiosity was strong. I sat sipping my drink and trying to make sense of the conversation. My thought was to stay as long as everyone behaved. Smitty offered several times to buy me beer, but I politely refused. One thing I noticed during the evening — no other soldiers came up to our table.

Later, Marianna laughed about it, saying she wasn't the least bit mystified. "Who would have the nerve to bother girls sitting with the military police!"

Conversation with Americans on a social level was a whole new experience for me. I envied Marianna's ability to speak English. The second evening I accompanied her, it was with the specific purpose of listening hard to the sound of English. Maybe, I foolishly hoped, it would start making sense after an hour or two. She just laughed when I told her of my intentions.

"Why do you think I go to the Gasthaus? I don't mind a little romance now and then, but that's not the reason."

"Then why do you?"

"Because it helps me improve my English. Most of the guys just like talking to a girl. I figure it's fair exchange!" She paused and looked at me for a moment, then went on. "I began learning English before the war ended. It was only a start, and I want to be good enough to quit the French. It's the Americans who pay the money. That's where I'm headed!"

Listening to Marianna, I wondered about her exact meaning. Was she intending to work for the Americans or find some G.I. to take her to America? I left the question unspoken. Sitting with her the second evening at the inn made me more frustrated. The next day, Madame took me aside to suggest I not go with the girl again. I readily agreed, though it had nothing to do with her fear for my morals. The girl and her family would soon be gone, and I'd already decided to buy a language book and study English on my own.

Forced into being a cook in my early teens, I felt competent in the kitchen long before the Montuirs had entered my life. Yet, it amazed me what I didn't know when Madame put on an apron. During our year together in Kirchheim, she'd taught me many things, starting with the making of wonderful coffee. Until Madame, I cared little for real coffee. A typical brewing method in German kitchens at the time was to put coarsely ground coffee into boiling water. The result never appealed to me. Madame followed a Swiss method that used a finely ground coffee. Hot water was poured over the coffee in a special cone-shaped holder lined with a paper filter. The result made me a coffee lover. It was just the start.

"Fresh oysters are good for love-making!" Madame insisted.

"Then I don't need them."

"You will," she argued. "Now eat!"

I hadn't yet developed the required assertiveness to fight off some of Madame's efforts to 'educate Anni.' Being a full-time member of the family in Wetzlar, I was introduced to traditions not experienced in Kirchheim. She did all the food shopping, and every Saturday morning, without fail, she stopped at a seafood shop for oysters in the shell and at the butcher shop for filets mignons. My task was to scrub the closed shells with a stiff brush until every crevice was clean. Shown how to crack them open, I then removed the empty shell half, neatly arranging the remaining halves on a serving platter. These became the hors d'oeuvres. Everyone, including the children, had to partake by bringing each shell to the lips and slurping down the contents. When my protests fell on deaf ears, I found that lemon juice helped in overcoming my disgust.

The Saturday ritual continued with a dinner of filets mignons. Again to my discomfort, the steaks Madame prepared received only nodding acquaintance with the bottom of a frying pan. The mere touch of a knife instantly brought blood into view.

"My steak hasn't been cooked thoroughly," I complained the first time.

"Anni, a proper filet mignon should only be seared on top and bottom. Rare beef provides the strength you need. I wouldn't be alive today without it. Now eat before it gets cold!"

Mostly I could react with at least tolerant obedience, but there were times I didn't. Dealing with strange foods like snails, oysters, and rare beef was one thing, ignorance turned out to be a far more sensitive issue.

❧

Returning from early shopping one morning, Madame presented me with a large basket of long yellow string beans. I'd never before seen the vegetable, and she offered no real information. Setting the basket on the kitchen table, she rushed off leaving the skimpiest of instructions. "I have to run and take care of more errands. Get these ready for me to cook when I get back."

On her return, I presented the result of my labors — a small bowl of beans painstakingly extracted from the long lumpy pods. "I really don't think there's enough for everyone to eat," I said, holding the bowl out for her to see.

"What have you done to the beans?" Her eyes went wide and her face turned red. She seemed not to be breathing at all.

"What's wrong?" I said, getting nervous about her reaction. "These are all the beans I could get out."

She threw up her hands and stomped out of the kitchen. Slowly, I began to understand. The beans I worked so hard to open and empty were intended to be eaten whole, just like the slimmer green beans grown at home. Now my face was red with embarrassment and it made me mad — at myself and at her for not explaining what they were. I went into the living room to confront her head on.

"Madame, I've never worked on beans like those in my life. You know many of your foods are new to me. You should have said how you wanted them prepared."

"You don't know yellow beans? I — "

"Tell me where you bought those beans," I said, interrupting her. "I'll go and get more with my money!"

"No, no. We have another vegetable. Let's just forget about the beans." She was back to her usual calm manner, and went on. "I'm as much to blame. You should have had better directions."

I accepted her apology, but decided to sulk anyway.

"Are you still mad at me?" Madame's unexpected question came about three days after the bean incident.

"What makes you think I'm mad?" was my terse reply.

"Oh, that's easy. Always, when you're angry with me, you say nothing for three days. Yes, always three days. The children — you talk to them, but even they see you're mad at me. Little Regine says, "Mama, is Anni mad at you again?" Today is the third day. I think we should be friends again."

Stung by the truth, I grasped for words. "I'm not mad. I just don't like misunderstandings." Or being thought dumb. But I didn't say it.

The incident was over, with a happier atmosphere in the house quickly restored. Neither of us wanted disharmony in the family.

Just weeks after moving into the villa, we had to pick up and leave. The French army returned the property to it's rightful and delighted owner, and the Montuirs were assigned an apartment in the French housing compound near the city's center. Several huge apartment buildings formed a long U-shaped complex of dependent housing. Each block had three floors for twelve apartments. The fourth floor, a full attic with dormer windows, was divided into bedrooms, toilets and showers for live-in maids. I alone occupied the entire floor in our building. For a private person it was a perfect situation, but it could be scary at night.

All the maids' rooms were entered from a long center hallway. At either end, a door and stairwell led to the apartments below. One set of stairs was all I needed, and it concerned both Madame and I that anyone could come up the opposite end without discovery. Locking the hallway doors was considered a fire hazard, and was prohibited. It wasn't a big worry for me. Most of my time was spent two floors down. At night, however, I followed Madame's suggestion to lock my room door, even when visiting the toilet three doors down or the bath, yet another door away.

My room was large enough for a single bed, a small wardrobe and chest of drawers, a writing table with a mirror, and a chair. Other than keeping it clean and neat, I made no effort to decorate — not even a photo adorned the place. And, since the window was high from the floor, I didn't bother with a curtain. When I did retire early to my room, it was usually to write Ida. Sometimes it had to be a letter to Leo telling him to stop writing me.

In his latest letters to me, along with the poetry, he'd written of being sick and unable to work at his job in a Ludwigshafen steel mill. I suspected he was attempting to win my sympathy, and I responded coolly at first. Then a letter from Ida came confirming Leo's poor health, and guilt took over. My next correspondence with him must have seemed downright warm, though I strove to keep the message to a simple 'get well' wish.

I felt no homesickness at all in Wetzlar, something even I was surprised about. Being away from Leo was probably behind part of it — I hoped he'd fall for someone else in my absence. Other than that, I had no reason to be glad about leaving Kirchheim. I missed family and friends, though probably not as much as they hoped. Still, one day in October, I jumped at the chance for a surprise visit home. Over dinner one evening, Adjutant Montuir told Madame that a bus was being sent to Kirchheim the next day to pick up more wives and children.

"It won't be a full bus load," he added, nodding toward me. "Anni could go along for a quick visit and be back in the evening."

Excited at understanding his French words, I jumped in. "How long would I have?"

"Oh, two hours at most," he said in German.

"I'll go!" My reply came totally without thought. Only then did it occur to me that Madame hadn't approved, and I turned somewhat red-faced.

"Yes, you can go," she laughed. "Just be sure to come back!"

There was not time to inform Erich and Ida. I was glad in a way. Word of my visit could reach Leo, and I had no intention of seeing him. There was already a chance he might be hanging around Breitstraße, moping and crying on Ida's shoulder.

I went with Adjutant Montuir to his installation early in the morning to board the bus. A handful of young soldiers were already seated toward the back, so I sat near the driver. Any concern in my mind about the soldiers misbehaving during the trip was quickly eliminated when the driver, a German employee, turned to glance at me after we got on the road.

"You must be some valuable cargo," he said, smiling.

"Why would you say such a thing? I'm just going home for a quick visit."

"I'll tell you why! The Adjutant came on board before he let you on. He told those guys back there to stay put and keep their 'filthy hands off of the young lady' all the way to Kirchheim!"

"He didn't!"

"Ja, he did. That makes you important!"

"Perhaps, but I think his wife gave him the orders." I had to smile, thinking of the Madame ordering her husband to ensure my safe passage.

Pulling into the Schloßgarten some three hours later, I was struck by how small everything looked to me. I certainly hadn't grown any taller in Wetzlar, and that made the sensation all the more peculiar. Walking up Neumayerstraße toward home, all the houses and apartment buildings looked almost tiny. Even the Catholic church tower appeared shorter. After the short trek up Breitstraße, I turned the door handle. It was locked. My knocking brought no response.

It was soon lunchtime and I had no key, and no idea where Ida might be.

Elfriede lived not quite a block away, and I decided to visit her. I didn't want the trip to be entirely wasted.

While I wouldn't be turning down Langstraße toward the old city, I did glance that way as I started to cross. There was Ida, not fifty meters away, standing in the middle of the street with a shocked expression. In one arm, she held little Brunhilde. On the other hung a shopping bag. I laughed and ran to her, happy to have surprised her after all. I took the girl from her, linked arms, and started explaining my flying visit as we walked home.

Ida listened quietly to my stream of talk about life in Wetzlar, and made fast work preparing a fine meal. Holding Brunhilde in my lap gave the little one a chance to rediscover her aunt. In no time, the girl was smiling and trying to talk to me. It all made me see how much I missed home and family. The emotion was dampened when Ida suddenly turned our talk to Leo. She told me that he didn't look good at all. The doctor told him it was a case of extreme exhaustion. He simply had no energy for anything.

I asked her how she knew all that. "Oh, he comes to the house a lot in the evenings," Ida answered. "Sits where you are now and cries about you being so far away. Can't you be nicer to him? Give him some hope you'll marry him? He'd probably get better and be able to work again."

"I'm not going to marry him, and I can't tell him any such thing. I've tried being nice about his condition, urging him in my letters to take care of his health. Nay, I won't promise marriage."

"But, why? He loves you."

"I don't love him!"

My two hours passed all too quickly. An otherwise happy visit had ended on a sour note. I'd hoped to avoid any discussion over a relationship that should have ended months before. Ida's report left me with an uneasy feeling that Leo wasn't about to let me go.

❧

The bus was nearly filled to capacity for the return trip, but there were no soldiers, just wives and children heading out to join husbands and fathers in Mainz and Wetzlar.

Leo, of course, found out almost immediately about my visit home. An angry letter greeted me a few days after my return, and another apologetic note followed a day later. The second was filled with pleas for forgiveness, and of his understanding about how little time I had at home. The first letter, he explained, was from a sick and hurt man. I threw both letters away.

❧

By law, the Montuirs had to give me one half-day off during the week. Madame informed me of this soon after our arrival in Wetzlar. We decided on Wednesday afternoons, though I must admit I found it difficult at first. I'd never had a job where I could just stop and walk away from my duties in the middle of the day.

It took some mental adjusting to feel comfortable. In time, I learned how to enjoy the free hours without guilt. Fortunately, I met Frau Lott, a part-time day maid for another family in the building. A lifelong Wetzlar native, and old enough to be my mother, she invited me right away to visit her home on Wednesdays. It was from her that I gained many insights about Wetzlar's fascinating history. She also kept me posted on events and exhibits at the museums I might be interested in, and about landmarks of interest. The most spellbinding for me was Pfaffengaße 10, an historic house from German literature. It's hard to imagine growing up in Germany without having learned about Goethe, our great writer and poet. He spent part of his younger years in Wetzlar and later published "Werthers Leiden," a story based on people and places in Wetzlar.

It was fun going into the city center just to walk about, window shop, and admire the old architecture. Sometimes I'd pick up a magazine to read while enjoying coffee and cake at a quaint cafe. It was always best for a single girl to look occupied while having coffee alone at a sidewalk cafe.

Chapter Thirty-Nine

As Christmas approached, Madame informed me that the family would go home to France over the holidays. Since it was not something they did every year, she explained that another change was in the wind, making it important to go. Her husband had told her that the military grapevine was warning of massive transfers to a place called Indochina. It was later to be called Viet Nam.

I'd planned to ask for a week off at Christmas. Her news allowed me an extra week. When I boarded the train for Frankfurt and points south, new snow was turning the grey city white. The Indochina rumors were still only rumors, but I wondered if I'd still have a job on my return. I couldn't worry about it. I was going home for Christmas.

I had many purposes in going home. Nothing was more important than being with my family at Christmas, and I had been invited to a wedding. There was also the recent letter from Ida telling about the Americans returning to our area in a big way. The Pfalz was to be reoccupied by U.S. soldiers, though some French forces would remain. The separate occupation zones were no longer. American flags would fly once more in our Pfälzer cities and towns, with the major centers located in the Kaiserslautern area. Soon, every Pfälzer would recognize the names: Western Area Command or WACOM — and the 12th Air Force at Ramstein nearby.

On that Christmas of 1951, I had a special interest in the American take-over of Weierhof, just five kilometers from Kirchheim. When I arrived home, the old Mennonite settlement and school was being transformed to suit the needs of an artillery battalion. Apartment buildings to house dependents were nearing completion just outside the compound walls. Some Germans in my town, and in nearby Bolanden and Marnheim, were still sore about losing to the Americans, but most were delighted at the prospect of work for good pay. I was one of them.

Elfriede had written to invite me to her wedding over the holidays. She and Manfred were finally going to tie the knot. A couple of days before Christmas, a small group of family and friends gathered at St. Peter's Kirche for the ceremony. Of course, my friend made a beautiful bride and he a handsome husband. I was full of joy for them. Later, at the wedding dinner held at her parents' house, Elfriede and I shared a private moment.

"It's your turn, Annchen. Have you had a change of heart about Leo? Ida has told me how he wants to marry you. Any chance?"

"None at all. I can't marry someone I don't love. Never."

☙

My hope to break clean from Leo during my visit fizzled as soon as he walked in. I was shocked by his physical appearance. He was clearly ill and I feared the worst if I demanded an end to the affair. The closest I came was when he presented me with a gift. In the wrapped package were a pair of fake alligator dress shoes. I had no gift for him and it took a moment to find my voice.

"Why would you buy me shoes? How could you know my size?"

He laughed. "Ida told me the size. Guessing had nothing to do with it."

"That's not it. Haven't you heard giving shoes is bad luck?"

"Ach, rubbish! Just an old wives' tale!"

The shoes should have been refused, but I kept and wore them. Normally I wasn't a superstitious person, but in this case, I wanted the tale to be true. Putting them on served to remind me that the break had to be made, and soon.

☙

I had expected to have a number of people and events to catch up on during my home visit, but a ghost from the past came as a shock.

Right after the house had settled down from the Christmas festivities, Erich told me of the surprise visit of our Onkel Raul from France to the Breitstraße. It had happened just days before I came, and I was sorry to hear it because I'd always wanted to meet him.

"It was just luck that I was at home," Erich said. "Ida doesn't understand French at all and he couldn't speak German."

"Didn't he bring Tante Dina? I would have wanted to finally meet Mama's sister."

"Tante Dina died not many months after Mama. She had strokes," my brother said sadly. He knew how I talked of going to France one day to meet her and the son Jean, who was my age.

"Onkel was sorry to have come so late bringing the news," Erich continued. "He said something about losing our address and going first to Marnheim. Onkel Adam told him about Mama dying and where we were living. His son Jean is serving in the French army in Algiers. He left the address with us."

"I'd like to have it, but Erich you remember how Mama worried so about

Dina, especially after our army invaded France."

"Ja, ja. I can tell you about that. Onkel Raul sat right here in the kitchen crying as he told us. He said the war at first brought hatred and threats to Dina from those who knew her birth country. But the two of them fought back the accusations, and after a few months everyone was convinced of her loyalty to France, and the trouble stopped."

I was relieved that Dina had survived the war alright, but I found it sad that Mama died not knowing what happened. And poor Dina — she never knew about her sister's awful illness and death. I promised myself to have Madame help me write to Onkel Raul and cousin Jean right away.

Returning to Wetzlar on January third, I threw myself back into the daily routine. Most evenings I stayed in the apartment until bedtime. Madame actually liked for me to do so, as the Adjutant often had to go back to his post after supper and returned late.

"Anni, I've decided to buy a sewing machine." We were sitting in the living room knitting knee socks for the twins when she spoke.

"But Madame, you don't know how to sew. You told me that some time ago."

"Ah, but you do. I've been thinking you could remodel some of my dresses. Perhaps make some things for the children as well."

Madame bought a used treadle machine, and I really didn't mind the added work. Helping her clean, cook, and look after the twins wasn't that great a burden. To tell the truth, I couldn't understand why a healthy housewife needed a paid helper. For me, it was a luxury I'd never want, even if I was rich. But to say so openly wouldn't have been smart — I needed the job.

Along with making alterations, I taught Madame some of the basics on the machine, it was good that I did. February was hardly a few days old when the Adjutant's orders came down. He and many of his comrades were being shipped to Indochina. Madame and the children had to go home to France, and I was out of a job. In a way, I was relieved. It was time again for something new.

"What will you do at home, Anni?"

"Oh, I'm sure to find something."

"That Leo fellow, will you marry him?"

"That's all finished. I'll just find a job, perhaps with the Americans returning to our area."

She grunted. "The Americans with all their money!" Her voice had taken on a harsh tone. It shocked me and it showed.

"Oh, don't mind me," she continued, a little calmer. "But we French have a right to be upset with our rich, powerful 'Uncle Sam.' For a long time now, our enemy is treated better than France by the Americans."

I was unaware she felt so angry at America or, for that matter, that she felt envious of my country. We rarely talked politics. The historic hatred between our nations clearly made the Madame sensitive about America's new generosity toward Germany. I couldn't get mad at her though, for it also occurred to me that her criticism arose out of frustration and fear. The man she loved would soon face extreme danger in a war France was already losing badly in a place all would soon know as Viet Nam.

On the day for goodbyes, I promised myself not to be sentimental, but considering how much I adored little Regine and Jean-Jacques, and for all the Madame's kindnesses, it was a tall order. My train would depart in the afternoon, so she wanted to prepare a last, special lunch. Standing in the living room after, and holding my one suitcase, she suddenly began shaking and crying. The twins, standing by, were distressed to see her so upset. When she held her arms toward me, I placed the suitcase on the floor to embrace her, and started bawling myself.

After a minute, she pushed me out at arm's length. "Why are you crying? You're the one who's leaving me!"

"I know," I said, laughing and crying all at once. "You have to stop first, or I can't."

I hugged her again, kissed the twins, and walked out the door. At the entrance gate of the compound, a bus would soon pick me up for the ride to the train station. I didn't look back.

At home, I found the apartment blocks completed at the new U.S. Army installation at Weierhof, and promptly applied for work as a maid. It wasn't my plan to continue as a domestic servant — it was simply a matter of starting somewhere and staying only until my English improved. I also didn't know what kind of better jobs were possible with the Americans. I'd heard of German girls working as secretaries, but that required more than good English. At the time, secretarial schools existed only in large cities.

I was sent to a Sergeant-Major Crawford for an interview. He accepted my qualifications and started me right away as daytime help for his wife and small daughter. This time my direct employer didn't pay me. The army paid me through the German labor office. The amount was a most welcome surprise — 130 Deutschmarks a month. It was nearly double what Montuirs had given me. The new wages, over thirty-two dollars in American money, was a real increase. Even contributing to expenses at home, I could buy personal necessities and save a little money as well. The distance between my house and Weierhof was so short, I could walk or ride my bicycle. On rainy days, there was bus service.

My new work domain was a spacious two-bedroom affair. The army provided all furnishings, including fine Rosenthal dinnerware and a silverplate service for eight. Household things like bed and bath linens, cooking utensils, everyday dishes, vacuum and the like, were provided by the occupant.

The apartment should have been very easy to maintain, but I didn't find it to be. For starters, the Crawfords had no vacuum. I was handed a straw broom to clean the living room carpeting. One of the few cleaning aids they bought was laundry soap, but there was no washing machine. Prior to my arrival on the scene, the laundry was washed and ironed at the base facility. With me, the Crawford's saved that cost, and I was back to scrubbing clothes in the bath tub. It wouldn't have been all that bad, except for one thoughtless habit of Mrs. Crawford's — she changed her cute little cotton dresses two and three times a day. After a few hours of wear, she expected the dress to be washed again. Of course, allowing the dress to drop to the floor and remain there until I found it didn't help the garment stay clean and wrinkle-free. I doubled my effort to learn English.

The sergeant's wife had an amazingly slim figure for a mother of a six-month-old girl, the perfect model for those light print dresses I had to carefully wash and iron. Her face was more cute than pretty, but she did have beautiful heavy hair worn in the fashion of the day — puffy on top and combed straight down to a flip at shoulder level. Two small barrettes held the hair in place on the sides. To achieve this look, she put the hair in big rollers every night, rollers that were left in place until minutes before her husband arrived home to prepare lunch. Mrs. Crawford didn't cook. In my presence, only the Sergeant cooked, and I never learned if he really could. Lunch, the one meal I had with them, was always soup from a can and white bread. Both were strange foods to me. I thought the bread was so soft and airy it could easily replace cotton pads, but the soup was better than Madame's raw oysters.

The lady of the house usually spent the afternoons with female friends drinking coffee at the post exchange snack bar. Less frequent were shopping trips to Kaiserslautern, where the army had built a huge shopping center in a suburban area called Vogelweh. In 1952, stories in our local newspaper said that Vogelweh was well on it's way to becoming the world's largest military dependent housing area. For Germans, the best news was that thousands of them were being employed in every work area from housekeeping to electronic engineering.

Sometimes, when the sergeant wanted to take his wife away for a weekend, he'd ask me to stay over Saturday and Sunday to care for the baby. I usually agreed. He either paid me extra, or gave me time off in the week. I was also allowed to bring Brunhilde with me, a treat for us both. And if they went away for the weekend, it meant I wouldn't have to face a pile of used condoms on their bedroom table Monday morning. I was quite shy about sex, and leaving soiled condoms for me to dispose of embarrassed and angered me. The first time, I'd brought the wife into the room and pointed at the table. She claimed not to understand even the simple English I could speak.

"Oh," she responded, without a flicker of embarrassment. "Just throw those in the trash."

I boiled inside, but continued to dispose of the sergeant's little trophy piles. I used the broom to sweep them down to the floor, then several feet across toward the door and into a dust pan. I could have swept their insult directly from table to pan, but I hoped she would see my method one day and learn my disgust. If she ever did, it made no difference.

I redoubled my efforts at English. I needed someone who would speak the language with me, and I found a candidate directly across the hall from Crawford's.

A couple with six children, aged one to ten, hired a German maid from a nearby village. I hadn't known her, but soon got acquainted. Lotte was older than I, in her mid-thirties, and a university graduate. When she told me, I must have looked stunned. Having my education cut off after the eighth grade, I probably deserved no better job than as a maid, but a university graduate who spoke perfect English?

"Aren't you aware of how some of us are treated?" Lotte was being persecuted for past involvement in the Nazi party.

"I'm sorry." It was all I could think to say, though I could have told her that I did know. My music teacher Karola Kiefer had been sent to prison for the same reason.

"Don't be sorry," she replied. "I'm glad to have even this job, in which I have to clean shit out of drawers on Monday mornings."

My mouth dropped open.

"Ja, it's true," she said. "The Jaspers like to sleep their weekends away, paying little attention to the children. Some of them let loose in the lower drawers on chests, the dining room buffet, and kitchen cabinets. Naturally, I clean it up."

And I thought I had my complaints. I told Lotte about the condom situation, and was surprised she thought I had it worse.

"That's direct adult behavior, and inexcusable," she declared. "Little children should be forgiven when they're not properly supervised."

"It's still not right that someone with your education should have to work in such a job."

"I'm patient. This will blow over someday. Besides I have a soul mate right here in this building! You must know him!"

"I don't think so."

"Ah, my dear Fräulein Klein, you must open your eyes to the people around you. The man who stokes the furnace in the basement was a professor at the university in Mainz. How can I feel sorry for myself?"

We continued to talk at the bus stop outside the gate after working hours. I was being given a lot to think about, but it didn't end there. As the bus approached, Lotte added something more to consider.

"I'm thinking," she began. "Your sergeant what's-his-name. He's not at all attractive. Actually, a little strange looking. Still, there's his pretty little wife. Maybe those condoms on the bedside table are meant to tell you something. I'd watch out!"

It was the beginning of Lotte's interest in me. Once I told her of my desire to get a better job, she agreed to spend some spare time helping me practice my English. The professor in the basement joined in. I supplemented their verbal lessons by trying to read the comics in the American Stars and Stripes daily newspaper that came to the apartment. The drawings did much to help me understand the words in the little balloons. I soon graduated to looking into the romance magazines that Mrs. Crawford brought from the PX. The more words I learned, the more eye-opening the illustrations became.

About the only thing Erich and Leo agreed on was their opposition to me working for the Americans. My brother's general dislike of Leo, however, hadn't diminished. He couldn't fathom why I allowed him to continue visiting.

My protests that I was only offering friendship left Erich scratching his head and predicting a bad end. I should have realized he knew the male psyche better than I and should have listened to his advice. Stupidly, I'd convinced myself to wait until Leo regained his health. I thought my stubborn resistance to marriage would send him packing without a blow-up. I hated confrontations.

❧

My cousin Ernst, a son of Adam in Marnheim, had been an infrequent visitor to Breitstraße One since returning from prisoner of war camp in 1949. About my brother's age, Ernst had a terrific impact on me in childhood. He was the one who liked to stand on the roof of a shed and perform for the neighborhood children. It was all very impromptu and outlandish for a small farm community, but we children and the few adults who stopped to watch got a kick out of it. Many were the times I looked on as he stood on the roof top, high above my head, to recite poetry or tell some fantastic tale. The stories were always full of flourish and drama, with Ernst playing each character to the hilt.

I saw Ernst and his brothers and sisters many times over the following years. Ernst was third oldest among the seven children, and with his fragile and artistic nature, he was completely different than the rest. Entering his teen years before the war, dreams of a life of poetry and art had to be set aside for reality. Onkel Adam insisted that he and his older brother Hans train in the family saddlery and upholstery business.

By 1942, Hans, Ernst, and even Onkel Adam were in the Wehrmacht serving their country. My uncle came home before the war ended, and Hans shortly after. Ernst wasn't released until much later. The Klein house became one of his favorite places to visit, and I got to know and appreciate my cousin 'of the roof top' all over again. If it was nice weather when he visited, we'd often go sit on the low wall bordering one side of the Ziegelwoog, the small lake just down from the house and around the corner. There I learned of his passion to leave for any big city where he could study literature and art. He always brought along examples of his latest efforts to read or show me. My cousin still loved to write poems, but he now had a deep interest in drawing as well.

"I had time in prison camp to develop my hand at drawing. What do you think?"

It was clear he loved the older rustic architecture found around our area. The drawings were beautiful and I told him so. "These are so good, you don't need more schooling!"

"Ah, but I do. There's so much more to learn, but — Papa's against it!"

419

"I'm sorry. You're so good with your poems and drawings. Maybe Onkel will still come around and let you go. At least, you should keep trying to make him understand."

"I don't know. Maybe."

A kind of gloom descended over our warm place in the sun. The breeze rustled the long, leafy branches of a large willow tree standing alone on a tiny island across the lake. We both stared at the thousand silvery green arms swaying in the wind, struggling to touch the water below. I wondered what was in his head, if he felt trapped like I did. I couldn't ask, but I thought of us as two willow branches, always blown helplessly about by the whims of nature and man.

I finally broke the silence. "When do you find time to draw and write?"

"Ach, almost always at night, in my room. Papa wouldn't put up with me doing anything like that in the daytime."

I thought it was sad — an adult son, a former prisoner of war, still obedient to the will of his father. It was almost time for Ernst to head back to Marnheim, and I had a brainstorm. "Ernst. When can you come back over?" The question came out of me with a sudden rush of excitement.

"Well, I — perhaps in a week or so." He'd been startled by my brash approach, and smiled. "Why?"

I'd asked without really thinking it over. Now I was stuck and had to go on with my idea. "It's foolish really. I can't say I have any talent, but I've always loved drawing and, well, don't laugh. It's not like anything you do."

"What is it? Why do you hesitate?" He began to chuckle.

"Please, don't laugh. I have this wish to be a clothes designer. Every chance, I sketch my ideas for dresses and coats, even shoes." Ernst's eyes had widened, but I rushed on. "Sometimes Ida laughs, not because I'm so bad, but — well, I guess you have the same problem. She thinks I should forget my impossible notions and get married. Maybe, she's right. You can tell me. Would you look at my stuff?"

"Naturally, I'll be happy to look at what you've done. I must tell you, I'm not surprised to learn of another artist in the family. Just knowing it lifts my spirits. I look forward to next week. And I promise not to laugh!"

The deaths of his brothers Heinrich and Wilhelm had made it possible for Onkel Adam to take over the Herbst homestead, where I was born in Marnheim. He needed the room of the big house and the shop building with all the children still at home. In his stubborn mind, he wanted to involve the entire family in building a new business dynasty in upholstery and leather work. Though Ernst and others told him, he wouldn't believe that the days were numbered for such family trades.

☙

True to his word, on my cousin's next visit, he asked to see my sketches. I found an excuse to go into the courtyard, not wanting Ida's input about the matter.

Studying several drawings intensely, he looked up to meet my eyes, smiling. "These are good. No, very good! I'm not sure I agree with what you want women to wear, but I do see what you're aiming for. Your lines and proportions are just fine. Here — " He laid one of my sketches on a work bench. "Have you got a pencil? Wait, I brought one with me."

With rapid motions, he added shading to my design for a flowing cape with hood. "You're almost there. What's needed is more attention to putting in shadows and creating highlights to give depth to the drawing. See?"

I could indeed see the improvement. Handing me his pencil, the next few minutes were spent showing me how and where to apply shading to my drawing of a leather handbag. The result was so pleasing, I could have kissed him. I thanked him instead, and asked if he'd talked more with his father. Right away I was sorry. The light died in Ernst's eyes, his smile gone.

"Ah, my father," he said after a strained moment. "Well, my father shouts that I must rid my mind of crazy ideas. His sons must follow in the business. It's tradition for us in the peasant class, he said. Only the rich can afford the artist's life!"

"You can't believe that, Ernst! I've read of many from the working class who succeeded as writers and painters."

"Ja, I know. But what can I do? I have no money, and father would need to help me, at least at the start. Sometimes, I'm so unhappy I could just leave anyway." He stopped, looking at me for understanding. I did understand, but had no wisdom to share. Finally, he sighed. "But I can't even do that. Mama says it would kill her."

☙

I've often thought of that conversation and wished I had known the right words to say. I was so young, too inexperienced to recognize his desperate state. When I came home from Weierhof three days later, Ida was sitting at the kitchen table crying. Erich was there, and he told me.

421

"Cousin Ernst is dead."

"Oh, nay — don't say that!" I had shouted out denial, but I knew it was true.

"It wasn't an accident," Erich said. "He hung himself in the old barn."

"Mein Gott! That's where we all played as children!" I don't know why that memory flew into my head, but it did. Ernst had chosen a place filled with so many happy memories to die.

Through all my sorrows and humiliations, I would've never considered suicide. The thought had never entered my mind, not even fleetingly. I didn't understand how he could have done it, and leave behind all who knew and cared about him.

Funerals were nearly always hard affairs, but Ernst's was tragic. Onkel Adam moved about like a robot, not really seeing anything or anyone. My aunt became so hysterical, she had to be physically restrained. I had to think of Mama, who had also been fond of Ernst, but more so because again the school children sang while a single violin played her favorite hymn.

"Harre meine Seele — " ('Rest my soul — ')

☙

Six months later, I attended another Herbst funeral in Marnheim. It was for Hans, Ernst's older brother and best friend. He'd become mysteriously ill shortly after the suicide, and had never recovered. The loss was even sadder, as he had become engaged to a beautiful girl. She and Tante Elise had nursed Hans to the end. Tante and Onkel Adam could not be consoled. And again, I heard the violin play while the children sang.

"Harre meine Seele — "

☙

It must be told that within a year, Onkel Adam was dead. Once more, I walked to Marnheim to bare witness and hear the terrible beauty in the songs of the children with a single violin in the hilltop cemetery. My uncle had never recovered from the lost promise of two sons. He wasn't old, and he didn't seem to be sick. He just died.

"Harre meine Seele — "

Chapter Forty

I remember only that it was a warm evening in 1953 when Leo came at me with a knife. It had to be summer, because Erich wouldn't have been sleeping with only briefs and a skimpy undershirt in cold weather. That's exactly how he appeared, rushing through the kitchen door in answer to my screams.

Neither Leo nor Erich liked my working in Weierhof, but their reasons were entirely different. My brother's objection came from his belief that the Americans, the French, and the English would be leaving Germany soon. "When that happens, so many Germans will need jobs, you won't stand a chance! Go now, and apply with some German firms."

Erich had not considered that women weren't treated the same as men in Germany — not yet. A man could find a job easier, even without higher level schooling or apprenticeship training.

Leo's objections were more personal. He thought a German girl working for Americans was no better than a prostitute or worse. In spite of my growing anger, he began concentrating on that angle. His evening visits and talk, after Ida and Erich retired, increasingly turned to how I was 'ruining my reputation.' That summer evening he went too far.

"We should get married right away, before the neighborhood starts calling you a whore."

"What??" I was flabbergasted.

He was pleased by my reaction. "That's right. I've already heard some talk around. I can tell you, it's not good. They say, 'What can we expect from the daughter of a man living in sin!' Mind you, I defend — "

"Shut up!"

In the months following my return, Leo's health had noticeably improved. Along with it, came a bigger push to get me to the altar. Up until that moment, his attempts had been limited to joking around the edges. No more, and my angry response made him jump up from where he sat at the kitchen table. I'd been sitting opposite him, knitting. Throwing the needles and yarn down on the table, I remained seated and threw caution to the wind.

"You shut up about my father. And, yes, it's time to stop your talk of marriage. There'll be no marrying you, not ever!" I was spitting the words out, unable to stop. "I should have made you see that a long time ago! Get out of here and don't come back. Our friendship is finished!"

My wrath caused him to back away, until he leaned against the kitchen cupboard. When I paused to allow him time to exit the door, he found his voice. "You know we have to marry. It's the only way to protect you. Everybody agrees — "

"Stop it! I told you we're finished. Get out and don't set foot in my house ever again. In a haze of anger I saw the cupboard drawer open and his hand bring out a sharp knife. "Put it back," I shouted, standing up.

He ran toward me and shouted. "You can't say that —"

I screamed, fell back on the chair, and tried to jerk away, but his fist with the knife struck my face. I felt a sharp pain around my nose, and saw blood spill down my front.

It must have been an awful scream. Erich came crashing through the door just as Leo stepped back, throwing the knife to the floor. The sight of that knife and my bloody condition was all it took. He grabbed Leo. "What have you done to my sister??"

"I'm sorry. I didn't mean to — " Leo was very afraid.

I'd recovered enough to know that he hadn't stabbed me. When I jerked back, the blade had missed, but his fist hadn't. Still bleeding heavily, I ran to the sink for a cloth. Erich was still shaking my attacker and insisting on knowing my condition. So much bigger than Leo, he looked like he was shaking a rag doll.

Stemming the flow of blood, I finally said. "Let him go, Erich, I'll be alright. The knife missed me. I just want him to leave and never come back."

My brother had waited a long time to hear those words. He pushed Leo through the door. "You heard what she said. Get out, and don't bother us again." He continued the same message down the stairs and out the front door.

Returning, Erich looked in on me as I tried to clean up both myself and the trail of blood on the floor. The nose bleed had slowed to a trickle. "Are you going to be alright?"

"Ja, ja. I'll be fine. I ruined a good blouse, and your sleep but thank you anyway. Go back to bed. Ida's probably wondering what happened."

"Ach, it's time you got rid of him. One way is as good as the other! Ida won't be shocked. She's been predicting the whole affair would end with one or the other of you dead."

What a comforting thought to sleep on.

ॐ

The next morning, they both looked at my face with some amazement over the breakfast table. I'd slept well, considering what had happened. My nose and the area around it were sore, but there was little discoloration or swelling.

"What?"

"Oh, nothing," Erich said, grinning. "Except that most people who get slugged in the nose like that wake up with black eyes."

"He didn't hit me that hard. You know how easy I get nose bleeds."

"Not ever as bad as last night!" He turned to Ida at the stove. "You should have seen the bloody mess in here."

"I wanted no part of that scene." It was Ida's last word.

Cutting off a slice of bread, my brother began to speculate. "I think Leo is a poor loser. He won't come back to the house, but he has a lot of crummy friends. You can bet they'll start badmouthing our name."

How I wished the affair had ended much earlier. "I'll handle it. Somehow."

"You sure? People will believe anything they hear about a girl working for the Americans."

"Well, I'll make sure they also hear that my hero was a German who came to the rescue in his skimpy underwear!" Ida laughed. Erich didn't.

Walking usually helped to clear my mind of nagging problems, so I walked to Weierhof that morning not realizing rain was expected by afternoon. When it came, I was forced to take the evening bus back to Kirchheim. Standing at the bus stop, I overheard two other German workers talk about a girl from Bolanden who'd just been hired for the telephone switchboard. She was a known prostitute, and they were laughing about the Americans hiring such a girl. My reaction was different. I knew of the girl too, and it made me mad. I had no reason to know there was a switchboard in Weierhof. I'd been in the military compound only once to apply for the maid's job — but I figured if that girl could qualify as an operator, I could too.

The following morning, I asked Mrs. Crawford for a half hour off and headed for the main gate, all the time praying that my English was good enough. The guard pointed to the headquarters building. Entering, I saw a girl working in an office off the hallway. She was German, so I felt at ease asking if a place was still open in the switchboard. She nodded. "Here, fill out this application."

When I handed it back, she looked it over and told me to check with her the next day. I did, and was sent to the main Signal Corps office in Kaiserslautern to be interviewed by a woman army officer. I knew that it would be the hardest part. Traveling in by train, I told myself that my bluff was doomed to fail. My English skills were still far from perfect. The presence of a translator in the major's office puzzled me at first, but after several questions, which she said I could answer in English or German, I was approved to start the following week.

The short notice I gave to Sergeant Crawford no doubt surprised him, but he accepted on one condition. His wife had a special request for me to take care of before leaving. When I learned what it was I nearly refused, then thought better of it. If it makes her happy, and allows me to leave without complaint, I was ready to do most anything.

Mrs. Crawford took me into the bathroom, wrapped a big towel around her shoulders, sat on the stool, and handed me a toothbrush and tube of shampoo. I was to take her hair, section by tiny section, and scrub all the scalp revealed with the toothbrush and shampoo. Not a centimeter of scalp was left untouched. In my three years of service as a maid, many things were asked of me, but none stranger than shampooing a woman's head with a toothbrush.

❧

Monday morning, I walked with apprehension into the headquarters building to start a new job. I felt like a fraud about to be found out. Going down the long hall, I heard music, big band music, coming out of radios in the offices I passed. A sudden surge of happiness tingled through me and brought a smile to my face. Hearing that music and seeing relaxed and smiling faces somehow made me feel at home.

I walked into the switchboard and introduced myself to Hilde, the supervisor, and Karin, the operator on duty. It was good that my spirits were high at that moment. One look at the switchboard with its dozens of patch cords said it all — I had a lot to learn.

I can't say Hilde was upset that I'd been hired, though I sensed in her a kind of indifference. She trained me quickly and efficiently, yet did so without warmth or tolerance. When I later discovered that she had hired the Bolanden girl only to be over ruled by the major in Kaiserslautern, it all became clear. I tried to not let it bother me. We were four operators and a supervisor, dividing up a 24-hour day. I was determined to remain as one of the four.

Soon allowed to work alone, I was put on rotating work shifts. These were the usual day, evening, and late night turns running the switchboard. My biggest problem for a long time wasn't with English itself, but understanding the people who spoke it.

Naturally, a new girl in the building caused a stir among the males who worked there. During my first week, it seemed that every one of them, officers and enlisted men alike, had some excuse to drop by for a look. They didn't need a reason. After all, our door was normally open, and the men's restroom was right across the hall. I got a kick out of the attention and, at the same time, found myself introduced to English spoken with many accents.

Every evening at five, the huge building quickly emptied of everyone, except the duty officer, a night clerk, and the telephone operator. The officer only stopped in now and then, leaving the clerk, a corporal named Bob in the front office, and me at the other end of the hall. The first time I worked late shift, an accent gave me a scare. By eight o'clock I was feeling satisfied having handled all the calls with no mistakes. Another red light came on and I plugged a cord into the incoming line.

"Weierhof, may I help you?"

Not a single word the man spoke made sense. I was convinced the language was not English, and it was certainly not German. "One moment, please," I said, and raced down the hall yelling for Bob. He ran out of the office, probably thinking someone was attacking me. Seeing that I was alone, he lowered the rifle in his hand and listened to my frantic plea for help. "I'm in awful trouble. There's a man on the line and I can't understand a word!"

Bob joined me at the switchboard and picked up my headset. My nerves were nearly shot as he talked to the party. "Yes, sir. I understand. I doubt anyone would be there this time of night, but I'll have the operator connect you." Smiling, he handed back the set. "Just give him the motor pool. If it doesn't answer, connect him to transportation headquarters in Kaiserslautern."

Bob waited for me to take care of it, and then tried to calm me down. "Hey, don't worry about it. That was one of our guys in France. Worst Texas accent I've ever heard."

"I just know I'll lose my job over this."

"Don't give it another thought. You'll get used to the way we talk. Wait till you run into someone from Mississippi. Your head will spin like a top." With that said, he left, laughing all the way down the hall, the rifle slung over his shoulder.

The incident provided my first clue to the special attitude held by most GI's in Weierhof. It was a small military outpost, and as such, everyone there was 'family.' Unless a person, American or German, behaved badly, they were helped and protected.

A few days after my long-distance encounter with the Texan, I got a real shock. After showing my pass at the gate, I started walking toward the headquarters building to begin a week of day shift. That's when it happened. Loudspeakers mounted on posts and buildings all over the camp came alive. "Good morning, Fräulein Klein. Isn't it a nice day?"

Stunned, I stopped in my tracks and looked back at the gate guard. He just laughed and shrugged. It wasn't his doing. Obviously, someone in the front office had seen me coming. Though more than embarrassed, I smiled and waved toward the front office. I'd been accepted into the family.

Over the five years that followed, I slowly began to believe again in Papa's 'green twig.' The 1950's were still a period of rebuilding lives in Germany, and always with the chill of the 'cold war' threatening the effort. For myself, I had to find a way to restore the relationship with young Peter, and find peace with my father. Meanwhile, the respect I received from my American employers gave me the fervor to push on to become the best I could be at my job. It also helped me deal with the 'reputation' question that continued to hang over German girls working for the former enemy. Such attacks could be worse against girls who married Americans. But that's another story.

Shortly after starting my new job, I came home to find nine-year-old Peter in my bedroom behind a locked door. Erich was at home and could have easily found a key to unlock it, but he decided to let me handle it. Since my young brother didn't live with us, and wasn't even supposed to visit our house, it had to be a serious problem. He wouldn't tell Ida and Erich anything after running upstairs and into my bedroom. When I got there, he'd been sitting in the room two hours.

"Peter? It's Annchen. Please open the door."

"Nay. I won't!"

"How can we talk this way? Please, Peter let me in."

"You'll send me back to Papa. I don't want to." He began to cry again.

"Let me come in. I promise not to send you back."

All was quiet for a moment, then I heard him moving. He'd been sitting on the floor with his feet propped against the door. The lock clicked, and I turned the handle. What greeted me was a tear-stained but determined face. I closed the door behind me and put my arm around shoulders that were much higher than I remembered. He was growing into a fine-looking fellow.

I sat down with him on the bed. "Tell me everything. Surely, Papa wouldn't hurt you!"

It would have been difficult to convince me that our father could have done anything to his own flesh and blood. As Peter's story unfolded, my belief wasn't entirely confirmed. After Papa had suffered the stroke, Frau Rolf had assumed disciplinary control over his young son. When I learned of her methods of punishment, and that Papa allowed them, I was filled with anger. What Peter told me was outrageous.

"Frau Rolf locked me in a pig stall," he said. "Sometimes she kept me there for hours, whenever I made her mad. Today, I crawled through a window to get out. Please don't take me back."

My promise not to send him back to Langstraße was a risky one. If Papa came to our door and demanded his return, there would be nothing we could do short of going to court. No Klein or Herbst had ever solved a family problem through a judge. I left Peter in the room and went to the kitchen. Erich had to hear the story and help me make a decision. I knew if I fought to keep the boy, it would be an unfair burden for he and Ida, who were already struggling. But once they heard my report, both were as upset as I was, and immediately agreed to fight for Peter. Before involving the law though, I wanted to confront Papa and demand custody.

I went back to Peter to explain my plan, and took the relieved boy back to the kitchen where Ida had set out a plate for him. Over the supper table, an agreement was made between Erich and I. He and Ida would provide food and shelter, and I would take care of clothes, school expenses and the like. It was good I had my new job — the move from maid to telephone operator had doubled my monthly income.

At almost seven o'clock I left for Frau Rolf's house. I wondered why she hadn't sent her daughter Ingrid looking for Peter. Surely they must have known he would head up to the Breitstraße. It was Ingrid who opened the door to my knock. She said my father and her mother were in the sitting room, but didn't mention Peter's name. When I entered, it was as if both had been waiting in silence, staring at the opposite wall. For some reason, seeing them sitting like that made my anger grow.

"Peter is at our house right now," I began. "And that is where he's going to stay. It's disgraceful what you've done to him. Here's a bag. I want all his clothes to take back. Erich and I will look after Peter from now on."

I expected Frau Rolf to snap back at me. She wasn't known as an even-tempered woman. But the both of them just glanced at each other, and Papa nodded. "Ja, it's good. Take the bag, Berta."

Without a word or a look, she accepted the bag and left the room. Standing there, looking down on my little father, I tried desperately to remain angry. He didn't really look at me, not with the straight, honest eyes I'd always believed in. In the gloomy stillness, my knees were turning to rubber. All resolve to hate what he'd done to his family was fading. "Why did you let that woman treat Peter so terribly? My God! Locked up for hours, and in an animal stall! How could you permit it?"

I waited for an answer, and it finally came. I saw that it was hard for him to speak, and only then remembered his stroke. The words came slowly, "You couldn't understand. It's good. You keep Peter. Let him — visit me."

"Like you let him visit us!" I had to stay mad, or risk breaking down in tears watching Papa struggle.

Frau Rolf returned with a bag that didn't appear very full. She put it on the floor a few feet from me and stood near Papa, refusing to look me in the face. For the first time, my father's eyes met mine. They pleaded for me to understand the situation, but I couldn't. There was no forgiveness. I picked up the bag. "I won't stop Peter from visiting. I just think it'll be a long time before he wants to."

Just a few weeks later, Erich asked me to speak to Papa again. There were rumors that Breitstraße One had been sold. Being the oldest, and the one helping to pay the mortgage, Erich should have made the effort himself. But he had promised Ida never to speak to his father again. It was heartbreaking to me, as I remembered how Erich had loved and respected his father the same as I. Both of us felt powerless to deal with the reasons behind our dilemma.

While Papa didn't drive his truck for hauling anymore, he would often bring it up to the Freier Platz to park overnight, as Frau Rolf didn't have a courtyard where it could be parked. Aware of the evening ritual, I walked down to wait for him at the base of the tall memorial statue that stood in the center of the plaza.

It was getting dark when he pulled in and, I ran to climb into the passenger side. "We need to talk, Papa."

If he was surprised by my sudden appearance, it didn't show. "Ja, Annchen," he replied, turning off the engine. "Why do you wait for me here?"

"Erich has heard that you're selling the house. Is it true?"

"Why doesn't Erich do his own asking? I've never refused to talk with him."

"Papa, please. You must know how it is with Ida."

"Ja, ja. That's a problem. Well, you tell him I don't want to sell."

"Please don't! You know I love that house, but — "

"But what, daughter?"

"It's that, well, Erich wanted to know if you are selling, would you let him buy it?"

It seemed like a long time before Papa answered, as though he had worn himself out with the little already spoken. "The house is not for sale."

"I'll tell him." I reached for the door handle, stepped down, and looked back across the seat. The man behind the wheel looked so small, so exhausted. "Papa, I — thank you."

I felt awful about questioning my father, and for a split of a second, I wanted to express my regret about the whole mess. I couldn't, and again wondered what happened to the man who always talked of the 'green twig.' I made my way back to the house.

"Do you believe him?" Erich said.

"How can you say that? I've never known Papa to lie."

"Times have changed him," he answered. "I hope you're right."

I was wrong. Two days later, a realtor knocked and requested to be allowed to show the new owner the house. I felt like someone had slammed me against a wall. Our father, the man said, had filed for bankruptcy, forcing sale of the house.

"But why didn't he let us buy the house?" I said.

"I couldn't answer that, Fräulein. If we may come in, I'll explain the terms, and when you must be out."

I left the intruders with Erich and Ida and went to my room. I didn't cry. The old numbness was back, completely blocking my tears. I only knew that the one person I totally trusted had betrayed me. There was a knock on my door — the realtor wanted to show the room. I walked out of the house and into the garden until they were gone. I could hear Erich's raging through the open kitchen window.

Peter came into the courtyard, home from school. I briefly explained what had happened as we went upstairs. Ida and Erich were sitting at the table.

"You don't have to say it," I said numbly. "Papa lied to us — lied to me. What I don't understand is why. I could have taken the truth from him. If he

431

had to sell the house to pay creditors, he could have told me. He didn't have to lie!"

"It's a sad thing to find out your father's a liar." Erich's voice was calmer than I expected. Seeing tears well up in Peter's eyes, I shook my head at Erich, warning him not to go on.

"Enough said," he agreed. "One good thing, under the law, we can't be forced to leave here until I find another house."

❧

It took all of October and November to find something in the scarce housing market in 1953. Erich finally found a nice place near the top of the hill at Breitstraße 65. We got moved in just in time for Christmas, but before that happened, I had some other business to look after.

Erich thought, and I agreed, that something should be salvaged from Papa's crashing fortunes — not for him or me, but for Peter. With Erich's support, I went to court to save some inheritance for the boy. Mama had brought parcels of land into the marriage. These, I told the judge, should be set aside for Peter when settling my father's debts. He agreed, and it was done.

❧

The military world I encountered in Weierhof was foreign but exciting. My prior contacts were always with individual soldiers, not the vast machine in which they are mere cogs. Given the job of keeping all parts connected to the whole was scary and fascinating at the same time. The telephone is by its nature an instrument of intimacy, and when ninety-nine percent of the telephone users were male, some interesting moments and direct benefits fell on the operators.

Anytime a telephone receiver was picked up in the compound, a red light appeared on the board in front of me. No phones had dials, and therefore, all calls came through the board. Even calls within the headquarters, from office to office, had to be connected by an operator. The system also enabled us to know from what location the call came even before plugging in.

The mess sergeant always identified himself and his location before asking if the operators would like some dessert treat. We knew it was the mess hall calling when we plugged in. The girls would joke privately, 'Don't call, and just bring whatever you've got that's good to eat.'

Unless it was an outright gift, like chocolates, most operators paid for whatever treats they requested of the boys to buy at the PX. We felt lucky to be asked. It wasn't permitted for German employees to buy directly, so if a fellow offered to buy with my money, I saw nothing wrong. As for gifts of chocolates, the first time it happened put me on edge.

The heavy cables coming out of the board went up to the ceiling, over to the center of the room, and straight down into a hole in the floor. The floor section around the small hole was removable to allow work on the lines. Normally, the section was in place to prevent accidents. I was shown how to lift the section up if asked by one of the signalmen working in the basement, and then promptly forgot about it. A few weeks into my employment, while working alone at night, I heard a strange tapping, and looked everywhere around the room trying to figure out the source. After a few minutes a red light appeared on the board in a spot that rarely lit up. I plugged in.

"Hey, this is Joe in the frame room below you. This Anna?"

I was finding Americans particularly adept at tossing my name around to suit their taste. Anything from 'Ann' to 'Annie,' but rarely 'Anna' pronounced the German way.

"Yes, sir. This is Anna." The light indicated the frame room phone, but I didn't know any 'Joe' among the signal group.

"I've been trying to get your attention to open the cable hole. I have something for you. Lift off the lid!"

I left the board and went over to where the cable disappeared into the floor. I was soon staring down into the face of a young man with curly blonde hair.

"Hi," he said, smiling. "Reach your hand down. I want you to have a box of chocolates. Call it a late Valentine's present."

"Nay — uh, no," I blurted, surprised by his offer. "Thank you, no. I couldn't take chocolates from a stranger. Besides, I don't know what you mean. What is Valentine's?"

I had not heard of Valentine's Day. His laugh didn't help my embarrassment. "You haven't heard of the day when men give their sweethearts candy?"

"No. It sounds nice, but you're not my sweetheart!"

"Ah, you're new around here. All the operators are sweethearts to the guys. Nothing serious, just our way of saying that it's nice having you around. Go ahead, reach down and take the box, or I'll have to get the ladder and bring it up."

"Alright," I said, sticking my hand into the hole. Bringing the box back through the opening, I saw that it was big enough for ten people. Joe was still standing there when I started covering the hole. Then I remembered something important.

"Thank you! I'm going to leave the chocolates here for everyone to enjoy."

"Do that," he laughed. "But you are first!"

I smiled at him and closed the hole. The operators were definitely spoiled by the men — a decent bunch of fellows, from the officers to the lowest private. The same can't be said for everyone in Weierhof. There were those faceless callers from various phones in the compound, some innocently attempting to get a date, others offering everything from filthy proposals to heavy breathing. If I wasn't too startled to pull the plug instantly, most of these callers quickly hung up, probably realizing I knew which phone was being used. It was an advantage of the switchboard operation. Fortunately, such calls didn't occur that often — we were just too small a place to escape detection for long.

❧

The mess hall serving the post was across the street from our building. The mess sergeant was a friendly soul, and smart about his cooks. Except when he had one of the cooks deliver an urn of coffee in the mornings, things like desserts and sandwiches only made it half way to our door.

"You come out and meet my cook outside in the street," he said. "I don't want him going in your building. He'll take all day coming back."

Often it was I who went into the mess hall to pick up the food. I remember being amazed at the huge dining area, empty when I saw it, and all shiny and clean from floor to ceiling. The only time I visited the mess hall with people eating was when the sergeant invited all the operators to share in the Thanksgiving dinner, my introduction to another American tradition.

Hilde watched the board when it came my turn to go over. I was very nervous, and prayed I wouldn't trip and fall in front of a roomful of men. I sighed with relief when I saw only a few G.I.'s still eating. One of the cooks came up to me at the door.

"You must be one of the operators."

"Yes, sir, the sergeant invited me."

"I know, and you don't have to call me sir. I'm just a lowly cook. Come, I'll show you to a table."

The table was in the officer's section. Two lieutenants were chatting over coffee, and both nodded and smiled. The cook went away, promising to return. In short order, he came back with a plate heaped high with steaming food. I recognized none of it, except the beautiful yellow corn. I knew corn, but Germans grew it for animal feed, not for people. I must have stared at the bounty before me with doubt on my face.

"Let me tell you about a Thanksgiving dinner," my server began. "We have here turkey meat with giblet gravy over bread dressing. In this little bowl is cranberry sauce. This is sweet corn and over here…"

I let him finish the tour, thanked him, and picked up a fork. I forget how many times he returned to urge me on. I was already full and there was still half the food yet to eat. Hilde had said I should leave room for something called pumpkin pie. That hadn't been offered yet and my brain said "leave!" The cook, however, looked so disappointed with my appetite that I felt compelled to forge ahead.

With the plate finally clean, the cook refilled my coffee cup. "You sure there's no room for more dressing and gravy? Turkey?"

I shook my head, hoping not to belch or throw up on his nice white outfit. He whipped around to a nearby table and reappeared with another plate. "Here you go. Pumpkin pie to top off dinner!"

For someone who made a practice of eating small amounts at meals, I was convinced the pie wouldn't go down. But, looking up at my generous host, I finished it off in record time. Enjoying pumpkin pie would have to come much later, on a less full stomach.

❧

The following Thanksgiving, 1954, I skipped the dinner. I was working the three to eleven shift, and it seemed foolish to go in three hours early. Nonetheless, the day taught me a lot about the loneliness of young men far away from home. It was both strange and touching.

After eight o'clock, my board had quieted down for the night. It was like that on holidays — not much talking on the phone. The few men who had to be on duty called only when necessary. Of the rest, half were probably in Worms or Kaiserslautern wasting their time in bars or walking the streets. The other half were satisfied to read or play cards with friends in the barracks. The snack bar and library closed at ten o'clock. It was another slow holiday evening, and a good time to catch up on my knitting.

At around nine, a light blinked on. It was the little guard house on the gate, and I wondered what he might want. Probably some problem with a drunk soldier or one of the 'painted girls' demanding to see some guy. In either case, the Officer-of-Day was called.

"Operator. May I help you?"

435

"Uh, this is the guard on the gate."

"Yes? Do you want the O.D.?"

"Well, uh, no. It's just that there's not much going on like usual. You know, it's Thanksgiving and, uh — "

"Yes, I know," I interrupted, wishing I knew where this was all leading.

"I can't help thinking of my family back home. By now, everyone's sitting around full of turkey and pie. My wife and two little ones are there, with Mom and Dad, and my brothers and sisters. I sure miss them!"

By this time I was glad I hadn't pulled the plug, but didn't know what to say.

"Please, would you talk to me a few minutes, so I can get over feeling sorry for myself."

"If you like." It hadn't been a question, but a plea, and I didn't have the heart to refuse.

"Tell me about yourself. Have you been here long? Are you someone I know?"

"Oh, no. I know you, but I'm sure you hardly notice me coming through the gate. Doesn't matter. It was nice, though, when you kind of smiled in my direction. Reminded me of Sue. Don't get me wrong. I'm not saying you look like my wife. Just sometimes, she'd smile at me for no reason at all. It made me think of her when you did."

I had to leave my lonely caller a couple of times to make connections, but when I returned, it was clear all he had on his mind was family. He said so much about his wife and two little ones, I could almost picture them. Then, there were Mom and Dad, and the youngest sister in her last year of high school.

"Good thing, too," he was saying. "Dad's getting along in years and wants to retire soon. I hate being so far from them. The next year is going to be rough. It sounds unpatriotic, and I don't say it to just anyone, but it's not right for a man with children to be drafted."

"Drafted?" I'd heard the word, but just couldn't think of the meaning.

"You know, forced to come in the army."

"Ah, yes. My father was drafted. Twice."

"You mean in the Wehrmacht?"

I was surprised he knew the word. "No, he was taken into the Luftwaffe. Papa was in his forties, and we thought he was too old to be, as you say, drafted."

"Well, you just made me feel a lot less sorry for myself."

For the first time, I laughed, and so did he. I looked at the clock. We'd been talking for over an hour. In another half hour, the night shift started. I'd agreed to stay and work it, too, for one of the girls.

"I guess I've taken enough of your time," he said. "What I want to say is — thanks. You have a nice voice, and it was great you listened." He paused, and only his breathing told me he was still there. "Would you do me one last favor?"

"I don't know."

He had obviously screwed up his courage for something, I just wasn't sure I wanted to know what.

"Please, don't get me wrong. You're going to think I'm crazy, but it's nothing bad. Maybe you'll understand. Sue, my wife, well, every night at bedtime, she always said, 'Good night, honey.' Could you say it to me? I'll hang up then."

It was crazy, but something told my brain to do it. With nervous fingers around the cord, I took a deep breath. "Good night, honey." The plug came out, and the light went off. Sitting back in my chair, my emotions were mixed. For one thing, I was glad he wouldn't be on duty when I passed the gate in the morning. I could understand loneliness, and I wanted to believe he just needed a sympathetic ear. Many of the fellows who worked in the building talked about missing home all the time. Maybe it wasn't so bad if one young husband and father, so far from home, went to bed that night with my voice in his ear. Maybe he really could pretend it was Sue saying, "Good night, honey." I hoped so.

Chapter Forty-One

The year that had passed between the two mess hall Thanksgiving experiences, was marked only by ordinary events. I felt close again to young Peter, and my attachment to little Brunhilde had grown as well. The three of us would spend endless hours walking in the forest when I wasn't working. Sometimes, I'd take them by train to Kaiserslautern to shop and walk around the busy downtown. There were still empty, bombed-out places — Kaiserslautern had suffered over sixty percent destruction in the war. Rebuilding was on a fast track, but it would be another few years before all the gaps were filled in. The children didn't seem to want to know what had happened, and I didn't want to talk about it. Peter was already learning about the war in school, and Brunhilde would be there soon enough.

&

I continued to be unmotivated about romance. One reason, I suppose, was what gathered outside the Weierhof gate on any day or night. The 'painted girls' waited for soldier boys who would provide cigarettes, bar soap, and sex. Some of the girls were prostitutes, so money was also a factor. A few of the girls had higher dreams of marriage and a trip to America. Very often the G.I. was already married with a family waiting at home and a wedding band in his shaving kit for the duration. I got to hear of many girls who never made it to the boat, and worse, were left in a pregnant state.

Illegal abortion was big business, and orphanages were filled with babies whose mothers feared the procedure or the law. They had good reason to be afraid. Only the lucky ones survived unscathed. Injury or death happened because women, for whatever reason, could only look to the back alleys for abortion.

For me, it all came down to maintaining my self-respect. Not long after Mama died, my father took me aside for a warning. "Without your mother, you won't always have a place to run for proper guidance. Being a girl, you won't feel able to speak to me freely about some things. I can only tell you to conduct yourself so as not to bring shame on the house."

I got the message, but wondered why girls had to follow a different code than men did. Papa's later decision to move in with Frau Rolf had added to my confusion. Disappointment had led to my running after fun on the dance floor, not really immoral behavior in itself, but it had left an opening for Leo. The smear campaign he put on for months afterward was my penalty. It was all the more reason to tread carefully around the men in Weierhof.

There was nothing easy about it. In the headquarters alone, there were a score of appealing unmarried young men. Take away half who weren't interested in me, still left enough to consider. The first months saw me far too shy to go beyond accepting an invitation for coffee in the snack bar. In time, I agreed to dinner dates, but not in any of Kirchheim's Gasthaus' (inns). Leo's attempts to hurt my name in town were too fresh. There were plenty of other villages nearby with nice places to eat. Of the three or four who asked me out, none got out of line. They were all nice mates for someone, just not for me. I was beginning to want to see the world without male company. There was one man though, who almost made me change my mind.

It was Joe, the very same who'd given me the box of chocolates. I had no idea that he was the supply officer until days later when he suddenly showed up at the door of the switchboard. His head nearly reached the top of the doorway.

Neither Hilde nor I could miss seeing the tall man at the door, though I was busy handling calls. As the Chief Operator, Hilde sat at a small desk near the door taking care of paper work. She also relieved operators for meals and breaks during the day.

"Hi, Hilde, how's it going?" He said it without actually looking at her. His eyes were on me. "And you must be Anna."

I nodded, and wondered why he was making such a point of it. Hilde was her usual ingratiating self when dealing with the Americans. "Hi, Lieutenant Whitley," she said, smiling. "Can I help you with anything?"

He just shook his head at her, grinning. "You don't remember me, do you?" The question was for me. I didn't, but he rushed on, apparently unconcerned about it. "The box of chocolates through the hole in the floor, that was me."

He sure looked different towering over me, instead of the other way around. "I'm sorry. You don't look the same as the other night." He laughed, and I went on. "Thanks again. I wish I could offer you some, but the box is empty."

"No, no. That's okay," he said, laughing again. "Supplies are my business. I know where to get more chocolates."

A light on the switchboard came on, and I turned to make a connection. When I looked up again, he was gone. Hilde gave me a quizzical look, and I shrugged.

Over the next weeks, it seemed that Joe Whitley had to go by our door frequently, always managing to poke his head in for a cheery greeting. But every week, another box of chocolates would arrive.

Some of the other girls thought our chocolate supplier was a heartthrob, but I didn't quite see him that way. He was friendly, generous, and not bad to look at. He just didn't turn me on. Maybe it was the blond hair. At the time, I was very prejudiced about things like that. Leo had reinforced the feeling, since he, too had blond hair.

Joe's interest in my direction went unnoticed — by me. Other concerns, like family matters, distracted me, and I didn't consider myself his type anyway. Except for keeping myself clean and my hair fresh and shining, I wore little or no makeup. Whenever I tried make-up, the results never pleased me, and off it came. Because making nice clothes was necessity and passion all in one, I did fear weight gain and losing my shape. Walking or riding a bicycle nearly everywhere, helped in that regard, but there wasn't much I could do about a mouth too wide or a nose a little too big — or did I want to.

Joe's rather indirect approach didn't help my awareness of his intentions. The post library was in the room next to us at the end of the building. Users went into it by way of an outside entrance, but there was a connecting door to the switchboard, kept closed during the week. On Sundays, Margo, a German woman hired as librarian, liked to keep it open to get at our coffee, and to chat when things were slow. Joe spent a lot of free time in the library, and unbeknownst to me, made sure he visited when I worked Sundays. Suddenly he'd be there in the doorway, striking up a conversation. The switchboard was off-limits after business hours and on weekends, and while Margo freely came in and out to rob the coffee pot, Joe wouldn't step over the threshold. He didn't have to, I sat only feet from the door. Assuming he visited with all the operators who worked Sundays, I just thought of it as another chance to practice my English in conversation. What a shock to find out from other girls that Joe never showed up when they pulled weekend duty.

One morning on a lovely spring day, Joe suddenly stepped through the doorway. The expression on his face left no doubt that he was excited. "Hilde, could you relieve Anna for a few minutes? I need her to do something."

"Of course, sir, it's almost time for her break anyway."

With a big grin, he motioned for me to come over to the door, and I couldn't refuse. When I got next to him, he opened a hand to show me two little silver bars, very much like the gold ones on his shoulders.

"I've been promoted, Anna. From now on it's First Lieutenant Joe Whitley. I'm second to no one now, except the Captain, of course. What have you got to say about that?"

"Congratulations, Joe. I'm really happy for you. I'll be glad to shake your hand. I don't know what else…"

"You can pin them on," he laughed. "That's what else! It's tradition."

"Hilde could put them on for you."

He leaned toward me to whisper. "Ah, but don't you think Hilde is a little too short?"

She wasn't, but when he stooped down, I took a silver bar and replaced the gold. Going around to the other side, I noticed Hilde looking at us, her chin dropped in surprise. Finishing, I smiled. "There you are. It looks real sharp!"

"The next part of the tradition is a kiss, right here!" He pointed to his left cheek.

"Oh, alright, if it's a tradition." I planted a kiss, and wondered what Hilde thought about it.

"Thank you," he said, then whispered again. "Now, are you busy tonight? It's also tradition to celebrate."

I protested. "Lieutenant Whitley, I don't go to bars!"

"No, no! The officer's club in Kaiserslautern is not exactly a bar, and they even have a band for dancing."

That did it. How could I turn down a chance to dance in an American club? Still, I didn't want it to be too easy for him. "This is a weekday. I can't stay out late, and you know the train doesn't — "

"I have a car."

Looking into his big grinning face, I had to give in. "Alright, I'll go."

We set a time to pick me up, and he bounced out the door. I was taken by surprise that he knew how to get to my house.

Apparently, it seemed, he's walked around Kirchheim more than most G.I.s. Then again, the Bachelor Officers Quarters were in a confiscated villa on the Glaserstraße, not far from my street.

"Well, it looks to me like you have a serious romance going," Hilde said haughtily.

"What — that? He just wanted someone to pin on his new bars. It doesn't mean a thing!"

"Oh no? Maybe you don't know that officers always have their sweethearts pin on new rank insignia!"

"Well, I'm not his sweetheart!" Returning to my place at the board, I found myself strangely embarrassed. It seemed that I had said the same thing to him the night he passed the chocolates through the hole in the floor.

&

That evening, Joe introduced me to shrimp cocktail, then treated me to dinner with wine, but best of all was being back on the dance floor. His dancing was passable, though not great. I didn't care, it was fun listening and dancing to a live band again.

"Did you have a good time?" Joe had pulled the car up to the stone archway of my brother's house.

"Yes, of course. Thank you very much. And again, congratulations." I leaned over to give him a kiss on the cheek and met his lips head on. It was nice, but I felt no passion.

"I'd like to see you again," he said. "Maybe a movie or sightseeing in Heidelberg. I don't care."

"Let's talk about it in a few days. Alright?"

"That's fine with me."

&

Spring turned to summer, and I'd found a new friend. His kisses still created no sparks, and his hands behaved. It was a relief not having to fight off sexual demands. Joe wasn't demanding or pushy, and best of all, he didn't endlessly talk about himself. Joe would ask, then really listen to what I said. With each date, I found myself increasingly attracted to him in a comfortable sort of fashion.

His interest in me, my family, the Donnersberg area, and Germany was boundless. Very often we'd go to a movie in Weierhof or Kaiserslautern to dine out at the officer's club. Sometimes we went to see the sights in Mainz or Heidelberg. After learning about my younger brother, Joe happily invited Peter to come along on the tours. They hit it off quite well, considering the language problem. I became the translator, and not the best one at that.

Our romance had it's simple pleasures — long walks in the forest, and Sunday afternoons listening to classical music on his record player at his bachelor officer's apartment in the villa. His taste in music jumped around a bit, from modern jazz to classical. He liked big band music, though not as much as I did. We had no disagreement about classical music. We'd snuggle on his bed, the window open to bright sunshine and gentle breezes, as the music of one of the masters flowed over us. He never invited me into his bed, and I pondered over this disinterest at times. I was quite satisfied to kiss and cuddle, but his meager overtures toward the sexual made me wonder if I was somehow lacking in appeal. A single attempt to learn the answer caught us unprepared to handle the awkward moment.

I have mentioned that his quarters were in a confiscated villa in Kirchheim. It was one of the fancier estate homes of the wealthy, built after the turn of the century. On the Sundays I visited him, the building was usually abandoned by most of the other officers. They preferred to be elsewhere on a day off. The situation enabled wonderful privacy for lots of things, including a luxurious bath for me. It was his idea. Showing me around the second floor on my first visit, he opened a door off the hallway into the biggest bathroom I'd ever seen. Devoted entirely to the art of keeping the body clean, the walls and floor were covered with gleaming tile. Along one wall, were fancy sinks with cold and hot water faucets in a row. There were some shower stalls and one long, beautiful bath tub nearby. Joe laughed at my wide eyes.

"Bet you've never seen a bath tub this big." He actually got in it, fully clothed, as he talked. "I'm six-three, and I can lay down flat without my head or feet touching the ends."

For a girl raised on heated bath water from the top of an iron cook stove, the sight of such a wondrous tub with its gold-plated hot and cold water faucets, must have put envy and desire all over my face.

"Would you like to take a bath?"

"Well, I —" I didn't know what to say, or what he had in mind.

"Hey. Don't worry. I'll go get a bath towel and a bar of soap, and you can have all the privacy you want."

He quickly returned with a towel and soap, showed me how to work the faucets, and left again. I stripped off my clothes while the tub filled. I cautiously stepped into the heated water and sank slowly down into it. I must have languished in luxury for a half hour and more. It may have been longer, since Joe had to knock on the door to jerk me from my reverie.

"You still alive in there?"

"I'll be out in five minutes," I shouted back.

On my third visit to his quarters, we discovered a sad truth. The day was beautiful enough to sit out on the flower-filled balcony, and we sipped wine and listened to Vivaldi through the open French doors. We would just relax and listen to music, interrupting now and then to speak.

At no time did we speak of love, as in 'I love you' or 'Do you love me?' But he had told me several times of having written his parents about me, along with several photographs of us together or of me alone.

"You want a bath before the other guys start coming in?"

"Yes, if you think it's okay."

"Go ahead. I've got some requisition forms to finish up. Then we can drive over to Kaiserslautern for supper."

I grabbed a towel and a bar of soap, and whistled a happy tune all through a bath. I soon returned to his room, dressed again. The ends of my hair were still wet, so I sat on the edge of his bed shaking and toweling them dry. It was no surprise when he came over and started kissing me. Throwing the towel on the floor, his hands went around my waist, pulling me close. Suddenly, they slipped under my sweater, and just as quickly retreated. I had to laugh at the startled look on his face.

"You don't have a slip on!" His shock at touching smooth, bare skin made me laugh harder.

Other than the usual bra and underpants, I wore a white sweater over a black and white checked skirt. "I don't wear slips on a warm day. Why would you expect a slip?"

"No reason," he stammered. "I just thought — well, I didn't want to give you the wrong idea!"

"About what, touching the bare skin on my back? Come here, I don't mind." And I didn't. I thought it might help to make his kisses less boring.

Starting in again, and with his hands roaming over my lower back, he did warm up, and put more effort toward something resembling passion. Being rubbed in the same confined area got a little irritating though. I pulled back, and in one movement, removed the sweater.

"Now you have a bigger area to touch," I announced, sitting there in my skirt and bra. He stared. His expression was one of wonderment, like a child who opens a gift expecting socks, but finding instead, a glowing, magical stone to touch and make wishes come true. Bringing his hands to my bare shoulders, I offered, "This is no different than kissing someone in a bathing suit."

"I don't think I've ever kissed anyone in a bathing suit," he answered, beginning to move his hands over and down my back. Fingers brushing over the bra clasp brought another reaction, "How do you open that thing?"

I turned to face him, my mind racing. No man, not Leo or any other man, had seen my bare bosom. Shame had nothing to do with it. I considered my breasts perfect for my shape, not too big or too small. Still, I'd never felt compelled to bare my breasts to anyone. Mere seconds had passed since Joe's question.

"It's easy," I said, my hands flying back, releasing the clasp. Bringing the bra straps over my arms, I put the garment on the bed.

It had been a rash move on my part, but motivated by the nagging question: Does he or doesn't he find me physically attractive? Hesitantly, he reached out, cupping my breasts with each hand, and gently massaged their soft fullness for a long moment. I expected to be pulled in an embrace and smothered in kisses, but instead his hands dropped away and he sat back, looking most uncomfortable. I returned his gaze, undoubtedly with an expression that began as a question and ended with outright disgust for allowing myself to be misled and shamed.

"Uh — you know, I did tell you I'm a minister's son," he reminded. "What do you say we get ready and go to dinner?"

Our ride to Kaiserslautern was quiet. Sitting across from each other at the club, we knew that it was our last meal together. Since neither of us spoke about it, I could only speculate as to his reasons, but I knew mine.

About three weeks later, I was told that Joe was to be transferred to another post. In the interim, we spoke during encounters in the hall, and it was always brief and polite. His leaving made life easier for me — the one man to see and touch my uncovered bosom was gone. I was at first angered over Joe's misleading behavior, and I again put up my guard about romantic relationships.

Months later, I ran into him on the street in Kaiserslautern. While we chatted only a minute, he was quite anxious to tell me of finding a 'very nice American girl' to date.

While I suspected he was trying to hurt me, I put on my sincerest face. "I'm really happy for you, Joe. Good luck!"

I realized that I wasn't without fault in our failed romance. He may have been bothered that I kept him away from Erich and Ida. The matter was never discussed, but I should have told him that both of them were adamantly opposed to my dating any American. They had known about us, couldn't stop it, and thought the worst.

Just for fun, Ida and I allowed ourselves the occasional visit to a fortune-teller's house in the old city. Frau Schneegans laid the cards for a small donation. In return, we got an hour's worth of entertaining information about our futures. I can't say whether Ida believed in it any more than me, but we did enjoy her predictions. Before television filled leisure time for older women and teenage girls, visiting a Wahrsager was one of the things done for entertainment. Other people approached it with more serious intent.

Young women liked to hear about possible husbands, babies, and that sort of revelation. Frau Schneegans offered the same to me, but only one of her predictions made me sit up.

"Fräulein Klein, someday you're going far, far away from here. It won't be real soon, but you'll go. Believe the cards! The cards say it's true."

"Going away could be exciting. But, I wouldn't want to stay away. What do the cards say about coming back?"

She studied the layout, adding one card and then another. "The cards don't reveal any return."

⁊

Christmas of 1954 was a truly white one. Heavy snowfall had begun on the weekend before, and I got the notion to take Brunhilde and Peter for a snowy Sunday outing in the forest. As expected, they were enthusiastic when I brought my old big sled out from storage. At four and a half, Brunhilde was no load at all for Peter and I to pull up the hill to the Schillerhain, where we'd enter the forest. Peter was ten, and more than a sport about a snowy jaunt in the forest.

Getting to the forest was easier from my brother's new house at the top of Breitstraße. Another fifty meters, and the road forked off to the Schillerhain and access to a main entry into the forest.

Before reaching it, we passed the hotel with its broad promenade and gardens, now almost unrecognizable under a heavy cover of snow. The health spa sanitarium was not far away, but for the patients who were usually out enjoying the park, the winter scene had to be viewed from the inside.

The start of the "Lang Schneise," the local name for the wide lane that begins the forest journey, was located near the soccer stadium, and we were soon there.

The day was windless, and I'd noticed on leaving the house an incredible stillness, caused by the blanket of heavy snow. The quiet intensified as we followed the lane deeper into heavier tree growth. It wasn't really cold or hard-going, but I had brought along some pocket candy to re-fuel our energies. Moving into the forest, away from houses and streets, my heart was lifted by the visual reminders everywhere of winter's beauty. I'd been away much too long from a snow-covered forest. The sun was hidden by an overcast sky, and

I could tell more snow was on the way.

I had no concern about additional snow. All of us were warmly bundled, including head cover. We could laugh at a few flakes of snow. Watching Peter scoop up snow balls to aim at imaginary wild boars, I saw ahead the small hut, a popular resting point for patients from the sanitarium who ventured that far in better weather. The rustic wood structure was also nice for hikers surprised by sudden storms. A door off the covered porch was never locked. Through it was a single room with a couple of windows. The hut meant an end to the straight and level wide lane, some two kilometers from Schillerhain.

The lane here narrowed considerably, and intersected with other more rugged trails. From the hut, a stranger needed a map identifying the markings on trees. Each trail had its own symbol, and the map provided direction and destination. It was too easy to get lost without the guide. For day-long outings, even a native is wise to add the markings to knowledge passed down over generations. Every Pfälzer knows that the deep forest is a bad place to lose one's way.

Our trek wasn't intended to be long. We left the house around one-thirty, and I'd planned to be home by four-thirty, before evening dark. In my head, our route was all laid out. At the hut, turn right, go to another trail, and again to the right. From there, I thought, we'd follow the path back to the road to Rockenhausen, cross over into the Judenthal, and return home.

"Annchen?"

"Ja, Hildchen. Are you cold?" Despite the fact she was my niece, I never insisted that she address me as 'Tante.' I stopped to check her condition on the sled. Peter was just a few steps ahead.

"I'm fine," she said, only her face showing to the elements. "Tell us a story!"

"A story? What would you like to hear?" I asked, but already knew the answer.

"Rotkäppchen," she squealed loudly. She loved Little Red Riding Hood, and asked me to tell it so many times that I began changing small details. 'That's not right,' she always corrected.

Peter had his say. "Aw, that's a fairy tale for babies. Tell us about someone my age!"

We'd made the turn at the hut several minutes before, and I didn't want to miss the next one. Peter had given me the idea for a perfect story, but telling it while pulling a sled up and down hills on a path that swerved around trees and bushes wasn't going to be easy.

"Alright, Peter. Help me pull and I'll tell about another Peter when he was just your age."

"You're not going to give us one of those tales where you change the characters' names to Peter and Brunhilde! I don't want to hear it!"

Again, I laughed. My old story-telling tricks had been exposed. "Ach, is that what I do? Well, not today. This is a true story about a ten-year-old farm boy living in the Alps long ago. When he got older he wrote famous books about his life. Someday I hope you read them. His name was Peter Rosegger, and my old teacher, Herr Lawaldt, would read his stories around this time of year. There was one about a Christmas Eve, when Peter got lost in a snow-storm trying to get home. Would you like to hear it?"

They did, and I proceeded, getting quite caught up in my memories of sitting in Herr Lawaldt's class at Christmastime.

Finally, I stopped on the snowy path to put a big flourish on the end of the tale, and received fine applause for my effort. New snow was falling as I looked around us. A shock suddenly ran through me. I hadn't the least notion where we were. Nothing in sight seemed familiar. Wrapped up in the story, I'd missed the other path. Looking at the children in my charge, I put on my best smile to cover my concern. "The snow's coming down harder than I expected. Maybe we should take a shortcut here for home."

I felt we had to go right again, trail or no trail, so I urged Peter in that direction. Fortunately, the tree growth allowed fairly easy passage — there was plenty of room to maneuver the sled around obstacles. I just had to remember to keep in a straight line. Peter was a great help. He instinctively stayed on course. However, after twenty minutes, the snowfall made it hard to see. Something was terribly wrong.

We should have hit the Rockenhausen road, or at least come near it, where I could better recognize our location. There was nothing up front or to the left or right that gave me any comfort. We were all turning white in the blizzard of snow.

"Peter," I hollered, "come back." Trying to be as light about the situation as possible, I reached into my pocket for the candies. "Here, take a couple of these. You, too, Hildchen."

I couldn't believe how fast the snow came, quickly filling in our own tracks. I was so frightened, it was a struggle to keep my wits and my voice calm. "Listen, you two. I think, instead of going the way I originally wanted, it's probably best to follow our own tracks back. Peter, let's see how good you are in finding the way we came. I'll be right behind you."

"Sure. It'll be fun!"

I was glad he thought so. Between the curtain of falling snow and the fading daylight, it was hard for me to make out any tracks in the ground cover. Going along at a much faster clip, Peter had turned the problem into a game. "Over this way," he'd yell, and race on. "Here's the trail we were on!"

I thought about all those old American western stories that had fascinated me as a child — how the Indians were used to scout the way through wilderness. Peter was my Indian scout. Soon I heard his voice again. "The hut is just up ahead!"

The snow was coming down even harder, but once my feet hit the wide lane it didn't matter. I could walk it with my eyes closed. At the Schillerhain, the road down to the Breitstraße was a long and winding downhill run. In my joy at seeing it, I had a fun idea and called Peter back.

"Thank you, Peter. You did a great job leading us back. Climb on the sled behind Hildchen. Let's end our jaunt with some real fun. That's it, move up and wrap your legs around her so I can get on, too." The road had been plowed, but the new snow made it perfect for what I had in mind. Shoving off, I put my legs around the children, my feet on the front guide, and away we zipped, laughing and screaming down to Breitstraße and home.

It was dark when we reached the house. That stone archway sure looked good to me. The children ran ahead and were already peeled out of their wet things by the time I'd walked into the kitchen. Erich was sitting at the table reading while Ida put the final touches on supper. She was the first to speak, "You were gone a long time. I was worried. In another few minutes I would have sent Erich out for you!"

Turning a page of his paper, Erich looked up at his wife. "Ach, you're such a worrier. Anna knows the forest almost as well as me. You don't have to worry about her getting lost, right sister?"

Glancing at my two rosy-cheeked companions smiling up at me, I inwardly sighed with relief.

"Right, Erich."

Chapter Forty-Two

In mid-January of 1955, the Weierhof switchboard closed. A new dialing system, installed by the Signal Corps crews in less than a month, had made operators obsolete. Erika, Margie and I agreed to a transfer — we would be working in the main switchboard in Kaiserslautern. Hilde and two other girls decided against it. Hilde had been a supervisor in Kaiserslautern before. I suspected she had a good reason for not returning. For me, the army's offer was quite attractive. It included a pay increase and reimbursement of train fare expense. Weierhof was among the first of the small army posts to automate phone service. Upgrading would continue. While some girls lost jobs in the process, the demand for operators actually went up in Kaiserslautern, the ever expanding communications center for Western Area Command. WACOM, as people called it, was the American army's military designation for an area encompassing roughly all of the Rheinland/Pfalz.

Because of the travel involved, working the day shift meant leaving the house in Kirchheim before five-thirty in the morning and returning around eight o'clock in the evening. Sometimes I could stay over to do some big city shopping, catching the last train at eight-thirty and arriving in Kirchheim closer to ten o'clock. The Nazi success in blowing up our rail bridge link to Marnheim made the work day long. German Railways were forced to provide service to Marnheim from my town and other surrounding villages to make the train connection. Many were the icy winter mornings that saw me slipping and sliding my way down to the center of Kirchheim to catch the bus. Trying to remain upright and still tuck my blouse or zip my skirt closed while on the run could be hazardous. I often wondered of some of my early-bird neighbors had to shake their heads as I rushed by. In my head, I could hear Papa's reprimand, "You'll never get on a green twig playing catch up with the clock!"

My destination in Kaiserslautern was Kleber Kaserne, located on the east side of the city. One of the city's main streets, Mannheimerstraße, was the major access to Kleber from the city center. Further out on Mannheimerstraße, another big American barracks called Panzer Kaserne housed the huge headquarters of Western Area Command. A major city cemetery lay opposite from Kleber, a favorite place to take a lunch break and feed the squirrels. Within walking distance was a suburban rail station where I got off the train coming into work. Kaserne means barracks, and Kleber Kaserne, built for the German army in 1914, encompassed some forty acres, making it quite large for an urban military barracks.

It was at Kleber that I'd interviewed with the female army major two years earlier. I was so nervous that day that my memory had kept only one image of the place — that of an immense fortress. The center parade ground, bordered on all sides by narrow streets, looked bigger than a soccer field. Surrounding everything were massive buildings or high walls closing off the outside world. Soldiers and German workers could enter and leave by designated and guarded gates on the east and west ends. As the command's communications center, all foreign workers at the time had to have security clearance and carry passes. Other sensitive operations, like the army intelligence offices, were also located in Kleber.

In general, all unmarried soldiers, and those with wives who remained stateside, lived in second and third floor billets in the buildings where they worked. One building had the Bachelor Officers Quarters. Single female soldiers (WAC) were all billeted at Panzer Kaserne. All soldiers with families lived on the economy or the growing Vogelweh dependent housing area across the city.

If the new girls from Weierhof were tense upon arrival the first day, chief operator Anneliese Klarner quickly put them at ease. She gave us two days to observe and ask questions before going on schedule. Some forty-five girls worked in the main switchboard covering the three shifts. Everyone, except the day supervisors and the chief operator, rotated shifts. Day shift had the greatest number of operators on duty, while late shift from three to ten o'clock had five, and night shift only three. Though I was always scheduled, it was impossible for me to work the three to ten shift, as there was no bus or train service home after eight-thirty. However, because late shift was the shortest — at seven hours with eight hours pay — switching with another girl was never a problem.

The very size of our new work place was something to get used to. Thirty switchboards, bigger and more complex than Weierhof, and four desks for information calls filled up one long room. The chief's desk and master board stood elevated behind the line at the midway point. During business hours, about twenty-eight regular boards and three information desks were always occupied. I found working information a bit boring, and preferred the more active job of connecting people long distance. Local point-to-point calls were dialed, eliminating the need for operator assistance, except for information. Otherwise, the primary job was connecting my party with someone in other parts of Germany, France, Italy, Belgium, Holland, England, and elsewhere. I loved it.

With such a large group of women, there was quite a mix of characters and ages. Most were born German, but not all came from the Pfalz. In the break room, a blend of many German accents could be heard. We all spoke 'High German,' but the regional overtones and prejudices still prevailed in speech and opinions. A handful of girls from the eastern states, and especially those who escaped the Russian east zone, could barely hide their disdain for the 'uncultured peasants' of the Pfalz. This attitude didn't come out often, because the backlash might be two or more 'peasants' switching to pure Pfälzisch dialect. No one liked to be excluded. And, there was also the matter of favors. Nothing in the rules said I had to trade my highly desired late shift hours with an uppity Prussian. Such leverage made all the difference in maintaining a level of politeness among so many women sitting side by side all day.

There were two or three refugees from outside Germany who worked with us. I enjoyed working with a woman from Lithuania and another from Holland, but the one I came to know best was Frau Wolansky from Russia. A widow, she was by far the oldest in the group. Both her German and English abilities were passable, though the words came out with a heavy Russian accent. Inge Trunk, from the closed switchboard in Pirmasens, soon joined our team. She struck me as the true German blonde of Hitler's dreams, pretty facial features and all. She wasn't born in the Pfalz, something I could quickly forgive because of her grand sense of humor. Along with Frau Wolansky, we made the best of long overnight hours.

Just months after my transfer to Kaiserslautern, the chief had recognized the compatibility of Wolansky, Trunk and Klein, and joined us for night duty once a month. I was named 'operator-in-charge,' but that was only because of my slight seniority over Inge, and Frau Wolansky didn't want the job. Staying alert for ten hours, through the night and into early morning, was hard enough on young minds and bodies. Frau Wolansky, in her late fifties, caused Inge and I to make a deal. We'd send our Russian co-worker to the break room for an early nap, usually after one a.m. In about two hours, she'd return refreshed. Inge and I could then afford to take a break without fear of her falling asleep at the switchboard.

Our system worked well, except during "Red Alerts." As shift supervisor, I'd learn of the 'surprise alerts' by way of a special phone at the chief's desk. The barracks' duty officer frequently stopped by the switchboard early in the shift to identify himself, and to tell us where he could be found during the night. Now and then his remarks would include a warning of an expected alert. He could offer no exact time, but they usually occurred between two and five. Frau Wolansky would take her nap earlier, and Inge or I would make a pot of strong coffee. When the special phone rang, the three of us had to be fully awake.

There were different kinds of alerts. Some were only for selected military units in the command. Less often, the entire WACOM participated in the immediate 'war readiness' posture. In answering the phone, I'd be given a list of units to connect for a conference call, plus a code number. Going down the list, I repeated the code to each sleepy person, with the order to stand-by for the duty officer. Once I had everyone ready, I brought him in and closed my key-switch. But the fun had only begun. The first call resulted in the lighting up of all three switchboards as the alert message spread to other units outside Kaiserslautern. Handling the influx always increased the pulse rates of three operators already made hyper by caffeine.

The efficiency of the switchboard was closely monitored during war exercises. Operators not up to par heard about it in short order from Fräulein Klarner. I was never completely satisfied with my alert performance, but always got a passing grade.

Our chief never ceased to puzzle me. She was the first single career woman I'd ever encountered. Fräulein Klarner could be friendly and intimidating all at once. Short brown wavy hair, combed back like a man, gave her a well-groomed look, and a well-endowed bosom topped an otherwise trim body. Business suits complimenting her figure were the norm, and she usually didn't wear the jacket at her desk, revealing sleeveless tops. She was always well tanned, summer and winter. Home tanning lamps were fashionable at the time.

On the whole, I considered her a model boss, though not easy to get to know privately. Strict, fair, and even charming on the job, an invisible barrier went up when soliciting personal information outside work. She didn't ever ask about my life, and I couldn't ask her. The only time we crossed swords was when I had approached her about a supervisor opening, certain that I was ready for the added responsibility.

"You're qualified in many ways for the position," she said. "However, at this time, I won't consider you."

Shocked and hurt, I had to know why. "I don't understand, Fräulein Klarner. Haven't I worked hard to prove myself?"

"You're one of my better operators, and you do a fine job leading your night team. It's just, well, you're not very tolerant of other operators who make mistakes."

"But I'm more critical of myself," I protested.

"I know, and you shouldn't be."

"I have to be critical about my performance. How else can I become perfect!"

Standing by her elevated desk, our eyes were at the same level, though she was sitting. In response to my last remark, an almost stunned expression passed over her face, and she quickly looked away. Finally, a smile slowly formed as her eyes again met mine.

"Perfection, Anna, is a wonderful goal, but don't ever think you'll get there. No one can be perfect, and thank God for it! It'd be too intolerable for the rest of us."

Those words, coming from someone I thought nearly perfect, were unsettling. I wanted to argue, but didn't. On my lunch hour, I avoided the break room, choosing instead to walk the parade field and cool my head. My pride was ruffled, but Fräulein Klarner had succeeded in making me look in the mirror. She knew I didn't really believe true perfection was possible. What I needed, and got, was a sharp warning that my approach toward the goal was far too radical, and was often hurtful to others. The lesson remained with me, but I was still determined to do my best.

Looking back, I can admit to pushing matters to the limit when I felt challenged. If my party in Kleber wanted an army office in Verona, Italy, and all of the main routes were clogged, I didn't readily admit defeat. The choices for the caller were to hang up and wait until I could get through, or to hang on for a wild ride. It was amazing how many opted for the crazy trip through several remote switchboards in three countries. Some of the smaller military switchboards had G.I. operators, and other places employed local Italian, French, Dutch and British girls. It could be hard understanding their English at times, but I found it fun.

Back then, long-distance calls often involved building connection. A caller in Baumholder wanting Frankfurt could find himself in our hands, then on to Worms, up to Mainz, and finally to his party. We had direct lines to most major places such as Frankfurt, but during business hours, overloading forced us into alternate routing. I learned some of the more innovative linking of switchboards on slow night shifts. I'd just plug into an outgoing line and start hopping from one faraway switchboard to the next. Each operator along the way had different capabilities, and were usually happy to exchange notes. Aside from sharpening my knowledge on routing calls, the excursions gave me new insights about other people and places — and my English ability benefited.

The three of us in Kaiserslautern received more late-night calls from soldier-operators in lonely outposts than we made to them. There were lots of small missile sites, ammunition dumps and isolated radar stations to keep us busy all night, if the duty operators in those places had the notion. None of them talked about military information, so leaking vital secrets didn't enter into it. The female voice and a listening ear constituted the sole attraction. A few of our married operators claimed they politely cut short such calls when they worked the shift, but if time allowed, and it suited me, I'd go along with a man's simple desire to pass an hour in conversation. Inge did likewise, as did Frau Wolansky.

Inge and I laughed to think of their reaction, had some of the guys known that one of the voices belonged to a woman old enough to be a grandmother. Only once did I overhear Frau Wolansky come close to revealing her age to a caller. It had to be one of the rare fellows with an indecent tongue, for she suddenly shouted, "I vill not haff zat talk! How you say such ding to vooman! Is forbidden speak to old vooman so!" She jerked out the plug, then seeing the two of us with mouths agape, she just shook her head. "Bat boy. Wery bat boy. Such naughty talk!" (Her outrage still rings in my ear.)

Her late husband would have been proud of her. It was to be expected that a few 'phone guys' would get up the courage to want a date. For me, there were two good reasons not to accept. I'd heard only bad news from some of the girls about blind dates, and there was really little personal time to spare for the risky. On rare occasions I accepted a lunch date with someone I knew in Kleber. The closest I came to going on a blind date was with a Captain Hodding of the army intelligence office.

One night I picked up an incoming line from the Kleber Bachelor Officer's Quarters, and heard the familiar request for a wake-up call. Getting the name and number, I promised to call.

"Saturday nights must be slow on the switchboard." His comment was a clear invitation to talk, and it was fine with me.

"Yes," I replied. "But I don't mind. I brought my knitting along."

"Knitting? You're not one of the old grandmother types with her little basket full of yarn?"

"And why not?"

"Nah, the voice is too young for an old lady. Which one of the operators are you?"

"You ought to know, sir, being with army intelligence, that I'm not allowed to give my name. You wouldn't want me to lose my job."

"Yes, yes, I know the rules," he chuckled. "But you must give me your operator number. With that I only have to open a file drawer for the name."

"You can have my number if there is a complaint, sir."

"My complaint is you won't say your name, Fräulein!"

"Sir, you are assuming I'm an unmarried woman." By this time, I knew we were both enjoying the give and take. "You can't tell by my voice if I'm young, single, or a gray-haired mother with ten children!"

"With that many children, shouldn't you be at home caring for them?"

"Ah, but they've all left home and have families of their own. That's why I have this nice job where I can knit little sweaters for my grandchildren!"

"What a line! I've got to check you out. What'd you say your number is?"

"I'll tell you in the morning, sir. Good night!" I popped the plug out, but not before hearing his laughter.

At seven a.m. I promptly placed the call. The receiver was lifted after a single ring. "Good morning, sir. This is operator fifteen with your wake-up call."

"Just a minute," a grumbling voice said after a long pause. "Hold on there — want to write this down." I then heard him mumble. "Ope--ra--tor fifteen. Alright then, thank you," he said, obviously writing down the information. "Well, fifteen, how would you like some music while I shower?"

"Music?? How can — "

"I'll just put the receiver down by the record player," he said, rushing on. "What do you like, maybe some Mozart?"

"I like Beethoven."

"Beethoven! This early on a Sunday morning? Ah, here's something. A little water music from Händel. Good, huh?"

He put down the receiver before I could object. I had other wake-up calls and connections to make, but could switch back into the captain's line at any time. Soon the music ended, and he was back.

"What did you think? Could you hear alright?"

"It was fine, sir." It was just a little white lie. "Do you always listen to classical music? Nothing else?"

"That's right. Nothing else. Most of the rest is junk!"

"I wouldn't say that, sir. All music has something to offer." I glanced at the clock. Before he could challenge me, I continued. "I have to go now. The day

456

shift girls will be in soon."

"Okay, operator fifteen. Next time we talk, I'll know a lot more about you. But don't worry. It'll be our secret!" He laughed, and I said goodbye.

I didn't care if he looked at my security file and found my name — I followed the rules.

❧

"Isn't this operator fifteen?" I recognized Hodding's voice right away. Only a week had passed, and I was back on the day shift. Obviously he knew my voice, so there wasn't much sense in denying it.

"How are you today, Captain Hodding?"

"I'm still working on your name," he said mockingly.

His request was for a connection to another intelligence unit in Stuttgart. After a few minutes I noticed the incoming cord light flashing. The line light to Stuttgart was out, and my local caller wanted me back.

"Yes, Captain? Do you need another number?"

"No, not at the moment, I just wanted to thank Anna Klein for her help. Bye now."

He had checked me out, but it wasn't anything I could be mad about. The captain's interest didn't appear threatening, just a game he could play because of his position. In a way I was impressed, and felt complimented. Besides, Germans were accustomed to having police officials know their names and where they lived. It wasn't something we could question.

❧

Hodding and I ran into each other, via the switchboard, many times in the following weeks. Nothing more than joking remarks were exchanged. Then, after one of his calls, the cord light blinked off, but before I could disconnect his line began flashing again.

"Yes, sir?"

"About time for the night shift again, isn't it?"

Our work schedule was posted on a bulletin board in the switchboard room, and even he would have to get approval to come in to study it. At least, I hoped so.

"Captain Hodding," I finally replied. "I'm not sure you should have that information. I'd like to talk, but we're very busy."

"The other girls can handle it for a minute or two. Just keep saying 'Yes, sir,' and no one will think you aren't working."

457

"The chief could listen in — "

"She's not going to check up on an old hand like you. Now just repeat 'Yes sir' to questions. Would you like to have dinner with me tonight?"

"No, sir."

He laughed. "No, no. You're supposed to say the other thing. What's the problem, got other plans?"

"Yes, sir."

"That's more like it! Okay. You'd probably rather meet in a public place for a cup of coffee?"

"Yes, sir."

"How's the main train station when you come in to work the first night?"

"Yes, sir."

"Alright! I have a car, so I'll get you to work by ten. When does your train arrive?"

"Eight-fifteen, sir."

We met in the huge downtown train station, as arranged. I'd told him of my planned attire, and he'd mentioned a lobby location. Spotting him across the waiting room, I was struck by how sharp he looked in his uniform. Reality, however, soon quieted my pounding heart. Walking toward him across the wide expanse of terrazzo floor, anticipation withered as he became shorter and shorter.

He smiled warmly as we shook hands, and we walked to one of the station restaurants for the promised coffee. We did our best to disguise our mutual disappointment. With no hope of a romance between us, a kind of relaxation set in to restore the cheerful banter we'd had on the phone. We still liked each other, so it wasn't the worst possible ending. Naturally, Inge wanted to know what he looked like. Since we were both fans of American movies, she got the picture right away when I said he may sound like Burt Lancaster, but he looked like a skinny Frank Sinatra.

In the break room, particularly during lunch, opinions on any subject could fly in as many directions as there were girls present. Such loud gab sessions didn't appeal to me, and as a result, I was labeled 'shy.' I'd often shove down my food, then leave for a walk. In very nice weather, Margie or Inge and I carried our food to the cemetery, picking up shelled hazelnuts on the way to feed the squirrels. It may seem crazy to eat where the dead rested under tombstones, but it wasn't. With so many trees, it was more of a combination of forest, park and cemetery, with park benches everywhere. Lots of people took their lunches there.

On one subject there was nearly universal agreement among the girls. We all loved AFN, the American Forces Network radio, especially after Kaiserslautern got its own local station. Before that, we had to bring in AFN-Frankfurt to hear all the great record shows. It was very powerful, so there was no problem getting the signal. The programs were broadcast on the regular frequencies, and while intended for the Americans, could be heard by anyone with a radio.

There were few young Germans who didn't listen to the record shows, which were aired four times a day. All allowed requests and dedications, which resulted in an overload of the current love songs played over and over. Of these, I think the song "Why Don't You Believe Me" was typical — clearly a plea from some German girl to her soldier boyfriend. Thankfully, the disc jockeys had a rule not to follow one girl singer with another. Without it, all the lovesick or otherwise motivated girlfriends would have made listening unbearable.

Most of my co-workers, like me, wanted to hear the male singers and good band music. We weren't above using our unique position as operators to put through requests under the table. Another rule had it that requests must be written. We phoned. Most of our wishes were directed at the noon show, "Rhythm on the Rhine," so we could listen over lunch hour. There are many female singers I enjoyed, but I wouldn't waste a request on them. At the time, my choices were always for the big bands, and sometimes a male singer like Frankie Laine, Mario Lanza, Jerry Vale, and even Frank Sinatra.

AFN-Europe, with its regional studio stations in most large cities, and many more transmitters, had a far greater impact than just the official mission of serving Americans. The music and news programs reached everyone.

This sign stood in front of a sizable building housing the Kaiserslautern affiliate of the American Forces Network. I would become very acquainted with the radio station that had as many German listeners as American.

Chapter Forty-Three

It was in Weierhof when I first met First Lieutenant Ed Girvin. He was just one of the many men I passed in the hall at headquarters, or helped when placing calls. As I remember, he was with an Ordnance unit and had an office near the front door. His clerk, Bob, was the same corporal who had come to my aid in the Texan phone call incident.

The Lieutenant was married, though his wife Phyllis didn't join him from the states until late 1954. Before her arrival, he had the reputation of being a loyal husband. I know that any remarks to me were always brief and polite. He was tall and lanky, and I liked him because he talked slow, which made it easy for me to understand his English. Phyllis was petite in every way, with her dark hair styled in a soft, shoulder length bob. It framed a face almost devoid of make-up — a natural, healthy complexion and a ready smile made her pretty without it.

I became acquainted with Phyllis in the fall, shortly after she'd joined Ed, and moved into a small apartment in a village near Weierhof. To celebrate their reunion, they invited his clerk to bring a date to accompany them to a concert and dinner in Kaiserslautern. Bob asked me. I can only speculate on the reason. We were casual work friends, and to my knowledge, he dated no one. Perhaps when Lieutenant Girvin told his corporal to find a nice girl for his wife to chat with, Bob just reached out to the nearest girl who didn't wear make-up.

The concert, in a downtown Kaiserslautern dinner theater, presented the Vienna Boys Choir. It was a beautiful program, followed by an equally fine dinner in a restaurant below the auditorium. I liked Phyllis instantly. Bright, gentle, and thoughtful, she had a kind of self-motivation I admired, and a self-confidence I wished for. We were kindred in one respect — we both had a desire to learn and understand the world around us. She wanted to know all she could about the people and history of the Pfalz.

By the end of the evening, I hoped Phyllis wanted to see me again, but didn't count on it. How pleased I was when she called soon after to arrange another evening, without Bob and Ed, who had late duty in Weierhof. Later, it so happened that the Girvins were transferred to Kaiserslautern at about the time as I was, and our evening visits took place in their Vogelweh apartment. I slept over because of my train situation, and though I felt bad intruding into their privacy, she always quieted me. "It's easier," she would say. "We can talk and not worry about the time."

Ed wasn't assigned to Kleber Kaserne, so I no longer saw him as before. Phyllis, however, got a job as secretary to the WACOM commanding general in the nearby Panzer Kaserne, and we met frequently via the switchboard. I was invited every month or so for an overnight stay. At first, Ed would mysteriously leave after supper. By the third visit, his absences were explained by a beautiful long, low cabinet sitting in the living room. Many hours of his free time had gone into making it as a surprise gift to Phyllis. He acted like a kid showing it to me, proudly opening each door to reveal a radio, record player and tape recorder, and a storage space for records.

That the Girvins loved music was evident from the start by their interest in attending the Vienna Boys program. And, being great fans of composer George Gershwin, they delighted in helping me learn about his music and genius. I'd heard many Gershwin songs over the years, but being educated about them as a body of work really opened my eyes and ears. Our evenings together always had some music appreciation. They also showed me photos from trips they had taken around Germany, especially skiing at Berchtesgaden in the Alps. The photos and my hosts' enthusiasm made me yearn to travel, but I knew it would be awhile before I could. Travel had to wait until it was certain I'd found a green twig.

One evening, Phyllis asked me if she could provide me with any magazines to assist me in my never-ending effort to be more fluent in English.

"Thank you, but I have one or two magazines that the Signal guys pick up in the PX."

"That's good. What are you reading?"

"You remember I mentioned the Mrs. Crawford I worked for? She introduced me to the romance magazines."

Phyllis exploded. "Romance?? Anna!!"

For a moment, I feared being tossed out the door on my ear. I could see I'd said something to lower her esteem of me. Even Ed looked up from his reading when she raised her voice. I didn't know what to say. "I know they're silly stories, but the English is simple and easy to follow."

Phyllis soften her expression, and almost smiled. "Yes, simple and too direct about certain things. Come with me. I'm going to give you some magazines that'll be a lot better."

I followed her into the bedroom, where she opened a closet and handed down a short stack of magazines called the Ladies Home Journal. "These you can read and learn about things more important than dumb romances."

I took them, glad for her interest and continuing friendship. When we settled down again on the couch, Phyllis looked at me quizzically.

"Anna, can I ask — you never mention anyone. Do you have a special someone?"

"Phyllis!" Ed had raised his head again, surprised by his wife's prying question.

I had to laugh. "It's alright. I'm not trying to keep men friends a secret. The answer is no. My sister-in-law is fed up with me over it. I can't help that. I had one bad experience by getting serious. Right now, I've got a job I love, my little brother and niece — I'm happy."

"In Weierhof, didn't Lieutenant Whitley take a shine to —"

"Ed!" Now it was Phyllis' turn to be surprised. "At least I didn't mention names!"

I'd forgotten that Ed knew Joe Whitley. Months earlier his words may have made me blush, but I had long gotten over Joe. Instead, I smiled at my companions. "Yes, there was a time when I thought something would happen with Joe. Let's just say, I was willing to give it a chance. Joe couldn't make up his mind."

"That can be really frustrating," Phyllis said.

"It was, and yet, I can't blame Joe too much. I'm another one who has a hard time making a decision. I don't know what I'd do if two guys said they loved me, and I cared for both of them!"

Ed chuckled from his easy chair. "Oh, my," Phyllis blurted, uneasily.

"What?" I said.

"Well, Phyl, you started the conversation."

Clearing her throat, she looked from him to me. "I guess I did. The truth is I couldn't make up my mind either when it came to choosing a husband. For a long time I dated two fellows — Ed was one — and both asked me to marry, almost on the same day. It was awful! I cared for each one. I thought they were both terrific. Actually, they knew each other, and were friends on top of it. What was I to do? My answer was to get in bed, put the pillow over my head, and cry.

"Fortunately, my dear mother came along and made me rinse my face in cold water to clear my head. She said my problem was no different than what she and many women have had, with two men on the hook. She said, 'Marry the one whose love is greater than your own!'

"Of course, that didn't make sense to me at all. How could I possibly know who that was? Her answer was to laugh and say, 'If you can't figure that out, then you're not ready for marriage.' She then told me to go for a long walk and see what came to me.

"I did, and as you can see, I found the answer to who I should marry. I've never regretted the decision. So, should you face the same dilemma someday, think of what my mother said. It worked for me."

I felt a real loss when the Girvins returned to the United States later that year. Their friendship had come when I needed it most.

At 65 Breitstraße, progress toward a better life was measured at a steady, cautious pace. Erich's business was tied to Germany's furious rebuilding program, but there were no guarantees. During construction periods, success was based on two factors, profitable low bidding and low maintenance costs. He learned how to submit good bids in a hurry, but his mechanical ability is what kept the dream going. A tough decision in the early years wisely conserved resources in slow times. Deep winter brought a halt to most construction, and while there could still be the odd hauling job, he simply turned in the costly truck license and canceled all insurance. Until a better all-weather truck could be acquired and winter job prospects improved, he preferred to cut his losses to spend the time renovating the house.

When we'd moved in, the place had an apartment which was occupied. Under law, the people couldn't be evicted, but they soon left, making it possible for us to spread out. Ida and Erich took the biggest room for their bedroom, and I claimed a smaller room adjacent. That left two nice rooms, and I convinced them to allow my friend Anni, from Oberwiesen, and her husband Herman to rent the space. The two had recently married, and badly needed a starter home. Herman Koch was a local boy, who, in my judgment, had luck on his side in capturing the heart of Anni. She was the sister of Kurt, my first romance in the old dancing days. It was to their house our group almost always went for refreshments during the dance breaks.

Anni's brothers, Kurt, Adolf and Theo, came to the house along with Herman to remodel the two rooms into an efficient living space. From them, Erich learned new tricks in burying electrical conduit in stone walls. The entire house soon got new hidden wiring and better switches, outlets and lighting.

Around this time, Margie, a co-worker and train mate, declared the daily commute a burden, packed up her things in Marnheim, and moved to

Kaiserslautern. I wasn't exactly delighted by my long days either, but she had a different situation, with no family or other ties to Marnheim. Without a traveling companion, an unexpected problem arose — falling asleep on the evening train. Staying awake in the morning couldn't be easier. The car was loaded with boisterous factory workers. But the late evening return run was deadly quiet. The factory people used an earlier train, and what company I had amounted to a handful of likewise weary stragglers, all strangers to me. Without a chattering Margie next to me, nodding off became a bad habit.

The conductors were usually good about calling off the stations loud enough to rouse me. Other times, it was the jerk of the train starting up that had me scrambling to jump off as my car reached the end of the platform. One summer night, neither the conductor's warning nor the jerky movement of the train leaving Marnheim station shook me from slumber. But as the train slowly approached the last village houses, an alarm of some kind sounded in my brain. I instantly recognized those houses, and ran for the door. The car was empty except for one elderly woman with a pile of store packages next to her. I heard her say something like, "You can't get off now!" But I managed to open and make it through the door despite the swaying of the car from one set of tracks to another. I braced myself on the handrail and put my feet on the bottom step.

Bright moonlight was all that made my frantic plan work, as I clearly saw the path along the track begin to blur. Too late, I thought, but jumped anyway. Landing on both feet, God's hand must have helped me stay upright. I stumbled just a few steps, then stopped to wait for my heart to slow. That's when I saw my bus rolling along a distant road heading for Kirchheim. Thankful to be alive in Marnheim and not spending the night on a Worms train station bench, I walked the five kilometers home.

☙

Finding late evening company in the kitchen on my return from work was not unusual. Erich's boyhood friends, like Helmut Gass and Werner Diehl, never seemed to be without tales to share and topics to debate. Helmut, at the time, received disability money from the government. He had parts of both hands missing, blown off in the war. Since he didn't work, he seemed to have lots of time to spare. Erich and Ida didn't appear to mind his company. He was nice enough and had some interesting opinions, especially on politics.

By 1955, the Conservative and Liberal parties were well-established, with many fringe parties of various stripe trying to be heard as well. There seemed to be a constant round of elections going on, with local, state and national campaigns held at different times. Able to vote, I was generally confused by all the rhetoric, and the heated debates in our kitchen didn't help. Helmut liked the Communists, and did his best to convince everyone that its goals would make Germany great again. He wasn't alone. I heard others talk about the wonderful 'equality' we'd all have under Communism, but it was soon outlawed in West Germany, forcing local believers to observe Communist achievements from a safe distance. As for my vote, I usually followed Erich's conservative lead. Election outcomes, I discovered, were never entirely satisfying.

Germany's defeat in the war, and the death camps, were not topics for discussion in our kitchen, or in any house I visited. The silence wasn't intentional. After the initial shock of losing in such a devastating way, the natural instinct to survive immediately took over. Ordinary people had little time or energy to dwell in their bitterness. There were radical persons in the population, however they were without a platform and enough followers to threaten the peace. This time the victors, and especially the Americans didn't leave us to our own devices after the last battle. The outcome of 1918 was a lesson not forgotten.

With survival came the urge to rebuild lives and fortunes, something Western Europe, and Germany in particular, did well. Undeniably, after centuries of going to war every few years, the old cliche 'practice makes perfect' gives real perspective to the most recent gross destruction on humankind. As always, the persons left standing had to clean up the mess and get on with life. For the time being, we mainly kept our thoughts to ourselves. Talk was for the politicians. After years of living under dictatorship, common folk had much to learn about 'freedom of speech.'

It was not easy to forget that as Hitler's war ground on, those posters in every city and village warning about the enemy listening came to mean the real enemy to fear was one's own neighbors. A careless word of criticism, as conditions worsened, could put the speaker in danger of a visit by Gestapo. Whether it was for political or economic gain, turning people in became commonplace toward the end, and the dirty game flourished under occupation for the same reasons, or for revenge.

I personally knew one woman in our neighborhood who had the scary experience of being hauled off to Landau to face false charges. Her accusers were two neighbor women seeking revenge over some petty grievance. They had told the French that she had been a Nazi leader. My former music teacher, Karola Kiefer, had already been convicted and imprisoned in Landau. Only when the French brought Karola in to identify and testify against the accused woman, was it discovered she had never been a Nazi leader, just a simple housewife who had joined the party to avoid problems during the Nazi fervor.

There were plenty of reasons to speak little of the war in our homes, and the revelations about the mass murder of the Jews in the concentration camps received even less open discussion. Of course, there was a constant saturation of news and comment in the press and on the radio, especially during the Nuremberg trials and the ongoing hunts for those Nazis who had operated the death camps. After the initial shock of seeing the terrible photos and films of the camps, the people around me didn't seem to know what to express. I think many grew tired and frustrated at being personally accused in the tragedy, much of it from Americans. Any and all attempts to deny prior knowledge always met with contemptuous disbelief. It didn't take long for such attacks to cause only silence. Choosing not to always talk of the Holocaust with family and friends wasn't the same as denial. How could the overwhelming fact and horror of it be denied?

While the horrendous consequences of orders issued and carried out by Hitler's dictatorial regime will forever stain the German nation, German people were no better or worse than the rest of humanity. History teaches that mass murder for ethnic or racial reasons is nothing new for mankind. I read Anne Frank's diary in 1955 in a continuing quest to seek answers to my country's behavior. Anne was my age, and like me, a dark-haired girl, with similar hopes, dreams and habits. She adored her father, fussed with her mother, kept notes and a diary, hung up pictures of movie stars, and a dozen other traits which made me feel kinship with her. Anne's murder truly brought the genocide of millions into the realm of personal loss for me. But, like Anne Frank, I have to believe in the basic goodness of people.

❧

According to a diary entry of mine, it was a Saturday night around two a.m., and I was just hours into the first of three night shifts. The date was October 15, 1955. As usual, Inge and Frau Wolansky were my partners in picking up the occasional calls.

"Operator, may I help you?"

The response rolled down the line at me in the recognizable manner of someone affected by too much drink. I was surprised that he'd identified himself and was still in the officer's club at that hour. His request boiled down to wanting to know the outcome of a football game back in the states — the payoff on a bet rested on the information. What he asked for was 'any connection' to get the score. Trying to explain that sports scores were not a part of our service, I hit on the idea of simply putting him off. I got his phone number and promised to check out the possibilities.

I was later told that at about the same time, a taxicab pulled up to the studios of AFN-Kaiserslautern in Vogelweh. A soldier got out of the cab, unlocked and entered the front door of the building. In the darkened lobby was a sofa, his bed of choice for what remained of the night. Recently assigned to the radio station, the tired corporal had forgotten about being scheduled for the 5:30 a.m. sign-on in place of the regular announcer. The slip in memory had cost him the high price of cab fare from a downtown Kaiserslautern night club for a quick nap. A German engineer was scheduled to come to work around five o'clock and would wake him.

I'd told Inge about my weird caller, probably hoping she'd encourage me to search to the ends of the earth for the game score. She laughed, but argued against any effort. "Forget it! He wouldn't remember asking, even if you did find the answer. That's not our job anyway. If it's so important, it'll be on AFN."

"You're right," I said. "It's a looney idea. But now I feel bad having told him I'd try."

"Ja," she said, smirking. "I know how you hate failure."

I settled back to knitting, picking up the occasional line light, and chatting with my two mates on either side. Yet, something Inge had said kept percolating in my head.

At four o'clock, I couldn't stand it anymore. "Inge! You gave me an idea. AFN would have the score. I'm trying their number!"

"What? You can't do that! The station doesn't go on the air until later, you crazy girl. I'll bet no one is even there."

"Oh, I think there is," I replied. "I talked to their morning man once. Al, I think his name is. He told me about how he sleeps in the attic."

"Sleeps in the attic?"

"It's too long a story. I just know he's there — "

Plugging into a Vogelweh line and dialing, I had the last word. "He won't mind." The number began ringing. How could Al mind? After all, I'd once helped him place a difficult call.

I couldn't have known that the ringing I heard had set off a loud buzzer alarm through the halls and studios of the radio station. I would learn after the receiver on the other end was picked up.

"Yes! Hello. AFN — AFN Kaiserslautern." The answering voice was loud — didn't belong to Al — and it wasn't very coherent. Soldiers are supposed to also identify themselves. A name and rank was given, but I didn't catch it.

"Good morning. This is the operator. I'm sorry to bother you. I have a caller on the line needing information." I lied.

"Wait. Wait a minute, operator. I've got to turn on some lights and find a seat. My head is spinning." In the background, I could hear a thrashing around, a yelp of pain and some groaning. Finally, the sound of a chair on squeaky wheels. "Yes, operator, I'm back. What the hell time is it, anyway?" Before I could answer, he continued. "Oh, my God! Ten after four. I've only been asleep two hours!"

I suddenly felt guilty, and didn't know what to say to fill the momentary silence. My hand was on the plug, ready for a fast exit from my intrusion.

"Okay, okay. You have your job to do, operator. What is it your caller needs?" His voice was now calm, and actually quite pleasant. I figured he had to be one of the announcers.

"Spencer, Tim, Corporal, United States Army!"

The humor in his tone relieved my guilt. "A lieutenant at the officer's club wants to know the final score of a college football game. Can you give me that information?"

"Ah, well, I guess the lieutenant doesn't realize that our station has access only to local news and sports scores. You'll have to tell him to listen for the network news report from Frankfurt at seven o'clock."

"Thank you, I will. Again, I'm sorry to have awakened —"

"Hold on, operator! Don't hang up on me. Pass the message along and come right back. There's no way I can get any sleep now. You're going to have to keep me awake for the next hour and a half. Besides, I kind of like the sound of your voice!"

"I guess it'll be alright," I answered. "I like your voice, too." I hadn't meant to say the last out loud, though his voice really was pleasant.

"I'll pass along the information and come back." I closed my key for a moment, paused, took a deep breath and let my fingers open the key once more. "Hello, I'm back."

"Good! Let's start with your name and how many children you have."

I laughed. "Sorry. You can only have my operator number, which is fifteen. And I'm called a Fräulein. You do know the difference between a Frau and a Fräulein?"

"I do indeed. Well, Fräulein Fifteen, let's begin!"

Chapter Forty-Four

The heat of a bright spring sun, tempered by cool breezes, helped celebrate the beginning of a new life on May twenty-fourth, 1956. It was a Thursday morning, and our appointment with the Registrar of Kaiserslautern had been set for ten o'clock. Only seven months earlier, an audacious phone call to a radio station had unexpectedly sparked a romance and changed my life.

Marrying couples wanting God's blessing usually sought it right after the civil ceremony at a city hall. Because of a scheduling conflict between the German Registrar and the Army Chaplain's office, the church ceremony for us was delayed for two days. The glitch was just another humorous inconvenience for two people who had been well-tested by months of military and civilian red tape. We joked about having two anniversaries to celebrate each year.

Standing before the Registrar, a short bear of a man who roared rather than speak in normal tones — it was all so anticlimactic that we both had to struggle to keep from grinning like idiots. What surprised us was the trauma experienced by our witnesses. Tim and I had asked my landlady, Frau Kreuz, and one of his friends from AFN, Ed Starr, to stand with us. Apparently, the duty was more than they expected.

I had moved to Kaiserslautern, renting a room from Frau Kreuz, soon after becoming engaged in February. Ed was a young Jewish man from New York. A charming and talented announcer, he was one of the many pulled away from a budding career at home to serve a two-year military obligation. Frau Kreuz and Ed Starr were as unalike in age and background as could be found for our witnesses. Yet, in the matter of facing a German bureaucrat, their reaction was the same.

When the four of us arrived at the old city hall on Steinstraße, the wide public hallway inside looked to be as ancient as the building's exterior. My soon-to-be husband had smiled. "What a dark place to marry on a beautiful day!"

Reaching the right door, we found a secretary in a small office that was as equally undisturbed by the twentieth century, except for the telephone and typewriter. How surprising it was when we were escorted through another door into a totally new and modern office. The floor, walls, ceiling and furnishings were all up-to-date and brightly lit. Even the inside of the old door had been given a modern facade. Dominating the room was a desk big enough for three people, but only the heavy-set Registrar was seated behind it. Standing to the side was a translator, another requirement when marrying a foreigner.

The female translator indicated we should sit in the chairs placed in front of the desk. Ed sat on Tim's right, and Frau Kreuz took the chair on my left. The Registrar had yet to speak. He seemed busy perusing a thick file opened on the desk before him. It was our file, and I knew it was full of all kinds of documents, all designed by American and German specialists in marriage prevention. Along with these were the usual health examination reports, police records, and a report on my moral character from the army chaplain, who had interviewed me. All papers had to be translated and submitted in triplicate.

The most time-consuming was the security clearance check by army intelligence on me and my family, back to and including my great-grandparents. We were told that this alone could delay final approval for several weeks, since the investigation was handled by an intelligence unit outside our area. Welcome help came from my friend Captain Hodding in Kleber. He couldn't do anything about the findings, which didn't worry me anyway, but he did make sure my papers didn't find a home in someone's pending file.

Tim took my hand, gave it a reassuring squeeze, and smiled. He was also thinking of the long three-month application process, accomplished against a background of opposition from many sides. During the 1950's, American and German authorities put in place many discouragements for soldiers who wanted to take home German brides. They undoubtedly served a good purpose in some respects, but were no more than a nuisance to anyone intent on marrying. At least that's the way it was for us, once I overcame obstacles in my mind and the protests of my family. My personal 'D-Day' had come on February tenth. Weeks of inner turmoil boiled down to one hard choice — lose Tim or stay with the family. With Tim, the future held promise, great risk, and separation from family. In my family, there was comfort with the old and known, yet I felt stifled and unfulfilled.

Late Saturday morning, February eleventh, we walked into Seiler's Jewelry in Kaiserslautern. Two gold bands were selected. Later, in privacy, we'd put them on in a bond of engagement. I was fully committed to the unknown with Tim Spencer. War with the family would continue, but now I could face the torment and not waver.

Without warning, the stout Registrar stood up behind the massive desk, and ordered us to stand and step forward. His tone of voice made me think the man must be a holdover Nazi bureaucrat, the kind that could really scare anyone. Frau Kreuz had the same reaction. The poor woman dropped her purse to the floor when she jumped up so quickly. The order was translated in softer female tones for Tim and Ed.

I couldn't see Ed's face, but I was worried about Frau Kreuz. She looked ready to faint each time the man spoke. I thought it a curious reaction, since it was her own language and the words were no more threatening than reading the ingredients for apple pancakes.

The man's brutish manner didn't bother me, but I did wonder about Tim and Ed, along with Frau Kreuz. About the time we were being told to 'honor the marriage bond,' I quickly glanced at them. Tim, in his nice, new navy blue suit, looked quite self-assured and happy. Ed's eyes, though, were glazed, and he shook from head to toe. I nudged Tim, who put a comforting hand on his friend's arm. But when Ed handed the rings to Tim, his shaking fingers dropped them both. Hastily retrieved, the ceremony managed to close before we lost our witnesses completely.

No sooner were we pronounced 'man and wife,' than a warm smile spread across the Registrar's face. Warm and sincere congratulations, and handshakes all around, had instantly replaced his stern manner with one more akin to a father of the bride. Frau Kreuz and Ed were still glad to get out of there.

Two days later, Tim and I got married again in the Kapaun Chapel in Vogelweh. Chaplain Hansen spoke the words, and his wife played the organ. Our witnesses, and the only other people attending, were Erich and Ida. While I had worn a simple dark-blue suit to city hall, for the church ceremony I wore a calf-length, baby blue satin and taffeta dress. A white satin skull-cap, without veil, adorned my head. We hadn't asked for any special songs to be played or sung for us, and I'm sure the Hansens had to wonder about the empty pews. Had they known about my family opposition, or Tim's situation at the radio station — rapid turn-over had left him with few friends to invite, except for Ed Starr, who had to work that day.

If Erich and Ida were nervous, it came from opposing the marriage. They had only agreed to come by rationalizing that greater shame would come from 'failing family loyalty.' Rather than pit relatives against relatives, I decided to ask only Erich and Ida. Oddly, Tim faced a similar situation at the radio station — a few of his fellow workers opposed marrying Germans. Knowing he was in line for chief announcer, a neutral course was chosen.

Papa wasn't there. Any good sense I had now failed me completely. I didn't invite him out of fear that Erich wouldn't come. It had reached the point of choosing between my brother, who had given me shelter, and a father I adored, but who I felt had betrayed his family. Tim had tried to change my thinking on it, but unfortunately, a change of heart didn't come in time to share my wedding day with Papa. I continue to have deep regret about that decision fifty years later.

ȣ

Our marriage was followed a few weeks later by a month-long trip through Austria, Switzerland, Italy, France, Holland, and other parts of Germany. It was a time when a grand tour was still possible with a small car and a tiny budget. Salzburg and Vienna were the first big stopovers, and it was in Vienna that Tim revealed his plans to stay at AFN another three years. We were out for a late evening walk, and had just passed the famed opera house. This news caused me to stop in my tracks. He roared with laughter, put his arms around my waist and led us into an impromptu dance all the way down the block. Other late strollers passed us and didn't seem at all shocked by two dancing, singing idiots.

"Are you sure, Tim? Really, really sure?"

We found one of Vienna's famous little coffee bars nearby, and settled down with two espressos at a table. I was overjoyed with his decision, but I knew the sacrifice he was making — plans of finishing university studies and getting on with a career in broadcasting.

"Yes, yes, yes," he chuckled. "I didn't say anything before because some things needed to be checked out. It's been on my mind since we walked out of Seiler's with the rings." He paused to enjoy my startled look. We had gotten the rings more than four months earlier. "You'll find I don't rush decisions on such things."

"Tim! You asked me to marry after only two months."

"True," he laughed, "but thinking about you twenty-four hours a day, seven days a week, made it seem forever!"

I couldn't argue with that. After two weeks of only telephone conversations, we spent some part of nearly every day together until I finally said yes. "But what about your plans to complete school?"

"I'll still have the G.I. Bill waiting for me, if you think you can stand to have an old student around the house. Besides, I can't think of a better place to spend another three years! AFN is radio the way it should be, so I'll be able to do something challenging and enjoy Germany all at once."

"I know you love it here, but in the army?"

"AFN isn't the army. At least, not in the sense of the usual military stuff you know about. We have a rack of rifles in the back room of the station, but not one of us has fired a weapon or marched since basic training. If it stays like that, I'll be able to deal with wearing the uniform and remembering my military etiquette for three more years."

But I knew there had to be more than just liking a job and being in Germany to make an un-military person re-enlist. "You have other reasons, don't you? Is it my family?"

"Excuse me just a minute." Tim stepped over to the counter to order and bring back refills. The small espresso bar wasn't all that busy at two in the morning, though a few young people stood around or sat at tiny tables sipping drinks and talking quietly. Returning, he carefully put the small cups of steaming thick brew on the table. I would learn in the years ahead that he had a way of changing the subject until he decided how to answer.

"Might as well stay alert tonight. There's not much chance for a good night's sleep anyway."

His words were followed by a sexy wink that only he and I understood, and we soon laughed ourselves into tears. The temporary craziness had nothing to do with our sex life, but rather where we'd rented a room.

"Ah, so it goes," Tim finally said, catching his breath. "I should write a travel guide for honeymooners called 'Delightful Surprises for the Un-reserved.'"

On arrival in Vienna, we had gone looking for an affordable hotel room downtown. Usually, we stayed in less expensive private homes offering a clean bed and homecooking. But in this case, we'd wanted to be able to walk to the many attractions in the old city center. We'd finally found the perfect place, around the corner from the main street with all the expensive hotels. Except for size, our hotel appeared just as clean and nicely appointed, in an old world sort of way. We should have been suspicious though, when the clerk sharply questioned our real relationship. My passport still had my maiden name, but we had documents proving our marital status. The clerk took them and disappeared behind a door for a few minutes. We could only wonder what it was all about. No one had questioned us so rudely before. We could tell he wasn't happy about it, but on his return, we were allowed to register.

The room, as spacious and nice as any I'd seen, was on the fourth floor, with a view to the busy street in front. It was early afternoon, and we'd decided on a nap before a planned evening on the town. Around five o'clock, we dressed, and while I touched up my hair in front of the mirror, Tim opened the drapes.

"I'll be — if that doesn't beat all!" He'd nearly shouted the words, then began laughing.

"What?"

"Come here. Now I know why we were questioned. Take a look!"

I saw several women of varying ages and dress standing outside the hotel entrance, propositioning men who passed by. Only about one out of ten tries was successful, and the couple would disappear into the building. I suddenly found myself very embarrassed and angry. We had checked into a hotel full of prostitutes, and on my honeymoon!

When I turned to Tim to vent my rage, he had fallen back on the bed in a fit of laughter. At first I was shocked by his behavior, but a strange ticklish feeling welled up inside me, and I found myself caught up in his arms and the hilarity of it all.

"Oh, God help me," Tim said. "No wonder we got such a beautiful room, and so cheap!"

Thinking about it again over coffee, it struck us as wildly — and ironically — funny. But Tim still hadn't answered whether my family had played a role in his willingness to stay on for another three years. He had tried hard over the months to get Erich and Ida to accept him. The language barrier made it tough. They didn't know English, and he wasn't fluent enough in German. I had attempted to explain this man from Indiana, U.S.A. to them many times, but without success.

"Now, your question about the family." Our moment of laughter had ended, and he must have been reading my mind. "The answer is yes and no. I don't want us to leave Germany knowing your family has the wrong impression. So far, words haven't worked, so maybe time and actions will. I have a feeling Ida, in particular, thinks you're four months pregnant, and had to marry me. Another five months should dispel that suspicion and make the road a little easier.

"And there's something else just as important. While you're still here, they should learn that marrying an American isn't some kind of betrayal to family and country. I think they will, and I'm going to have fun sticking around watching it happen."

Tim loved a challenge. That was one special fact I'd learned over our whirlwind courtship, but I couldn't help having doubts. "It's such a mess, Tim. You may regret ever meeting any of us."

"Cut it out. You're sounding too much like your mother. Remember what you told me about your Papa? How he always talked about getting on a 'green twig?' Well, I understand him perfectly, and someday I'm going to insist you introduce me to your father. I won't be satisfied otherwise.

"Tim —" I didn't go on. He knew the story of Mama and Papa and what happened to tear the family apart. I had even used the situation to ward off his proposals of marriage. Obviously, it didn't work, but I still could not see how reconciliation with Papa was possible.

"I know what you are thinking, Frau Spencer. Don't worry. We'll climb one mountain at a time. First your brothers and Ida, then Papa Klein. Okay?"

♺

A month later Tim re-enlisted. He was promoted to sergeant's rank not long after, followed by an appointment to chief announcer at AFN-Kaiserslautern. I continued working at the Signal Corps switchboard. We stayed on with Frau Kreuz, sharing the bath and kitchen. Tim enjoyed living near the downtown, I was happy when, around our first anniversary, we were assigned an apartment in Vogelweh. Once again I had room to breathe, and could roam from kitchen to bath to bed in privacy.

Nearly every week we spent some time visiting the family at 65 Breitstraße. Tim had been right. With no baby in sight by the fourth and fifth month, the atmosphere in Ida's kitchen eased considerably. He was also gaining on the language, which helped the healing process along. We began joining the family for Sunday dinners, and at Christmastime and New Year's. Some of Erich's male friends never came to terms with my American husband, but it didn't matter. We had supporters among my relatives like Tante Lisbeth and Tante Sannchen. When we weren't visiting the Kirchheim family, almost all of our free time was given over to exploration.

Tim wanted to see and touch as much of the Pfalz and Germany as our schedules would allow. Often, we had no plan. "I like to be surprised," he'd say. Pointing the car south, west, north or east, we'd just follow the back roads for surprises, and were frequently enchanted with what we found. In truth, it was a new experience for me as well. Growing up in the Pfalz, I'd been well-educated in it's history and had seen many places. Never, though, had I just wandered slowly over the length and breadth of a land I claimed as mine. Naturally, I remain partial to the Donnersberg region, but the many weekend excursions with Tim had opened my eyes to the full meaning of being a Pfälzer.

Again in 1957 and 1958, Tim and I took a month to return to favorite areas in countries visited on the honeymoon trip. And over time, I came to understand my husband's great love for broadcasting. Words like boring or dull were never a part of the vocabulary at the station. The military make-up at other AFN stations may have been different, but in Kaiserslautern army and air force personnel filled announcing jobs. At the time, an air force first lieutenant was commander, aided by an army sergeant first class and a German civilian secretary. Across the hall, an American civilian held forth as program director. His secretary was another German girl. In the control room, military engineers were assisted by German employees. Another American civilian held the post of chief engineer. Five full-time announcers took care of all local programming except news. Local news and sports were handled by a civilian newsman.

One newsman was Ed Gress, a civilian who worked there about a year before going on to become a news correspondent in the Middle East for CBS Radio in the States. It was Ed who changed my husband's direction in broadcasting. He often called on Tim to replace him for on-air local and network reports. For some reason, Ed thought Tim should forget about the entertainment side of radio and concentrate on news gathering and reporting. It was good advice.

❧

By the spring of 1958, with Tim's non-stop urging, I finally agreed to a meeting with Papa. We decided to ask him for a weekend visit to our Vogelweh apartment. The first step had to be introducing him to my husband. For that, we drove to Kirchheim and Frau Rolf's house. On the way, I was given a pep talk.

"This is tough for you, I know," Tim said. "Just think about all we've talked about. I'm meeting the man for the first time, yet from everything you've told me, I can't believe he meant to hurt you. Consider how he must have felt when you sided against him. You chose brother over father. Then came the tragedy of the little girl killed by his truck. Not long after that, a severe stroke from which he's not really recovered. With his world collapsing, there was no choice but bankruptcy, and in those circumstances, you can't necessarily choose the buyer of the house."

Everything Tim said made sense. Peter still visited his father, so Papa obviously knew of my marriage. I suddenly felt foolish showing up two years late. Taking a deep breath, I knocked on Frau Rolf's door. She answered, and though shocked to find us on the doorstep, we were invited in. Papa was sitting in the kitchen. He looked so frail, but on seeing Tim, he immediately stood to extend his hand. My husband took it with both hands.

"Papa, I'm far too late with my manners. For that, I'm sorry. I want you to know my husband, Tim."

476

"Guten Abend, Tim." His 'good evening' came slowly, but in a warm manner reserved for family and good friends.

Frau Rolf offered drinks, which I declined but could have used. "We can't stay. I just wanted to introduce Tim and ask Papa if he would visit us in Kaiserslautern for a weekend. Do you feel well enough to do that, Papa? We have less than a year before leaving. Tim wants very much to know you."

My father looked at Tim, then at Frau Rolf, and back to me. "Ja, I can do that."

It was arranged. The following weekend we'd pick him up early Saturday and return him to Frau Rolf on Sunday night. My pleasure would have been complete, had I not seen the cane next to his chair. Frau Rolf noticed my surprise.

"Your father had another stroke a month ago. It was mild and didn't paralyze, but he's weaker and needs a cane."

I felt stupid for not knowing, and worse for not having been there. After leaving, I wondered aloud how Papa was going to manage three flights of stairs.

"Don't fret about it," Tim said. "I'll carry him up, if I must."

It wasn't necessary. Mounting each step slowly, Papa had insisted, with a weak laugh, that he needed the exercise. We had thought at first of showing him the radio station, but the climb up to our top floor dwelling was enough exercise.

That weekend, we talked constantly, or at least I did. It hurt me to see how hard it was for Papa to speak. I could hardly watch him sitting on the sofa, only a shadow of the Seppel I loved and wanted back. All my grievances against Papa, whose body and spirit no longer served him as before, had vanished. Talking kept me from thinking about all we had lost.

He was interested in my husband's background and work. Of course, I told him about my job in Kleber Kaserne, and of our plans for the future. He seemed pleased by it all, especially Tim's love for the family and our country.

As for his illness, my father avoided the subject, and acted as though he expected full recovery. He listened carefully when I talked about Peter. I expressed concern that with my departure to the United States, his future looked bleak. The boy was already feeling like a fifth wheel in his brother's house. Ida had finally given Erich the son he wanted, named Axel.

Peter was fourteen years old, and would soon be finishing the eighth grade. Someone had to help him go on to the field of work he wanted. Papa agreed, and promised to look into it. With his health problems, I momentarily regretted bringing up my worry. I thought a solution was beyond the scope of a man who seemed to have lost his Seppel powers.

A few weeks later Tim and I stopped by Langstraße to see Papa. To my complete amazement, he told us of having arranged for Peter to live with him again at Frau Rolf's house. It would only be for a few months, until after confirmation in the spring of 1959. The most surprising news, however, was my father's success in getting Peter accepted into a four-year school operated by the German telephone system in Neustadt, room and board included. It was Peter's dream to become an engineer in electronics. I was speechless, and could only smile with renewed admiration for Papa. He still had the touch, and had once more had come through for his family. The final days in my homeland were near, and to know that Peter was taken care of gave me peace of mind.

In the fall, I ended my employment with the U.S. Army. Tim wanted me to spend more time with my people around the Donnersberg. Weeks before the Christmas holidays, we began a new paper chase, preparing and gathering the documents for my visa application. While not as complicated as the marriage process, it was scarier. When the army gave approval to marry, there was a caveat at the bottom of the page: "This approval in no way guarantees entry into the United States."

The last hurdle was a day-long shuffling between offices at the U.S. Embassy in Frankfurt. There were X-rays, interviews, and still more questions. The last two hours were spent in a huge waiting room. People came, and others left, and I noted that some were in tears. Tim sat with me the whole time, keeping me calm and confident. At five o'clock, my name came over the loudspeaker. A gentleman handed me a document with a long number on it and the word "Approved."

Tim's deployment orders came in January. We were to leave on the twenty-eighth of February by ship from the port of Bremerhaven. During the second week of February, Erich drove with Tim to the port to turn in our car. It was his first trip north to the sea since the war's end. They stayed overnight, and returned by train. I spent the time in Kirchheim. Peter had already moved back to Papa.

On the twenty-sixth, Tim borrowed a car and we went one last time to the family in Kirchheim. Of course, at Erich's we all joked around to cover our feelings, but the three-year grace period was over. The time had come to leave, and I was ready. Our last stop was with Papa, where we found Peter in bed with a bad cold, but he kept insisting that was fine. Finally, I turned to gently hug Papa. I knew we were both sad, but there were no tears, just promises to write. And, for the last time, I heard him say, "Sei brav, Annchen."

Epilogue

The U.S.N.S. Geiger left Bremerhaven for New York on schedule. It was the same ship that had brought Tim to Europe four years earlier. After we settled into a small cabin high above the main deck, it was a short time to departure. I asked Tim to find the way to an outside gangway — I didn't want to have a last view of my country through a porthole. In minutes, we were standing by a railing and looking down over a now nearly empty wharf. An army band had earlier played "Auf Wiedersehen," and now its members were loading onto buses. The song isn't German, and hearing it had little impact on my mood. I'd already said my goodbyes to the family, and had had three years to prepare for the moment of leaving. Most important, I knew I could return.

The ship's whistles began blowing, and we soon detected movement. A shiver ran through me, but only because the turning ship allowed the cold March winds to reach our place at the railing. An earlier bright sun had fooled me into leaving my sweater in the cabin. Tim solved the problem by wrapping his arms around me from behind, and without a word, he sheltered me from the cold as I stood and watched until there was nothing left to see but water.

The expected nine days en route became eleven, when dangerous storms tossed the Geiger about like a toy and forced us hundreds of miles off course. I saw the Statue of Liberty on the morning of March eleventh, 1959.

Looking back over the time since, I can report that Peter did very well in school, and went on to build a rewarding career with the German telephone system. After his schooling in Neustadt, he chose not to return to Kirchheim to live, but moved instead to the other side of the Donnersberg and the village of his future wife, Christa. By choice, they live in a more peaceful and charming Heimkirchen, though it meant a daily commute to Kaiserslautern, where he was to become an executive with Telecom, the commercial communications service of the government operated system. In the 1980's, he was forced to retire on disability after two heart bypass operations within a ten year period.

Erich retired in 1989, having operated a prosperous trucking business for many years. With retirement, my older brother built his dream house at the very edge of his beloved forest, and next to the new home of his son, Axel. As a member of the district's official hunting club, he continued his volunteer work with the forestry service in looking after the welfare of the forest animals. Assigned to oversee a large section to the north of Kirchheim, he was responsible for removing animals killed in road mishaps, provide feed during hard winters, and keep a count of the deer and wild boar populations. The forest was his sanctuary. On several trips to Germany, following our 1985 visit, Erich took Tim and I deep into the forest to show us the places where he felt at peace with God. He had built platform perches high in trees overlooking boar wallows. He told us of some of his all-night vigils on the rough platforms, armed only with a flashlight to count the wild pigs in their muddy ritual.

At Christmas time in 1993, Erich informed us that he'd been diagnosed as having prostate cancer, and that it had been discovered too late for a cure, though many efforts would be made to bring it under control.

In the early months of 1994, after several phone talks, I made the decision to go with Tim to Germany for a four week visit with Erich. I'd told my brother that I would rather be with him when we could still talk, and go for walks together in the forest. We couldn't know how long he would live after the visit, but Erich agreed that I shouldn't plan to fly over just for a funeral.

Through our month-long visit in September, Erich and I made time to talk of many things, present and past. After more than forty years, he could finally speak of Mama and her last days, and why he couldn't view her in death — it reminded him too much of the victims in the death camp photographs. He felt the same about me seeing him toward the end. And for my ears alone, he expressed regret over the breakup with Papa. With those burdens out of the way, we were free to remember aloud all the good and bad times growing up and finding our way as Seppel's children. As Papa would have, we spoke mostly of the good and happy times.

Over the year and a half after that last trip to Germany, we spoke weekly on the telephone. By Christmas of 1995, we spoke of the end coming nearer — his strong resonant voice had weakened though his mind remained sharp. Since the doctor was willing to come to the house each day, it was Erich's wish to die at home.

Our last phone conversation was on Sunday, May nineteenth, 1996, five days before my fortieth wedding anniversary. Erich expressed amazement that the years had passed so quickly, and was intently interested in our celebration plans. I promised him I'd send photos of the occasion right away. "I won't be here," he said.

We'd been talking for twenty minutes, and I knew he was tiring. Even so, his words struck hard and I could barely speak. Finally, I did manage, "Ich liebe Dich, Erich."

"Ja, ja, and I love you, Annchen."

The words were all the more special because he had never spoken them to me out loud. I bit my lip, then heard him say, "Goodbye."

On the morning of May twenty-seventh, I received a phone call from Peter. "I'm sorry to tell you that we've lost our brother."

Erich had gone into a coma the day after Tim and I observed our anniversary, and had quietly slipped away in the arms of his son Axel two days later. For that, I was grateful.

Thirty-five years earlier, I had been in America only two years when word came of Papa's death on April 25, 1961. Erich then became 'Seppel' when Papa died. He was the fourth and last in the family line.

I kept my promise, writing to my father until his death. Letters to Peter at his school were more frequent, but I knew he went home often and would share these as well. Papa's last letter was mailed to us for Christmas, 1960. He had only recently come home from another bad spell in the hospital. No longer able to write, Frau Rolf's daughter Ingrid took up the pen for him. She wrote his words:

"Annchen, I have received your letter. It gives me joy to hear of your latest progress. I know you also write to Peter. Your brother is doing very well in Neustadt. Kurt Butz died a week ago and yesterday, Heiner Andres passed on."

(Papa had helped Kurt, who had lost both legs, to start his trucking business after the war, and Heiner was the neighbor and friend who couldn't stand to lose at cards. I know their deaths hit him hard.)

"This body won't let me work at all. November was a bad setback, but I'm home now and will get better. I have to, Peter is coming home for Christmas and I want it to be a happy time. I wish you and your husband a happy Christmas as well. When you put up your Christmas tree and turn on the lights, think on your Papa and our happy Christmas times together."

Ja, Papa. I will always remember — especially at Christmas.

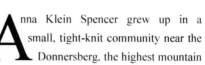

Anna Klein Spencer grew up in a small, tight-knit community near the Donnersberg, the highest mountain in Germany's wine-producing Rheinland-Palatinate (aka Rhineland-Pfalz) region. Throughout her childhood, she often heard people refer to her as "Seppel's daughter." In time, she learned why her father Fritz, as well as her grandfather Peter and great-grandfather Joseph, were better known as "Seppel." As Germany struggled through periods of war and economic crisis, Anna discovered how being Seppel's daughter was a source of strength and support for her and her family.

❧

Tim Spencer grew up in Fort Wayne, Indiana, during the 1930s and '40s — a period of economic strife and national sacrifice. It also was the golden age of radio, which inspired young Tim to dream of becoming a disc jockey — an aspiration he fulfilled with the Armed Forces Radio Services during his tenure with the U.S. Army in the '50s. While stationed in Germany during the Occupation he met and married Anna. In 1959, they moved to the U.S. where Tim transitioned into an award-winning career as a broadcast journalist. After 30 years on radio and TV, he left broadcasting to devote more time to creative writing.

CPSIA information can be obtained at www.ICGtesting.com
Printed in the USA
LVOW13s1954091113

360679LV00002B/452/P